THE FIERCEST DEBATE

Cecil A. Wright, the Benchers, and Legal Education in Ontario, 1923–1957

From its earliest days the Law Society of Upper Canada adhered to the traditions of English legal practice and education. In the 1930s and 1940s, however, some of the most cherished of those traditions were challenged in a bitter debate about the nature of legal education in Ontario. This book tells the story of that debate and one of its leading participants, Cecil Augustus Wright.

'Caesar' Wright was one of the first Canadian legal academics to attend Harvard Law School, and his Harvard background played a significant role in the development of his position in the controversy over legal education. The established lawyers who served as benchers of the law society insisted that legal training should be principally a matter of practical experience. Wright, who sought to bring American notions of the roles of lawyer and legal academic to Ontario, tried unsuccessfully to persuade the benchers that the job of educating young lawyers should be transferred to the universities. Decades of contention culminated in 1949 with Wright's dramatic resignation from Osgoode Hall Law School and his appointment as dean of the newly created Faculty of Law at the University of Toronto.

The debate between the benchers of the law society and the proponents of academic legal education touched the lives of many prominent lawyers and law professors, and its resolution permanently changed the nature of legal education in Ontario. Ian Kyer and Jerome Bickenbach offer an account of the conflict and a portrait of the energetic and often acerbic figure who has been called Canada's most influential law teacher.

C. IAN KYER holds a doctorate in history and practises corporate and commercial law with the Toronto firm of Fasken and Calvin.

JEROME E. BICKENBACH is an associate professor of philosophy and a lecturer in law at Queen's University.

The Fiercest Debate

Cecil A. Wright,
the Benchers, and
Legal Education in Ontario
1923-1957

C. IAN KYER
AND
JEROME E. BICKENBACH

Published for The Osgoode Society by
University of Toronto Press
Toronto   Buffalo   London

© The Osgoode Society 1987
Printed in Canada

ISBN 0-8020-3986-3

Printed on acid-free paper

Canadian Cataloguing in Publication Data

Kyer, Clifford Ian, 1949–
The fiercest debate

Includes index.
ISBN 0-8020-3986-3

1. Wright, Cecil A., 1904-1967.   2. Osgoode Hall Law School – History.
3. University of Toronto. Faculty of Law – History.
4. Law – Study and teaching – Ontario – Toronto – History.
5. Law teachers – Ontario – Biography.
I. Bickenbach, Jerome Edmund. II. Osgoode Society. III. Title.

KE289.K96 1987   340'.092'4   C87-094636-6
KF272.K96 1987

Contents

FOREWORD   vii

PREFACE   ix

Introduction   3

1   Wright as Student: Osgoode Hall 1923–1926   37

2   The Bar Associations and Legal Education   60

3   Wright at Harvard: The Shaping of a Legal Scholar   80

4   Wright as Teacher: Osgoode Hall 1927–1935   98

5   The Decade of Frustration: 1935–1944   134

6   The Summer of 1945   162

7   Negotiations and Manoeuvres   176

8   Confrontation   201

9   'An Honest to God Law School'   222

10   The Road to Compromise   241

Epilogue   264

APPENDIX: THE WRITINGS OF CECIL A. WRIGHT   279

NOTES   287

INDEX   331

PUBLICATIONS OF THE OSGOODE SOCIETY

1981 David H. Flaherty, ed. *Essays in the History of Canadian Law,* volume I
1982 Marian MacRae and Anthony Adamson *Cornerstones of Order: Courthouses and Town Halls of Ontario, 1784–1914*
1983 David H. Flaherty, ed. *Essays in the History of Canadian Law,* volume II
1984 Patrick Brode *Sir John Beverley Robinson: Bone and Sinew of the Compact*
1984 David Williams *Duff: A Life in the Law*
1985 James G. Snell and Frederick Vaughan *The Supreme Court of Canada: History of the Institution*
1986 Martin L. Friedland *The Case of Valentine Shortis: A True Story of Crime and Politics in Canada*
1986 Paul Romney *Mr Attorney: The Attorney General for Ontario in Court, Cabinet, and Legislature, 1791–1899*
1987 C. Ian Kyer and Jerome E. Bickenbach *The Fiercest Debate: Cecil A. Wright, the Benchers, and Legal Education in Ontario, 1923–1957*

Foreword

THE OSGOODE SOCIETY

The purpose of The Osgoode Society is to encourage research and writing in the history of Canadian law. The Society, which was incorporated in 1979 and is registered as a charity, was founded at the initiative of the Honourable R. Roy McMurtry, at that time attorney general of Ontario, and officials of The Law Society of Upper Canada. Its efforts to stimulate legal history in Canada include the sponsorship of a fellowship and an annual lectureship, research support programs, and work in the field of oral history and legal archives. The Society publishes (at the rate of about one a year) volumes that contribute to legal-historical scholarship in Canada and which are of interest to the Society's members. Included are studies of the courts, the judiciary, and the legal profession, biographies, collections of documents, studies in criminology and penology, accounts of great trials, and work in the social and economic history of the law.

Current directors of The Osgoode Society are Brian Bucknall, Mr Justice Archie G. Campbell, Douglas Ewart, Martin Friedland, Jane Banfield Haynes, John D. Honsberger, Kenneth Jarvis, Mr Justice Allen Linden, Brendan O'Brien, and Peter Oliver. The attorney general for Ontario and the treasurer of The Law Society of Upper Canada are directors ex officio. The Society's honorary president is the Honourable R. Roy McMurtry. The annual report and information about membership may be obtained by writing The Osgoode Society, Osgoode Hall, 130 Queen Street West, Toronto Ontario, Canada, M5H 2N6. Members receive the annual volumes published by the Society.

Disagreements over legal education have by no means been restricted to Ontario or to the twentieth century. The nature of legal education was debated in many parts of Europe and North America in the course of the nineteenth century. As the century drew to a close, the issue assumed its modern guise as part of a wider process of adjustment of disparate middle-class elements to the forces of urbanization and industrialization. Disputes arose between university faculties and legal practitioners over who should be responsible for training new lawyers; more significantly, the very nature of legal education became the subject of passionate debate.

In Ontario, these difficulties assumed a unique form in response to the nature of provincial society and the conservative traditions of the Ontario legal community. The issue came to the fore somewhat later in Ontario than in other locales; it involved an extended struggle between a powerful and entrenched professional body and Cecil A. Wright, a man of great determination; and, ironically, it gave new substance to enduring tensions between the legal community's pride in its British heritage and Wright's single-minded efforts to introduce American ideas and methods to the study of law in Ontario.

The Fiercest Debate is at once an analysis of a particular and specialized subject and a wider study of the forces of modernization and professionalization at work in a provincial society. Dr Kyer and Professor Bickenbach offer a fascinating narrative that will engage the reader and shed light on the development of the professional traditions of those who teach and practise law in Canada.

Brendan O'Brien
President

Peter N. Oliver
Editor-in-Chief

Preface

This book is the product of chance discoveries, happy coincidences, and a working partnership. When Ian Kyer came to the University of Toronto Law School in 1977, he felt that he was leaving his historical pursuits behind. When Jerome Bickenbach entered the school the next year, he too feared that he would have little time to think or write about the philosophy of law. Though we had both earned doctorates in our respective disciplines, we turned to law because employment prospects seemed so much better there.

Being unable to completely suppress his interest in historical matters, Kyer, along with a friend, David Petras, began systematically to explore the old buildings in which the Faculty of Law at the University of Toronto is housed. The results of their research into the history of the buildings were published in the law school newsletter every two weeks.

One day, with the permission of Dean Martin L. Friedland, Petras and Kyer made their way into the attic of Flavelle House, the main law school building. There, in a far corner of the very large attic, they found four or five boxes of old books and papers. Brushing away the dust, they discovered that several of the boxes contained notes made by Cecil A. Wright while he was a student at Osgoode Hall and Harvard University. Other boxes contained notes and manuscript pages in what they assumed was Wright's handwriting. They proclaimed to themselves that they had found the 'Wright papers.'

Months passed, and nothing further was done with the papers. Kyer became the editor of the *University of Toronto Faculty of Law Review* and in this capacity met Bickenbach, a first-year law student eager to work on the *Law Review*. One day, we discussed the discovery of the 'Wright papers,' and, after managing to get a key to the attic, we confronted the dusty and dilapidated cardboard boxes in which the papers were kept. Agreeing that the papers should be cleaned and properly stored somewhere, we took them down to the *Law Review* office, borrowed the custodian's vacuum cleaner, and began the job of cleaning the documents.

Having taken this step, we thought it only right that we inform the officials of the law school of what we had done. When we did, we were told by Dean Friedland that the boxes in the attic contained only a small part of the papers of Dean Wright that were stored at the school. The most interesting papers, he said, were in several boxes in the associate dean's office. We approached the associate dean, Ted Alexander, and received his enthusiastic encouragement to bring all of the Wright papers together into a usable collection. He gave us the four boxes he had in his office, and explained that there were additional papers in the basement of Falconer Hall. We spent many enjoyable hours reviewing the papers, putting them into clean file folders and archive boxes provided by the law librarian, Shi Sheng Hu, and compiling an index of them.

The project had been proceeding for some months when Ken McCarter, a third-year student, remarked when told of the papers, 'Oh, you mean the papers in the coffee room.' Knowing nothing of these papers, Kyer was taken to a small room in Flavelle House where coffee supplies were kept. There, on a shelf in the corner, were six old letter boxes, each marked 'Canadian Bar Review: Letters of C.A. Wright.' The boxes contained many personal letters, including some of the most interesting items in the Wright collection.

From a few offhand remarks and chance discoveries we had accumulated over one hundred archive boxes full of materials. Not all of the documents related to Wright; some were from the W.P.M. Kennedy era of the law school. Together, however, they made up a substantial body of material. It did not take us long to realize that we had the primary sources for a novel examination of legal education in Ontario. We had before us the materials we needed to tell the story of how certain ideas and attitudes absorbed by the young Wright during his year at Harvard Law School changed his perspective on law, the legal profession, and legal education, and how, animated by Wright's powerful and often acerbic personality, those ideas and attitudes helped to alter the structure of legal education institutions in this province.

This book was written with the co-operation and encouragement of many people. We first thank Dean Martin L. Friedland and his successors, Dean Frank Iacobucci and Dean Robert Prichard, for their continuing interest and initial financial support for our project. Professor Ted Alexander, who had at one time contemplated writing a book on Wright, deserves special acknowledgment for his enthusiasm and insightful comments in the formative stages of this project. A general thank-you is owed, in fact, to the entire faculty of the University of Toronto Law School and its student body during the years 1977–81 for their support. Cecil Wright's son William made available certain personal papers and provided much information and encouragement. The former president of the University of Toronto, James Ham, permitted us access to the papers of President Sidney Smith, and Harold Averill, an assistant archivist at the University of Toronto Archives, gave us considerable assistance in using those papers. (In return, we were able to arrange to have the Wright papers stored in the university archives.)

We must also thank the former treasurer of the Law Society of Upper Canada, Mr Justice John Bowlby, and the secretary of the law society, Kenneth Jarvis, for permission to review the society's files on legal education. In addition, many individuals graciously answered our questions, either in person or in correspondence. First and foremost, we wish to acknowledge the assistance of the late Right Honourable Bora Laskin, chief justice of the Supreme Court of Canada, in providing us with helpful comments and constructive criticism. John Willis corresponded with us and shared his recollections. W.P.M. Kennedy's sons, Gilbert and Frere, provided information and pictures. John J. Robinette, QC, Henry Borden, QC, Mr Justice John Arnup, Mr Justice Robert Reid, John Honsberger, QC, and Brendan O'Brien, QC, were all most co-operative in granting us interviews. We also wish to thank the *University of Toronto Law Journal* and its former editor, R.C.B. Risk, for allowing us to incorporate portions of our *Journal* article into the book.

The Osgoode Society gave us a generous grant to meet certain expenses of preparing the manuscript, and the Social Sciences and Humanities Research Council of Canada provided Bickenbach with a research grant that made it possible for him to take a year away from teaching to devote more time to this book.

Many people have provided expert secretarial help and enthusiastic assistance over the years that we have worked on this manuscript, including Julia Hall, Karen Beairsto, Tracy McGarry, Lesley Hunter, Corrine Wuschenny, and Aleli De Villon. The law firm of Fasken and

Calvin, where Kyer has been employed since 1980, has been supportive of this project in many ways. Phyllis Kyer deserves special thanks for her patience and encouragement.

Many others, too numerous to list here, have assisted us by reading and commenting upon all or part of the manuscript. We, of course, assume full responsibility for any errors that may be found in the book, and we wish to thank those readers for ensuring that there were not more. Special thanks are owed to David Shopiro, Kyer's father-in-law, and to Mr Justice Arnup, each of whom reviewed the first draft of the manuscript very carefully and took the time and trouble to correct the many grammatical and typographical errors that made their way into that draft. We also wish to thank the Osgoode Society's editor-in-chief, Peter N. Oliver, for his patience with us over the years, and for his many helpful suggestions along the way. Finally, both authors owe an enormous debt to Kathy Johnson, whose editorial skill and linguistic common sense are matched only by her cheerfulness and patience.

C.A. Wright as a young scholar,
University of Western Ontario, 1923

Osgoode Hall in the 1920s

Old friends and allies:
President Smith and Dean Wright in March 1948 at the installation of
George Hall as president of the University of Western Ontario

A contemplative W.P.M. Kennedy   Sidney Smith at the Wright home

Five treasurers of the Law Society of Upper Canada, May 1950:
left to right Shirley Denison, R.S. Robertson, Cyril Carson, D'Alton McCarthy,
Gershom Mason

The replacements, Osgoode Hall faculty 1951:
left to right Donald Spence, Allan Leal, John Falconbridge,
Dean C.E. Smalley-Baker, David Smout, Desmond Morton

Resignation publicity, January 1949:
left to right Stanley Edwards, John Willis, Bora Laskin, and C.A. Wright pose
for the press

W. Earl Smith, secretary of the Law Society of Upper Canada

Park Jamieson

The opening of Flavelle House, University of Toronto:
left to right Principal Alex Corry of Queen's, Lord Devlin, C.A. Wright,
Chief Justice J.C. McRuer, Dean E.N. Griswold of Harvard

The Fiercest Debate

... if the question whether English law can be taught at the Universities could be submitted in the form of a case to a body of eminent counsel there is no doubt whatever as to what would be their answer. They would reply with unanimity and without hesitation that English law must be learned and cannot be taught, and that the only places where it can be learned are the law courts and chambers.

A.V. Dicey, 1883

... law is a science ... all the available materials of that science are contained in printed books ... a University, and a University alone, can furnish every possible facility for teaching and learning law.

Christopher Columbus Langdell, 1886

Rightly considered there is no conflict between the educational functions of the office and the school, each is the complement of the other.

William Albert Reeve, 1889

Introduction

Bora Laskin, the late chief justice of Canada, wrote in 1969:

When ... Dr D.A. MacRae moved to Osgoode Hall Law School as a full-time lecturer in 1924 and that school began to strengthen its teaching faculty under newly appointed Dean John D. Falconbridge, while at the same time a concurrent system of law school and law office attendance was maintained in the only law school until 1949 permitted to qualify students in Ontario for law practice, a policy was set for a quarter of a century that ultimately engendered the fiercest debate on legal education that Canada has hitherto known.[1]

This is the story of that debate over legal education in Ontario. On the surface, the debate concerned the practical question of how best to educate prospective lawyers: should they be taught by professional law teachers in a full-time law school situated in a university, or should they be trained through extensive apprenticeship in the offices of a practising lawyer? Should they be lectured to, or should they be forced to engage in socratic dialogue to expose the legal principles embedded in judicial decisions? Should legal education be a matter of learning a trade from those already practising it, or should it involve a combination of theoretical learning and practical skills? If a combination of the theoretical and the practical was the best scheme, which aspect should be emphasized? Should practical training dominate, with lectures given only to supplement practice, or should the practical skills be learned only after the 'science' of the law had been systematically set out and absorbed by the students? But the controversy over the appropriate character of legal education – academic learning, practical training, or both – represented deeper questions, questions few Canadians had satisfactorily reflected upon: What was the role of the lawyer? What contribution could the teacher of the law make to the law, the legal profession, and society as a whole? Who could better determine the course that legal education should take, the practitioner or the law teacher?

The story of the development of legal education in Ontario is not only a history of conflicting philosophies of education, but a history of the evolution of the practical and academic legal professions, their functions, and their responsibilities. The legal profession is unique in the range and scope of its critical self-scrutiny; no other body has so closely examined the question of what constitutes the proper preparation for admission to the profession. The development of legal education in Ontario, for various reasons (some unique to the cultural background of the province, others common to Canadian institutions generally), brings into relief the conflicting attitudes, preconceptions, and philosophies about the profession that may not have been so clearly visible in other common-law jurisdictions.

The story of the career of Cecil Augustus Wright is in many ways the story of legal education in Ontario. 'Caesar' Wright, as he was known by friend and foe alike, has been called 'the father of Canadian tort law,' 'the architect of legal education in Ontario,' and 'the most powerful influence on legal studies that Canadian legal education has known.'[2] Wright's career spanned five decades. He was a student in the mid-1920s, when Dr Donald A. MacRae and Dean John D. Falconbridge began to change Osgoode Hall Law School from a trade school to an academic institution. In 1927 he joined the teaching staff of Osgoode Hall after a year at Harvard Law School, where he was the first Canadian to earn an SJD degree. In the 1930s and 1940s he lobbied continuously, in person and in print, for more academic instruction for law students. In 1948, when he was named dean of Osgoode Hall, he pushed even harder for reform. In 1949, when he was confronted by an uncompromising Law Society of Upper Canada, the governing body of the profession in Ontario, he spearheaded a revolt against the law society's control of legal education in the province and established a rival law school at the University of Toronto. In the 1950s, he fought to win official sanction for his law school, which was finally granted in 1957.

The debate between those who, like Wright, wanted a larger academic component in legal education and those members of the law society who favoured more practical training for law students was not merely a clash of personalities (although there is no doubt that Wright's combative personality contributed to the ferocity of the debate). It was, in Bora Laskin's words, 'a clash of principle,' or, more correctly, a clash of principles. The controversy that culminated in the public resignation of Wright and three other Osgoode Hall professors reflected attitudes towards legal education and the profession that had developed slowly over the course of centuries, first in England, then in the United States.

The benchers of the Law Society of Upper Canada staunchly upheld the principles that legal education must be practical in order to prepare the lawyer to serve society, and that the educational process should be controlled by those who practised the profession. In contrast, Wright and his teaching colleagues stressed the 'learned' nature of the profession and the need for the educational process to be developed and controlled by professional educators. In many respects the controversy represented a clash between American and English ideas about legal education. Although it is tempting to describe the establishment of university law schools in Ontario as the triumph of the innovative American approach over the traditional English approach to legal education and the profession, and although it is not inaccurate to describe Caesar Wright's endeavours as an attempt to 'Americanize' legal education in Ontario, it is none the less wrong to draw the battle-lines so starkly. Every revolutionary upheaval creates a new regime that incorporates aspects of the regime that was revolted against. In Ontario, a hybrid form of legal education developed and evolved in several stages, some of which were looked upon with admiration by observers in both the United States and England.

In many respects, too, the debate reflected a contest between differing perceptions of the role of the lawyer and his place in society. From the beginning the leading members of the Law Society of Upper Canada conceived of the society as more than an educational institution geared to train young lawyers; they also thought it the responsibility of the society to build and maintain a professional élite.[3] Wright and his followers shared that vision of the profession, which was fashioned for the most part in the 1920s by those American legal educators who saw the need to diversify the functions of lawyers, and in particular to train lawyers to serve as advisers to governments. This entailed, as we shall see, the development of a new 'sub-profession' – that of the legal educator who was both an academic and a political adviser.

To appreciate the unique history of legal education in Ontario, it is necessary to review the historical development of legal education in England and in the United States. From the twelfth and thirteenth centuries, law was, both on the Continent and at the great English universities of Oxford and Cambridge, a university discipline. The law that was studied, however, was Roman law and the canon law that drew so heavily upon it. Although as early as the twelfth century Roman law in England was a *cadaver juris*, in the universities there was life in it, since it formed the basis for training in legal dialectics and jurisprudence. In time, the Roman law of the universities was received back into the continental courts. Professor-made law, in the form of codifications and refinements of Roman law, formed the civil-law tradition still in place today in Quebec and Europe. Because of the role of the scholar in the development of civil law, universities in civil-law jurisdictions have always had a secure hold on legal education.

In contrast, the development in England of a 'common law' largely independent of Roman and canon law determined the course of legal education in that country and in the rest of the common-law world. The national law in England was the law of the courts, not the law of the universities and the academics. The common law had its origins with Glanville and the petty assizes of the late twelfth century. In the latter part of the thirteenth century, the Year Books appeared. The Year Books were compilations of law derived from notes made in court by law students and junior practitioners, individuals whose sole concern was the practice of the profession. The common law, given its origins and the absence of a text such as Justinian provided for Roman law and Gratian for canon law, was thought incapable of university instruction, and students of the common law were denied the systematic method of study offered to students of Roman and canon law. Although it did not lack intellectual content, the common law was regarded primarily as a trade to be learned.

Special institutions and methods of instructions had to be developed to train those who desired to practise in the common-law courts. The most prominent of these were for four principal inns of court – the Inner Temple, the Middle Temple, Gray's Inn, and Lincoln's Inn. They were self-contained and self-regulated bodies, and they came to occupy a permanent place in the professional culture of English law. References to the inns of court go back to the early 1300s, when Edward I directed judges to make provisions for apprentices of the law. Although little is known of the nature and function of the inns in their early years of existence, they were eventually entrusted with the task of preparing and admitting barristers, the select group of lawyers who argued in court.[4] Solicitors, who came in direct contact with the public and drafted wills, deeds, and other legal instruments, were not members of the inns of court, and rules regarding their preparation and fitness for practice were, from the beginning, established by statute. Until 1729, when apprenticeship training was introduced, solicitors were not given any organized education by the bar.

For nearly two hundred years the inns of court monopolized the teaching of English law. The inns also served to restrict the numbers of barristers. Admittance to the bar required the student to 'keep terms' at an inn, and the expense of doing so was considerable. Sir John Fortescue notes in *De Laudibus Legum Angliae*, written about 1470, that only 'Sons to Persons of Quality' were sent to the inns, not merely to make the law their study but also to 'form their manners and to preserve them from the contagion of vice.' It is likely that the discipline of the primarily oral exercises, coupled with the infrequent lectures by prominent lawyers, tamed the young men's spirits and enabled them to acquire practical experience of the rigours of advocacy.

For a variety of reasons, however, the inns ceased to teach law in the last quarter of the seventeenth century. All that remained, in a period aptly described by William Holdsworth as the 'decadence of legal education,'[5] were the formalities: the more or less meaningless oral exercises, the mandatory keeping of terms, and the payment of the necessary fees. Even in the universities, lectures required for the attainment of the bachelor or laws degree ceased to be given and were replaced by perfunctory Latin exercises and residence requirements. By the beginning of the eighteenth century, formal legal education had effectively ceased to exist in England. The result was that the student of law was left to teach himself as best he could. He was advised to follow Roger North's program of legal study set out in his *Discourse on the Study of the Laws*, written in the 1730s, which recommended studying the few texts there were, carefully 'commonplacing' legal principles and notions, and attending sessions of the courts.

Soon enough the law student, if for no other reason than to have other students to discuss the law with, was forced to rely on the system of apprenticeship, or articles, which, with the decline of the educative function of the inns of court, became popular. The system of apprenticing in the chambers of special pleaders, conveyancers, and equity draughtsmen became in time the most reliable method of practical legal training. As this regime of legal education gained ascendancy, it was common to find barristers who had gone through such a procedure expressing grave doubts whether formal education of the sort found in universities could be of any use to the student-at-law.

Apprenticeship was also made necessary by the lack of accessible legal literature. There were such works as Bracton's *De Legibus et Consuetudinibus Angliae* (1250) and *Coke upon Littleton* (1628), but these were not particularly helpful to the neophyte. In 1720 Thomas Wood sought to remedy the situation by completing a project Francis Bacon had begun nearly one hundred years before. The result was a digest-like volume called the *Institutes of the Laws of England*, the object of which was to make the law a 'scientific whole' – that is, to extract the basic principles of the common law and to present them, with commentary, in an orderly fashion.

Thomas Wood's effort failed; it was a dull statement of the law in the form of categorical propositions, and made no attempt to organize the common law in a usable manner. But Wood's work paved the way for another attempt that eventually led to a revolutionary change in the concept of legal education. In 1753 a young lawyer by the name of William Blackstone lectured on English law at Oxford. Blackstone's were the first such lectures given at an English university, and they soon became popular. Over the next five years Blackstone organized his lectures and published his *Commentaries on the Laws of England*. This work, like Wood's, was premised on the view that English law was not merely a collection of disjointed rules, learnable only in practice, but a rational and coherent whole that could be explained and studied as a university subject. In 1758, Oxford University, pursuant to the terms of the will of Charles Viner (himself a keen advocate of the systematic study of English law and the author of a twenty-four-volume abridgment), appointed Blackstone the first university professor of English law.

In the first volume of his *Commentaries*, Blackstone strongly criticized the apprenticeship approach to legal education. He found it astonishing that an area of knowledge of such importance was not taught systematically. The notion that students could acquire knowledge of the law in the service of an attorney or barrister Blackstone dismissed as ludicrous: 'If practice be the whole he is taught, practice must also be the whole he will ever know: if he be uninstructed in the elements and first principles upon which the rule of practice is founded, the least variation from established precedents will totally distract and bewilder him.'[6] How, Blackstone asked, could we allow the interpretation and enforcement of the law that vitally affects our property, liberty, and lines to fall into the hands of illiterate men? The only hope for the profession, he argued, was to make an academic education a prerequisite to legal study, and to make legal study part of a university education.

Blackstone's views on the nature and aims of legal education formed the basic creed of those who were to argue for the university law school for the next three centuries: law can be systematically taught, not merely as a body of practical rules but as a science; as a science, law can be taught only in a university setting surrounded by teachers and students of the other sciences. This being so, the argument went, professional law teachers must be skilled both in the practice of the law and in the science of the law and what we would regard today as the kindred social sciences. In addition, legal education needed a literature, the product of specialized legal scholars able to assess and recommend changes in the law. As we shall see, the university setting, the professionalization of legal academics, and the development of legal scholarship formed the core of demands made by the crusaders for university law schools.

Blackstone's aspirations for legal education for 'gentlemen of all ranks and degrees' came to an abrupt end in 1766. Exasperated by the conservatism of the legal profession, itself mostly untrained in the learned study of the law and unconvinced of the need for such training, Blackstone resigned his post at Oxford. The system of office apprenticeship continued, and, in England at least, the only marks left by Blackstone were the volumes of his *Commentaries*, which the student simply added to the short list of books he was required to master on his own.

In the first half of the nineteenth century several attempts were made to upgrade legal education for barristers. In 1842 the University of London took the bold step of appointing John Austin to teach the common law, but the profession paid little attention. Solicitors were organized into a profession by the creation by statute of the Incorporated Law Society. Soon thereafter, statutory requirements of fitness to practise forced the the law society to organize a series of lectures for its articling clerks. The lectures were sporadically given and poorly attended. This system of legal education, rudimentary at best, none the less gave law students some assurance of practical experience. But the costly system of residence at the inns of court effectively made admission to the bar a matter of birth and money. For the privileged few there was little reason to change the traditional scheme; barristers formed an élite class centred in London, and their numbers were maintained by a steady inflow of sons of the upper class. Fortunately for the profession, most of the young future barristers had had the benefit of a good general education, so that a certain minimal level of competence was likely to be achieved.

In the age of reform, however, such a system could not endure un-challenged. In 1846 Parliament created a select committee to inquire into the general state of legal education in England. Its report echoed Black-stone's complaints ninety years before. The committee took the position that emphasizing the purely practical, even mechanical, side of the law at the expense of the doctrinal side would soon prove fatal to the de-velopment of the law.

The consequence has been that in this country we have, generally speaking, but few examples of that important class of thinkers and writers who, in other countries, standing on the summits of the profession, and disengaged from the turmoil and labour of its daily technical duties, have, with its position and capacity, leisure also, and the opportunity to keep the profession up to the intellectual height, to which it should be the proudest boast to aspire. Also publicists and professors form a class apart, occupying the most honourable posts in their profession, and in the service of the state. Here such a class is comparatively unknown, and individual examples are rare; and yet few countries have, from the principles and forms of its government and constitution, greater need of such a body than ours.[7]

The select committee made two recommendations. First, the univer-sities should create schools of law and attract scholars; degrees in law should be offered, and the universities should foster a philosophical and theoretical training in legal principles, especially in the areas of juris-prudence and international and constitutional law. Second, the inns of court and the Incorporated Law Society should take it upon themselves to provide professional legal training. Compulsory lectures should be given regularly, and extensive examinations should be required.

The thrust of the committee's recommendations was that there should be a three-way division of responsibility for legal education. The uni-versities were to train legal scholars; the inns were to produce educated barristers; and the Incorporated Law Society was to produce competent solicitors. All three institutions responded enthusiastically, and over the next twenty-five years most of the recommendations were implemented. Oxford and Cambridge offered the degrees of bachelor of common law and bachelor of laws by 1853; the inns of court established lectureships and in 1852 created the Council of Legal Education to oversee the education of barristers; and the law society expanded its lecture program and took control of examinations for admission to the bar.

In many respects, these changes improved the state of legal education in England. But the committee's recommendations also served to entrench one of the greatest weaknesses in the English tradition of legal education. Because of the strict division of educational labour between the universities and the two professional organizations, the gap between the theoretical and the practical was widened. Few students wishing for a career as a barrister or solicitor thought it necessary, or for that matter even desirable, to begin their education with a bachelor of laws degree from a university, and few LL B candidates intended to practise law. The ruling bodies of the inns, or 'benchers,' insisted that as far as the learning of practical skills was concerned the student could do no better than turn to the law courts and chambers.

That the practice of English law could not be taught at the universities was self-evident: there was no one there to teach it. The select committee had insisted that the inns of court and the law society should teach practical professional skills, while the universities should teach the general theory of the law. For many decades to come, committees on legal education would reject the proposal that a university education be required to begin the study of law. They reasoned that university training was not relevant to professional studies and would unnecessarily lengthen the time required to qualify as a barrister or solicitor. What *was* required was between three and five years of unbroken apprenticeship. In short, the effect of the 1846 reform was to ensure the persistence of the institutional ignorance of the basic principles of the law that Blackstone condemned. The universities were geared to produce legal scholars, while the profession itself admitted students who were given what amounted to vocational training.

The English tripartite system of legal education continued into the twentieth century, and a distinction still exists between the academic instruction provided by universities and the practical training offered at schools controlled by the professional bodies. In 1971 the Ormrod committee discovered that the professional law schools had improved their teaching to the point that they were on par with the thirty or so universities and polytechnics that offered academic degrees in law. The committee recommended that the professional schools cease to offer academic degrees in law; but, following centuries-old tradition, the committee affirmed the need for extensive articling experience (or 'in-training') before a student could be allowed to practise law.

Over the centuries there has been vigorous criticism of the system of legal education in England. The great legal historian and Vinerian Professor at Oxford, William Holdsworth, remarked of the situation in the eighteenth century: 'It is indeed a curious paradox that in a state in which the wording of the constitution depended upon the law, a state in which the country gentlemen who sat in the House of Commons were legislators, and the peers were legislators and judges, a state in which the administration of the local government and of large parts of criminal law was entrusted to unpaid amateurs, no provision should be made for training in the rudiments of law the persons on whom these duties were cast.'[8]

More critical still was A.V. Dicey, who argued in 1871 that the training of barristers was so poor as to be embarrassing, that reading in chambers was an expensive sham practised on the apprentice, and that the education given at the inns of court was far too narrow.[9] In his inaugural lecture as Vinerian Professor in 1883, Dicey spoke strongly in favour of placing professional law teaching in the university, where the student could learn to analyse legal concepts and could be given the opportunity to see the law as a whole. For the next twenty-seven years Dicey made every effort to upgrade legal education, and in particular to supply a desperately needed legal literature.

In 1898 Dicey gave a series of lectures at Harvard University. He returned to England greatly impressed by the quality of the teaching of law at Harvard Law School. On his return to Oxford, Dicey published an article entitled 'The Teaching of English Law at Harvard,' which was subsequently published in the *Harvard Law Review*. In it Dicey discussed in detail the school and its teaching methods. Although Harvard, as a professional school, differed in aim from Oxford, Dicey enthusiastically endorsed the teaching methodology he found there, noting that 'the Harvard experiment' showed beyond a doubt that English law could be taught successfully in a university.[10]

Dicey was not the first Englishman to look to the United States, and especially to Harvard, for a model of legal education. James Bryce wrote in 1888, 'I do not know if there is anything in which America has advanced more beyond the mother country than on the provisions she makes for legal education.'[11] Most American legal educators proudly agreed. Speaking to the legal education section of the American Bar Association in 1895, the Harvard law professor James Bradley Thayer bluntly remarked, 'We, in America, have carried legal education much farther than it has gone in England. There the systematic teaching of law in schools is but faintly developed. Here it is elaborate, widely favored, rapidly extending. Why is this? Not because we originated this method. We transplanted our English root, and nurtured and developed it, while at home it was suffered to languish and die down.'[12]

The 'English root' was of course Blackstone. Colonial America had trained its lawyers with the English methods of self-teaching and apprenticeship. But Blackstone's *Commentaries*, and his vision of legal education, became immediately popular in America. It was Blackstone's great experiment in the university teaching of law, Thayer wrote, 'and the publication a little before the American Revolution, of the results of that experiment, which furnished the stimulus and the examplar for our own early attempts at systematic legal education.'[13] One immediate effect of Blackstone's influence was the establishment, after the Revolution, of chairs in law at American universities. The first such chair was founded through the efforts of Thomas Jefferson in 1779 at William and Mary College; the first incumbent was George Wythe, with whom Jefferson had studied law. In the same year Isaac Royall bequeathed property to Harvard College to provide the means by which to hire a professor in law.

Overall, however, these early attempts to develop law as a university subject were not successful. It was not until 1815, for example, that Isaac Parker was appointed professor of law at Harvard College. In the late eighteenth century, the student who wished to prepare himself for a legal career – and, increasingly, to realize his political ambitions – turned not to the universities but to the private law school. As the apprenticeship approach to legal education was abandoned, private schools opened to meet the demand for legal training. Practitioners who had shown themselves to be particularly successful as teachers responded to the growing demand for legal instruction. The most famous of these schools, and by far the most successful, was the Litchfield Law School, established in 1784 by Tapping Reeve and James Gould, practitioners who had drawn eager students to their offices in Litchfield, Connecticut, for a decade. The Litchfield Law School produced a long list of extremely successful graduates until the 1830s, when many such schools were overshadowed by the growing university law schools. None the less, in the United States the private law school, which typically offered part-time classes conveniently held in the evenings, remained a popular form of preparation for admission to the bar.

From the beginning, legal education in the United States was not the exclusive province of professional organizations with statutory powers and responsibilities – in striking contrast to the situation that existed in England and, as we shall see, in Canada. This early period has been described as the 'laissez faire' or 'Jacksonian democracy' period of American legal education. There was a market for legal education, and various types of institutions moved to satisfy it. In addition, probably as a conscious rejection of the elitism of the English bar, regulations from admission to the profession were often minimal and not rigorously enforced. From 1851 to 1933 the constitution of Indiana, for example, provided that every person of good moral character who was a voter was entitled to be admitted to the bar.[14] The egalitarian ethos of the United States ensured that there would be strong pressure against erecting barriers to entry to the profession, especially since the practice of law was often the first step to a career in politics or business. This free-enterprise approach to legal education was part of the larger American vision: anyone, regardless of social position, through industry and self-sacrifice, could enter the ranks of the wealthy and politically powerful.

Of course, the vision of equal opportunity was not always translated into practice. De facto restrictions on the opportunities for blacks and women to enter the legal profession were accepted as a matter of course. More important, however, even the empty expression of equal opportunity was not looked upon with favour by all members of the legal profession. In some important respects, the gradual move towards the university law schools, coupled with the professionalization of the lawyer's role, was a shift towards (or back to) a legal elitism, even though this change was for the most part motivated by a concern about the quality of preparation for legal practice. From the beginning it was the Harvard Law School that took the lead.

In the first dozen years of its existence, enrolment in Harvard Law School averaged nine students a year. In 1829 Justice Joseph Story was elected Dane Professor at the school. Story reorganized the school and, like Dicey at Oxford fifty years later, began the slow process of increasing the prestige of the school with the hope of legitimating university legal training. In most states, admission to the bar required, at most, a period of apprenticeship. All legal education took the form of lectures by practitioners and judges, some of whom, like Justice Story, continued to serve on the bench. But by the 1850s and 1860s legal education in American universities was showing signs of life; in 1860 there were twenty-one university law schools in existence, each of which found itself combating the scepticism of the legal profession over the value of professional legal education in a university setting.

By this time the face – and future – of legal education in the United States was being changed by a revolution in teaching methodology. In the early 1870s the 'casebook method' was introduced at Harvard Law School. This innovative teaching device usually is credited to Christopher Columbus Langdell, although there is some reason to suspect that the originator of the method was Harvard's newly appointed president, Charles W. Eliot.[15] The casebook method, which Eliot had first recommended for the training of scientists, involved the replacement of lectures by an 'inductive' analysis of concrete cases with the aim of identifying general principles. The law teacher's task was changed from that of setting out the principles and practices of the law to the considerably more challenging one of selecting and presenting cases that embodied or exemplified legal principles and, through a process of careful questioning, drawing out these principles from the responses of his students.

Langdell was Eliot's personal choice for dean of the law school when that post became open in the early 1870s. After having practised law in New York for sixteen years, Langdell came to Harvard eager to follow Eliot's lead and to set legal education on a completely new footing. In 1891 he published the first casebook, *Cases on Contracts*. The law, he wrote in the introduction, must be considered as a science consisting of certain principles or doctrines.

To have such a mastery of these as to be able to apply them with constant facility and certainty to the ever-tangled skein of human affairs, is what constitutes a true lawyer; and hence to acquire that mastery should be the business of every student of law. Each of these doctrines has arrived at its present state by slow degrees: in other words, it is a growth, extending in many cases through centuries. This growth is to be traced in the main through a series of cases; and much the shortest and best, if not the only way of mastering the doctrine effectively is by studying the cases in which it is embodied ... It seems to me, therefore, to be possible to take such a branch of the law as Contracts, for example, and, without exceeding comparatively moderate limits, to select, classify, and arrange all the cases which had contributed in any important degree to the growth, development, or establishment of any of its essential doctrines; and that such a work could not fail to be of material service to all who desire to study that branch of law systematically and in its original sources.[16]

Years later, in an address to the Harvard Law School administration, and with the success of the casebook method secured, Langdell elaborated on its virtues. Since the law is a science, and since cases are the experimental data of the science, legal education must be limited to the university; he boldly rejected the notion that law was 'a species of handicraft ... best learned by serving an apprenticeship to one who practices it.' Langdell was convinced that 'law can be learned and taught in a university by means of printed books.' For him books were not just another tool to be used in the work of a lawyer's office, or at attendance upon proceedings of courts of justice. On the contrary, printed books were 'the ultimate sources of all legal knowledge.' Given this, 'a university alone [could] furnish every possible facility for teaching and learning law.'[17]

For the student, Langdell's method meant an opportunity to participate in judicial reasoning. No longer could the student merely record legal doctrines presented in lectures and then demonstrate the accuracy of his memory by regurgitating them on final examinations. The student must work through the law; he must learn a method of classifying judicial opinions, distinguishing superficial similarities, rejecting ill-reasoned cases, discovering inequities, and deriving general conclusions. Throughout the course of his education he would be tested by means of hypothetical situations that required him not only to use legal generalities, but to turn his mind to the inconsistencies and anomalies in the law and to suggest how the law ought to deal with human affairs.

The casebook method, which one observer called 'an entirely original creation of the American mind in the realm of law,'[18] not only revolutionized teaching methodology but changed the character of the university law school and began the process of·'professionalizing' the teachers of law. Langdell felt his method required a higher calibre of student, and, with Eliot's blessing, he began to raise the school's admission standards. The nature of the law school, or at least its reputation, also changed. Langdell's casebook extracted cases from many of the jurisdictions of the United States; the assumption was that the principles presented by these cases cut across state lines, thus undermining the view that legal education should differ from each state. It was not long before Harvard, under Langdell's inspirational leadership, was viewed as a 'national' law school. This effectively began a competition for students among the existing university schools, in which the question of teaching methodology was in the forefront. For the next fifty years other schools sought to challenge Harvard's teaching approaches and its conceptions of the nature of law and the social responsibilites of lawyers.

The most important consequence of the Eliot–Langdell revolution was the rise of the profession of law teacher. The first of this new breed was Langdell's student, James Barr Ames. Ames was appointed assistant professor in 1872, a year after completing his LL B at Harvard and without having practised law. Ames adopted the Langdellian method and extended it to all the common-law subjects. Soon, with William Keener's appointment at Columbia and a succession of appointments of Harvard men at other universities, the casebook method began to attain supremacy. Harvard consciously geared its curriculum to the production of law professors. In 1895 President Eliot told Harvard's Law School Association that the 'experiment' had succeeded: 'In due course ... there will be produced in this country a body of men learned in the law, who have never been on the bench or at the bar, but who nevertheless hold positions of great weight and influence as teachers of the law, as expounders, systematizers and historians. This, I venture to predict, is one of the most far-reaching changes in the organization of the profession that has been made in our country.'[19]

The rise of the 'scientific' teacher of law was made necessary in part by the demands of the Langdellian method. Before 1870, the law teacher had been a practitioner who lectured in his spare time; but the casebook method demanded more time than busy practitioners were prepared to set aside. Moreover, as a 'science' the law was a scholarly undertaking that required, and thus produced, experts. In time, these 'new professionals' enhanced their power in areas of politics and social reform. The law professor became the law reformer, and the gulf widened between the practitioner and the professor, situated in his 'legal laboratory' behind university walls. The development of the legal professoriate was to have a profound effect on the nature of legal education and on American society itself.[20]

At the same time, the offspring of the Litchfield School – the small private night schools – continued to prepare those who could not afford university training for admission to the bar. The seeds of conflict had been planted. A growing and aggressive class of highly educated teachers, who defined their roles in terms of the 'scientific' nature of their expertise and the university environment in which they taught, desired to secure a monopoly over legal education. But the legal practitioners, many of whom lacked university legal training, distrusted university professors as mere theoreticians and resisted every effort to make admission to the bar more difficult. The night schools, which purported only to prepare their students for bar exams, also fought to keep the university monopoly from being established, and were supported in that effort by many practitioners. The situation was further complicated by the emergence of a powerful new group of practitioners – the corporate lawyers from the large firms who catered to the needs of the business élite situated almost exclusively in large cities. Significantly, corporation lawyers, more and more the product of schools like Harvard, often sided with the university law schools in what had become a continuing debate over the need for university legal training.

But it was the conflict between the university law schools and the proprietary night schools that became the main concern of the American bar associations. First, a slow but sustained campaign was initiated after the Civil War by practitioners and legal academics from the twenty or so university law schools to raise the professional standards of bar admission procedures. Since, general speaking, there were no formal requirements to be met before a call to the bar, the crusade at first was aimed merely at convincing the state bar associations to lobby state legislatures to require some period of apprenticeship or legal study prior to admission.

This effort led to the creation in 1878 of the American Bar Association, which dedicated itself and its resources to the campaign to raise standards. Although the ABA represented no more than 5 per cent of the sixty thousand lawyers practising in the country, its membership constituted a powerful élite in the profession. Some have argued that the principal motivation of the ABA lawyers was to rid the profession of undesirables – specifically Jews, immigrants, and blacks.[21] But this intention, if it existed, was masked by the association's public statement of policy: to raise the technical standards and the ethics of the profession.

It was not until the 1890s that the battle heated up sufficiently to come to the attention of all practitioners. Pressure from Harvard and elsewhere began to mount to raise the standards of admission to the bar. The night schools retaliated with the so-called Abraham Lincoln argument. The argument took two forms. First, it was asked, why require three years of university education before a call to the bar when Abraham Lincoln, Chief Justice John Marshall, and other prominent figures had done so well without such training? The second form of the argument would surface in Canada in a different context fifty years later: not every capable man or woman could afford to pursue, on a full-time basis, extensive university training; nor, for that matter, would a general practitioner in a small town need such sophisticated training. A few highly motivated individuals might want an academic education, but what of the average student who was interested only in opening up shop in a small town? For a long period this argument was not unpersuasive, and university supporters often seemed lost for a rebuttal.

In 1892 the American Bar Association established its section on legal education as a forum to discuss these and other educational concerns. The new section soon became the special preserve of the university law teachers. At the annual section meetings such prominent figures as Elihu Root, William Howard Taft, Harlan F. Stone, Woodrow Wilson, John H. Wigmore, Samuel Williston, and other luminaries, usually university scholars, dominated the discussion. The tone of these debates was captured by Justice David J. Brewer's remarks to the 1895 section meeting: 'If our profession is to maintain its prominence, if it is going to continue the great profession, that which leads and directs the movements of society, a longer course of preparatory study must be required. A better education is the great need and the most important reform. The door of admission to the bar must swing on reluctant hinges, and only he be permitted to pass through who has by continued and patient study fitted himself for the work of a safe counselor, the place of a leader.'[22]

By 1897 the ABA had issued a recommendation that three years of study in law schools be required by all states prior to a call to the bar. In 1900, under pressure from the academic lawyers, the ABA created a separate organization, the Association of American Law Schools. From the beginning the AALS represented the views of the academics, and often these views clashed with the majority position of the bar association. Membership in the AALS was restricted to those institutions offering two years of full-time study. In 1905 membership was further restricted to institutions offering three-year programs, and finally, by 1912, all part-time non-university law schools were simply excluded from the AALS.

In 1910 the Flexner report on medical education was published. Commissioned by the council on medical education of the American Medical Association, it bluntly recommended that all medical schools not directly tied to universities be driven out of business by state licensing regulations.[23] The report had the effect of reducing, in one decade, the number of medical schools and medical students by nearly 50 per cent.[24] In 1916, Walter Wheeler Cook of Yale, the president of the AALS, made an impassioned speech urging the ABA to follow the doctors' lead and establish a council on legal education. His colleague at Yale, Henry Wade Roger, was the chairman of the ABA's committee on legal education that year, and the council was formed.

Encouraged by the effects of the Flexner report, the ABA commissioned the Carnegie Foundation for the Advancement of Teaching to produce a similar study for the legal profession. The foundation assigned the job to Alfred Z. Reed.[25] Reed was critical of the night law schools, though sympathetic to their objectives. Arguing that there was a need in the United States for several kinds of lawyers and that a differentiated bar probably was inevitable given the ethnic and economic diversity of the country, Reed did not believe that the attributes of the university law school should be made the standard against which all other law schools should be judged.

The ABA and the AALS responded by joining ranks and rejecting the thrust of the Reed report. The council on legal education now assumed the task of pushing for reform. Originally, the council included the deans of Harvard (Roscoe Pound), Columbia (Harlan F. Stone), Northwestern (John Wigmore), and Minnesota (W.R. Vance). Since the council was heavily packed with academics, it was not surprising that the general membership of the ABA felt that it would soon force the issue of admission standards and refuse to recognize any opposition to the move. The executive committee responded by refusing to fund the council, and it was abolished in 1919. Having learned their lesson, the schoolmen, led now by W. Draper Lewis of the University of Pennsylvania, tried a new strategy. In 1920, on Lewis's motion, Elihu Root, the highly respected past president of the ABA, was elected chairman of a special committee on legal education.

The special committee reported in 1921; the result of its report was a series of compromise resolutions adopted by the membership of the ABA. The schoolmen got what they badly wanted – a declaration that one could obtain an adequate legal education only in a full-time university law school. They also got a recommendation that two years of college education be required before admission to law school. The opposition succeeded in getting night law schools legitimated, as long as they could show that they were offering 'equivalent' hours of law study. But the stroke of genius in the Root report was the recommendation (concurred in by the ABA) that the council on legal education be revived and assigned the task of publishing yearly lists of 'ABA-approved' law schools in the United States. By 1925, this list was identical to the list of member universities of the AALS.

The delegates to the 1921 meeting were far from unanimous in their enthusiasm for the Root report. Dean Edward T. Lee of the John Marshall Law School of Chicago expressed the fears of the night schools when he argued that the effect of the resolution

would be to place the control of legal education through the country in the hands of the deans of a few large day law schools who have the fate of the law teachers in their hands. It would close the profession of the law to all save the leisure class of youth with means sufficient to obtain college and law school training, and would bar hundreds of naturally well-endowed, zealous and industrious youths from attaining an honorable ambition. It would result, in large communities, in the establishment of legal factories with a few lawyers at the head and all others mere clerks cut off from the hope of entering the profession. Finally it would discourage legal education throughout the country, decrease legal knowledge everywhere, and deprive masses of people in our large cities, many of them of foreign extraction, from access to our courts and legal aid for want of lawyers familiar with their language and distinctive customs.[26]

Lee was hinting at a worry that was not ill-founded – namely, that the effect of the universities' victory would not be simply a better-trained and more educated bar; the resolution would also have the effect of producing an elitist bar that would not serve poor, black, or immigrant communities satisfactorily. The elitism of the Root recommendations is illustrated by the fact that barely 5 per cent of would-be law students who would be affected by the changes in pre-legal education completed college.[27]

The ABA recommendations and the subsequent pressure for higher standards in pre-legal and legal training did not have an immediate effect. Some of the state governments that controlled admission to the bar were vigorously opposed to standards that they viewed as being imposed by the eastern establishment. None the less, by 1935, thirty states required two years of college before legal training; by the outbreak of the Second World War nearly all states did. The ABA recommendation favouring law school training was of little significance, since very few students came to the bar with only law-office experience. Still, the battle for the entrenchment of the university law school had been largely won. Today, part-time and night schools continue to provide legal education in the United States, but they have been overshadowed by the university law schools.

The ferment over legal education in the United States in the late nineteenth and early twentieth centuries had only an indirect impact on legal education in Ontario. One important source of American influence was Caesar Wright's exposure to Harvard in 1927; prior to the 1920s, however, developments in the United States had little discernible effect on Canadian legal education. This was not because Harvard Law School was unknown to those responsible for legal education in Canada. Rather, few Canadians believed that the experience of legal education in the United States was relevant to Canadian circumstances. From the beginning, the English-speaking provinces preferred the English approach to legal education.

In the second half of the eighteenth century,[28] this preference was the result of the circumstances that led to the establishment of the bar in the English-speaking provinces. Immediately after the signing of the Treaty of Paris in 1763, the royal proclamation introduced into the old province of Quebec the civil and criminal law of England. The next year the courts of King's Bench and Common Pleas replaced the French judicial institutions. The French offices of avocat, procureur, notaire, and arpenteur were not formally abolished, and, with the reintroduction of French law in civil matters by the Quebec Act of 1774, the French-Canadian lawyers continued practising more or less as they had before the conquest. The privilege to practise in this period came directly from the government by way of licences. After the American Revolution and the passage of the Provincial Articles of Peace in 1782, the legal community in the old province of Quebec pressed for admission requirements. The only system of preparation conceivable at the time – articles of clerkship for five years in the office of an advocate – was officially recognized by the Ordinance of 1785. In 1791, old Quebec was divided into Upper and Lower Canada, and the first act of the first Parliament of Upper Canada ([1792] 32 Geo. III, c.1 [UC]) introduced the English civil law. No other changes directed to the legal profession were instituted.

Although the Ordinance of 1785 continued to govern the legal profession in Lower Canada until 1849, in Upper Canada it was suspended for two years in 1794 and repealed in 1797 and 1798. Initially, there were only two members of the bar competent to plead English law – the attorney-general, John White (an English barrister), and Walter Row (who had recently arrived from Montreal). Three more Upper Canadians began their training under the ordinance: John Ten Broeck, Walter Butler Wilkinson, and William Weekes.[29] In 1794 an act was passed authorizing the governor to grant licences to practise as attorneys to as many as sixteen British subjects. John White and the first chief justice of Upper Canada, William Osgoode (who had been called to the bar at Lincoln's Inn in 1779) could at first find only six suitable candidates, although the full complement of sixteen was soon achieved.

Early Ontario, it appears, did not so much adopt the English approach to legal training as retain it. While the post-revolutionary United States rejected many English traditions, the settlers of Upper Canada, many of whom were loyalists or anti-republicans fleeing the United States, were anxious to carry on English traditions. In particular, the English practices that created a social élite of lawyers emerged early in Upper Canada's development. Only the distinction between barrister and solicitor failed to survive, although even that did not wholly disappear until the middle of the nineteenth century.

The bar in Upper Canada thus moved naturally to English traditions. From the viewpoint of the British empire, all Canadian courts were lower courts of the English Privy Council; English barristers were consequently viewed as automatically qualified to plead before a Canadian court, and it was but a short step – usually taken without conscious thought – to the view that indigenous Canadian barristers should meet the English standards of qualification for practice. In the United States, with its constitutional division of power, the judiciary was independent, and one of its roles became that of admitting lawyers to the bar. In England, that role had been assigned to the bar itself, and was exercised under statute by the governing organization that spoke for the profession. Upper Canada, mimicking England, soon found itself in need of a similar professional organization.

In 1797 the Law Society of Upper Canada was created following a meeting of lawyers convened according to the terms of an act of the legislative assembly of Upper Canada (37 Geo. III [1797], c. 13 [UC].) As that prolific historian of Canadian legal institutions, Mr Justice William R. Riddell, remarked, 'In every line of this Act, the hand of an English Barrister is manifest.'[30] The act separated the professions of 'barrister' and 'attorney' (later called 'solicitor') and specified different periods of articles for each. The titles of 'treasurer' and 'bencher' were brought from the traditions of the inns of court into the Canadian legal profession to designate the officers of the law society. Similarly, the governing body of benchers was called 'Convocation.' The law society was empowered to enrol 'Students of the Laws,' and the first student's name was put on the books of the society in 1801. Students of the law were not required to pass examinations either before entering articles or before being admitted to the society with full privileges to practise law. The student's master, or principal, was solely responsible for his education and, after five years, his acceptability. The law society was quick to institute a complex schedule of fees to be paid by the student at various points in his career.

By 1822 a total of 112 students-at-law had been enrolled, and 65 had been called to the bar. The 1797 act had empowered judges of the Court of King's Bench to admit barristers of England, Scotland, and Ireland as well as of any North American colony to practise in the province. This was not met with favour by the profession, since the inevitable result would be a dilution of the law society's power. The legislature was sympathetic. An act of 1822 made the treasurer and the benchers bodies corporate. The object of this move was in part to give the law society power to hold land and erect a building, known as Osgoode Hall, to house the society and various courts. John Beverley Robinson, the attorney-general, took advantage of the opportunity to make the law society more closely resemble an English inn of court. Through Robinson's efforts, the law society was vested, pursuant to the act, with the exclusive power to admit persons to the practice of law in the province.

The act also took the first step towards eliminating the significance of the distinction between barrister and solicitor by removing from the law society the power to create solicitors. Since the law society had virtually complete control over the legal profession in the province, only the status of barrister was of any significance in practice. In 1857 the law society regained the power to admit solicitors, by which time the distinction between the two kinds of lawyers had effectively disappeared. Speaking as a true product of the English tradition in Canada, Riddell described the final step in the monopolization of control by the law society: 'No Court can hear a Barrister who has not been called by the Society. No Court can admit a Solicitor without the certificate of the Society. The Society is the sole judge of the fitness and capacity of either, and the legal profession is master in its own home.'[31]

By 1832, when the construction of Osgoode Hall was completed, Upper Canada had its own inn of court. Following tradition, the benchers required students-at-law to keep terms at Osgoode Hall. This led to problems that were unique to Canada and that were repeatedly to plague the traditionalists. In Upper Canada not every student-at-law was pleased with the notion of travelling to York (later Toronto) to 'keep terms' at Osgoode Hall. Many aspired to practise in small communities such as Barrie or Windsor. As the years passed, suitable articles were more easily obtained in communities other than Toronto, and the benchers were reluctant to institute compulsory lectures for students because of the bitter complaints from students who lived outside Toronto. One student was moved to write that term-keeping for those in remote sections of the province 'partakes of the character of an absolute outrage.'[32]

Yet by the middle of the nineteenth century it was becoming obvious that law students in Upper Canada required some sort of formal training to supplement their articling experience, however inconvenient it might be to those from remoter areas of the province. As early as 1834, Convocation, responding to student requests for lectures, asked the governor of the soon-to-be-opened King's College that provision be made for a professorship of law.

When the college finally opened its doors, a professor of law was indeed on the staff – William Hume Blake, later the first chancellor of Upper Canada. Blake was appointed the first professor of common and civil law in the University of King's College in 1843, and his duties as a lecturer competed with his job as a solicitor to the law society and his responsibilities as judge of the Surrogate Court. Blake, and occasionally two practitioners, William Henry Draper and James Christie Palmer Esten, lectured in law until 1848. D.B. Read, writing some fifty years later, recalled that 'Mr Blake was a fearless dissector of decided cases, and never failed to illustrate a proposition by the highest principles of philosophical trust.'[33]

By 1850 the college had become part of the University of Toronto, and lectures were being given by Skeffington Connor, Blake's partner. The law society apparently was not enthusiastic about the arrangement, and discouraged students from attending what it saw as increasingly 'academic' lectures. The university responded by abolishing the chair in 1853. The next year an arrangement was made with Trinity College whereby students were allowed to attend lectures given by John Hagarty, John Hillyard Cameron, and Philip Van Koughnet.[34] In 1855, Convocation began to finalize the required texts for bar admission examinations, and for the first time made provision for compulsory lectures to be given at Osgoode Hall itself.

These first attempts at instituting formal lectures set a pattern for the next several decades. Although the law society was reluctant to invest its own funds in educational ventures (in 1834 it had asked the governor of the province for aid in establishing a lectureship at Osgoode Hall, pleading financial hardship), it feared losing control over the education of its students and therefore was unwilling to allow any of the province's universities to take over the role. Still, law students clearly felt the need for some type of formal training, and the profession itself worried that articles alone might not afford a guarantee of fitness to practise. One contributor to the newly established *Canada Law Journal* wrote in 1855: 'A young man whose only qualifications for entering on the study of the law is the ability to read and write, may be articled to an Attorney: – spend five years copying and serving papers, or idly kicking his heels against the office desk, or in doing the dirty work of a disreputable practitioner. At the end of this time, armed with a certificate of service, he claims to be sworn in as an Attorney of Her Majesty's Courts.'[35]

By 1858 two permanent lecturers had been appointed by the law society. They were S.H. Strong, who lectured in equity, and J.T. Anderson, who lectured in law. In 1862, Convocation decided for the second time to open a school of law at Osgoode Hall, to be regulated solely by the committee on legal education. The law society established a system of scholarships 'open to the son of every man in Upper Canada, no matter how lowly his station or straitened his circumstances.'[36] The lectures were continued over the next few years, and Edward Blake (William Hume Blake's son and a future premier of Ontario) and Alexander Leith (who had adapted for use in the province a part of Blackstone's *Commentaries*) were appointed lecturers. The law society may have been provoked to reactivate its school of law by the decision, two years earlier, of the board of governors of Queen's University in Kingston to put into effect a project first conceived in the 1840s: the establishment of a law school. Two local lawyers, I.J. Burgess and W. George Draper, had agreed to lecture there, and John A. Macdonald's law partner, Alexander Campbell, was appointed dean. The law society refused to waive its requirement that students spend four terms in Toronto, making the program at Queen's unattractive to students. Furthermore, Queen's was not willing to supplement the pay of the instructors, who relied entirely on class fees, and the venture collapsed after two years.[37]

Yet in 1868 the law society abruptly discontinued the lectures and its own law school in favour of frequent compulsory examinations. Financial difficulties were given as the reasons; the benchers claimed that 'the advantages to be derived from [the law school] were not commensurate with the expenses.' Moreover, the benefits of the lectures apparently had proved questionable and 'productive of little but disorder and "skylarking." '[38]

The next attempt to formalize legal education took place in 1872, when the law society treasurer, John Hillyard Cameron, QC, and Chief Justice Thomas Moss persuaded their fellow benchers to reopen the law school. Partly to still the objections of those students who did not reside in Toronto, the benchers made attendance at the four weekly lectures voluntary. In addition to the two-year exemption to the five-year articling requirement that had been granted to university graduates since the 1840s, the benchers offered a further exemption of six, twelve, or eighteen months for those who went through the school and passed the required examinations.

In his inaugural address, Cameron told the hundred or so students in attendance that the law society had always taken its responsibility for legal education seriously, and noted that the inns of court themselves were beginning to establish lectures. Stressing the need for more formal lectures to deal with the increasing body of legal doctrine, Cameron suggested that the modern student's reading would have to be much more extensive, 'reaching even to the law of the United States.'[39]

The second law school to be established at Osgoode Hall maintained the pattern of the first; lectures were given on real property, general jurisprudence, commercial and criminal law, and equity during the mornings so as not to interfere with the articling students' office duties. The concurrent system, as it came to be called, was obviously a modification of the pure apprenticeship approach. In 1876 the editor of the *Canada Law Journal* reprinted a lecture given by Theodore Dwight of Columbia Law School in New York in which the advantages of the university law school, and the Harvard casebook method, were forcefully set out. In this first published Canadian reference to the u.s. scheme of legal education, the editor commented that Dwight's remarks, however interesting, did not describe an approach to legal education that was applicable in Ontario. The editor noted that 'our method[s] of teaching, examination, admission to, and most of all, retention in practice, both as solicitors and barristers, are worthy of study by our New York neighbours.'[40]

The new law school did not last long. By order of Convocation it closed in 1878, this time not because of under-attendance and 'skylarking' or a lack of funds (the law society was if anything turning a profit from the lectures).[41] The reasons for closing the school, although not clear from the minutes of Convocation, probably had to do with the pressure exerted by the out-of-town profession. Whatever the reason, the decision was not a popular one.[42] The University of Toronto offered to affiliate with the law society and take on the task of presenting lectures, but that proposal was not taken up by the society. The law students sought to remedy the situation by sponsoring a series of lectures delivered by leading barristers under the auspices of the student-run Osgoode Hall Legal and Literary Society. The society had been founded two years before, apparently with only modest assistance from the law society, and was designed to further the scholarly study of law by encouraging essay-writing and public speaking. It was most successful in organizing lectures by prominent members of the bar. Ex-lecturers John S. Ewart and T.D. Delamere spoke on Saturday evenings without remuneration, and by 1880 the student council had organized thirty-two lectures by eight Toronto lawyers.[43]

The students eventually petitioned the law society to re-establish the school, arguing in part that it was unfair that their educational needs were not provided for when they contributed nearly half of the law society's revenues. The benchers responded in 1881 with a plan to re-establish the school for a two-year period. Soon thereafter the 'Law Students' Department' of the *Canada Law Journal* blithely reported, 'The revised Law School is hard at work. The Chairman of the School, Mr. Thomas Hodgins, Q.C. opened on 13th inst., with an interesting lecture on Constitutional Law, a subject with which he is very familiar.'[44]

Unfortunately, attendance was disappointing in the first year – an average of 34 of the 220 students apprenticed to Toronto practitioners attended the voluntary lectures. But Convocation decided to open the school for another year, and it continued to operate on a year-by-year basis until 1888, when the University of Toronto once again proposed to collaborate with the law society in the establishment of a law faculty.

There had been occasional quiet speculation in the profession about the wisdom of the law society's resolve to maintain its control of legal education. Some Ontario lawyers suggested that Ontario should look to the example of Dalhousie Law School in Nova Scotia, which had been founded in 1883 by Richard Weldon, a man who was clearly inspired by Harvard Law School.[45] One editorial in the *Canada Law Journal* noted that 'it is, we think, to the University of Toronto, and not to the Law Society' that the profession should look for improvements in legal education in the province.[46]

Since 1881 the law society had been on record as saying that it was eager to encourage legal studies in all areas of the province. A few years later, lawyers located outside of Toronto thought they might try to take the law society at its word. In 1885 the secretary of the Middlesex Law Association in London petitioned Convocation for recognition of the newly established law school at Western University (later renamed the University of Western Ontario). Although leading members of the Middlesex bar offered to give lectures, and although thirty-eight students were registered for the first year, the law society refused to accept the examinations of the London law school as equivalent to its own.[47] The University of Ottawa, Victoria University, and, for the second time, Queen's University also took steps to open law schools. None was approved by the law society.

In 1888, perhaps encouraged by what it took to be a change of mood in the profession, the Senate of the University of Toronto, 'for the advancement of legal education,' proposed the establishment of a faculty of law under the joint management of the university and the law society.[48] The proposal called for a four-year program, the first two years of which were to consist of full-time attendance at the university, and the second two years of which were to be spent in articles. The university was careful to note that the law society would have the final say over admission to the bar. In response, the law society formed a 'Committee on the Establishment and Maintenance of a Law Faculty' in February 1888 to study the proposal.

Judging from the tone of some of the letters to the editor of the *Canada Law Journal*, the university had misjudged the views of the established Toronto bar. J.A. Worrell wrote that the proposed period to be spent under articles was 'ridiculously short' and wondered about the value of 'a two years' dabbling by a schoolboy of sixteen in the depths of international law and Roman Jurisprudence.'[49] A barrister scoffed at the 'new and short road to the bar' and rejected the idea of forming an alliance with any other teaching body, insisting that the law society 'should not lower its dignity by becoming the mere handmaid of Toronto University.'[50] Less strident voices argued that the scheme would give an unfair advantage to the Toronto student and might lead to both an inadequate university and an inadequate course of practical study. The other Ontario universities also responded. Queen's University rejected the proposal, arguing that the university's role should be to provide only pre-legal education. Trinity College and the University of Ottawa merely expressed their displeasure at Toronto's apparent intention to reserve the potentially lucrative market in students for itself.[51]

The committee made its report to Convocation in December 1888. Predictably, the committee thought it 'not desirable to enter into any arrangement with any university for the joint education of students, nor to shorten in any way the period of study or service of students.'[52] Having scotched the possibility of joint endeavour, the committee then recommended the reorganization of the law school at Osgoode Hall to improve the quality of lectures and make them compulsory, and the hiring of a principal, two lecturers, and two examiners. The underpinnings of a permanent law school were thus secured: the law society, probably to block any further attempt by the University of Toronto to encroach on the field of legal education, was finally in the business of training students for admission to the bar.

The benchers passed the recommendations of the committee on 15 February 1889, and asked the legal education committee to implement them so as to be ready for lectures by the fall of 1889. The legal education committee busied itself with curriculum decisions and the selection of the principal. After failing to persuade the long-time equity lecturer S.H. Strong (later a chief justice of Canada) to accept the post, Convocation settled on the relatively unknown William Albert Reeve, MA, QC. Somewhat surprisingly, given the benchers' view of American legal education, Reeve was immediately instructed to inspect (with benchers Edward Martin, QC, and the Honourable Charles Moss) law schools in New York, Massachusetts, and other northeastern states to acquire information on current systems of legal education and report back to Convocation. The visits profoundly affected Reeve's views on legal education.

The committee, it should be noted, had recommended the continuation of the full five-year period of articles (three years for university graduates). The law school at Osgoode Hall was merely intended to provide lectures before or after the business day to supplement office training. The lectures were, above all else, to be practical. William Riddell's comment in 1916 that the benchers would have been much better satisfied if the university had established 'a real and practical faculty of law with a curriculum satisfactory to us'[53] is probably an accurate assessment of the mood of the benchers at the turn of the century. But what they had in mind by a 'practical faculty of law' was very different from what any university law school in the United States was offering.

The central importance of 'practical office training' was an unquestioned article of faith for most of the members of the legal profession in Ontario, and it was to remain so for nearly sixty years. At the beginning the reasoning was straightforward: universities taught academic law; fields such as Roman law, constitutional law, and international law were their proper domain. Although these subjects were valuable to the training of a legal scholar, they in no way prepared a practising lawyer for his craft. The legal profession was regarded essentially as a trade, and only on-the-job training could prepare the student for his work. The law society was always prepared to admit that not all practitioners provided the same level of training to their articled students, and indeed that some merely used the student as a form of cheap (and sometimes free) labour. These difficulties could be overcome, the benchers argued, by appealing to the practitioner's sense of professional duty, not by handing over instruction in practical matters to the academics. To do that would be to abdicate the law society's obligation to the public. It was perfectly possible at the time for a bencher to argue that, overall, the system of preparation for the bar in Ontario was far superior to that in most American states, especially those in the grip of 'Jacksonian democracy' and its attendant doctrine – that it was the inherent right of each citizen to become a lawyer. The benchers viewed the Harvard, Yale, and Columbia law schools in much the same light as they saw the Oxford and Cambridge law programs: admirable academic institutions that could not be presumed to be in the business of training future lawyers. At the same time, of course, the law society had always taken legal education very seriously. The society offered a complex arrangement of entrance exams, apprenticeship, term-keeping, lectures, and bar exams, and often helped the students in their attempts to organize special lectures, moot courts, and other supplemental activities. Yet the aim of the benchers was always to ensure that the bar was a meritocracy, an élite, whose members were principally located in Toronto.[54]

The reorganized Osgoode Hall Law School was opened on 7 October 1889. The treasurer, the Honourable Edward Blake, introduced Principal Reeve to the 120 students in attendance in Convocation Hall. Reeve's inaugural address was an attempt to persuade the benchers of the virtues of academic training in the law.[55] Reeve reached back to Blackstone's critique of wholly practical preparation for the bar. Although Reeve argued that there was no conflict between the educational functions of the office and the school, and indeed that they were complementary, the general tenor of his remarks indicated his desire to emphasize the importance of the role of the school. The law student could become dazed and bewildered by the sheer number and variety of legal decisions. But, he said,

the remedy for all this is proper teaching, by which the reasoning faculties will be cultivated and allowed their due share in the matter by which the great fundamental principles of law will be discussed until they are properly understood and so impressed upon the minds as to be available for daily use through life, so that the student or young lawyer when a new case is presented to him, instead of at once flying as a matter of course to the reports to search until he finds a case exactly similar in its facts, and considering it hopeless to do anything else until that is done, will first sit calmly down, and applying the test of general principles form some opinion of his own, not of course to take the place of authority, but to enable him to intelligently apply such authorities as he finds ... But another truth which is practically acknowledged everywhere, is that every science which needs a study of books to acquire it, needs also a teacher to assist the study, as witness our colleges and schools of theology, of medicine, of military and naval science, of technology, of the fine arts, of pharmacy, of agriculture. It would seem strange indeed if the profound and universal science of law were the only one in which a student might safely be left to his books without a school.[56]

Reeve's speech reflected the teaching of Langdell; the language was similar, as were the sentiments. Reeve spoke briefly about changes in the school's curriculum. Almost by way of apology for the addition of suspiciously academic subjects such as private international law and constitutional history and law, Reeve quickly added, 'The aim has been, while making somewhat liberal additions to the course of study, to add nothing except what may be justly considered a part of the education needed to fit the lawyer to properly practise his profession in this Province.'[57] As for methodology, Reeve made a veiled reference to the Harvard casebook method:

One word as to our proposed methods of instruction. The word lecture is used by us in a somewhat elastic sense. It will cover recitations, discussions and oral examinations. Different lecturers will always have somewhat different modes of conveying instruction, and it is perhaps well not to push any one mode to extremes. In some of the leading schools in the United States, recently visited, the lecture in the strict sense of the term is not the prominent feature which it once was. Speaking for myself, I am convinced that, as an every-day means of conveying instruction, there are more effective modes than the smooth, unbroken delivery of lectures or essays upon legal subjects, valuable and desirable as those are upon occasion. If our law is founded upon reason, it is by the exercise of reason that we must hope to master it, and without at all undervaluing the aid of memory in gathering in stores of knowledge, in this as well as in other departments of learning, I attach the highest importance to the cultivation of the reasoning faculties. To be compelled to think is the paramount need of the student of law, and the oral examination by the lecturer of the student from day to day and the frequent discussions of questions by the students among themselves, together with constant explanations by the lecturers of points not fully understood, I believe are better methods of securing this object than a steady adherence to the plan of reading or delivering uninterrupted lectures, strictly so called, during which the student may think as much or as little as he pleases.[58]

Concluding with the mandatory praise of the profession in Ontario and a prediction of the great future of the school, Reeve remarked that Osgoode Hall Law School was blessed in being governed by the profession itself, men 'capable of appreciating the needs of the students, and keenly alive to all that affects the interests and honour of the profession.'[59] Ironically, it was precisely this control over legal education that was to prevent the changes in approach to legal education that Reeve optimistically pointed to in his address.

The school's enrolment grew and tuition fees were steadily increased. Few changes occurred in the profession or the nature of legal education during the early years of Osgoode Hall Law School. One revolutionary step, however, was taken in 1891. In the summer of that year, Clara Brett Martin petitioned the committee on legal education to be admitted as a student, the first woman in Ontario to do so. The committee recommended that her petition not be granted. Ten years before, an editorial written on the occasion of the refusal to admit women students at the inns of court in England remarked that to deny admittance to women to 'the rough and troubled sea of actual legal practice, as it appears to us, [was] being cruel only to be kind.'[60] The law society apparently took the same view. None the less, times had changed, and in 1892 Convocation was persuaded, with the help of Sir Oliver Mowat, the attorney-general of Ontario, to revise its rules and admit Miss Martin. At the conclusion of her studies in 1896, once again over the strong protests of the benchers and with the aid of legislation, Miss Martin was called to the bar.

Lectures at the school were scheduled to begin at 9:30 in the morning and 4:30 in the evening in order to leave the main part of the day free for office work. Principal Reeve sought to increase the number of lectures and broaden the range of topics covered. But these and other changes, including the appointment of staff, were ultimately in the hands of the members of the committee, which kept a close eye on the 'practical' content of the school's curriculum. The committee was even responsible for the texts to be covered, and only in 1893 did it allow examinations to include material covered in lectures as well as in texts. Whether Principal Reeve could in time have persuaded the committee to allow such academic decisions to be placed in his hands is unclear. In any event, any attempt on his part to reform the school's administration was brought to an end by his unexpected death in May 1894.

By the fall of 1894 Reeve's replacement had been selected. He was Newman Wright Hoyles, QC, 'a gentleman by birth and instinct.'[61] The Hoyles administration lasted for twenty-eight years; during that period almost no innovation – apart from the decision to make all three years of training compulsory – took place in legal education in Ontario. Although he apparently was well-liked by his students (who gave him the name of 'Daddy' Hoyles), Hoyles never seriously questioned the pedagogical approach of the school that he had inherited. Like Reeve before him, Hoyles was sent on a tour of law schools in the United States. Unlike Reeve, however, Hoyles was not impressed, even by Harvard, which at the time was acquiring a reputation as the best law school in any common-law country.

In an address to the legal education section of the ABA in 1899, Hoyles described the system of legal education in Ontario in a manner that strongly suggested that the universities of the province and Osgoode Hall were engaged in a co-operative educational venture, a dubious proposition at best. He remarked that 'the combination of a liberal academic or allegorate training with the sterner and more practical studies of the School [Osgoode Hall], cannot fail to produce better read and more accomplished lawyers, and to raise appreciably the standing and increase the usefulness of the legal profession in Canada.'[62] Hoyles told his American audience that nearly half of the students coming to Osgoode Hall were university graduates, mostly in political science. The impression Hoyles gave was that the profession saw the ideal preparation for the bar as a three- or four-year university degree in political science or a related field, followed by three years of combined articles and law school lectures. The law society, however, did not require a university degree, so the 'matriculate' preparation for the profession consisted of a two-year period of 'office work,' wherein the sixteen- or seventeen-year-old student tried to pick up practical experience while performing menial office chores, followed by three years of concurrent articles and lectures. For a substantial number of law students, legal education was almost entirely a matter of so-called practical office training.

Although Hoyles did not present an entirely accurate picture of legal education in Ontario, it could not be denied that for the student who began his legal studies at the University of Toronto at the turn of the century the opportunities for acquiring a sophisticated background in law were reasonably good.[63] Provision for a faculty of law had been made as early as 1819, when King's College was being contemplated, and requirements for the degrees of bachelor of common law and doctor of common law and later bachelor of laws and doctor of laws were continuously on the books of the University of Toronto, although few of those degrees were actually conferred in the nineteenth century. Until 1888 special examinations for the LL B degree were offered to University of Toronto graduates and to barristers of seven years' standing. Although the university curriculum in law usually was restricted to the 'academic' subjects of constitutional law and history, Roman law, and international law, from time to time, doubtless to give the program legitimacy in the eyes of the law society, more practical subjects such as real property, contracts, landlord and tenant law, mercantile law, and wills were also offered.

In 1888, when W.J. Ashley was appointed professor of political economy and constitutional history, he was given the task of revamping the University of Toronto Faculty of Law. A month before the benchers announced the opening of the new Osgoode Hall Law School in 1889, the provincial government, by order in council, announced the establishment of a faculty of law at the university. Two distinguished professors were appointed, the Honourable Mr Justice William Proudfoot (hired to teach Roman law) and the Honourable Mr David Mills, a respected lawyer and member of Parliament who would later serve as minister of justice and as a justice of the Supreme Court of Canada (constitutional and international law). The same order in council provided for a series of lectures to be given, without remuneration, by some of the leaders of the bench and bar, including the Honourable Mr Justice Hugh MacMahon, the Honourable Edward Blake, QC, the Honourable Samuel H. Blake, QC, Dalton McCarthy, QC, B.B. Osler, QC, and Charles Moss, QC. The law society allowed attendance at these lectures to count in lieu of attendance at those given at Osgoode Hall. But the late nineteenth century was in general a period of doldrums for the University of Toronto, and the university's grandiose scheme was stillborn. Only a few lectures were actually given, and the university once again proved itself unable to move successfully into the field of professional legal education. Retrenching in the Department of Political Economy trimmed the Faculty of Law to a single professorship. That post was held by Mr

James Mavor and later by A.H.F. Lefroy. As the twentieth century began, modest LL B and LL M programs were nurtured and offered to members of the political science and economics and history departments.
In 1906 the new Conservative government of James P. Whitney appointed the Royal Commission on the University of Toronto, chaired by
Joseph Flavelle (whose home on Queen's Park Crescent now houses the
University of Toronto Law School). The commission recommended 'that
a Faculty of Law should be established in the University, and that, if
possible, arrangements should be made with the Law Society by which
the duplication of the work which is common to both in the courses of
instruction may be avoided.'[64] As before, however, the law society turned
the offer down. Students taking four years of law and law-related courses
at the University of Toronto were required to sit through three more
years at Osgoode Hall.

Principal Hoyles was the only full-time teacher at the law society's
school until 1919, when he persuaded Convocation to appoint as assistant principal John Delatre Falconbridge, who had joined the school
as examiner in 1904. The move was intended to relieve Hoyles of his
administrative duties. E. Douglas Armour retired in 1910 after twenty-
eight years as a part-time lecturer, and was replaced by John Shirley
Denison. The committee continued to keep a close watch over the school.
In 1910 the committee reminded the lecturers that they should 'endeavour to impart to the students the methods of practically applying the
principles of law, to the elucidation of which their lectures must of
necessity more particularly be directed.'[65]

Principal Hoyles retired on 25 May 1923 at the age of seventy-nine.
The school had changed little during Hoyles's tenure as principal. But
many voices were being raised in the early 1920s in strong criticism of
the scheme of legal education in Ontario. Those favouring change were
encouraged by the appointment of John D. Falconbridge as acting principal, for Falconbridge was a noted legal scholar, who often sided, if
somewhat cautiously, with the 'university-minded' elements in the
profession. The advocates of change, had they been able to see into the
future, would have been encouraged by the entrance into the law school
in 1923 of a nineteen-year-old student, the holder of a bachelor of arts
degree from the University of Western Ontario, whose career was to
help change the face of legal education in Ontario. That student was
Cecil Augustus Wright.

1

Wright as Student:
Osgoode Hall 1923–1926

Cecil Augustus Wright was born on 2 July 1904 in London, Ontario, the fourth child of Thomas Augustus Wright and Emily Rosana Wright (née Whitehold). Thomas Wright, an Englishman born in 1867, was the secretary-treasurer of a flour and feed mill. A precocious child, Cecil Augustus finished primary school at the age of eleven, and at fifteen he scored first in the matriculation examinations at London Central Collegiate Secondary School. In that year, had Wright been over the minimum age of sixteen, these credentials alone would have qualified him to enter the books of the Law Society of Upper Canada as a student-at-law. It is unlikely that Wright was tempted, since his performance on the examinations earned him a $125 scholarship plus two years' free tuition from the Board of Governors at Western University.

At Western, Wright concentrated on the study of economics, history, and political sciences. In his first year he won the W.W. Tamblyn Prize in public speaking; in his second, the Typographical Union Gold Medal in English composition; and in his third, the Board of Governors' Scholarship in political science. When he graduated in 1923, Wright virtually monopolized the convocation ceremonies: he received the Edward Blake Prize for political economy and University Gold Medals in history and political economy.

The Western *Gazette* convocation supplement of 1923 includes a photograph of a thin, bespectacled Wright, beneath which appears the following description of his musical skill as a violinist and his oratorical abilities, written in the usual style of college yearbooks:

CECIL A. WRIGHT

'While vanquished, he could argue still.'

All who know Cease are convinced that, for enthusiastic endeavor, he has kept in his heart as a motto, Caesar Augustus' message to Rome, 'Veni, vidi, vici.'

This year marks the conclusion of a brilliant career in his course of Honor History and Economics, during which period he has consistently led his class. In his final year, the History and Political Science Club has strengthened under his efficient guidance, so that he leaves his Club well established at Western. Prominent in musical circles, he was one of the founders of the Glee Club, and has also been a member of the Little Theatre Orchestra.

Upon Cease's shoulders have devolved most of '23's debates, and in this telling ground he has proved himself a worthy probationer for his future career in law. With such intellectual and oratorical gifts, we may expect his ability to be speedily recognized among the legal fraternity of this province.

While the nickname 'Cease' did not stick (given his middle name of Augustus and his strong personality, it is not surprising that he came to be known as 'Caesar'), the prediction of speedy recognition of his legal ability certainly came true.[1]

Although family members say that he toyed with the idea of becoming a professional musician, there is no evidence that Wright gave much serious thought to any career but law. After graduating from Western, Wright moved quickly to the next stage of his education. The Proceedings in Convocation of the Law Society of Upper Canada, dated 18 October 1923, include his name among those of persons who, having paid the fifty-dollar admission fee and the hundred-dollar tuition fee, were accepted for the first year of studies at the law school.[2] Wright was admitted as a 'graduate,' a category that included students who were graduates of a faculty of arts or law of a degree-conferring university in His Majesty's dominions, holders of a diploma from the Royal Military College, Kingston, or graduates of the faculties of applied or practical science from Toronto, McGill, Montreal, or Queen's universities.[3]

'Graduates' formed one class of students-at-law; the other class was made up of 'matriculants' and included, prior to amendments of August 1925, anyone holding a certificate of pass matriculation (that is, a graduate of an Ontario secondary school), and anyone able to pass the examinations of the University of Toronto (or the equivalent in another province) prescribed at the end of the first year of studies in the Faculty of Arts (this was often called 'senior matriculation'). A matriculant was required to serve under articles of clerkship with a practising solicitor before entering the law school; a graduate could enter the school directly.

Once at the law school, both the matriculant and the graduate were required to spend most of the day at a law office under articles and to attend lectures at 9:00 A.M. and 4:40 P.M. In effect, legal education in Ontario was, as it had been for decades, almost wholly a matter of service under articles. The time during which a student was in attendance at lectures was deemed by the law society to be part of his articles. Articles of clerkship were a contractual matter between students and practising solicitors; a student, assisted if necessary by the law society, was required to find a solicitor willing to serve as his articling principal and enter into an agreement with him. The agreement was supervised by the law society, which was given, by statute, the sole authority to regulate and administer all of the details and procedures of legal education in the province.

The entering class of 1923 was a large one, numbering 165 students, up from 129 in 1922 and 119 in 1921. First-year attendance tended to fluctuate from as low as 70 to as high as 165 in the 1920s, in part because matriculants, who were eligible for admission for up to four years after completing pass matriculation, arrived at the school in irregular numbers. Nearly half of Wright's entering class qualified as graduates. These young men came to Toronto in search of solicitors with whom they could article, hoping to put in a month or two of work before classes began on the last Monday in September. Wright entered into an agreement of articles with the firm of Johnson, Grant and Dodds, and began his clerkship in their downtown office in the Bank of Hamilton Building.

In 1923 the law school was located, as it had been for decades, in the east wing of the original Osgoode Hall building on Queen Street. Quarters must have been cramped for the 391 students attending lectures that year. Indeed, many aspects of the law school were less than satisfactory. In a 1924 *Canadian Bar Review* article, John Shirley Denison pointed to several difficulties with the school and its administration. Denison had been a part-time lecturer since 1910, and in 1925 he resigned to devote full time to his practice. In the 1940s, as treasurer of the law society, he would become Wright's most powerful and unrelenting critic. The article expressed the teaching staff's grievances, and is an interesting early statement of the attitudes toward legal education that Wright and others would come to oppose vigorously. Denison began by noting some of the more obvious shortcomings in the physical plant of the school:

The equipment consists of three class-rooms built years ago, and much too crowded now, a library of about 2,500 books, two small common rooms, one for men and the other for women, and cloakrooms in the basement. The principal has a room and the lecturers and demonstrators share one amongst them. Convocation Hall is used by permission for dances or debates, and the main library is also available for students under certain restrictions. There is no gymnasium, campus or other place for exercise. Any sports must be arranged for outside. Apart from dances or debates the writer only once saw students amusing themselves at Osgoode Hall, and then his unintended entrance broke up a foursome engaged in African Golf.[4]

The school even lacked a name, Denison remarked (it was not until March 1924 that the benchers officially approved the name 'Osgoode Hall Law School').[5] All these deficiencies, Denison concluded,

[explained] one of the chief needs of the School, a real esprit de corps. There is no outside interest in the School, therefore it has not been held in much esteem. People are not proud of attending or of graduating from it. Our profession is efficient and businesslike, law is administered without undue delay, we do not impede justice with useless technicalities, and the standard of honour and behaviour is high. Surely a school which has functioned for a generation and has contributed to these results and its record is a proper source of pride. It is time to bespeak greater professional interest in and constructive criticism of its work.

Had Denison stopped there, it would have appeared to the profession that his only complaint was that the law school lacked a proper school spirit, something that might have been created by proper entertainment facilities rather than by higher standards of education. But he proceeded to list more cogent criticisms. He noted that class size had increased to 100 or 150 students and that part-time teachers, including himself, did not have the time to do more than lecture to students with whom they could never hope to interact on an individual basis. This overcrowding had its cost, Denison insisted: training in the law in Ontario was becoming superficial.

The love of learning, Sir Edward Coke's 'delight' in the study of the law, is not developed, and we are not creating a class of lawyers, who by research, study and authorship are equipped for introducing or criticizing reforms in a scientific spirit. No great native progress in law reforms is possible without much learning, and that this is lacking in Ontario is shown by the fact that our important statutory improvements and codifications have been borrowed from England. This field of law school work is as yet entirely untilled in Ontario.

Here was a different and more damning criticism of the benchers' law school. These and similar sentiments were to dominate the ongoing controversy over legal education in Ontario, and many years later Wright would quote Denison's remarks, directing them rhetorically against Denison himself.[6]

Denison's public expressions of dissatisfaction with the law school were the first to go beyond mere complaints about facilities and pay. He gave voice to a concern about the failure of the law school to create learned Canadian lawyers. None the less, as his later views confirmed, he was not worried about the law society's complete control over legal education, nor was he at odds with the law society's insistence that office training form the most significant part of the process of legal education. Quite the contrary: he was a firm believer in office training, claiming that it was the 'crying need' of legal education in the United States. Although Denison faulted the school for its lack of esprit de corps, he made it clear that the Harvard approach to legal education, and specifically the casebook method of instruction, were not the answers to Ontario's problems. Nor was he enthusiastic about raising admission requirements. If the road to the profession was made too difficult, there would be pressure to seek some other approach to the training of lawyers, thus endangering the law society's 'strict and beneficial control over its members.'

Like many practitioners with an interest in legal education, Denison sought both to increase the intellectual content of the process of legal training in Ontario and to maintain the law society's control over that process. Denison and others were unable, or perhaps unwilling, to consider the possibility that the law society could not muster the intellectual and financial resources necessary to provide the kind of education that would foster and develop Canadian legal scholarship. It is unlikely that Denison would have perceived any conflict between educational quality, in the sense of proper preparation for practice, and the law society's control over legal education.

None the less, Denison was willing to criticize the law society. In his article he noted that the society's revenue from student fees in the years 1919 to 1923 was $443,958 (some 60 per cent of total revenue), while the cost of running the school, excluding administration, for those years was $140,303. The surplus funds were spent on other professional concerns. Surely, Denison argued, given the importance of legal education, the law society could see its way clear to extend the school's activities and facilities. If nothing else, it could well afford to hire more staff.

Denison's concern about the need for more instructors was justified. In the school year 1923–4, 621 hours of lectures in twenty-four subjects were given. John D. Falconbridge, the only full-time lecturer, gave 198 hours of lectures in eight different subjects. The rest of the teaching load was carried by Edwin George Long (who taught five courses), Arthur Roger Clute (three courses), Samuel Hugh Bradford (two courses), and Albert Nash, a senior partner in the accounting firm of Clarkson Gordon, who taught a first-year course in bookkeeping. There were also five non-teaching examiners (including a future chief justice of Canada, John Robert Cartwright), and two practice demonstrators, Christopher Robinson and Harold Foster. The entire staff, except for Falconbridge, consisted of practising lawyers; Arthur Clute also lectured at University College at the University of Toronto. Besides teaching nearly a third of the courses given at the law school, Falconbridge was saddled with the bulk of the administrative duties and served as liaison between the teaching staff and the legal education committee of the law society. The argument for more teaching staff was strong indeed, and it was made even stronger by Falconbridge's request that the benchers increase the number of lecture hours from 621 to 762.

John D. Falconbridge was formally appointed acting principal (at a salary of six thousand dollars per year) by the Legal Education Committee in the middle of September 1923. Because of this late appointment, he was unable to initiate any curriculum changes in the year Wright was first enrolled at the school. The courses Wright took and the texts he read in that year were the same fare that had been offered at 'Hoyles's School' for the past three decades. Indeed, the only important difference in the curriculum of first-year subjects set out in the 1923-4 calendar was that Falconbridge based his first-year contract law course not only on the enduring English text *Anson on Contracts*, but also on C.S. Kenny's *A Selection of Cases Illustrative of the Law of Contracts*.

Kenny's *Cases on Contract* had been published in England in 1922, and was based on a collection of cases edited and first published in 1896 by G.B. Finch, an English lawyer who, according to Kenny's preface, wished 'to adopt the methods of the Harvard Law School, which he had visited.'[7] It is ironic, but typically Canadian, that in this instance Harvard's influence on Ontario legal education appears to have come by way of England. A more direct introduction of the casebook method occurred the following year, in the form of Falconbridge's own mimeographed casebook on the sale of goods. This work was subsequently published in 1927, and may be counted as the first Harvard-inspired casebook compiled and published in Canada.[8]

Besides the Kenny casebook, Caesar Wright's first-year materials reflected the standard late-nineteenth-century English-textbook approach to legal education. Wright studied real property with Denison and read E.D. Armour's *A Treatise on the Law of Real Property*, first published in Ontario in 1901 and based on the standard nineteenth-century Leith and Smith edition of Blackstone.[9] Samuel Bradford taught Wright jurisprudence and common law, the texts for which were the English classic *The Elements of Jurisprudence* by Thomas Erskind Holland, first published in 1880, and John Indermaur's *Principles of the Common Law*, published in 1876, one of the standard texts in use at the inns of court. (Both of these ponderous volumes were dropped from the curriculum the following year in favour of the more modern *Salmond on Jurisprudence*.) Constitutional history and law was taught, as it had been for a decade, by Edwin Long, who assigned Sir J.G. Bourinot's *A Manual of the Constitutional History of Canada* (1901) and A.H.F. Lefroy's *Leading Cases in Canadian Constitutional Law* (1914). Both books were vintage volumes – the Bourinot text was first published in 1888. Lefroy had modelled his *Leading Cases* on the English pattern: instead of offering for discussion cases that might not state current law, but were there to show the evolution of leading principles, Lefroy collected cases that stated the law applicable at the date of publication. Thus, nearly all of the cases were decisions of the Privy Council; the lower-court Canadian decisions failed to qualify as 'leading.' The remainder of Wright's first-year curriculum – criminal law, practice, and procedure and statute law – concentrated on statutory material and forms. The case-law was for the most part English. Cases from the United States, as well as from other Commonwealth countries, were absent from most of the readings, and Kenny's *Cases on Contract* included no Canadian or Commonwealth cases whatsoever. Canadian content, such as it was, came in the form of the Judicature Act and the rules of practice (which were based on English statutes). It was only in Falconbridge's *Cases on Sale of Goods* that a student at Osgoode Hall was able to read a substantial number of Canadian cases: of the 172 cases included in Falconbridge's casebook, 49 were Canadian.

The strong emphasis on English cases at the law school was no more than a reflection of the fact that English law was 'practitioner law,' the law actually cited in courts. The law society was wholly dominated by practitioners, and the explicit aim of the law school, as far as they were concerned, was to provide the student-at-law with information directly useful to him in the law office. A consideration of the law of contracts in the United States was quite unnecessary: the Toronto practitioner went to court with Anson, not Williston, under his arm.[10]

The circularity of thinking evidenced in the law society's program did not escape those keen on reforming legal education. It was easy to argue that Canadian law was on the whole uninnovative. Canadian lawyers seemed ready to wait for English jurists to make changes in the law, which could then be cited and relied upon with confidence in Canada. A practitioner-oriented legal education was an education in English, not Canadian, law. In effect, the student was being taught law as if it were outside of domestic control. Moreover, he knew no other law with which to compare the English precedents. Canadian judges, trained under a strictly English regime, were not willing to consider u.s. or Australian precedents or novel arguments based on them. Counsel, eager to win cases for their clients, were not willing to risk their legal arguments by trying to draw 'foreign' analogies. The circle was completed when practitioners insisted that the law taught at the law school should be relevant to the chores of the students working in their offices. New generations of lawyers trained in this manner simply replaced their predecessors at the bar and bench.

It was clear enough to the reform-minded academics that changes in the content of legal education were necessary in order to break out of the pattern: circumstances in England and Canada were not always the same, and Canadian law would benefit from some of the legal innovations found in other Commonwealth jurisdictions and the United States. The problem was evident, but the solution was not. There were few professional legal academics in Canada; most teachers were practitioners. Still, many people were dissatisfied with the content and structure of the courses that were taught at Osgoode Hall, but the question was whether reforms should come dramatically or gradually. The new acting principal opted for a policy of gradual change.

When John Falconbridge assumed the post of acting principal of the law school in 1923, he was in a unique position to push for reform, which he clearly wanted. Born in Toronto in 1875, he was the son of Sir Glenholme Falconbridge, chief justice of the King's Bench of Ontario, and Mary Phoebe Falconbridge, the daughter of Robert Baldwin Sullivan, who had been a judge of the Court of Queen's Bench and later of the Court of Common Pleas of Canada.[11] John graduated from the University of Toronto, studied law at Osgoode Hall, and was called to the bar in 1899. He practised in Toronto for seventeen years, the last twelve with the firm of Cassels, Brock, Kelley and Falconbridge.

From the beginning of his career, Falconbridge was a practitioner at heart, although his scholarly talents led him to contribute to the literature. His first book, *Banking and Bills of Exchange*, published in 1907, was written for the practitioner. In 1909 he offered his services to the law school at Osgoode Hall on a part-time basis. He grew to enjoy teaching, but it was not until 1917 that he retired from practice to devote his time to teaching and writing. His strong practical background, coupled with his international reputation as a scholar and legal writer, made him the obvious choice to replace the retiring Principal Hoyles.

Falconbridge was a principal in whom the benchers could put their trust, and his requests – more books for the student library, more lectures, and, in time, more permanent lecturers – met with far less resistance than they would have had they come from a more 'academic' principal. The benchers' first response to Falconbridge's expressed intention to reform the law school was, in the circumstances, grounds for some measure of optimism. In June 1923, the legal education committee created a special committee 'to look into and consider the matters pertaining to the Law School generally.'[12] The special committee included Featherstone Osler, treasurer of the law society, who died soon after his appointment and was replaced by the new treasurer, Frederick Weir Harcourt. Following a tradition set by his predecessors, Falconbridge travelled at the law school's expense to the University of Michigan Law School to learn firsthand what he could of educational developments in the United States. On his return Falconbridge participated in the discussions of the special committee, and appears to have had a considerable impact on the subsequent report (although it is difficult to say how much of that impact reflects the developments Falconbridge saw in the United States).

The special committee made its recommendations to Convocation on 20 March 1924. The report hinted at a change in attitude on the part of the benchers, a turning away from the stagnation of Hoyles's years to a new and more vigorous school under Falconbridge. It appears that the committee granted all of Falconbridge's requests. New courses in the history of English law, agency, bankruptcy, and company law were added to the curriculum, and other courses were consolidated. The sessions of the law school were extended to the end of April, and the number of lecture hours increased to 762 per school year. Falconbridge was officially made principal; the law school was given its official name; promises were made to expand the student library; and the legal education committee was advised to develop closer relations with the teaching staff. In response to Falconbridge's urging that the casebook method of instruction be formally acknowledged as preferable to the lecture method, the legal education committee noted that methods of instruction 'must of course be left generally to the discretion of the individual member of the teaching staff' (an important concession in itself), and gave its guarded support to the casebook technique: 'Your Committee believes that, to some extent, the old system of lecturing might advantageously be replaced or supplemented by some method of instruction which will demand a larger share of intellectual effort from the students, and that the teaching staff should be encouraged to try experiments with this object in view. In some subjects, at least, it would seem worthwhile to substitute for ordinary lectures the discussion of cases by the students under the direction of the lecturer.'

The most significant sign of a change in attitude, however, was Convocation's approval of the appointment of another full-time lecturer. Falconbridge had argued that the staff should consist of himself (with his title changed from 'principal' to 'dean') one other full-time lecturer, three part-time lecturers, and three practice demonstrators. The position of examiner – a holdover from earlier days when, following the tradition instituted by the English inns of court, student exams were set and marked by law society officials who had no teaching role – was to be abolished.

Given the strong symbolic flavour of many of the changes put into effect – the change in Falconbridge's title, the naming of the law school – it is clear that Falconbridge's intention was to develop a different image of teaching at the law school and of the institution itself. But his desire that his teaching staff have some measure of control over setting and grading exams was designed to make their professional status more than symbolic. Some members of the special committee were more than a little apprehensive about the subtle changes Falconbridge was insisting on, and took steps, if not to stop them, then to try to slow down the process that these initiatives represented. As dean, Falconbridge was given the job of supervising the law school, yet all of his decisions about curriculum and lecture hours were 'subject to the approval of the Legal Education Committee.' In addition, the important hiring power was never contemplated by the committee to belong exclusively to the dean. The benchers were determined to control all major administrative decisions. At one point, to further secure control by the practising bar, Bencher Michael Herman Ludwig, chairman of the legal education committee, moved an amendment to rule 118 of the rules of the law society that deans and full-time lecturers must be barristers of not less than ten years' standing, a move clearly intended to ensure that the teaching staff at the law school be right-thinking practitioners. The motion failed.[13]

The early efforts at restructuring required the appointment of a full-time lecturer, and Falconbridge's choice was Donald Alexander MacRae. On 17 April 1924 Convocation empowered the legal education committee to negotiate with MacRae 'with a view to securing his services as full-time lecturer at the Osgoode Hall Law School.' MacRae was appointed in May 1924 at a salary of $6,000. At the same meeting, Falconbridge's salary was increased to $7,000 (a not insubstantial figure, given that a puisne judge sitting on Ontario's High Court made less than $9,000 in the early 1920s). The academic year 1924–5 thus found Osgoode Hall Law School staffed by two prominent full-time legal scholars. Denison, Bradford, and Clute continued as part-time lecturers (although Denison had already submitted his resignation effective July 1925) and long-time practice demonstrators Christopher Robinson (who died later that year) and Colonel Harold Alexander Foster continued in their jobs. Falconbridge had won the first battle quickly, elegantly, and without casualties.

The strategic significance of acquiring the services of Donald A. MacRae would not have been lost on those who were in the process of agitating for higher standards of legal education in Canada. MacRae was one of a select group of legal educators in Canada who had come out strongly for the concept of the 'university law school.' His views on admission requirements, curriculum, and university-level legal education were well known to the profession at large and to the benchers in particular. That Falconbridge was able to persuade the legal education committee to appoint MacRae is evidence of the trust the benchers had in Falconbridge.

MacRae was born in Prince Edward Island in 1872. After leaving school and working for seven years in a clothing store, he entered Dalhousie University and graduated with a degree in classics and the University Medal. In 1899 he earned his MA and in 1905 his PH D in classics from Cornell. From 1900 to 1905 MacRae taught Greek at Cornell. When he moved to Princeton as an assistant professor, he became a preceptor in

Greek. During his four years at Princeton, MacRae developed an admiration for the scholar–statesman Woodrow Wilson, an association that may have turned his mind away from classics and towards the law.

At the age of thirty-seven, MacRae left Princeton and returned to Canada to study law at Osgoode Hall. One can only wonder at MacRae's choice of Osgoode Hall over Dalhousie Law School, a school he would have been more familiar with and which enjoyed a high reputation, possibly better than 'Daddy Hoyles's' school. MacRae may have been drawn to the city of Toronto, with its large and powerful law firms, although it is reported that his move to law was partly motivated by 'the intention of becoming a law teacher if the occasion ever presented itself.'[14] After his call to the Ontario bar in 1913, MacRae began to practise with the Toronto firm of Baio, Bicknell and Co.

MacRae's career as a practising lawyer lasted exactly one year. In 1914, after the retirement of Richard Chapman Weldon, who for thirty years had been the dean of Dalhousie Law School, MacRae was appointed to that position. The rapid elevation from junior lawyer to dean of one of Canada's foremost law schools was unusual, to say the least. Still, in the circumstances, the move was understandable. The legal academic community in Canada in 1914 was practically nonexistent. Dalhousie's president, A. Stanley MacKenzie, apparently wanted to acquire the services of a proven academic rather than someone with teaching experience in law. The law school had suffered something of a decline in the last years of Weldon's deanship, and President MacKenzie thought that it should be headed by someone with many years of university teaching behind him. In that respect, MacRae was a good candidate. Moreover, as MacKenzie frankly admitted, it was unlikely that the three-thousand-dollar salary would have convinced an established lawyer to leave a lucrative practice.[15]

The fact that MacRae's academic credentials rather than his experience as a practising lawyer got him the job at Dalhousie helps to show how fundamentally different the law schools at Osgoode Hall and Dalhousie were. Osgoode Hall was a practitioners' law school – in effect, a trade school for those who intended to enter the legal profession as barristers and solicitors. Dalhousie Law School was an institution with a very different history and tradition. Dalhousie was Canada's first common-law university law school; it had opened its doors in 1883. (Three Quebec university law schools were founded before Dalhousie: the Faculty of Law at McGill University, founded in 1853, the Faculté de Droit at Université Laval, 1854; and the Faculté de Droit at Université de Montréal, 1873).

From the beginning, the Nova Scotia Barristers' Society and Dalhousie University agreed to co-operate in the business of preparing lawyers. The university was to undertake the task of providing a legal education, the purpose of which was to combine instruction in practical legal skills and a general liberal education in the law. The barristers' society, which operated under legislative authority to control preparation for the bar, just as the Law Society of Upper Canada did, restricted its attention from the outset to the period of articles and the bar admission examination. In Nova Scotia, articles of clerkship were a one-year affair; moreover, that year could be postponed until after the student finished his studies at the law school.

In the early part of the twentieth century, when other Canadian law schools were established, there were two distinct models they could turn to for guidance. On the one hand, there was the Osgoode Hall model – a school controlled and operated by the provincial law society, with a program of concurrent lecture and office work. On the other hand, there was the Dalhousie-McGill model – a university law school with a consecutive program of three years of full-time law school followed by one or more years of articling. The result was a series of compromise schemes and shifts from the Osgoode Hall model towards the Dalhousie model.

The differences between the Dalhousie and Osgoode Hall law schools were startling. The law school in Halifax was the creation of a small group of academically minded lawyers concerned about the lack of formal instruction in law in the province. Rather than maintain the English apprenticeship approach – which, given the English traditions they shared with Ontario, they could very well have done – these men turned instead to their university. The university was the likely place to look, since, unlike the much more prosperous bar in Toronto, the Nova Scotia bar could not afford to set up its own school.[16] For its part, Dalhousie University was as eager as Toronto, Western, and Queen's had been in the late nineteenth century to develop professional faculties. The educators at Dalhousie were successful in their bid primarily because they were lucky enough to receive a series of gifts from a benefactor, George Munro, a Nova Scotian who had made his fortune in publishing in New York. One of those gifts endowed a chair in constitutional and international law, a position soon filled by Richard Weldon, who came from Mount

Allison University, where he had taught mathematics and political science. Weldon's academic background (he had received his PH D in international and constitutional law from Yale), coupled with his lack of practical experience in the law, moulded the law school at Dalhousie for its first thirty years.[17] The curriculum at Dalhousie, which appears to have been consciously modelled on those of Columbia and Harvard law schools, included courses in international law and other 'academic' subjects that would have been quite foreign to the Ontario benchers' conception of preparation for admission to the bar.

In 1914, when MacRae began his deanship, Dalhousie Law School had recently undergone a general house-cleaning at MacKenzie's hands, in co-operation with the Council of the barristers' society. The teaching period was extended, the minimum entrance requirement was raised from attainment of a high school certificate to completion of one year in an arts college, and certain curriculum changes were made. After MacRae's first year as dean, the First World War began to take its toll on enrolment, which dropped from its all-time high of 58 in 1914 to 39 in 1915, and finally reached a low of 20 in 1918. MacRae used the opportunity to create and implement a revised curriculum, which was put into place during the war. The curriculum was MacRae's major contribution to legal education in Canada. As we shall see in the next chapter, this curriculum, recommended by the Canadian Bar Association, was to serve as a model for law schools throughout the country.

In his ten years as dean, MacRae brought Dalhousie to a position of leadership in legal education in Canada. By 1921 MacRae, with the blessing of the barristers' society, raised the minimum law school entrance requirements to two years of university study. He also expanded his full-time teaching staff to three by hiring John Read and Sidney Smith. He encouraged his new teachers to contribute to legal scholarship. Still, despite his successes at Dalhousie, MacRae was probably discouraged by his inability to get from the university the money he felt he needed to run his law school properly.[18] He was not hesitant to leave Dalhousie for the wealthier Osgoode Hall when Falconbridge made him a lucrative offer. As John Willis suggests in his history of Dalhousie Law School, MacRae was a 'kindred spirit' to Falconbridge.[19] Their moves to reform legal education in Ontario were important ones, although there was much left to do. Both men were committed to a gradual, non-confrontational approach to reform. Falconbridge in particular was gentlemanly but remote, and took little pleasure in his administrative duties.[20] At Osgoode Hall, MacRae, who was then forty-nine years old, seemed to settle into his teaching, leaving educational reform to others. MacRae taught the first-year course in the history of English law that Falconbridge had added to the curriculum. The course was MacRae's creation at Dalhousie, and it is very likely that Falconbridge fought to have it added to Osgoode Hall's curriculum as a favour to MacRae. Almost at once MacRae began to work on his treatise on evidence law, which appeared in the 1928 edition of the *Encyclopaedic Digest*. Although his move to Osgoode Hall was strategic, forming as it did the first (but not the last) link between Dalhousie and Osgoode Hall, MacRae's reformist activities appear to have ended when he came to Toronto.

Falconbridge's initial steps to institute reforms at the law school during Caesar Wright's first year there count not as the beginning but as the climax of the first important country-wide campaign to bring legal education in Canada into line with the standard advocated by legal academics in the United States in the first two decades of the twentieth century. The Canadian movement was led by Falconbridge, MacRae, R.W. Lee, and H.A. Smith, the last two of whom were English scholars sojourning in Canada at McGill University Law School. The movement needed a forum independent of the provincial law societies. That need was met by the provincial and county bar associations that had come into existence some years before. In the 1920s these organizations, sometimes unanimously, sometimes not, urged reform in the strongest possible terms.

The remaining two years of Caesar Wright's student career were as successful for him as they were for the school's reform-minded dean. Having led his class in his first year at Osgoode Hall, Wright went on to stand first in his second and third years as well; he won a $100 scholarship for his efforts in his second year, and the $400 Chancellor Van Koughnet Scholarship as well as the less lucrative, but none the less prestigious, $15 Clara Brett Memorial Scholarship in his third and final year. Wright managed to score a total of 945 marks out of a possible 1,000 in his final examinations, a remarkable feat which Falconbridge proudly brought to the benchers' attention when the decision to hire Wright was being made in 1927.[21]

In his second year at Osgoode Hall, Wright was among the first group of Ontario students to use a Canadian casebook – Falconbridge's preliminary mimeographed version of *Selected Cases on the Sale of Goods*. Bencher G.F. Henderson of Ottawa announced in the February 1926 issue of the *Canadian Bar Review* that Falconbridge intended to 'publish at an early date' his selection of cases on the sale of goods. Henderson remarked that Falconbridge 'frankly admits his indebtedness to Williston's Cases on Sales,' but chose to adopt 'a fundamentally different arrangement of the subject.' Space considerations, he reported, made it necessary for Falconbridge to omit U.S. cases. Henderson's assessment of the value of this volume suggests the mild ambivalence that the older lawyers must have felt towards the venture: 'While this book is intended, primarily, for the use of students, every busy lawyer knows the practical advantage of a convenient collection of cases on a particular subject, and in view of the fact that the particular subject covered by this selection of cases is a fertile field for litigation, the convenience of the book in Court should be very great.'[22] Henderson was unaware that a Langdellian casebook was intended to be not merely a compendium of current decisions, but a tool for leading students through a line of legal argument.

Wright also took courses on bills and notes and equity from Falconbridge in that year, and agency and partnership (for which two English texts were required), criminal procedure, and evidence from MacRae. For the last course MacRae used the English *Cases and Statutes on the Law of Evidence* by Ernest Cockle, the fourth edition of which had been published that year.

In 1923, speaking as convenor of the legal education committee of the Canadian Bar Association, MacRae was less enthusiastic about the casebook method of teaching than Falconbridge. He had recommended that the case method be 'judiciously' used and that the lecture technique not be superseded. Cockle's *Cases on Evidence* was something of a compromise between the two techniques, and as such would have appealed to MacRae. It was not a Harvard-style casebook, in which, generally speaking, cases are selected more as examples of legal reasoning than as 'leading' cases setting out current law. In Cockle's book, selected cases, heavily edited, were set out with the aim of presenting the 'textbook' rules. So that no mistake was made, the statement of the rule in each case was printed in bold-face type.

Arthur Clute introduced Wright to the law of torts, the branch of the law to which Wright contributed most in his scholarly life. Clute used the third edition of C.S. Kenny's *A Selection of Cases Illustrative of the English Law of Tort*. Kenny's casebook, like Cockle's, was closer to the English 'leading case' model than to the Harvard model. Many years later, in the preface to the first edition of his own torts casebook, Wright explained the difference between the two approaches:

It scarcely need be said that this is not intended as a collection of 'leading' cases

– whatever that term may mean. Cases have been chosen, whether they be English, Canadian, Australian or American, which raise either a problem of fact which should challenge inquiry as to the method adopted by the court before which it came up for solution, or a method of dealing with a familiar problem which casts light on or raises doubts concerning methods which through repetition have been 'accepted' although not necessarily definitive.[23]

In his third year at Osgoode, Wright saw another result of Falconbridge's steady, cautious reform of the law school. At the meeting of Convocation on 5 February, Falconbridge announced that a third full-time member of the staff was urgently needed. Shirley Denison had resigned and Falconbridge was keen on replacing him with a full-time instructor. At the time, Dalhousie was the only law school in Canada to satisfy the Association of American Law Schools' minimum requirement of three full-time instructors, something Falconbridge made certain the benchers were aware of. The request for a third instructor was Falconbridge's attempt to satisfy all of the AALS's requirements so that Osgoode Hall could become an 'approved' law school by U.S. standards. Falconbridge recommended Sidney Earle Smith, then teaching at Dalhousie; and at the 25 February meeting, Convocation appointed Smith to a position to commence on 1 July 1925 at a salary of $3,600 a year.

Sidney Smith, born in 1897 in Cape Breton, entered King's College at Windsor, Nova Scotia, at the age of fourteen. After receiving his BA degree, he set his sights on Dalhousie Law School, but the First World War interfered with his plans. After active service in France, he returned to Windsor and an articling job. While articling, he completed his MA degree at King's College. He graduated from Dalhousie in 1920, finishing second in his class; first place went to Vincent MacDonald, who in 1934 would succeed Smith as dean of Dalhousie Law School. After completing law school, Smith was persuaded by Dean MacRae to do post-graduate work at Harvard Law School, and Smith and another Canadian, James Power, were admitted to Harvard as special (non-graduate) students who were not entitled to take degrees. Even this concession required considerable persuasion, for Harvard did not then recognize Dalhousie's LL B degree as a suitable qualification. Not until 1925 was MacRae able to persuade Harvard officials to allow Dalhousie graduates of 'high rank' to be considered for admittance.[24]

At Harvard, Smith took basic courses, including contracts from Samuel Williston and trusts from Austin Wakeman Scott. Smith was introduced to the casebook method, and the experience made him an uncompromising advocate of it. It was not surprising that on his return to Dalhousie to take up the teaching post Dean MacRae had promised would be waiting for him Smith adopted the casebook method in two of the subjects he was assigned to teach, contracts and trusts. Smith used the casebooks he was familiar with, Williston's *Cases on Contracts* and Scott's *Cases on Trusts*. He gratefully acknowledged this debt to Scott in the preface to his own *A Selection of Cases on the Law of Trusts,* which was published in 1928.[25]

The casebook method did not meet with immediate success among the students at Dalhousie. Smith contemplated resigning when his third-year trusts class refused to engage in the discussion required by the casebook method. Undoubtedly, the students were not used to the process of discussing judicial reasoning. G.F. Henderson, who reviewed Smith's mimeographed version of his casebook in 1926, may have put his finger on one of the reasons for the students' disquiet. By third year, many of Smith's students would have spent four years working in the offices of a practising lawyer, and it is understandable that the needs of the law office would have become those of the students-at-law. In his review Henderson noted 'one drawback about these books from the practical lawyer's standpoint: The cases were selected by the Law School Professor to form the basis of discussion with students, and sometimes a badly decided case is chosen for the simple reason that it is badly decided and leaves the door open for the kind of criticism which is useful in educating the student.'[26] It is likely that the resistance to Smith's casebook and his method of teaching came from students who could not see the practical value of reading and discussing cases that were badly decided. Henderson tried to justify the inclusion of badly reasoned cases by saying that 'counsel does not always choose not to cite a case which appears to be in his favour because it is badly decided.' Henderson was missing the point, but Smith and others who used the casebook method had to face the attitude expressed by Henderson: the ultimate value of a law book was in its practical usefulness to the practising lawyer. Smith's students apparently relented in time, and became accustomed to the technique and to the burden of work it required of them.[27]

With his former teacher and mentor, Donald MacRae, already teaching at Osgoode Hall, Sidney Smith probably was not reluctant to leave Dalhousie and join the Osgoode staff in September 1925. He took over Shirley Denison's courses in real property, personal property, sale of

land, and wills. He also assumed part of Dean Falconbridge's teaching
load by taking over his third-year trusts class.

Smith stayed at Osgoode Hall until 1929, when he was replaced by
John Josiah Robinette. In that year Smith was offered the deanship of
Dalhousie, a post he accepted on the condition that a fourth full-time
teacher be hired and that the staff be better paid.[28] In Smith's four years
at Osgoode, he and Caesar Wright laid the foundation of a lifelong
friendship, a friendship that ultimately was to have a significant impact
on the controversy over the Law Society of Upper Canada's control of
legal education in Ontario.

Falconbridge, with three full-time teachers in place at Osgoode Hall,
was preparing to make a case for a fourth. His ties with Canada's most
successful university law school, Dalhousie, could not have been closer.
The students' library was being slowly enlarged; Falconbridge had managed to extract from the benchers a positive statement of the value of
the casebook method of teaching; and the number of lecture hours was
rising steadily (from 621 hours in 1923–4 to 852 in 1926–7). Falconbridge
was beginning to feel that his views on the needs of the school were at
last being taken seriously by the benchers.

With these victories in hand, Falconbridge began to push to raise
admission standards. The importance of this effort, as with many of
Falconbridge's initiatives, was partly symbolic and partly real. Clearly,
it was easier and more interesting to teach students who had a liberal
arts education. The success of the casebook method depended on a
classroom of students with sufficient imagination and critical sense to
make the discussion profitable, and it was to be hoped that such students
eventually would make better lawyers. These were important factors in
the move to toughen the educational requirements for admission. But
it was also symbolically important, at Osgoode Hall and elsewhere, that
the image of the trade school be dispelled; one of the ways of doing so
was to have it be known that the students were of university calibre and
were qualified to pursue a bachelor's (or even a graduate) degree in any
university.

In 1926 Sir James Aikins, the president of the Canadian Bar Association, told his members, 'The Association, through its committee of
legal education, is continuing with success its effort to raise the standard
of requirements for admission to the profession.'[29] In May of that year
the Ontario Bar Association met in Toronto and the entrance standard,
at the law school was the principal issue for consideration. R.J. Mac-

Lennan and F.H. Barlow, legal education activists who had no direct connection to the law school, moved and seconded a resolution calling for the entrance requirement to be raised to the CBA's recommended standard of completion of two years of university. Falconbridge and MacRae, who probably had orchestrated the event, rose to speak to the question. Justices Orde and Riddell, two of the most highly respected jurists in Ontario, also addressed the issue. Falconbridge risked the ire of the benchers when he said, 'I don't know that bricklayers require much more general education than is provided for legal education.'[39] It had recently been learned that New Brunswick, the only province with a lower entrance requirement than Ontario, had raised its admission standard to completion of two years of university studies. That news was not kept from the membership of the OBA for long.[31] Under pressure, the benchers reconsidered their position. Facing the fact that their school had the lowest entrance requirement in the dominion, the benchers decided to raise the standard to that recommended by the CBA. Because of his zeal and leadership in this effort, Falconbridge's reputation rose among the university-minded. The editor of the *Canadian Bar Review*, Charles Morse, lauded him in print for 'the successful issue of his labours' on behalf of the cause.[32] At long last the state of legal education in Ontario, as in Canada at large, appeared to be improving. One benchmark of this improvement was an interim report of the Carnegie Foundation issued in 1925, in which A.Z. Reed, North America's foremost expert on legal education, noted that in some respects Canada was ahead of the United States in the field: in 1925, seventeen American states had no educational requirements of any sort and seven did not even require a period of legal study prior to admission to the bar.[33]

Falconbridge's labours were paying off. Most of what he asked for, he received. Indeed, it appears that only one of the moves he supported (if he did not initiate it behind the scenes himself) failed during the years Caesar Wright was a student at Osgoode. Late in 1924, the Ottawa lawyer E.R. Cameron, from all appearances on his own initiative, brought forward a motion before the Senate of the University of Toronto. The motion requested that a committee be appointed to meet with the benchers to discuss once again the possibility of establishing a law faculty at the university. Cameron said this law faculty should not displace the law society's school, but rather should be geared to train advocates and judges. The benchers' school, Cameron argued, would produce 'lawyers to whom the highest professional honours will not be paid, but who will perhaps be the best moneymakers.'[34]

The wording of the proposal made it likely that Cameron's suggestion would not be taken altogether seriously. But it was ingenious, since it neatly answered the old-school benchers' contention that legal education should be geared primarily to the general practitioner, the legal yeoman who, without pretensions to scholarship or political leadership, was engaged in the day-to-day practice of the law.[35] In Cameron's proposal, the other side of that coin was revealed: if the law school was designed for the commonplace lawyer, clearly a form of legal training for academically distinguished lawyers was also required.

The university Senate passed Cameron's motion. M.H. Ludwig, the chairman of the law society's legal education committee, was sent by Convocation in October 1924 to meet with the university's representatives. In December of that year a joint committee was established; its members were Mr Justice C.A. Masten of the Appellate Division of the Supreme Court of Ontario; Frederick W. Harcourt, a former bencher and later treasurer of the law society; Michael Ludwig; and John Falconbridge. Out of these meetings a plan was devised. The university would modify its existing course in politics and law to permit a candidate for the bachelor of arts degree to choose half of his third-year subjects from courses offered in Osgoode Hall's first-year program. After that, the student would go immediately into the second year at Osgoode, at which time articling would commence.[36]

The proposed joint program was very different from what Cameron had suggested. It was strongly favoured by Falconbridge for obvious reasons: not only would it encourage those intending to go into law to take a BA from the university, it also would develop a closer relationship between the law society and the university, a relationship that might in time lead the benchers to transfer the whole of legal education to the university.

The proposal was immediately shelved by the legal education committee. In late June 1925 Michael Ludwig wrote to Dr James Brebner, the registrar of the university, informing him that the committee could not support or recommend the proposal. Ludwig had not been in favour of the proposal from the start. He pointed out that the proposal would mean that in some cases a year of office attendance would be dispensed with. In addition, the program would not be available to graduates of other universities – a justifiable objection. The joint program, like so many past proposals involving the University of Toronto, was stillborn.

Nevertheless, the proposal was not without its effects. In 1926 a new undergraduate program was introduced at the University of Toronto –

the honours degree in politics and law.[37] The course was intended to follow the general outlines of BA courses in jurisprudence offered at Oxford, Cambridge, and Dublin. It focused on Roman law, the history of English law, English and Canadian constitutional law, jurisprudence, international law, and – rare in Canada – Canadian administrative and municipal law. It is perhaps odd today to think that all of these courses were viewed by lawyers as being of limited practical importance, and indeed as having little to do with the law. But such was the opinion of most members of the profession.

The program at the University of Toronto was the brainchild of one of the most innovative actors in Ontario's legal education drama, William Paul Maclure Kennedy. Kennedy, with Norman A. MacKenzie, a pre-eminent international law scholar,[38] and J.F. Davison, taught Canada's only university program designed exclusively as an academic course in legal theory. Charles Morse described the program in an editorial in the *Canadian Bar Review*: 'The course primarily aims at training legal scholars and jurists, and in sending out into Canadian life a group of men and women fundamentally interested in law as a science. Incidentally, it is a first-class pre-legal training for those going to the law schools, where, indeed, those who have graduated in it have already acquired honour and distinction.'[39]

Charles Morse's description of what was to be known as the 'Kennedy Law School' suggests that Kennedy intended to establish a program that would precede legal training. It was, Morris wrote, 'something analogous to what [the University of Toronto] offers in its honour pre-medical science BA course to future doctors.' More specifically, the program could be integrated with the training given at Osgoode Hall Law School. The student would acquire, 'first, specific training in the science of law and politics; then, if the student selects the legal profession as his life's work, training in its "clinical" work in a Law Society.' Many successful lawyers (including Bora Laskin, G. Arthur Martin, and W.G.C. Howland) were to follow this two-stage program. Some twenty years later the Kennedy School was to be transformed, at the hands of Caesar Wright, into a Harvard-style university law school. In a sense then, Cameron's visionary, if somewhat jocular, proposal came to eventual fruition in spite of its apparent failure.

Falconbridge's success during the years Wright was a student at Osgoode Hall were the result of his personality and the respect the benchers had for him. Equally important was the growing disquiet felt by a distinct minority of the profession in Canada over the existing system of legal education. Many established practitioners were uninterested in educational reform; it was not uncommon for those lawyers to argue that the education they received could not have been all bad, since it produced so many outstanding lawyers, including themselves. The few legal academics in the country were, naturally enough, concerned about their particular sub-profession. Certainly much of the unease originated with Canada's small population of law teachers, who saw themselves as educators first and lawyers second. But another group of lawyers, who were not themselves law teachers, were seriously interested in the problems of legal education in Canada. These lawyers often gravitated to the various national, provincial, and local professional organizations that provided a forum to discuss legal education and other problems in the profession. In retrospect, it is clear that Falconbridge and the other activist academics, MacRae, Lee, and Smith, used these forums with considerable skill to debate the question of legal education in Canada and, most important, to bring pressure against the benchers in Ontario and the law societies in other provinces. As a result, Falconbridge's initial successes with the Law Society of Upper Canada can be properly understood only against the background of the discontent registered by the voluntary associations of practising lawyers and legal academics. It is to this aspect of the story that we now turn.

2

The Bar Associations and
Legal Education

A gregarious lawyer living in Toronto during the first two decades of this century could satisfy his craving for the company of his fellow lawyers by belonging to as many as five different professional organizations. He would, of course, have to be a member of the Law Society of Upper Canada, and in time he might be elected to join the select ranks of the benchers, or sit on one of the law society's seven standing committees. In addition, he might join the Toronto Lawyers' Club, the York County Law Association, the Ontario Bar Association, and the Canadian Bar Association, voluntary associations that came to perform a very useful function in promoting improvements in legal education.

From the earliest days of the Ontario profession, lawyers from outside Toronto felt alienated from the Law Society of Upper Canada. Although benchers of the society were elected from all parts of the province, the concentration of lawyers in Toronto meant that most of them were from Toronto.[1] If a lawyer from, say, Belleville or Fort William felt disfranchised and resentful, he might consider joining a local organization that would provide a forum in which he could voice his complaints. The county law associations, for example, were already in place, ready to be moulded to the needs of local lawyers. Ironically, those associations, which were the source of membership for both the Ontario and the Canadian bar associations, had been established by the Law Society of Upper Canada itself to collect fees from local lawyers to establish and maintain central libraries in county seats.

Although many practitioners wanted to retain and reinforce the autonomy of the local bar,[2] most felt that the individual associations were impotent, and argued for a federation of county law associations.[3] The first attempt to organize a province-wide association came in the summer of 1899, when representatives from six county associations met at Osgoode Hall to discuss the possibility of creating a federation of county associations.[4] These informal meetings continued annually until 1905, when a resolution was passed declaring that it would be to the advantage of the legal profession of Ontario to form a provincial bar association. In 1906 the Ontario Bar Association was officially created, with an initial membership of about fifty. A.W. Clarke, QC, MP, was elected president.

At its second annual meeting, which took place in 1908, the association, then numbering 257 lawyers,[5] was ready to set its agenda. The acting chairman, F.E. Hodgins, KC, made it clear in his opening address that the matters open for consideration and discussion by the OBA were not to be thought of as being pre-empted by the powers and responsibilities of the Law Society of Upper Canada: 'If you look at the Act which deals with the formation of the Law Society, you will see that there is nothing in that which would cast upon the Benchers the necessity of considering the various questions which this Association considers from time to time ... there is nothing in that which indicates that they are to take into consideration or that they only have the right to represent the bar in questions on which the bar may be concerned, and its relations either to one another or to the public.'[6] The law society had no inherent jurisdiction over the relationship of the bar to the bench, legal ethics, the procedure and administration of justice, or law reform. Sir Aemilius Irving, still the treasurer of the law society in 1909, expressed his strong approval of the OBA and its aims. It appeared that the law society and the Ontario Bar Association would be able to live together in harmony.

Although Hodgins had, by implication, put questions concerning legal education beyond the purview of the OBA, it was not long before the annual meeting became a forum for discussing these issues. This was inevitable. Legal education was always a topic of interest, and it was difficult for any formal or informal gathering of lawyers to avoid discussing and disagreeing on some aspect of preparation for the bar.

On the agenda at the 1911 meeting – in addition to such uncontroversial matters as the abolition of dower, whether jurors' allowance should be increased, and whether Crown attorneys in cities with a population of more than fifty thousand should be allowed to continue private practice – was a motion to discuss legal education. The motion, which probably was made by Falconbridge, who had begun to attend the meetings in 1909, resulted in the passage of an amazing resolution. The membership resolved to discuss at its next meeting 'the advisability of transferring the educational functions of the Law Society to a properly organized and constituted Faculty of Law of the provincial university [that is, the University of Toronto], the president and lecturers of the Law School to be the dean and professors of such Faculty.'[7]

The motion could only have been intended to be provocative, since the suggestion that the law society's educational functions be transferred to the university certainly would not have obtained a hearing in Convocation. The university had made similar proposals – all of them considerably more deferential to the law society – and had been rebuffed. The tone of the resolution is noteworthy: not only was the OBA entering into an arena known by everyone to be within the purview of the law society, it was doing so in the most confrontational manner possible. Unfortunately, we do not know whether the proposal was ever discussed at the 1912 meeting, since no report of that meeting is available.[8]

In 1913, Viscount Haldane, the first lord chancellor of Great Britain to visit North America while in office, addressed a meeting of the American Bar Association in Montreal. Apparently, this auspicious event persuaded some members of Canada's legal profession to give the dormant Canadian Bar Association another chance.[9] The Canadians may have been embarrassed in front of their American colleagues by their lack of a national bar association. In any case, after the ABA's Montreal meeting, Manitoba's minister of justice, C.J. Doherty, asked Sir James Aikins, KC, MP, the president of the Manitoba Bar Association, to take on the job of convincing other provincial associations of the value of a national bar association.

The first meeting of the Canadian Bar Association was held in Montreal on 19 and 20 March 1915. The *Canadian Law Journal* gave the meeting extensive coverage[10] while downplaying the OBA meeting that also was held that year. The Toronto-based *Canadian Law Times* ignored the CBA meeting and devoted its attention to the OBA gathering.[11] (This division of loyalty remained intact until 1922, when both the *Times* and the *Journal*, after forty-two and fifty-eight years, respectively, of publishing, combined to form the *Canadian Bar Review*.)

One of the stated aims of the CBA was to encourage a high standard of legal education. The prospect of a national forum for discussion of the problems of legal education caused legal educators such as Falconbridge and MacRae to turn their attention to the Canadian Bar Association. From this point on, the CBA and the OBA were to compete for the role of leading critic of legal education in Canada.

The CBA committee on legal education was created at the first meeting of the association; H.A. Robson, founder of the Manitoba Law School, was appointed chairman. The committee set itself the task of investigating law-school admission requirements, the period and course of study, the transfer of students from one province to another, and admission to the bar. There was no suggestion that the committee would prepare a report of its findings.

The war made regular bar association meetings impossible, and it was only after the Armistice of 11 November 1918 that both the CBA and OBA experienced a rebirth. Legal education was one of the prime topics of discussion for both associations, and legal education committees of both groups presented reports at the annual meetings. Falconbridge and MacRae, perhaps anticipating the flood of new students returning from active service, thought the time opportune to press again for educational reform.

The report of the OBA standing committee on legal education, probably written by R.J. MacLennan, was primarily an argument for the addition of a second full-time instructor at the law school.[12] The argument was based on the unspoken premise that Harvard Law School's teaching methodology was the best if not the only model for Ontario to follow. The committee drew back from its provocative pre-war suggestion that legal education be turned over to the University of Toronto. Instead, it noted that 'to remove the Law School from Osgoode Hall would have the tendency "to cut off legal education from the living body of the law." '[13] The difference in attitude between the 1911 resolution and the 1918 suggestion for moderate reform was the result of a change of personnel on the committee and a change in Falconbridge's strategy. Falconbridge, who was the obvious choice for the additional full-time position at the law school, realized that his effectiveness as a reformer would be undercut if the Ontario Bar Association maintained its hard-line stance. The accompanying editorial in the *Canada Law Journal* was even more cautious. The Harvard Law School approach undoubtedly had its merits, the editor, Henry O'Brien, wrote, but in Ontario something more practical and less scientific was desirable, since 'a mere teacher, who has not been in active practice, however profound his knowledge and in other respects efficient, cannot be as useful an educator as one who, perhaps less scientific and less learned, is able from his own experience to make clear difficulties and to be helpful in the explanation of matters likely to arise in the conduct of litigation.'[14]

The report of the CBA committee on legal education, in contrast, was more specific and less equivocal in its approach.[15] The committee's two major recommendations were (1) that every candidate for admission to study be over eighteen and a graduate of an approved university, and (2) that the course of study consist of attendance for three uninterrupted years at an approved law school, followed by service for at least two years in the office of a practising barrister or solicitor (or one year if the student was a university graduate). The report, a draft of which was published prior to the meeting,[16] was based on the earlier discussions of the Robson committee.

The chairman (or convenor, as he was called) of the committee on legal education was Robert Warden Lee, who with Falconbridge and MacRae led the academic reform movement. Lee, like MacRae, came to law from a background in classics. A graduate of Balliol College at Oxford, Lee spent a brief time as a civil servant in Ceylon, where he became acquainted with Roman–Dutch law.[17] He was called to the bar at Gray's Inn in 1896 and went to Oxford as a law tutor, a position he held from 1899 to 1914. In 1914 Lee emigrated to Canada to serve as dean of the Faculty of Law at McGill University, holding the post of professor of Roman law. He discovered that since Quebec had retained its civil-law tradition McGill was the ideal location for a centre of comparative legal studies, and in his seven years as dean, before returning to Oxford as the Rhodes Professor of Roman–Dutch law, he laid the foundations for the only Canadian law school geared to the teaching of comparative law.[18]

Although he had been trained in England, Lee was an advocate of the Harvard approach to professional legal education. In an article published in 1916, he set out what he took to be the three forms that legal education could take: a student could be trained in the practice of law; he could be trained in the law which he is to practise; or he could be trained in the law.[19] In Canada, the first form predominated, and was maintained by the reliance on apprenticeship in law offices. If the sole aim of legal education was to train the student to practise law, Lee argued, then there was little need to require him to spend any time at all the classroom: 'You cannot teach a man in your class-rooms to practise law, any more than you can teach him to play the fiddle by lecturing him on fiddling.' For Lee, however, legal education involved teaching the student the law that he would practise as well as teaching him the science of the law. These were the proper aims of a legal education, and they could be satisfied only in a university environment.

Expanding on his views a few years later, Lee wrote that the preparation for law consisted of two distinct processes – learning law and learning to be a lawyer.[20] Canadian law societies had tended to concentrate on the latter (which Lee acknowledged was an essential element of a legal education) while ignoring (or worse, ineffectually attempting to provide) the former. Learning the law could not be a part-time affair: 'The student who runs away to the office as soon as the lecture is over gets little good from the lecture, and, I should suppose the student who runs away from the office to attend lectures does not take full advantage from the office either.'[21] Law school study and office attendance, in short, should be consecutive, not concurrent; moreover, if law teaching was to be taken seriously, the job should be reserved for those who were suited to it and able to give it their full attention. One need only look to Harvard, Lee argued, to see the value of developing an institution devoted to the teaching of law:

Why has that institution risen to its present commanding position, why is it famous the world over, why has it shown the way to many other law schools in the United States of America, which by following its lead, are able to compete on equal terms for pride of place? Simply because some fifty years ago, a man of genius called Langdell advised, and a man of vision called Eliot approved what was then a new departure in legal education. I attach less importance to the method than to the spirit which animated it; which was essentially nothing but this – concentrated and continuous effort on the part of teacher and student directed towards the desired end.[22]

Lee was a committed 'university man,' and it was not surprising that as long as he headed the CBA's legal education committee the law society was kept on the defensive. Lee's strategy of heaping praise on Harvard law school would be used by Falconbridge, MacRae, Smith, and, in time, Wright. It was impossible to gainsay Harvard's prestige; as a result, the benchers found themselves having constantly to defend the view that Ontario had no need for a scholarly and prestigious law school – not the easiest argument to make publicly or in print.

The 1918 CBA report brought to the fore one of the major targets of the attack, Ontario's system of concurrent law school and office attendance. The battle lines were drawn between those who, like Lee, favoured a consecutive approach and those who favoured the existing concurrent approach.

The discussion that followed the tabling of the 1918 report occupied most of the next two days[23] and aired many of the arguments for and against the concurrent approach, arguments that were to be repeated for the next thirty years. Falconbridge began the discussion at the 1918 meeting by echoing Lee's rejection of the concurrent scheme: 'A man cannot serve two masters. Either he will really devote himself to his law school studies, in which case he will cheat his employer by absenting himself from his office, or he will devote himself to his office work and neglect the law school. He cannot do the two things any more than a man in any other walk of life can do two things satisfactorily.' MacRae, in a lengthy speech, stressed the 'utmost importance' of the recommendations under consideration and argued for a standardized scheme of education throughout the country along the lines Lee had suggested. MacRae was in agreement with Lee and Falconbridge that the concurrent system did not work, but in his view it would be better to have the office experience precede full-time law school attendance. Isaac Pitblado, speaking from his experience in Manitoba, congratulated Lee and his committee on the report and emphasized the importance of higher standards of admittance. Eugene Lafleur, a prominent Quebec lawyer, noted that from the standpoint of the employer the concurrent system was not satisfactory: the student would have to interrupt an office task to attend a lecture.

The opposing arguments came, for the most part, from the Ontario delegation. Angus MacMurchy of Toronto argued that if law school was divorced from the articling experience the student would be deprived of the useful instruction that his articling principal could provide. J.F. Orde of Ottawa was concerned that the minimum age of eighteen would keep worthy aspirants out of the profession. G.F. Henderson of Ottawa claimed that the concurrent approach in Ontario worked splendidly: 'The student who goes to the lectures and then can come back to the law office, and apply in practice what he learns at the lectures, will have a better understanding of the lectures than the student who is not able to put the theory into practice.' In a published response to Lee's report, Henderson was blunt: 'Law is essentially practical, and it is better to have a limited store of knowledge with the ability to use it to practical advantage, than a greater knowledge without that ability.'[24] This sentiment was echoed by other voices from across the country: Mr Justice Mellish of Saint John remarked that 'law study in a school will not make a lawyer. It may make critics, but it won't make practising lawyers.' The Saskatchewan lawyer J.A.M. Patrick pointed out that 'the example of the servitude of a law student has been handed down to us for hundreds of years, and I do not think we should set it aside without some good and sufficient reason.'

It is clear enough what the arguments on each side amounted to. In the post-war period the conception of what law was and ought to be was in the process of change, a change reflected in the jurisprudential battles being waged in the United States between 'progressive' and 'conservative' elements. Both sides expressed plausible views about the nature of the law and the character of the legal profession. The difference was that the academically minded believed that the law was not just a practical profession but a 'scientific' field of study of substantial complexity that was strongly affiliated with the social sciences. The practitioners envisaged the law from the standpoint of how they practised it: there was some theory to learn, of course, but that theory made sense only if viewed from the perspective of the lawyer in practice. The debate over legal education was nothing more or less than a debate about the nature of the legal profession itself. Neither side denied that the other had a point – law was obviously both a practical matter and a theoretical subject amenable to scientific treatment. The problem was which of the two conceptions was to dominate at the level of instruction.

Lee's report was held over until the 1919 annual meeting of the CBA, where he presented it in a modified form. At the 1918 meeting the 'consecutive' approach to legal education had been understood to mean that a student would spend three uninterrupted years at the law school, followed by two years in a law office. The revised recommendation was that 'the course of study ... consist in attendance at the office of a practising barrister ... for a period of five years ... provided ... that the obligation of office attendance shall be suspended during the period of the year in which a student is duly following a course of study at an approved law school.'[25] The compromise seemed acceptable, and the report, with the amendment, was adopted without discussion.

From the perspective of those whose main concern was to require full-time attendance at law school, the change was not important. It did, however, make the proposal more palatable for some, since it allowed the so-called interpolated approach to be implemented. The student would attend law school full time during the eight-month school session, and then fulfil part of the articling requirement during the summer. In 1919 Dalhousie was the only law school in Canada operating under this optional interpolated scheme. (The school eventually abandoned it in 1934, following Saskatchewan's lead, and went to the purely consecutive approach.) The interpolated approach had problems of its own, but it did have the advantage of giving students the opportunity to earn a modest sum of money doing law-related work over the summer.

It is difficult to assess the impact of Lee's report. Especially in western Canada, newer law schools were in a state of flux and willing to experiment. Whether the CBA was influential in that experimentation is not clear. It appears, however, that the Lee report had many supporters in Manitoba.[26] That province was unique in having a law school jointly operated by the University of Manitoba and the Manitoba Law Society. With the full agreement of the Manitoba benchers, the trustees of the law school proposed a purely consecutive approach to legal education in 1919, and beginning in 1921 students were required to put in three full-time years at the law school, followed by one year of office training. This scheme (which, together with the six-month bar admission course, is in force in Ontario today), was modified in 1927 to a plan whereby the student would attend law school for two years and then proceed to two years of concurrent law school and articling. In 1931, Manitoba returned to the concurrent system, with the option of interpolation, and offered four hours of lectures during the mornings, leaving the afternoons free for office work. The program, unlike Osgoode Hall's, was four years in length for university graduates and matriculants alike.

In 1919, Falconbridge, MacRae, and Lee could hardly have expected to convince the CBA membership, let alone the Ontario benchers, of the virtues of the consecutive scheme. In 1919 the concurrent approach was the rule, and only the Saskatchewan, Manitoba, and Ontario law societies required law school attendance for admission to the profession. Full-time schooling was offered at Dalhousie Law School, and most prospective lawyers availed themselves of it; but even in Nova Scotia it was possible to become a lawyer merely by articling for four years.[27] Many of the small law schools in the West, some of which turned out as few as eight students a year, could not envision themselves as full-time university law schools in the Harvard mould: they simply lacked the resources. Over the years these schools would experiment with various arrangements, and, like the University of Manitoba Law School, would shift from one approach to another in rapid succession.

The Lee reports of 1918 and 1919 raised issues that were to be discussed often in the years that followed. More and more, the delegates from Ontario began to feel the pressure for reform. The law school at Osgoode

Hall was invariably the last to make any sort of change. But while the Lee reports had no immediate effect in Ontario, they could not be wholly ignored.

Perhaps feeling that the reformers had gone as far as they could on the question of consecutive versus concurrent arrangements, Lee changed his tack. He organized a subcommittee on curriculum that in the next two years would have a great deal of influence on Osgoode Hall. The subcommittee, which was composed of Lee, MacRae, Dean T.D. Brown of the University of Saskatchewan Law School, H.A. Robson of Manitoba, and W.F. Kerr of the Law Society of Upper Canada, wrote a report in 1919, which MacRae presented to the CBA in 1920.[28] Lee did not attend the meeting: he had accepted a one-year appointment at Oxford, which became permanent. He dropped from the Canadian scene, and MacRae took over the reins of the committee on legal education and the subcommittee on curriculum.

The subcommittee report presented MacRae's Dalhousie curriculum, with slight modifications, as the pattern for legal education throughout Canada.[29] The subcommittee report was adopted with only minor objections, and MacRae's curriculum gained the official sanction of the Canadian Bar Association. This was a minor victory for the university-minded members of the committee, and a personal triumph for MacRae.

For the next five years MacRae used the CBA committee to achieve two major ends – the adoption at the provincial level of the standard curriculum, and the raising of law school admission requirements. The first of these was an unqualified success. In 1921 MacRae could report that all of the provinces except New Brunswick, Prince Edward Island, and Ontario had adopted the standard curriculum in principle. The Ontario benchers could not object to the content of the curriculum, which was strongly weighted in favour of the kind of preparation a general practitioner in private law would need; rather, their concern was that implementing the curriculum would require more courses, and so would force them to hire more lecturers, something they felt they could not afford to do. But MacRae and the CBA succeeded in calling nationwide attention to the fact that Ontario was lagging far behind the other provinces, and when Falconbridge went to the law society's legal education committee in 1923 to ask for a curriculum change, he was able to use to his advantage the open criticism of the Ontario system.

MacRae's other objections generated considerable controversy, although it was not a particularly contentious topic. In 1921 Osgoode Hall informed the MacRae's CBA committee that admission to the status of student-at-law would henceforth require senior matriculation – that is, the student must have passed one year in a university arts program or passed exams in four subjects (English, French, history and Latin or mathematics) at the first-year university level. The next year MacRae and the CBA made it known that this standard was not good enough; the CBA committee recommended the completion of two years in arts at an approved university as the minimum admission requirement. The MacRae report of 1922 argued that two years minimum was the American Bar Association standard, and was the same as the admission require-ment for schools of medicine and dentistry. If the law school entrance standard was lower than that for medical school, some students might be tempted to enter the legal profession 'not because they have special fitness or liking for the study and practice of law but merely because they can save time and expense by choosing law.'[30] In retrospect it is clear that this last claim was specious, or at least devoid of factual foun-dation, but it was a shrewd approach: practitioners tended always to worry about overcrowding.[31]

The reaction to the recommendation was surprising. Although MacRae, Falconbridge, and Lee had decided not to push the troubling question of whether legal education and training should be concurrent or con-secutive, and indeed had not brought up the matter for three years, some members of the Ontario delegation were not about to let the issue rest. After MacRae tabled his report, M.H. Ludwig, speaking for the Ontario benchers, took the opportunity to return to the fundamental question of whether legal education was a matter of practical training or scholarly learning. Although Ludwig was eventually chastised by the chairman for going far beyond the topic at hand, his remarks were worth noting. The outburst appears to have been spontaneous; Ludwig and others were losing patience with MacRae's incremental approach to re-form, when the end envisaged seemed clear: the law society's loss of control over legal education. Ludwig's remarks show the state of mind of the majority of benchers at the end of the Hoyles era, as Falconbridge was about to step into the deanship. Rising to inform the membership that, in Ontario at least, the concurrent system was not seriously ques-tioned, Ludwig remarked:

We feel that a young man who gets a text-book and reads about a mortgage and has never seen a mortgage is not as well able to judge what a mortgage really is as the man who has seen it. The physical thing is the mortgage. He sees the form, the words, the language and then he has his textbook, and that makes a more lasting permanent impression than he gets when he simply reads in a book about a mortgage. The same applies all along the line with reference to all forms of documents – when he once actually sees the thing and what it looks like. It lands home in his mind in a manner that will serve him all through his career, so that we have rather stood against the idea that the universities should take the training entirely of our law students. We feel that there is too much of the theoretical about that proposal, and not enough of the practical, and I feel that so long as some of us older chaps are in harness and in authority in Ontario, the universities will not entirely, perhaps not at all, get the training of our law students.[32]

In 1922, when Ludwig made this speech, only the law societies of British Columbia and Ontario ran their own law schools; the rest of the provinces had made some sort of arrangement with provincial universities to take on the job of legal education, either entirely or in part. Clearly, Ontario's benchers felt that they were being pressured through the CBA to relinquish control over legal education. The pressure may not have been explicit, but it was none the less felt and strongly resisted. It should be recalled that it was Ludwig who, in 1923, proposed that lecturers at the school be barristers of at least ten years' standing. There was substance to Ludwig's suspicions, for Falconbridge's subsequent reform moves at Osgoode Hall were always made in concert with CBA pressure.

The Ontario Bar Association also had a role to play, and in 1922 it met to discuss legal education policy.[33] Four speeches devoted to the theme were given at the meeting: R.J. MacLennan's presidential address and speeches by Harlan F. Stone, the dean of Columbia Law School, Donald MacRae, and Ira A. MacKay, a Dalhousie graduate with a PH D in international law from Cornell, who was Lee's replacement at McGill Law School.[34] Both the presidential address and Harlan Stone's contribution were published, the latter in the first volume of the newly created *Canadian Bar Review*.[35]

In his address, MacLennan drew his audience's attention to recent developments in the United States, although he was not aware of their political and social significance. A few months earlier, the American Bar Association had met in Washington, DC, for the sole purpose of discussing legal education. Elihu Root's committee on legal education, destined to change the face of legal education in the United States, led the discussion. The Root committee had been created in part to reconcile the ABA with the American Association of Law Schools, which had vigorously argued for a radical upgrading of legal education. The Washington meeting was attended by representatives of forty-four state bar associations, several universities, and two Canadian associations – the Law Society of Upper Canada and the Ontario Bar Association. Edward D. Armour was sent to represent the law society,[36] and MacLennan represented the OBA. At that meeting it was agreed that to gain ABA approval the law school must require two years of university study before admission; require the student to spend three uninterrupted years at legal study; be possessed of an adequate law library; and be adequately staffed.[37] Few voices were heard to defend the night and part-time law schools, and the delegates, roused to an emotional pitch by speeches from Root and the chief justice of the United States, William Howard Taft, voted overwhelmingly to adopt the standards.

The 'glorious victory in the development of legal education'[38] was the beginning of the end for privately owned night schools in the United States; it was also the final move in the entrenchment of the control over legal education by the university professoriate. The motives behind the movement towards higher uniform standards were not always above reproach. Jerold Auerbach has argued, for example, that the greatest part of the hostility felt by the academics and practising lawyers towards the 'proprietary' and night schools was a resentment of foreign-born, Jewish, and black lawyers who had gained access to the profession through the less expensive night schools.[39]

If this is true of the United States, and Auerbach's evidence in support of this claim is considerable, there is almost no evidence to suggest that the Canadian attempts to standardize and upgrade legal education in the 1920s and later were similarly motivated by racism or xenophobia. It is foolish to suggest that such attitudes were unknown in Canada,[40] and it is not difficult to find in the *Canada Law Times* and other journals editorials warning of the 'dilution' of professional competence that would result if immigration policies were not tightened. Yet, if one may judge from the tone and substance of the views of those who strongly opposed attempts by Canadian legal academics to upgrade educational requirements for admission to the bar, the worst sin the academics in Canada could be accused of was empire-building. Even that accusation is in large part unfair: until the 1940s the legal academic community in Canada was extremely small, and educators were more concerned with keeping potential teachers from leaving the country than with building up large faculties.

In Canada, in contrast to what Auerbach suggests was the case in the

United States, there was no natural and permanent alliance between the corporate law firms and the élite schools. Powerful lawyers in Canada were as often hostile to the 'university-minded' academics as they were supportive of them, and there were no law schools in Canada comparable to Harvard, Columbia, and Yale that could plausibly hold themselves out as 'national' schools able to provide young talent for the powerful corporate firms located in large cities. Professional complaints about overcrowding to the contrary, there were far fewer lawyers per capita in Canada than in the United States: Ontario had 80 lawyers for each 100,000 inhabitants in 1921, while New York had 178.[41] Perhaps because of closer cultural ties with England, the Canadian lawyer was not as likely as the American lawyer to move into politics or business. In short, in the United States there may have been more at stake in the battle to maintain an élite bar by reforming legal education; in Canada culture and tradition tended to make for an élite bar from the outset, and Canada did not have a period of 'Jacksonian democracy' to be overcome by creating obstacles to entry into the profession.

The cultural differences between the two countries to one side, MacLennan's address shows that his motivation for an improved system of legal education in Ontario had little to do with the politically charged controversies that existed in Washington. MacLennan, who had not attended law school, argued for each of the Root committee's requirements from the perspective of one who believed his own preparation for the bar had been inadequate. He worried about the general quality of his own profession,[42] and felt moved to argue for a better-staffed and better-funded law school that would enable those already in the profession to continue their education. The law school could become a clearing-house for legal knowledge that could be made available to politicians and the general public. In his speech MacLennan spent only a moment expressing concern about the problems of too-easy access to the profession, an issue that loomed large in the United States. Overall, he seemed far less eager to erect higher educational barriers to entry to the profession than to give the profession reason to feel pride in its learnedness.

In contrast, Harlan F. Stone's address to the 1922 OBA meeting reflected the prevalent desire of American academics to 'cleanse' the bar of undesirable elements. Stone, who had been appointed dean of Columbia Law School in 1910, was noted for his scholarship and mastery of the casebook method.[43] Stone believed that legal education was composed of two distinct phases: the first, which could be accomplished only within the walls of a university, provided the student with a theoretical basis for subsequent practice; the second was simply practical experience it-self. Practical training, Stone believed, was no part of the business of a university law school. As dean, Stone had reorganized Columbia's cur-riculum to emphasize the scientific aspects of the law, which meant, in the 1920s, the sociological and political background against which par-ticular laws and statutory regimes could be interpreted. He was an advocate of interdisciplinary legal scholarship,[44] and persuaded William Underhill Moore to come to Columbia in 1916 to pursue his investigations into legal control as a form of behaviour modification. Stone's strong views of educational policy often brought him into conflict with Columbia's president, however, and in 1923, after a particularly acrimonious series of academic quarrels, Stone resigned to re-enter practice. He was soon appointed attorney general of the United States, and, not long after that, a judge of the u.s. Supreme Court. He was named chief justice in 1941.

Stone's address to the OBA probably represented the views of the radical wing of the American educational reformers of the 1920s. The address focused on the virtues of full-time university law schools, par-ticularly Stone's own. Such schools were staffed with professors who devoted themselves exclusively to teaching and scholarship and strict examinations were required for admission. Most important, the schools were well-equipped research centres. Stone assured his audience that at the 'leading law schools' the lecture and textbook method of instruc-tion had been virtually discarded in favour of the casebook method. In short, the United States was able, with its university law schools, to sustain the best system of legal education and produce the best legal educators in the English-speaking world.

After describing the glories of the American scheme, Stone enumer-ated some of the less desirable 'phases' of legal education in the United States. It behooved Canada to avoid the pitfalls into which the Ameri-cans, on occasion, had stumbled. The great advances of the 'leading schools' had been hampered by 'the democratic tradition that the Bar must be kept within reach of the great mass of the people,' a tradition that resulted in low-grade law schools and the 'inferior quality of the lower strata of the Bar' recruited from night school students. 'We have been depriving the world of the services of mechanics, tradesmen, and salesmen for which it had some need, in order to create an over-supply of inferior lawyers.' It was Stone's impression that 'the percentage of lawyers who are either foreign born or of foreign parentage has increased rather than diminished, and the great majority of them have come to the Bar by the easiest and most expeditious route.' Being foreign-born was, of course, not in itself objectionable, Stone added; but higher standards should none the less be demanded and put immediately into place in Canada, lest Canada suffer as the United States already did from a surfeit of inferior lawyers.

Stone concluded by noting that the Canadian bar, with its strong and highly organized law societies, was excellently placed to avoid these difficulties: 'unhampered by our extreme democratic tradition, what is difficult for us ought to be comparatively easy for you.' Indeed, he suggested that the requirement of extensive apprenticeship, if allowed to take place after law school, might be a desirable feature of Canadian legal education, having, as it did, a kind of filtering effect on the membership of the profession. In any event, Canada's strong law societies would surely make it possible for Canada to avoid the 'cult of incompetence masquerading in the guise of a spurious democracy.'

Stone's address seems to have been widely read by the university-minded educators in Canada, and the less savoury elements of his argument ignored. It is odd that those in Canada who thought that the articling experience was not nearly as important as law school education did not notice in Stone's address one reason the established bar held the opposite view with such vehemence: articling was a kind of social screening device; undesirables – women, racial minorities, and Jews – knew that they would have to struggle to find and keep suitable articling employment, and this knowledge discouraged them from even applying to law school. It is ironic that Stone looked to the Canadian law societies as the source of the profession's salvation. Most legal educators were of the view that law society control over legal education was the core of the problem and the cause of Canada's backwardness.[45] It seems obvious that neither the Canadians nor the Americans fully understood and appreciated the strengths and weaknesses of each other's educational systems.

When looking for Canadian authorities to support his views, Stone was able to find only one, an article that had been recently published in the *Canadian Law Times* by J.T. Hébert of the University of Saskatchewan Law School.[46] Hébert was indeed sympathetic to Stone's views, or at least to Stone's views shorn of his antipathy to the 'extreme democratic tradition'; but Stone was probably unaware that Hébert was for many years the only Canadian legal academic who was willing to express those views publicly.

Hébert had been educated at the University of New Brunswick and Harvard Law School, although he did not get a degree from Harvard.[47]

He had come to the University of Saskatchewan Law School from practice, and returned to practice, apparently overwhelmed by the academic
workload, in 1924.[48] He was remembered as a powerful personality
utterly devoted to the casebook method of teaching. Hébert's article 'An
Unsolicited Report on Legal Education in Canada,' was, at the time, the
strongest public statement in favour of the Harvard model in Canada.
Hébert ridiculed the apprenticeship approach ('the legal knowledge
acquired in this routine may be bounded by a nutshell and still leave
infinite space'), dismissed bar examinations as mere memory tests, and
called any favourable comparison between Canada's law schools and
the great American schools 'pathetically absurd.'

Hébert identified three causes of the unsatisfactory state of law schools
in Canada: the lack of a permanent professoriate; the lack of full-time
courses; and unscientific teaching methods. The defects were all closely
interrelated, Hébert claimed, and could be directly tied to the provincial
law societies' control over legal education. Drawing upon remarks made
by Lee, Falconbridge, and MacRae in the relative privacy of Canadian
Bar Association meetings, Hébert expounded at length on the virtues
of the case method of teaching. The case method, he wrote, develops
the legal mind

by training the student in legal reasoning: it makes him study the opinions of
the great lawyers of the past, and it compels him to reach his own conclusions
on the same or similar legal problems. It teaches him the law as it is, in a manner
which, interesting if not easy, indelibly fixes it in his mind, and gives him a just
appreciation of its application to the specific questions which are going to come
before him as a practising lawyer, and where the law is uncertain or unsatisfactory, it offers him the opportunity and the means to find out what it ought
to be.[49]

Hébert may have been the first legal educator in Canada to adopt the
casebook method in his teaching. He seems to have used Williston's
Cases on Contracts, which Falconbridge would also use three years later.
Hébert was unwilling (or more likely, given his workload, unable) to
develop a casebook of his own as Falconbridge eventually did. Hébert
published little, and never belonged to the CBA or attended any of its
meetings. His article, a unique document for its time, reflects a frustration that probably contributed to his leaving the teaching profession. As
we shall see, however, one of Hébert's students, J.A. (Alex) Corry, was

to play an important role in introducing Ontario's present scheme of legal education.

The following year, 1923, saw Falconbridge prepare to assume the deanship of Osgoode Hall. It was also the inaugural year of the *Canadian Bar Review*, which devoted many of the pages of its first volume to the debate over legal education. MacRae's last major report as convenor of the CBA committee on legal education was included.[50] That report took the form of a survey of progress throughout Canada in six areas: entrance requirements, standard curriculum, methods of teaching, production of teaching materials (especially casebooks), teaching staff, and remuneration of teachers. Ontario's entrance requirements (correctly assessed in the report as 'something less than the equivalent of senior matriculation or junior matriculation and one year in Arts') were lower than those of any province except New Brunswick. Manitoba and Nova Scotia had recently raised their admission standard to completion of two full years in a university arts program, and the report recommended that efforts to persuade law societies to raise their entrance requirements be continued. All of the provinces except New Brunswick, Prince Edward Island, and Ontario had adopted the standard curriculum.

When the report was discussed by the membership, McGill's new dean, Herbert A. Smith, noted, 'We in Canada have not yet succeeded in convincing one another within our own profession to believe in the necessity or even in the value of scientific, organized, academic legal education.'[51] Echoing remarks he had made two years before in an address to the Association of American Law Schools,[52] he described the legal profession in Canada as being in the same position regarding legal education as the United States had been fifty years earlier. Smith expressed amazement that in 1923 it was even necessary to argue for full-time university law schools; such an argument would be unnecessary anywhere else.

Herbert Smith, an Englishman educated at Oxford and called to the English bar in 1909, had been attracted to McGill by R.W. Lee, who was engaged in making McGill into a national law school specializing in comparative law. Smith had lectured for a number of years in the United States, and found the Canadian situation nearly intolerable. He was quite willing to inform the legal community of the 'inferiority' of Canadian legal education. In a 1921 piece in the *Canadian Law Times*, Smith criticized the provincial law societies for tending to dictate policy on curriculum and other law school matters to legal academics: 'Can anyone imagine that Harvard greatly concerns herself with the local requirements for practice at the Massachusetts Bar? Is it her principal function to keep up the supply of recruits for the law offices in Boston?'[53] Of course, the Canadian response to these rhetorical questions was that, whatever role Harvard saw itself as fulfilling, the law schools in Canada, because of the structure of the provincial bar, were of necessity concerned with providing lawyers for a local market. Still, Smith saw McGill Law School as a likely candidate for a 'national' law school, and he took the project of turning McGill into a national centre for legal scholarship seriously, against, as it is easy enough to see in retrospect, all odds. Early in his deanship he built up the faculty at McGill, producing by far the best international law program in Canada while continuing to make a considerable scholarly contribution to that field himself.[54] Later in the 1920s Smith was heavily involved in a project to establish an 'Imperial School of Advanced Legal Studies' in London – a kind of Commonwealth Harvard – which was for several years mired in administrative problems.[55] Along the way he managed to anger most legal academics in Canada, including Falconbridge, by telling the London Times that 'the general education level of the profession in Canada is far below that which prevails at the English Bar.'[56] Like Lee, Smith was soon drawn back to England, leaving in 1927 to become a professor of international law at the University of London.

When Ontario's special legal education committee met in 1923 and 1924 to consider the first round of changes that Falconbridge proposed, the new dean was well aware that the recommendations of the two bar associations were familiar to the members of the committee. Falconbridge may have reminded the benchers that the legal community in Canada was watching developments in Ontario. While they met, however, yet another association of lawyers was preparing to make its views known.

The Lawyers' Club of Toronto, a group of seventy-two young lawyers who had graduated from the law society's school within the past decade, supplied the committee with a strongly worded memorandum in July 1923.[57] The memorandum was signed on behalf of the club by F.H. Barlow and W.S. Montgomery. Five recommendations were put forward: (1) that more full-time professors be appointed to teach full-time students; (2) that practical experience be obtained by the student after law school; (3) that, except in rare cases, only graduates of universities be admitted to the school; (4) that the fees paid by the students be devoted to the students and the school; and (5) that the principal have full control over both curriculum and staffing.

In comparison with these recommendations, Falconbridge's requests seemed mild. It must be remembered that the chairman of the law society's legal education committee at that time was M.H. Ludwig, who at the 1922 CBA meeting had informed MacRae that as long as 'some of us older chaps are in the harness and in authority in Ontario,' the university would not be in the business of training law students. Ludwig would have been correct in thinking that his was the minority view at CBA meetings; but, as Falconbridge knew, he was in the majority among the Ontario benchers. Falconbridge's successes in 1923 and 1924 must be credited in part to the fact that the 'older chaps,' although not about to make radical changes to the school, and certainly not about to give up their control over legal education, were conscious of the unpopularity of some of their traditional views and were willing to make certain concessions if they could do so without losing face. This was why Falconbridge, in three years, was able to institute more reforms at Osgoode Hall than had been attained in the previous fifty.

Caesar Wright's years at Osgoode Hall, 1923 to 1926, saw remarkable changes in the school. Those changes came about through pressure from the various bar associations, which was in large part orchestrated by Falconbridge himself, with the co-operation of MacRae, Lee, and others. Falconbridge's cautious dealings with the benchers and his shrewd planning in concert with like-minded legal academics in the CBA and the OBA made this first revolution in Ontario's legal education possible. Falconbridge and MacRae helped to produce a new generation of university-minded legal academics. MacRae had groomed Sidney Smith, and now another candidate was on the scene – the brilliant graduate of Osgoode Hall, Cecil A. Wright.

There was little doubt that with his credentials the twenty-two-year-old Wright was meant for an academic career. The next step for him was to obtain a graduate degree in law. With more than a little pride, and probably feeling that his own efforts at patiently upgrading the law school had borne fruit, Falconbridge made an announcement in the 1926 Osgoode Hall student directory and handbook: 'A fact of more than passing interest is that Mr. Cecil A. Wright, winner of the Chancellor Van Koughnet scholarship in 1926, is now taking a year of graduate study at Harvard Law School, his degree in arts and his degree as barrister-at-law obtained with high distinction, being accepted as sufficient qualification to enable him to be a candidate for the degree of LL M at Harvard.'[58]

3

Wright at Harvard:
The Shaping of a Legal Scholar

In a *Toronto Telegram* article of 7 June 1926 entitled 'Large Class Finishes Osgoode Hall Course,' Caesar Wright was reported as heading the list of graduates with a standing of 94.5 per cent, 'one of the highest in the history of the law school.' The article goes on to say, 'It is interesting to note, in view of the present controversy for higher standards of entrance at Osgoode, that the two scholarship men are both university graduates, the one from Western and the other [H.M. Rogers] from U. of T.' Wright's home-town paper, the *London Free Press*, was more enthusiastic. In an article carrying the headline 'Brings Honor to His University,' the *Free Press* reported that 'honor has come to London and the University of Western Ontario alike, according to Dr K.P.R. Neville, registrar of the university, in the exceptionally high standing taken by Cecil A. Wright in heading the graduating class of Osgoode Hall, Toronto, this year.' The article concluded, 'Mr Wright has not yet decided definitely upon his plans for the future, but he is seriously considering taking a post-graduate course at Harvard University looking to the taking of a degree as a professor of law.'

Wright's choosing Harvard was no surprise; Falconbridge, MacRae, and Smith were all keen on sending him there to do graduate work. Indeed, it seems the pressure to choose this career path came from several sources. A *Telegram* article written on the occasion of Wright's appointment to the teaching staff at Osgoode Hall Law School claims that when Wright graduated from Osgoode Hall, 'it was decided to send him to Harvard for post-graduate work,'[1] suggesting that the staff at the law school took an active hand in Wright's career choice. MacRae wrote to Dean Roscoe Pound of Harvard recommending Wright: 'Both Mr Falconbridge and myself are very desirous of having one or more of our best students go to Harvard each year for graduate study. In selecting [Wright] as our first representative to you we are naturally indicating a special confidence that he is possessed of ability and scholarship which will do us credit.' It is likely that a teaching career for Wright was part of the long-range plans of the university-minded Osgoode Hall staff. As dean of Dalhousie Law School, MacRae had been instrumental in persuading Harvard to accept several Dalhousie graduates, including Sidney Smith, in its graduate program. In Smith's case, however, Harvard had been willing to allow him to take courses only as a special (non-graduate) student in 1920. At that time the Harvard officials were unconvinced of the rigour of Dalhousie's undergraduate law program, although, after repeated requests by MacRae, Harvard relented. If anything, Harvard officials were even more sceptical of the quality of the Osgoode Hall program in 1926. MacRae was called upon once again to plead the case for a Canadian law school to Dean Pound. As Wright said later, he and the Harvard people 'went into the Canadian situation rather thoroughly and it was with some misgivings that I was accepted.'[2] These misgivings had nothing to do with the size of Osgoode Hall Law School. In 1926 it would have counted as a reasonably large school, and was certainly the largest in Canada. An enrolment of 350 students made Osgoode Hall much larger than Dalhousie, and larger than the law schools at Cornell and Pennsylvania.[3] The worries Harvard officials had concerned the nature of Osgoode Hall, and in particular the kind of education it was providing.

As we have seen, American legal education had undergone a period of critical self-assessment that culminated in Elihu Root's report to the American Bar Association in 1921 recommending strict standards for u.s. law schools. Harvard Law School, a driving force behind the movement to upgrade American legal education, probably would have been doubly cautious about recognizing the Osgoode Hall degree until it was certain that the school could qualify as an ABA-approved school. Falconbridge had seen to it that many of the ABA criteria – higher entrance requirements, three years of full-time attendance, an adequate library, and a sufficient number of full-time instructors – were substantially satisfied at Osgoode Hall. Harvard officials, however, probably were disturbed by A.Z. Reed's definitive study of legal education in the United

States and Canada,[4] in which Reed reported that at Osgoode Hall, 'such systematic instruction in technical law as is provided is intended, as in England, for those who are simultaneously serving their office clerkships.' To those familiar with the standards at Harvard, Reed's assessment probably would have been interpreted to mean that the systematic study of the law provided at Harvard and other leading American law schools was not offered at Osgoode Hall. 'Systematic study of the law' at Harvard, of course, meant the study of the law by means of the casebook method rather than lectures. When Wright first entered Osgoode Hall in 1923, the English lecture system predominated at the school. Wright himself later described the teaching methods used during most of his law school career in disparaging terms:

The lecturer presents in dogmatic fashion a system of rules or principles which he states to be in force because of legislation or judicial decision. The lectures are presumably intended to be, and are as a matter of practice, taken down by the students as closely as may be – the completeness of a student's notes depending on his ability to write more or less quickly and the speed at which the lecturer speaks. In most courses of this kind, it is customary to have one text-book as the basis of the lectures, and in the main the lecturer follows that book.[5]

Between 1923 and 1926, however, many changes in the style of teaching at Osgoode Hall had taken place. By 1926 there were six Canadian casebooks in existence – Falconbridge's *Cases on Sale of Goods* and *Cases on Conflict of Laws*, MacRae's *Cases on Agency*, Smith's *Cases on Equity* and *Cases on Trusts*, and Horace Read's *Cases on Constitutional Law* – and all were in use at Osgoode Hall. Falconbridge, MacRae, and Smith all used one form or another of the case method, regardless of whether casebooks were available for the specific subject being taught. Still, because the benchers had made it known that they were sceptical of this approach and preferred the traditional lectures, the case method did not predominate and few if any of the part-time lecturers used it. This fact more than anything else probably contributed to the misgivings that Harvard had about admitting the young Wright. None the less, in the end, he was permitted to enrol in the LL M program.

The young, impressionable Wright must have been awed by Harvard Law School. In comparison with Osgoode Hall, Harvard was immense, with a total student population of 1,545. Harvard's graduate program was designed to produce academic law teachers. The program was well-enrolled: Wright was one of 64 graduate and special students attending in 1926.[6] Harvard's faculty numbered 30 and included such famous legal scholars as Roscoe Pound, Felix Frankfurter, Francis Bohlen, Austin Wakeman Scott, and Samuel Williston. The faculty enjoyed a degree of academic freedom unknown at Osgoode Hall. In addition, Harvard had a campus, proper teaching facilities, and an impressive library.

The intellectual and political climate of Harvard Law School must also have impressed Wright. During his year there Felix Frankfurter and others were beginning work on the Harvard Crime Survey, and were actively involved in the controversy surrounding the trial of Sacco and Vanzetti. Manley Ottmer Hudson helped to organize the Harvard Center of Research in International Law, and Roscoe Pound was a member of several government commissions investigating the administration of the criminal law in the United States. Wright's year also saw the emergence of a new and more activist u.s. Supreme Court. Justices Oliver Wendell Holmes and Louis Brandeis, both closely connected with Harvard, were attempting to change the traditional function of the judiciary by increasing the court's influence over social policies.[7] Wright had left a legal community that was insular and tradition-bound and joined one that saw its role as one of active participation in social and political change.

Administratively, Harvard was still in the process of revamping its graduate program when Wright enrolled. It was then offering both a master of laws (LL M) and a doctor of juridical science (SJD) degree. Wright initially was allowed to register in the LL M program. A student could be admitted to either program, depending on the graduate committee's initial assessment of the candidate, but in the end the real difference between the two programs was what was expected of the student in his examinations: the doctoral candidate was expected to pass 'with distinguished excellence,' while the master's candidate need only pass 'with high rank.'[8] (The distinction may have been a disguise for a more impressionistic assessment by those teachers who dealt directly with the candidate.) Neither degree required the preparation of a thesis. Rather, each involved one academic year of course work, with a twelve-hour course load per week, and end-of-year examinations. If the student enrolled as a doctoral candidate, he was permitted to substitute guided study in a particular subject for four course-hours' credit.

The LL M program was still in an experimental stage in 1926, and it is not clear how much leeway was permitted in tailoring the course of study to the abilities of particular students. In any event, because Wright's record at Osgoode Hall impressed the faculty, he was permitted to do guided study in advanced tort law as if he were a doctoral candidate.

In addition, he enrolled in Roman law (which appears to have been compulsory), comparative public law, and jurisprudence.[9] There is little doubt that Wright was far more interested in torts than in the more theoretical subjects he studied. By temperament he was a practically minded lawyer rather than an abstract thinker, but he was also a keen student surrounded by formidable scholars.

Wright studied Roman law under James Bradley Thayer, who was then an instructor in comparative law. Thayer was named for his grandfather, who had been Royall Professor at Harvard from 1873 until his death in 1902. Thayer was the son of Ezra Ripley Thayer, who served as dean of the law school from 1910 to 1915. This legal scion was a colourful character (he has been described as bearded and having the air of Napoleon III); he was not much older thanWright, having received his LL B from Harvard in 1924 and his SJD in 1925. Thayer was particularly interested in Roman law and the modern civil law systems based on it.[10] Wright's notebook in Roman law attests to the heavy demands that Thayer put on his students. A decade later Wright was to remark in a review of a text on Roman law that there was little usefulness in teaching the subject at the undergraduate level, since the importance of the topic became apparent only after a firm foundation in the common law was laid[11] – a belief shared by Roscoe Pound, who also taught the subject from time to time.[12]

Another of Wright's teachers, Professor Josef Redlich, seems to have cultivated Wright's interest in comparative law. Redlich, who led the comparative public law seminar, had just joined the faculty as the Charles Stebbins Fairchild Professor of Comparative Public Law after having taught for several years at the University of Vienna. While there he had served as a member of the Austrian Parliament and for a time had held the post of minister of finance.[13] Dean Pound had actively sought to hire Redlich in the hope that he, together with James M. Landis (also hired in 1926) and Thayer, would form the nucleus of a growing comparative law section of the Harvard faculty.[14]

Dr Redlich, an expert on English legal institutions, was also an authority on the use of the casebook method of legal instruction. In 1914 the Carnegie Foundation for the Advancement of Teaching had invited him to visit the United States and to conduct an examination of the merits of the case method as it was used at Harvard, Columbia, and elsewhere. In his final report, which was exhaustively discussed at the 1915 meeting of the Association of American Law Schools, Redlich concluded that the method – 'an entirely original creation of the American mind in the realm of law' – was both practical and effective in allowing students to do independent thinking about the law.[15] Redlich, however, did qualify his praise of the casebook method by suggesting that it might produce confusion and obscurity in the minds of the students at the outset, so that it would be wise to prepare them with lectures setting out the postulates, concepts, and terminology of the law.[16] Redlich also worried that legal scholarship might be directed away from the production of treatises because the amount of time required to produce and update casebooks was so great.[17]

Working under Redlich's supervision, Wright and a fellow Canadian, Harold Eric Carey from Manitoba, prepared a lengthy study entitled 'The Canadian Constitution and Judiciary,'[18] which, according to the title page, was 'a report submitted in a seminar of Comparative Public Law, conducted by Josef Redlich, J.U.D.' In this study, which was never published, Wright and Carey contrasted the U.S. judiciary's role in constitutional adjudication with the much more limited one of the Canadian courts. They concluded by stating that

Canada has already become accustomed to invalidating legislative Acts beyond the scope prescribed by the B.N.A. Act. Whether further restrictions based on theories of 'justice' or 'desired ends' will arise, depends on the willingness of the people to accede to the proposition that legislatures are but one agency through which they make for the social betterment of the Province and Dominion and that the judiciary is a totally distinct and separate agency making for the same good. Suffice to say that to date not even the Courts have considered their position in this light.[19]

Thayer and Redlich helped to form Wright's views on jurisprudence, although neither man was to become an adviser and confidant, and Wright was never to teach or contribute to the literature on either Roman law or comparative public law. The influence of these scholars was indirect: Wright seems to have been far more impressed by the fact that subjects like Roman law and comparative law were taught at a law school than by anything he learned in those courses. In his later polemical pieces on legal education, in which he made out his case for the university law school, he would underscore the importance of including in law school curricula 'academic' and comparative law courses.[20] MacRae's highly innovative standard curriculum, which was just beginning to find its way into Osgoode Hall Law School in Wright's third year there, was a considerable improvement over what it replaced, but it too was almost totally lacking in 'academic' topics. In his own teaching career Wright did not fight vigorously for the inclusion of Roman law or comparative law courses in the law school's curriculum; generally, his interests lay in more practical subjects, such as trusts and torts, and in the character of legal education. The more important Harvard influences came from Dean Roscoe Pound and Professor Francis Bohlen.

When Wright attended his seminar on jurisprudence, Pound at fifty-six years of age was a distinguished scholar, although his creative period was behind him.[21] Originally trained as a botanist, he had spent one year at Harvard Law School in 1889. After practising law in his native Nebraska and serving a few years as a commissioner of the Supreme Court of that state, Pound became dean of the University of Nebraska College of Law in 1903. In that year he published his *Outlines of Lectures on Jurisprudence*, the fourth edition of which formed the framework of the course Wright took in 1926. In his years at Nebraska, Pound wrote many of the jurisprudential articles that set out the tenets of sociological jurisprudence, perhaps the first wholly American jurisprudential theory. After two years at the Northwestern University School of Law and one at the University of Chicago Law School, Pound was appointed Story Professor of Law at Harvard in 1910 by Dean Ezra Ripley Thayer. When Thayer died in 1915, Pound became dean, a post he held until his retirement in 1936.

Wright's year, it appears in retrospect, was one of considerable activity in jurisprudence. It was a year of transition from sociological jurisprudence, which Pound advocated, to American realism, which was to dominate the American legal scene by 1930.[22] In the 1920s Harvard's pre-eminence was being challenged by the law schools at Yale, Columbia, Chicago, and Johns Hopkins. At these schools various educational experiments were begun in an attempt to use the techniques of the social sciences to further the ends of legal reform. Because of Pound's reluctance to move in this direction, Harvard soon found itself losing influence and research grants. Although the realist movement was to prove something of an intellectual dead end,[23] in the 1920s it challenged Pound's views with considerable force and energy. Situated where he was, Wright was exposed to a jurisprudence which, while losing influence elsewhere, was still being propounded by its creator. In his own writings, as we shall see, Wright never seemed to be able to come to grips with the difference between Pound's views and those of the realists: he would rely on the slogans and provocative claims of sociological jurisprudence or the realists as each suited his argumentative purposes, without attempting to distinguish the two schools, or indeed without pretending to contribute to the debate between them. Wright was too practically minded to be drawn to the abstractions of natural law and historical and positivist jurisprudence.[24]

Sociological jurisprudence grew out of a series of articles Pound published in the first decade of the twentieth century in which he called for a rejection of the nineteenth century's obsession with supposedly ineluctable legal rules and the 'mechanical application of those rules to changing social conditions.'[25] Legal conceptions, he argued, should be judged not by the niceties of internal structure, but by the results they achieved in practice.[26] Technology, industrialization, and the growth of cities made the mechanical application of legal notions born in an earlier era ludicrously out of date. By way of example, and echoing Oliver Wendell Holmes's dissent in Lochner v. New York,[27] Pound argued in 1909 that the 'sterile' application of the 'fossilized' legal rule of 'liberty of contract' had had the effect in previous cases of preventing various states from regulating the maximum number of hours an employee could be required to work. These decisions, according to Pound, ignored the social and economic realities of the situation: they ignored experience for the sake of logical consistency.[28] Pound recommended infusing the law with extralegal ideas so as to avoid the errors of 'mechanical jurisprudence': 'Let us look to economics and sociology and philosophy, and cease to assume that jurisprudence is self-sufficient … Let us not become legal monks.'[29]

The culmination of Pound's thinking on these questions appeared in 1911–12 with the publication of 'The Scope and Purpose of Sociological Jurisprudence.'[30] Here the basic tenets of a mature theory of law were logically set out, tenets Pound was to state, restate, and defend, more or less unchanged, for the rest of his long life. The correct perspective to take on the law, Pound contended was one in which law was seen as a 'social instrument,' an institution that could be improved by careful manipulation; law must be thought of as a form of 'social engineering.'[31] Towards this end, one must move beyond the mere description of the law as it is to the question of how it can be improved in the light of the realities of the various social situations in which it is actually employed.[32] But this attitude can develop only if the law is studied from the vantage point of the social sciences; those concerned about the law as a form of social control must be 'co-workers' with the social scientists.[33] The results of such investigations, Pound believed, would make the law in action not only more efficient, but also able to reflect actual social needs and concerns. The adherents of sociological jurisprudence were unimpressed by legal jargon and maxims; they sought to go behind the words to discover the genuine concerns those words hinted at, but often obscured. Pound proposed to replace talk of legal 'rights' with a theory of personal and social interests, a theory that would allow the judge to determine which interests set before him in a case should be legally recognized and how they should be weighed.[34]

In 1926, when Wright first heard him explain his views on the law and legal institutions, Pound had already begun to react against the challenges that were to form the basis of the jurisprudential school that more or less supplanted Pound's. Although the realists acknowledged Pound as one of their inspirations, their approach to jurisprudence reflected a different philosophical basis and an even more different practical stance. Whereas Pound was influenced by the optimism of the progressives and the pragmatists, the realists, writing after the horrors of the First World War, tended to show a profound pessimism and cynicism about the law, lawyers, and the judiciary. Whereas Pound saw sociology, political science, and ethics as the natural 'co-workers' of jurisprudence, the realists, at least initially, expressed scepticism about ethical values and shifted their concern to psychology so as to understand better the fundamentally irrational and biased behaviour of judges, with the aim of predicting trends in judicial decisions.[35] As the realist movement matured, some of the more sceptical elements were dropped in favour of sincere (although, in retrospect, somewhat naïve) attempts to bring the findings of all the social sciences to the service of the law.[36] But in the early days, realism, from Pound's perspective, overlooked the essentially ethical 'ideal element' in the law – the Ought that guided the jurisprudential search for the better Is. As early as 1923, Pound had vigorously argued that judges must take cognizance of political and ethical ideas as the end of the law, and that adjudication must function as a force of moral cohesiveness in society.[37] The realists were never to satisfy Pound that their view of the law recognized the importance of the ethical sphere.

Sociological jurisprudence, besides laying a foundation for judicial activism and clarifying the function of the courts, entailed a radically different approach to legal education. If law was a social instrument, a means of social engineering, then learning the law should involve an appreciation of both the end of the law and the means, as illuminated by the work of the social sciences, of achieving that end. Sociological jurisprudence, in short, suggested a move towards an interdisciplinary or extralegal approach to legal education. Indeed, this is precisely what the realists were to advocate: law, they argued, should be taught primarily as a practical discipline, with an emphasis on legal clinics and the use of casebooks and non-legal materials that reflected current research in the social sciences.[38] Pound did not accept that view of legal education, however, and throughout his tenure as dean was extremely reluctant to alter Harvard's curriculum, even when the experimental programs at Yale, and in particular Harlan F. Stone's social-science-dominated program at Columbia, were gaining momentum. Erwin N. Griswold commented on the irony of this in a tribute to Pound in 1957: '[Pound] was the great developer of sociological jurisprudence and he did much to change the basis for thinking about law in this country. Curiously enough, though, Pound did not direct himself particularly to the case method of teaching, nor did he undertake to develop the ways in which way teaching might well be modified in order to give adequate recognition to the sociological approach.'[39]

The irony of Pound's refusal to move towards the sort of interdisciplinary education suggested by sociological jurisprudence was, of course, of little concern to Wright in 1926. This was Wright's first exposure to fundamental questions about the nature of the law, and the subtleties of internecine jurisprudential battles probably were completely lost on him. On the specific question of curriculum, Wright would prove relatively conservative, and would later criticize Harvard for its failure to address itself to the need for practical legal training.[40]

There is no doubt, however, that Pound's lectures had a lasting impact on Wright. Twenty years later he described Pound as 'opening up the paths of European philosophies to the Anglo-American lawyer, not as something to be shunned, but as part of the progress of the human mind towards solutions of the "whether," the "ought" and the "why." To him jurisprudence had to be concerned with philosophy and law dealt with man and man's destiny in the world.'[41] In 1947 Wright described his reaction to Pound's lectures: 'I was privileged to attend Professor Pound's famous course on jurisprudence at the Harvard Law School. Like all others equally so privileged, the impact of his overwhelming knowledge and the wide vistas which he then laid before persons who, like myself, had been trained in the black-letter analytical jargon of Austin was an experience to which only the much abused adjective "terrific" can do justice.'[42]

There is little doubt that the impact of Pound's jurisprudential notions on Wright had little to do with the actual philosophical debates and historical surveys Wright absorbed as a twenty-two-year-old student at

Harvard. Although in Wright's later writings Pound's influence can be discerned, one will look in vain for a paragraph that seriously treats the kinds of issues that perplexed Pound. The influence was far more subtle. In his writings and speeches Wright could point to Pound's or to the realists' positions without bothering to distinguish between them, because, for Wright, what was important about the two camps was that both rejected the view that the law was a mere trade, a craft to be learned by memorizing lists of rules and applying them in practice. In his campaign for reform in legal education, Wright, like Falconbridge before him, had to respond to individuals such as M.H. Ludwig, who argued that legal education was essentially a practical matter unsuitable for a university environment. Such people thought, as Ludwig argued at the 1922 CBA meeting, that legal education was a matter of taking up a mortgage form in one's hands and reading it, and, having read it, knowing what to do with it.[43] Faced with these attitudes, Wright would naturally look back on the conception of law he was exposed to at Harvard, a conception that placed law firmly in the company of the social sciences. As a social science, law was a university subject; law could be taught only in a university environment. Of course, Wright did not himself teach law as a social science; but neither did Pound.

At Osgoode Hall, Wright had excelled in the study of torts; it was a subject that fascinated him, one characterized by factual situations reflecting problems of the utmost practicality that were often dealt with by the common law in mysterious and irrational ways. Torts was an ideal substantive area of study for someone like Wright, who distrusted abstractions but enjoyed the intellectual thrill of sorting out practical difficulties in a principled manner. Wright's nature made it almost inevitable that he would be drawn to the subject of torts, and to one of the dominant forces in American tort law, Francis Hermann Bohlen.

Wright later said of his year at Harvard that he 'was almost exclusively working with Bohlen.'[44] In 1926, Bohlen, at age fifty-eight, was the Langdell Professor of Law. He had joined the Harvard faculty the year before Wright's arrival, after over thirty years of teaching and scholarship at the University of Pennsylvania Law School. The appointment to the Harvard faculty came as the result of his great distinction in the field of tort law: Harvard then, as now, was able to draw brilliant scholars away from the universities where they had proved themselves. Soon after his arrival at Harvard, Bohlen's famous essays on tort law were collected and published as *Studies in the Law of Torts*. Wright was fortunate to have had the opportunity to study with Bohlen, for the year after Wright graduated he resigned his professorship at Harvard to resume teaching at the University of Pennsylvania.[45]

In assessing Bohlen's infuence on Wright – which, unlike Pound's influence, was both direct and substantive – it is important to appreciate Bohlen's position in the history of tort law scholarship. Bohlen stands as a transitional figure: he was to adopt certain attitudes characteristic of the developing realist school, but he remained unconverted to the overall realist theoretical perspective and relied instead on the 'conceptual' approach that characterized much of the torts scholarship of the late nineteenth century.[46] During Wright's year at Harvard, the realists, led in the area of tort law by Leon Green of Northwestern Law School, were in the process of experimenting with a novel approach to the subject. The conceptualists of the nineteenth century had arranged tort law into the standard categories of intentional harms, negligent harms, and strict liability, and set out the concepts of causation, duty, contributory negligence, assumption of risk, and vicarious liability in the form of principles. The realists favoured a classification based on the nature of the 'interests' involved in the specific circumstances of the tort litigation. Green's casebook, *The Judicial Process in Tort Cases*, published in 1931, organized cases into 'functional' categories, such as 'automobile traffic,' 'manufacturers and dealers,' 'passenger transportation,' and the like, with the idea of encouraging students to focus on the interests at stake in a lawsuit and not to view tort law as a mere collection of doctrines to be found in a text.[47] The 'interests analysis' was, in a different form, the creation of Pound; this aspect of realist scholarship, like many others, owed its origins to sociological jurisprudence.

Bohlen's *Cases on Torts*, first published in 1915, was more traditional in organization. None the less, the second edition, published in 1925, while retaining the doctrinal classifications of earlier treatments, moved in the direction of the realists' 'interest-balancing' analysis. Despite the heated attacks that he would later make on Green's work, Bohlen shared many of the realists' assumptions. Bohlen came to law convinced of the importance of social change and of the central role legal theorists should play on behalf of social progress. Like Green and the realists, Bohlen argued that lawyers and law teachers should 'look rather to what the law does than what the courts say,'[48] and that much of the legal machinery was unsuitable for the new problems of the day.

Bohlen may have lacked sympathy for the realist movement because he was nearly a generation older than the young turks who formed the ranks of the realists. In any event, his estrangement from Green, in particular, was due in part to Bohlen's participation in the American Law Institute's *Restatement of the Law*. Bohlen had been appointed reporter for torts in 1922, and was deeply involved in the project during Wright's year at Harvard. In fact, work on the *Restatement* was to absorb a large part of Bohlen's time until 1937, when he was forced to resign for reasons of health. Many of the realists felt that the *Restatements* merely entrenched the legal dogma of the past, so that at best they were irrelevant, and at worst would harm genuine legal scholarship.[49] Green himself would later write an acerbic attack on Bohlen's *Restatement of Torts* when it was completed in 1934.[50] Wright, however, viewed the *Restatement* as Bohlen's crowning achievement. Upon his return to Canada, Wright tried to impress upon his Canadian audience the value of the *Restatements* as a source of comparative law and, more important, as an example of what could be accomplished by a well-trained legal community willing to point the direction for legal change.[51] Wright never mentioned the realists' objections to the project, and it is not known if he was aware of them.

Bohlen never wrote a book-length treatment of tort law, although he produced articles on problems in torts and attempted to resolve them. Unlike the realists, who campaigned for a wholesale reorientation of legal scholarship on the topic, Bohlen's approach was to try to unravel the issues that a given problem presented and to offer constructive suggestions for reforming the law by refining concepts and principles. On occasion, he was to see his suggestions incorporated into the law. For example, a 1929 article presented arguments for departing from the doctrine of privity in negligence that were taken up by the English court in *Donoghue* v. *Stevenson*.[52] Bohlen's treatment of tort problems reflected his conviction that law was an instrument to be used to improve rather than hinder social interaction; the job of the legal scholar was not to unravel abstruse legal mysteries but to solve genuine social problems in the most efficient way consistent with fairness to the parties to the dispute.

The law of torts was to Bohlen one of the best examples of what Pound called the 'law as social engineering.' According to Bohlen, the torts scholar, the lawyer, and the judge must be flexible in order to take full advantage of all possible solutions. To develop this flexibility, one must first reject the 'belief in the existence of definite and certain legal rules which are automatically applicable to the facts of the majority of the cases.'[53] In this direction lie artificial distinctions, 'word magic,' and judicial utterances that completely ignore the purpose of tort law, which is to balance competing interests and to adjust losses. Legal rules, to be useful, must accord with social realities, realities that will change over time.

In 1926 Bohlen summed up the principle that guided him in his analyses of tort questions: 'There is no field of law in which rigidity and finality is less probable and less desirable [than tort law] ... The constant changes in the physical and economic environment of modern man, and even more in the values put upon the respective interests involved in the more important social and business relations, necessarily involve a constant change in judicial opinion.'[54] Like many of Bohlen's ideas, the notion that tort law must avoid rigidity and finality was to stay with Wright throughout his career. Bohlen was repeatedly quoted in Wright's articles on torts (partly as authority and partly, as we shall see, to bring the name of a leading American scholar to the attention of Canadian lawyers). One example of Bohlen's enduring effect on Wright is found in an article entitled 'The Law of Torts: 1923–1947,'[55] an article Wright wrote twenty-one years after leaving Harvard. In concluding a long critical survey of English and Canadian tort law, Wright felt obliged to set out a principle for the understanding of tort law, and he did so in distinctly Bohlen-like language:

[In the next twenty-five years] there will still be the pressure of new interests struggling for recognition and of old interests seeking protection against subtler forms of invasion. The task of the lawyer and of the judge is to approach those problems with an appreciation that there are no set answers, but only methods of exposing the basic social and economic realities involved. The extent to which the profession is willing to admit that the impact of physical forces, of ideas, of social ordering, of 'use and wont,' is as important as the concepts which create order and continuity in the living law, will mark the extent to which the law of torts will be responsive to the rapidly changing aims of individuals and groups of individuals in the atomic age.[56]

Wright went on to develop, and in many instances improve upon, Bohlen's views of tort law. Bohlen initiated Wright's thinking about the underlying social significance of tort law, but Wright was to apply, refine, and extend these ideas to create a vision of tort law that can with justice be said to be distinctly his own. Of course, Wright's own work in tort law was aimed at English and Canadian jurisprudence. It would have been inappropriate for Wright to carry Bohlen's views to Canada verbatim. Wright's own contribution to tort law was the product of both the Harvard influence and his own careful, critical treatment of the law. Wright could not have merely applied Bohlen to Canadian law, since he found it necessary to be an advocate for a position that Bohlen, in the United States, could take for granted: that there was something valuable in critical thinking about an area such as tort law.

It has been said of Bohlen that 'he was primarily the teacher of those who already knew some law and had brains'[57] and that he 'despised mediocrity and made short shrift of the stupid student,'[58] descriptions that later could have been applied to Wright himself. Wright had little to fear from Bohlen. Indeed, he found in Bohlen an intellectual mentor, a friend, and, in a few years, an adviser. In 1954, when Wright published his own torts casebook, he acknowledged 'with grateful appreciation the influence of the late Professor Francis Bohlen ... His brilliant analysis and keen perception made many things clear which had been obscure and it would be surprising if the present book did not reflect in some measure his thinking.' It was from Bohlen that Wright learned that 'principles in the law of torts were not as simple as they seemed when embalmed in a text book.'[59]

Wright had been permitted by the Harvard admission committee to do guided research in advanced tort law in addition to the other required and optional courses on the LL M curriculum. There is no reason to suspect that Wright had asked to work with Bohlen, or that Wright was familiar with Bohlen's work before he arrived at Harvard. It is conceivable that Sidney Smith, Donald MacRae, or even Wright's Osgoode Hall instructor in torts, Arthur Clute, had heard that Bohlen was at Harvard and had advised Wright to try to work with him. In any event, Wright did find himself studying with Bohlen on an individual basis, and that meant that a substantial piece of written work was required of him. Although Harvard's LL M and SJD graduate program did not expressly require a thesis, Wright's long paper, entitled 'Gross Negligence,' could easily have counted as one. Bohlen was pleased with it; it was an impressive piece of work Wright would have had reason to be proud of. Oddly enough, however, Wright appears never to have taken the steps necessary to publish it when he returned to Canada. To be sure, the law it contained was soon superseded by judicial developments, and one can easily imagine Wright hesitating to spend time revising it when so much of his attention must have been devoted to developing his courses at Osgoode Hall. Many of the substantive arguments presented in the paper surfaced in Wright's published articles on tort law over the next three decades.[60] While some of Wright's friends remembered that he had once written a long piece on gross negligence, it remained virtually forgotten until what is probably the only extant copy was discovered in Wright's papers. 'Gross Negligence' was finally published in the *University of Toronto Law Journal* fifty-six years after he wrote it and sixteen years after he died.[61]

As a piece of scholarship written by a twenty-two-year-old, 'Gross Negligence' is a polished thesis (although, when it was edited for publication, it was discovered that a surprising number of the footnote references were inaccurate). The piece reveals the influence of Bohlen on every page. Wright's recently acquired knowledge of Roman law also is prominently in evidence, and one can see Pound's influence from time to time.

'Gross Negligence' is a historical and critical analysis of the jurisprudence of 'the vague and nebulous definitions of gross negligence.' Wright traces the distinctions between the levels of fault to the distinctions in Roman law between *dolus* and *culpa*. He argues at considerable length that the notion of gross negligence has been employed by courts whenever it was felt that the application of the objective standard of fault would be too hard on the defendant. Difficulties would arise, Wright notes, when attempts were made to apply formulas purporting to be exact to an area of the law where precision and exactitude are inappropriate. Wright's initial diagnosis of the problems posed by the term 'gross negligence' reflects the kind of scepticism about legal reasoning typically associated with the realist school:

Somewhere in the course of our history a new phrase has been introduced. Subsequent judges facing a situation which they were either inadequate to work out logically, or desiring to give a result which could not be expressed in the form of precise rules (so dear to the heart of all too many a lawyer) discover among the case law this hidden treasure and without in many cases seeking its basis or original use, seize on it in a manner similar to the drowning man and his straw and fell that they have contributed not a little to the body of the Common Law. They are right, but their gift is generally not one of utility; it is usually one of the greatest confusion. As time goes on and successive tribunals toy with the phrase it begins to take on an importance never before dreamed of, until the day finally arrives when it is a veritable 'Open Sesame': the mere utterance is the solving of the problem. 'There is no privity,' 'There is a waiver.' How many times have rights depended on these magical utterances! And to these we believe another should be added to the Legal Hall of Fame – 'There is no gross negligence.'

Wright calls for the use of common sense, a seeking not of pleasing theories but of useful decisions. Courts must seek 'not words, but content, in the belief that the more simple and capable of understanding the greater the strength and utility of the law in achieving its prime purpose – the speedy and just solution of individual controversies.' This necessary understanding requires the lawyer and the judge to look behind the words to the factual situations which the words purport to characterize. By adopting an attitude of suspicion about the 'form of words' courts use to state their judgments, one may see lurking behind the legal jargon other legal categories which, though unexpressed and hidden, more often than not are the true determinants of judicial reasoning. In the case of gross negligence, Wright thought he discerned behind the 'blind adherence to a "form of words" ' categories of contract law that affected tort law. To disclose what is really at issue, and not to be mystified by the language used, is to begin the important job of solving problems in a fair and coherent manner.

This major theme of the article, which owed much to Bohlen, was a consistent presence in much of Wright's later work in tort law. In Wright's introduction to his casebook on torts, a large portion of which was separately published in the *Cambridge Law Journal* in 1944,[62] Wright advised students on how to approach the subject of torts. Under the heading 'The Necessity of Analyzing Commonly Used Expressions,' Wright noted: 'Frequently the use of legal "labels" to describe the results of a case in which compensation has been ordered obscures the true nature of the problem to be investigated for future guidance. Students approaching the study of torts should not be deterred by labels or tags from making a critical examination of the problem presented for solution, or from attempting to discover what they feel to be the true basis of decision.'

Throughout Wright's introduction, the advice he gives to students embodies the lessons he learned from Bohlen. 'The study and practice of law is concerned with discovering all possibilities of choice open to a court at a given time, so that the court may choose wisely and with full knowledge of the alternatives. If we conceive of law as dictating a result in every case, we deceive ourselves.' As a result, 'the cases in this book should not be read in isolation in order to memorize what a given court said or did – the search must always be, why did the court do what it did? might the court within the framework of existing common law method and principles have done something else, and how?'[63] In all this, Bohlen the torts scholar and the near-realist shines through.

In the spring of 1927 Wright wrote his examinations. He achieved an overall A average (only Pound gave him a grade lower than A).[64] All that remained was for his professors to determine whether Wright was to graduate with 'high rank' and be awarded the LL M degree, or with 'distinguished excellence' and be awarded the SJD degree. On 23 June 1927 Wright was awarded the SJD degree. He was now ready to begin his career as a law professor, the months at 'the legal foundry'[65] behind him.

4

Wright as Teacher: Osgoode Hall 1927–1935

The decision to add a fourth full-time lecturer to the faculty of Osgoode Hall Law School was made about the time that Caesar Wright was finishing his first term at Harvard. As early as June 1926 Falconbridge had once again gone to the benchers of the Law Society of Upper Canada to try to convince them that another full-time lecturer was urgently needed for the school. This time Falconbridge argued that it was essential to the efficiency of the school that the staff be increased – the teaching load would be eased, and instructors would be able to have more personal contact with the students. It had only been a year since Falconbridge had made a similar argument to the legal education committee of the law society, which had resulted in the hiring of Sidney E. Smith in February of 1925, and it is likely that the committee and its chairman, M.H. Ludwig, were on the whole unsympathetic to Falconbridge's request.

It is impossible to say whether, at that early date, Falconbridge and MacRae had Caesar Wright in mind for the fourth spot on the faculty. There is reason to suspect that his appointment may have been on their minds. After all, Wright was the most brilliant student the school had turned out in many years, and Falconbridge and MacRae had seen to it that Wright went on to do graduate work at Harvard. There may have been an element of truth in the London *Free Press* story of June 1926, in which it was reported that Wright was intending to go to Harvard Law School in the following year, and was 'looking to the taking of a degree as a professor of law.'

Whatever had been the reception of Falconbridge's request for another full-time instructor in June 1926, Convocation was in a generous mood when Falconbridge argued his case again in January 1927. He cited A.Z. Reed's recently published statistics on law schools in Canada and the United States[1] to show that the student–lecturer ratio was far higher at Osgoode Hall than at any of the leading law schools on the continent. Eventually, he won the benchers over, and on 17 January Convocation approved a recommendation 'that Cecil Augustus Wright, winner of the gold medal and Chancellor Van Koughnet Scholarship in 1926, be appointed a full-time lecturer in the Law Schol at an initial salary of $2,400 per annum commencing on July 1, 1927, subject to the rules of the Law Society as to tenure of office.'[2] A few days later, Falconbridge suggested that Wright's appointment might be viewed as an experiment in hiring the school's own leading graduates. Wright accepted the position soon thereafter.

Several months later, at the end of the school year, Falconbridge, in his annual report, informed Convocation that the number of lecture hours had increased from 852 to 900, and that the number of students expected at the law school the next year was somewhat higher than the year before. The three part-time lecturers, Samuel Bradford, Arthur Clute, and Harold Foster, were reappointed for the next year. Finally, Falconbridge reported that Wright's work at Harvard was 'gratifying.'[3]

In mid-June the local newspaper picked up the story of the new appointment at the law school. Wright's hiring shared column space with news that the year's star student had been selected to follow in Wright's footsteps and go on to graduate work at Harvard. The student was John S.D. Tory, the son of the supervisor for western Ontario of the Sun Life Assurance Company. One of Tory's uncles was the lieutenant-governor of Nova Scotia; another was the president of the University of Alberta. Tory won the same prizes and scholarships as Wright had the year before. It was reported that Roscoe Pound, accepting Tory as a candidate, commented, 'Mr. Wright [last year] fully justified your recommendation.' John S.D. Tory was to be a lifelong friend of Wright and a valuable ally in Wright's struggles to improve legal education in the province.

The *Toronto Star* interviewed Dean Falconbridge on the occasion of the announcement of Wright's appointment. Falconbridge used the opportunity to praise Wright and to engage in some mild propaganda for his ideas about legal education:

In my opinion, Mr. Wright is exceptionally qualified for the appointment which he has just received, not only by reason of scholarship and personal qualities, but also on account of his intimate knowledge of the problems of legal education from the students' point of view and the additional experience he is now acquiring at the Harvard law school. It seems to me fortunate for the school that he is willing to devote himself to teaching. I am convinced, also, that in the teaching of the law, as in most other things, the best results can be obtained by men who are devoting their whole time to the work, and that the most hopeful feature about the development of the Osgoode Hall law school in recent years has been the enlargement and strengthening of the full-time teaching staff. That does not mean, however, that there is not a place for part-time members of the staff, and in some subjects it is desirable that the teachers should be in close touch with actual practice.[4]

Always the gentleman and diplomat, Falconbridge immediately went on to smooth the feathers of the benchers: 'I should also like to refer to the obvious fact that the development of the school has been rendered possible only by the intelligent direction of the governing body, and in partiular by the sympathetic co-operation with the teaching staff of the legal education committee of which Mr. M.H. Ludwig, K.C., is chairman.' That Falconbridge made a special effort to mention Ludwig by name suggests Ludwig had put up something of a fight at the prospect of increasing the staff at the law school. Wright's appointment turned out to be the last substantial move towards reform that Falconbridge was able to make during his twenty-five years as dean. The faculty decreased to three full-time lecturers within five years, although the number of part-timers slowly increased. And seven years after Wright's appointment, the legal education committee and the benchers were to make it abundantly clear that Falconbridge's incremental approach would gain no further concessions from the law society.

In Wright's first year of teaching at Osgoode Hall he was responsible for three courses, with a total of 116 hours of lectures over the year. The load was not particularly heavy (Falconbridge, MacRae, and Smith each taught five courses, and Smith lectured for 221 hours), but it was Wright's first year and each course was a new venture for him. Wright taught one course for each year of the program: jurisprudence in first year, agency and partnership in second year, and wills and administration of estates in third year.

Jurisprudence had been taught by Samuel Bradford for many years; the course was assigned to Wright because of Bradford's failing health. Bradford had always relied on two classic texts, Holland's *Elements of Jurisprudence* and *Salmond on Jurisprudence*. Wright, fresh from Harvard, used a casebook he had put together over the summer which followed the familiar structure of Roscoe Pound's *Outlines of Lectures on Jurisprudence*. The course was a failure, and, although it had been a traditional part of the Osgoode Hall law student's first year curriculum for decades, it was dropped the next year and replaced by Crimes. In 1928 Wright wrote to Francis Bohlen describing his efforts at casebook compilation and mentioning his fiasco with jurisprudence: 'Last year, for example I prepared for classroom use ... mimeographed copies of embryo Canadian casebooks in Wills and Administration, Agency and (never breathe it to R.P.) Jurisprudence. This year, Jurisprudence – Thank God – is gone – in fact, I like to think that perhaps I killed it.'[5] Jurisprudence was not the sort of course that the practically minded Wright would have naturally been drawn to, and it was lucky for him, and probably for his students, that he never taught it again.

As he mentioned in his letter to Bohlen, Wright also put together casebooks for the two other courses he taught. Neither has survived, although we know that they were based on American casebooks. In 1929 Wright wrote to George P. Costigan of the School of Jurisprudence at the University of California in Berkeley and mentioned that he had used Costigan's casebook for courses in wills and administration of estates.

In the next couple of years Wright produced several mimeographed casebooks for the courses he was assigned. He collaborated with MacRae on an agency casebook, and compiled a casebook on first year contracts for the 1928–9 academic year. Contracts, agency, and wills and trusts were Wright's standard fare for many years at Osgoode Hall, and in each of these courses he used annually updated casebooks of his own construction. These were never published, although not because of any lack of effort on Wright's part. In the early 1930s, Wright wrote to Sir Isaac Pitman & Sons (Canada) Limited to try to sell his contracts casebook. In his letter Wright carefully described the differences between his casebook and the other student texts in use in Canada and England at the time. Wright optimistically promised the company sales of up to 1,000 copies in Canada, England, and elsewhere; none the less the publisher did not think the venture worthwhile. Wright's time was soon taken up with other activities, and not until 1954 did he publish his own casebook on tort law.

Although Wright used casebooks, he did not use the 'socratic' method of teaching. Brendan O'Brien, who was a student of Wright's in 1929, recalled that Wright never questioned his students. In O'Brien's words, he was 'a young, aggressive, self-assured fast talker.' Wright was extremely critical of wrong-headed Canadian and English decisions, and showed great admiration for American developments. In his early years of teaching Wright tried to retain his link to Harvard Law School and American legal scholars. Early on he had his name added to the list of law teachers who received drafts of the American Law Institute's *Restatements*, and he had the Harvard librarian, Eldon R. James, send him copies each year of the Harvard Law School examination questions.[6] Wright also corresponded with Pound, Frankfurter, Warren Seavey, and others at the law school. At one point he received a letter from Henry Hart, then editor-in-chief of the *Harvard Law Review*, saying, 'Dean Pound has suggested that it would be an exceedingly valuable thing for the Review to be able to publish an article by you.'[7] Wright did not follow up on this invitation, but it must have buoyed his confidence to be thought worthy of such an honour at a time in his academic career when he had nothing in print except a short case comment in the *Canadian Bar Review*.

Perhaps the headiest praise for the twenty-four-year-old Wright came from his old torts mentor, Francis H. Bohlen:

I wonder if you would be interested in teaching law in America. The situation is this. I have resigned from the Harvard Faculty and re-joined the Faculty of the University of Pennsylvania Law School. As everywhere else we are in need of able young men as teachers ... Would you consider taking a one year appointment with us as assistant professor for the year 1929–1930? I think you can get a year's leave of absence from your own shop. I am asking this entirely on my own ... but I want to be in a position to put your name before [the Faculty] and urge your appointment ... I, personally, am anxious to have you in my faculty and I feel sure that you would make good if you came down and that the appointment would be permanent.[8]

In later correspondence concerning the job offer, Bohlen told Wright that he had spoken of him to influential men at Yale and Michigan as well as to Dean Young B. Smith of Columbia.[9] Bohlen's greatest compliment to Wright, however, was of a more personal nature. In a handwritten postscript to his letter of 15 January 1929, Bohlen said: 'From my personal point of view, I want you here. I need just such a person as you to talk law to. I think we together can really get something worthwhile done.' A week later, after mentioning to Wright that he should come down for the weekend, Bohlen wrote: 'When I was at Harvard Seavey and I could talk over tort problems together. Here I have no one, and I need someone to discuss things with, largely to see whether my own mental hat is on straight and also to get, as I am sure I would from you, suggestions and corrections of my own views.'[10]

As things turned out, Bohlen would not have the opportunity to discuss law with Wright. In early February Wright telegraphed Bohlen to say that he was coming down to Philadelphia soon. Bohlen wired back to say that Pennsylvania had decided to hire an older man. Bohlen was apologetic and expressed disappointment at Pennsylvania's decision; he hoped that Wright did not feel that he (Bohlen) had misled him. Had the job materialized, Wright might well have taken it and been lost to Canadian legal education. Already, after only two years of teaching at Osgoode Hall, he was feeling frustrated by the Ontario legal education regime. In one of his letters to Bohlen he explained that 'a year's leave of absence ... along with several other notions that ordinarily are incident to any academic institution find no place here.'[11] Wright's private complaints about teaching at Osgoode Hall were not always to remain private, but, at least at the beginning, he carried out without objection the day-to-day chores of teaching, and slowly began working up material for publication.

At the end of Wright's first year of teaching at Osgoode Hall, Dean Falconbridge reported that Wright had 'devoted himself to the school with great industry and ability, and his work has been vey satisfactory.'[12] Samuel Hugh Bradford had died that past year, leaving only two part-time members of the teaching staff. Harold Foster had agreed to teach practice in all three years. The dean suggested to Convocation that a further increase in the full-time staff would be required in the next year or two. While it unlikely that the benchers would have been willing to consider adding to the faculty, by May of the next year they were faced with the need to replace one of the full-time instructors.

On the first of April, after only three years of teaching at Osgoode Hall, Sidney E. Smith accepted the post of dean of the law school at Dalhousie. The previous dean, John Read, had resigned to become legal adviser to the Department of External Affairs. Smith had not been unhappy at Osgoode Hall, although his teaching load had been extremely heavy (in his last year there he taught real property, equity, trusts, bankruptcy, and mortgages). He had recently been appointed assistant editor of the *Canadian Bar Review*, a position he continued to hold after going to Dalhousie, and was preparing his trust casebook for press as well as co-writing with Falconbridge *A Manual of Canadian Business Law*. These activities had established Smith firmly in the Ontario legal arena. He accepted the offer at Dalhousie (and a cut in pay from $6,000 to $5,000) primarily out of a sense of loyalty to his old school. In addition, of course, the prospect of being the dean of a major law school was an attractive one. As a condition of his accepting the post, he demanded and got from the university a commitment to raise staff salaries and to add a fourth full-time teacher by the 1930–1 academic year.

Smith's decision must have come as a great disappointment to Wright. In the few years that Wright had known Smith, both as a student and as a colleague, the two men had forged a strong relationship. Over the years, and despite the separation, they were to become even closer, and the friendship would be a significant factor in Wright's later campaign against the benchers. Falconbridge must also have been displeased by Smith's decision to leave. In a short piece in the *Canadian Bar Review*, Falconbridge said, 'It is difficult to imagine the law school without him.'[13]

Falconbridge did not have to look far for Smith's replacement. The man chosen was John Josiah Robinette. Born in 1906, Robinette had earned the gold medal in political science at the University of Toronto and, in 1929, the gold medal at Osgoode Hall. On 14 May 1929 Robinette was hired, at an initial salary of $2,400, to teach real property, equity, and trusts. He used Smith's casebooks on equity and trusts, and compiled one of his own on property. Robinette continued teaching on a full-time basis until 1932, when his appointment was changed to part-time. By then Robinette had been appointed to edit the *Ontario Reports*, and was becoming increasingly interested in practice. He eventually left teaching in 1936 to devote his full time to practice, and became one of Canada's foremost criminal and constitutional litigation lawyers.[14]

By 1930 the staff at Osgoode Hall had grown to a total of four full-time and four part-time instructors. Two changes in staff took place that year. Vincent MacDonald was another Dalhousie star student who, after a decade of trying his hand at practice, had taken the academic turn and become a regular contributor to the *Canadian Bar Review* on international law and editor of the *Dominion Law Annotations*. Now, after having taught part-time at Osgoode Hall for one year, he had accepted a full-time post at Dalhousie. Falconbridge wrote to M.H. Ludwig formally recommending Wishart Flett Spence for MacDonald's job. Spence was a gold medallist and Chancellor Van Koughnet Scholarship winner; he had been Osgoode Hall's third candidate for Harvard Law School (where he earned his LL M). The second appointment was that of James Chalmers McRuer KC, a practitioner, who was hired to teach criminal procedure.

In June 1930 Falconbridge wrote to James Baw, chairman of the finance committee of the law society, to ask that Wright's and Robinette's salaries be increased: 'As [they] are both contemplating taking themselves wives respectively, the time seems singularly appropriate for reconsidering the question of their salaries.' (Wright and Marie Therese Laughlin were married on 8 July 1930, and spent a honeymoon in Nova Scotia with the Smiths.) Falconbridge thought it appropriate to mention also that Wright had been considering an offer from Pennsylvania, which was 'tempting,' and that Robinette had received a job offer from the University of Toronto. Moreover, both Wright and Robinette had 'refused opportunities of going into practice on very advantageous terms.' The argument worked, and both men received a salary increase; Wright was now earning $4,500.

The 1930–1 academic year saw the beginning of a program of exchange lectures instituted by Falconbridge in an attempt to insure co-operation between the major Canadian law schools. A.L. MacDonald of Dalhousie delivered a series of lectures at Osgoode Hall on the liability of property owners; Dean P.E. Corbett of McGill gave three lectures at Dalhousie on constitutional developments; and Donald MacRae gave three lectures at McGill on legal history. The lectures were well received, and probably helped to fulfil the aspiration of Falconbridge and others for the creation of a legal academic community in Canada.

In the late 1920s and early 1930s, Falconbridge and other activist deans – Smith at Dalhousie, Corbett at McGill, E.H. Coleman at Manitoba, and F.C. Cronkite at Saskatchewan – were trying to use the momentum created by interest in legal education voiced by the CBA and other associations to continue the push for reform. This momentum was soon to dissipate, however. Despite substantial improvements in the conditions of the legal academic profession in Canada – larger salaries, more staff, better libraries, more publication, exchange lectures, and the rest – nothing could forestall the tremendous effects of the developing depression in Canada. As with any economic disaster, the impact on the legal profession was felt first by those on the lowest rungs – the students.

The first rumblings of trouble can be discerned in the reports of the legal education committee of the Canadian Bar Association. In 1928, John E. Read, then dean of Dalhousie, was the convenor of the legal education committee. The major topic of discussion was the current state of 'practical training,' which in Canada meant service under articles. Read introduced the topic by remarking, 'There has been a tendency for the requirement of services under articles to degenerate into a legal fiction.'[15] The various arrangements were surveyed: the concurrent scheme, which existed only in Ontario, whereby employment at a law office was undertaken at the same time as attendance at the law school; Manitoba's scheme of concurrent office employment and school attendance for the last two years of a four-year program, after two years of uninterrupted law school attendance; and the Saskatchewan and Quebec consecutive scheme, whereby one year of articling took place after three uninterrupted years of law school attendance. The last of these schemes was strongly favoured by the members of the CBA legal education committee, although the representatives of the benchers of the Law Society of Upper Canada expressed their worries about the undervaluing of the importance of practical training.

New issues also arose at this meeting, issues that were to dominate CBA meetings for many years to come. Ontario delegates emphasized that, whatever scheme was selected, careful consideration had to be given to the fact that the profession, at least in Toronto was seriously overcrowded. There simply was not enough articling work to go around. One Ontario delegate noted that what work there was could not be considered to be practical training in the law: 'Intelligent lady stenographers can do almost anything students can ... what is left for a junior student can be performed by an office boy ... it may well be questioned whether every law office is a safe place for a law student to obtain his practical training.'[16]

Previously, when arguments about overcrowding in the profession were aired by established lawyers, the complaints could in part be explained by the general desire of the lawyers to maintain their own income level. By the early 1930s, however, as businesses failed and legal work became increasingly scarce, the fears of overcrowding reflected more serious difficulties. The articling student was in a tricky position: to qualify as a student-at-law, he had to be employed by a law firm or sole practitioner; but in the 1930s, this was more easily said than done. First, an articling job had to be found (and kept). If a job was found, it rarely paid the student enough to live on. Then, if the student was lucky enough to find work and to support himself, the articling experience was likely, as the Ontario delegate had suggested, to consist of the kind of work a secretary or even an office boy could perform.

In the early years of the 1930s, then, the Law Society of Upper Canada found itself confronting the general economic pressures the country was facing, which required a reduction in the number of lawyers and therefore in the number of law students. Yet the law society did not want to drastically reduce the number of students it was allowing into the school.

Since the benchers were generally convinced of the importance of practical experience, they felt that they had some responsibility for making suitable articling jobs available to students. The obligation to provide these jobs was the more troubling because the only professional law school in the province was in Toronto, and the only practical locality for an articling job was in that city. The economic situation would have to be responded to, but the benchers could not agree among themselves what the response should be. To make matters more confusing, the benchers were also facing ongoing pressure from Canada's law teachers to increase the academic quality of legal education. That pressure ultimately was an economic pressure as well: as long as the law society had complete control over legal education, every improvement to the school was an extra expense, and one that might not be acceptable to the profession at large.

It seems apparent that Falconbridge's strategy in the 1930s was the same as it had been in the 1920s – namely, to keep pressing for reforms at the law school. Wright, who was seen (and who saw himself) as part of a new generation of Candian law teachers, took up the fight almost immediately. In the academic year 1930–1 Wright gave three public lectures that brought his name to the attention of the profession. The first was before the Ontario Women's Law Association at the University of Toronto. Wright spoke on parity in treatment of husbands and wives in divorce settlements, arguing, among other things, for the abolition of dower.[17] The other two lectures were to have a lasting effect on the profession. On the surface, they were merely examples of the kind of academic activity expected of a young, ambitious professor. In fact, both were carefully planned strategic moves in aid of 'the cause.'

In 1930 W.P.M. Kennedy's subdepartment at the University of Toronto, which for two years had offered an honours course in law, became a full department of the university. Kennedy immediately helped to organize the Law Club as a forum for invited speakers. The year before, Kennedy had invited A.L. Goodhart, who was then visiting at Yale Law School, to speak to his students. Kennedy, always eager to advertise his unique law program, thought that frequent lectures would help to spread the word. He may have been worried about the status of his special program, since in 1928 he had lost one of his Harvard-trained scholars, James Forrester Davison. Davison had left at the end of the academic year to finish his SJD at Harvard. Once at Harvard, Davison had turned down Kennedy's offer to return, saying that he was looking for a law school position: 'I still have a yearning for a full law school course which may perhaps be the immediate influence of the Harvard Law School.'[18]

Over the years, Kennedy's Law Club was to host an impressive number of legal dignitaries. The first speaker invited was Wright, who had probably been suggested by Falconbridge. Kennedy had recently begun to recommend to Falconbridge various students from his program who were interested in going to Osgoode Hall Law School, and lines of communication between the two deans were opening up. Wright accepted Kennedy's invitation, and on 21 January 1931 he spoke in the University College common room on the 'Modern Approach to Law, or Recent Tendencies in Law.' The speech was later pubished in the *Canadian Bar Review* under the title 'An Extra-Legal Approach to Law.'[19]

The article, Wright's first major publication, is a complex manifesto of Wright's views of law, legal education, and the profession. It is an impassioned piece, highly rhetorical yet persuasive. For the most part, the ideas in it are Pound's. Wright collected together the more iconoclastic notions about law in the air at Harvard and discussed a handful of problem areas that stood in need of rethinking. Reading the piece, one is struck by the fact that Wright is offering up a doctrine, with which he aligns himself, rather than discussing a jurisprudential position that, in the United States, was the subject of considerable controversy. There are no loose ends in the philosophy of law Wright espouses in his speech; it is a call to arms, and must have been extremely provocative to his audience.

Wright's vision of the law seemed simple enough. A new age had begun, Wright told his audience, one marked by a reluctance to view the law as 'a dissociated group of rules of absolute validity.' Rather, the modern view was that law was an instrument of social control, and the job of lawyers and legal officers was to determine what had to be done by means of the law and to proceed to attain those ends. 'The end of law must always be found outside the law itself, and as our opinions of that end change, so must change the content of the law.' In short, law must not be studied in a vacuum; one must determine extralegally what one actually wished to achieve through the legal system, and then develop the means for doing so. So viewed, the law became 'a living thing rather than the stagnant well of technicalities which it has always seemed to the man in the street.'

What the aim of the law should be, Wright continued, could not be determined from within the law. The aim was not absolute, since 'what is good to-day will not necessarily stand the test of changed living conditions to-morrow.' Reliance on rigid rules was folly. Wright expressed scepticism about the prospect of identifying an ideal for the law, and favoured a 'purely pragmatic or utilitarian approach' whereby the law was seen to exist for the protection of the claims and demands that were identified as actually arising out of social life.

With this provocative famework laid, Wright then went on to describe a collection of legal issues that demanded the commonsense approach he advocated. Wright mentioned Pound's 'interests' analysis of legal rights, Leon Green's demystification of the notion of proximate cause in tort law, Samuel Warren and Louis D. Brandeis's famous analysis of the right of privacy, and the American developments in quasi-contract or the law of restitution.

Turning to another of Pound's theses, Wright urged his audience to remember that the 'development of our law is but one phase of the development of our civilization.' Lawyers had to realize that the law must be functional in its handling of certain human affairs. In the case of business law, lawyers had to attempt to 'bring law closer to business, rather than business closer to law.' This required, again, an extralegal approach to law, a frank admission that the law could at best do no more than guarantee what is usual or customary. At the same time, however, the law had to repond to problems as they developed in social relations, rather than hearken back to the solutions of a prior day. Wright cited the American case of *MacPherson* v. *Buick Motors*,[20] where Cardozo J reconsidered older precedents in light of present-day conditions and, 'having taken a peep over the legal horizon and discovered another world,' was able to add new content to old concepts.

In conclusion, Wright stressed that law could not be taught dogmatically. 'There are no essential verities. Law can never stand still long enough to allow them to be extracted. What is law to-day is not necessarily law to-morrow. Hence law, like the movements of the earth itself can only be observed in operation.'

The article was Wright's challenge to the legal profession. He obviously intended that his message jar the established Ontario bar from its conservatism. By viewing law as a list of rules and doctrines, lawyers were not only behind the times, but were making it impossible for the law to solve the real problems that demanded real solutions. The consequences for legal education were clear: law could not be taught in the manner the benchers insisted it should be, as a collection of skills and rules that had to be learned by rote and applied precisely in practice. Another implication of Wright's vision was that legal reform came only from without; the resources of the law itself were inadequate to respond to real social problems. Legal reform, moreover, was not merely a matter of novel legislation; all lawyers could and must be legal reformers. Although in most instances there was room for a mechanical determination of the law – where certainty of result served the function the law ought to perform best – every case before a court was potentially one that called for an extralegal approach. That approach required a new type of lawyer, which in turn required a new view of legal education. Extralegal education, by its nature, was best carried out in a university setting. If the profession was left to teach law, what would be taught was the law of the day, not the law needed for tomorrow.

The themes in Wright's article were to be repeated in all of his published pieces on legal education. The argument for university-based legal education was not airtight: many of the realists, who saw the law in a similar light (indeed, who were cited by Wright in this and in other pieces as authority for his views), were soon to argue strenuously that legal education should be taken out of the university setting completely.[21] Ironically, when the legal education debate began to dominate the scene in Ontario, at times the battle lines were drawn between those who favoured 'practical' legal education and those who favoured 'theoretical' legal education. Wright and the other legal academics who insisted that law must be taught in a university setting were classified as advocating a 'theoretical' education. But in an important sense, this was precisely what Wright was arguing against: the 'extralegal sources to be tapped for law's content were, for Wright, the practical realities of business and everyday social life, not the abstractions of theory. But why should one expect the university environment to be more directly attuned than the practitioner's office to the demands of the practical world?

Wright never addressed himself to this problem in his views about legal education. In a sense, given the existing situation of legal education in Ontario, the battles that Wright and others were to fight in the next two decades did not require a consistent theoretical groundwork. The lecture delivered in January 1931 was Wright's first public attempt to express his dissatisfaction with nearly all aspects of Canadian law and legal institutions. That this dissatisfaction eventually took the concrete form of a challenge to the law society's control over legal education was a consequence of Wright's status as a professional educator: he saw the problems of legal education firsthand and on a day-to-day basis.

Wright's third public lecture was also motivated by reformist aims. The experiment in exchange lectures had been a success. It seems to have been a common assumption that one of the purposes of the exchange lectures was to continue the debate over legal education; at least, this was the view of Charles Morse, who wrote in a *Canadian Bar Review* editorial that 'a forum for the discussion of legal education in Canada has thus been created and a closer co-operation of the law schools should result.'[22] Wright was chosen to give a series of lectures at Dalhousie (Smith gave the lectures at McGill, and C.S. LeMesurier of McGill at Osgoode Hall). Wright's lecture at Dalhousie was scheduled for 16, 17, and 18 March 1931; his topic was 'Unjust Enrichment and the Common Law: Quasi Contrasts.' On the surface, the subject matter involved a fairly exotic area of the law which, though somewhat dry, was none the less a respectable subject for a professor from Osgoode Hall Law School. Yet the topic had been one of the examples Wright used in 'An Extra-Legal Approach to the Law,' and it had been chosen as his lecture topic in part for propaganda purposes.

In Canada in 1931, the topic of unjust enrichment would have given Wright the opportunity he wanted to compare American and English law. Although nothing has survived of those three lectures, it is easy enough to reconstruct, from Wright's training at Harvard and from his later writings, the gist of what he said. Wright would surely have informed his audience that in the United States a vast body of law on restitution dealt, in a commonsense and coherent manner, with a range of problems that arose frequently in business affairs. In England and in Canada, out-of-date doctrines and a slavish attachment to precedent prevented courts from making sense of the problems that were brought before them. As a result, American law solved certain problems to which English law had so far failed to respond. Wright doubtless would have mentioned that Warren Seavey and Austin W. Scott of Harvard were at that moment in the process of compiling the *Restatement of Restitution* (which was to appear in 1937), a resource that Wright believed Canadians should turn to for guidance.[23] The topic of restitution was a perfect weapon in the campaign of those legal academics who wanted to shift the profession's focus from England to the United States.

The strategic significance of Wright's lectures at Dalhousie can be seen in a letter Smith wrote to Wright on 14 February. Smith asked for a picture of Wright ('the intellectual contours of your physiognomy') for publicity for the upcoming exchange lectures. 'It is all grist for the mill in advertising your lecture, *the School*, and the *Cause*.' Wright sent his Osgoode Hall graduation photo, which made its way into the *Dalhousie Gazette* a month later. The *Gazette* reported that Wright 'was greeted by a capacity attendance of the students of the school at each lecture, while two former members of the Osgoode Hall staff, Mr. Sidney Smith, Dean of Dalhousie, and Mr. Vincent C. MacDonald, were also present.'[24] Wright probably left Dalhousie exhilarated both by the renewal of his friendship with Smith and by his own contribution to 'the cause.'

The rest of that academic year was uneventful. At the end of the year the benchers agreed to reappoint all four part-time Osgoode Hall instuctors for the next year. In his annual report, delivered on 19 November 1931, Dean Falconbridge informed the benchers of the success of Wright's lecture series at Dalhousie. He also presented Convocation with the traditional statistics on the numbers of hours taught at the law school. Robinette headed the list (with 192 hours), followed by Falconbridge (186 hours), and Wright and MacRae (180 hours each). Falconbridge cautiously avoided making any requests for more staff that year.

The academic year 1932–3 brought Dean Falconbridge's announcement of Robinette's desire to reduce his teaching load in order to devote more time to the editorship of the *Ontario Reports* and to his practice. The number of full-time staff was now back to three. At the meeting held on 15 September 1932, however, Falconbridge was able to persuade the benchers to appoint two additional part-time lecturers to ease the teaching burden: Henry Borden and Kenneth Gibson Morden were scheduled to teach one course each – Borden in equity and Morden in trusts. The teaching staff at the law school was increased to ten people, although only three were full-time instructors.

Borden, who had been born in Halifax in 1901, was the nephew of Sir Robert Borden, a former prime minister of Canada.[25] Like Sidney Smith, Borden had studied at King's College School in Windsor, Nova Scotia. He attended McGill University and received a BA in political science and economics in 1921. Borden was recruited by the Royal Bank and sent to Halifax for a year. While on his own in Halifax, he became seriously ill. One of his aunts spoke to Dean Donald MacRae at Dalhousie to see if it might be possible to find someone for Borden to room with. MacRae spoke to Sidney Smith, and as a result Borden and Smith agreed to share a bachelor apartment across the street from the law school. The two men had many discussions during that winter and spring, and, at Smith's suggestion, Borden gave up his work at the bank and enrolled at Dalhousie Law School. After two years of study at Dalhousie Borden was awarded a Rhodes Scholarship and entered Exeter College, Oxford, where he received a BA in jurisprudence in 1926. He was called to the bar in Lincoln's Inn in 1927 and returned to Nova Scotia, where he was admitted to practice. The relationship between Borden and Smith was further cemented by marriage. During Smith's summer vacation from Harvard in 1925, Borden introduced Smith to one of his cousins, Harriet Rand, who eventually became Mrs Sidney Smith. Borden later married Jean Creelman MacRae, a daughter of Donald MacRae.

Shortly after being called to the bar in Nova Scotia, Borden moved to Toronto where he joined the law firm of Warld, Grin, Fraser and Beatty. His father-in-law suggested that he might want to teach part-time at Osgoode Hall Law School. Osgoode Hall would pay him two hundred dollars a month if he lectured for five hours a week. Because of the depression, everyone at the law firm had taken a substantial reduction in salary. The law school offer seemed attractive, and Borden took the job. Soon afterwards, Falconbridge wrote to Wright, 'My own impression is that [Borden] will be an excellent appointment, provided he is prepared to use the case method with Smith and Read's book, and not to submit to the influence of his father-in-law.' Borden, as it turned out, did use the case method and his friend's casebook.

Through his law school post and his friendship with Smith, Borden and his wife became very close to Caesar and Marie Wright. The Wrights, Smiths, and Bordens spent a good deal of time together, and their friendship would prove to be important in determining the course of legal education in the province.

The change in staff for 1932–3 was not the most important development at the law school that year. At the end of the previous academic year, M.H. Ludwig, chairman of the law society's legal education committee, had decided that the time had come to reconsider the issue of requirements for admission to the law school. Since 1927 the standard had been the completion of two years of university. On 12 May 1932, the committee voted to reduce the admission standard to what it had been before 1927 – namely, pass matriculation and either honours matriculation or the completion of one year of university. The new standard was to go into effect in September 1932.[26]

The move to return to the earlier standard is difficult to understand in the light of the complaints of overcrowding and inadequately prepared lawyers that were constantly in the air. Although we know little of the actual debate that took place before the vote, there is some suggestion that the dominant argument was the 'poor boy' argument. The rationale was that the profession ought not to be closed to those lacking the financial means to afford two years of university prior to law school.[27]

The 'poor boy' argument, however determinative of the decision it may have been in 1932, was apparently not voiced the next year when the legal education committee decided to increase the fees required to enter articling from $50 to $100, and to raise the tuition fees at the law school from $100 to $150 a year. Although this move was inconsistent with what may have been the rationale for the lowering of admission standards, it was consistent with the prevailing view that the profession was overcrowded and with the benchers' desire to raise revenue.

The legal education commitee's initial response to pressures from both the profession and the academics may have lacked a clear rationale, but it did serve to remind the staff at the law school that the committee retained control over legal education in the province. In the next year, the committee's decision to lower the admission requirements met with sustained criticism. The 1933 report of the legal education committee of the CBA was written that year by F.C. Cronkite, the dean of the University of Saskatchewan Law School (MacRae had resigned from the post the year before). Cronkite expressed the frustration of many when he said that he had been proud to report a year earlier that the CBA's 1922 recommendation that law students complete two years of university had finally been accepted by all of the provinces. Now the Law Society of Upper Canada had seen fit to go back to the earlier standard.[28] Writing in an English journal, Dean Falconbridge admitted with some embarrassment that the relatively high admission standards that had prevailed in Ontario had, because of 'some difference of opinion among the benchers of the Law Society of Upper Canada,' been lowered again.[29]

The active debate over legal education in Ontario had begun again; what had been for several years a matter of negotiation and slow but real reform, primarily because of Falconbridge's quiet diplomacy, had once again become a public matter. Within a few months the law society's legal education committee was to make clear that it wanted the reformist policies of the past decade to be abolished. The established lawyers, Ludwig's 'older chaps,' would once again respond to criticism by turning back the clock.

In the meantime, relations between the Osgoode Hall staff and W.P.M. Kennedy's Department of Law at the University of Toronto were becoming strained. The tension was caused, in part, by Kennedy's personality and his desire to build up his department. Kennedy had fought hard for recognition of his program, and some teachers at Osgoode Hall – Wright in particular – were concerned that his efforts might make the creation of a professional law school in a university setting all the more difficult.

Bora Laskin, who entered the second year of the honours program in 1930; later recalled that there were some thirty students in the second year, and that those who went on to Osgoode Hall Law School remained a very cohesive group.[30] The physical accommodations were primitive at 43 St George Street, where Kennedy's school was located, but the four-man staff of Kennedy, Jacob Finkelman, Clyde Auld, and Norman MacKenzie generated a good deal of enthusiasm. Finkelman had just been hired that year, after having received his BA at Kennedy's school and graduating from Osgoode Hall Law School. Finkelman had the opportunity to go to Harvard Law School (Wright had written a letter of recommendation on his behalf), but accepted the job at the University of Toronto instead, and introduced a pioneering course on labour law. Clyde Auld, who taught Roman law and the history of English law, was a native of Prince Edward Island. He received his BA from McGill and his MA and BCL from Oxford. He served as a tutor in law at New College, Oxford, for a year, and then spent seven years practising law in England and Toronto before being hired by Kennedy in 1929.

Laskin recalled that his teachers at Kennedy's school aroused in him an interest in law as part of the social sciences and the humanities. This had always been Kennedy's intention; indeed, it is very unlikely that he had ever had any wish to create a professional law school that would produce practising lawyers. In 1929, when he was trying to persuade J.F. Davison to return to teaching at University of Toronto after his year at Harvard, Kennedy responded to Davison's hint that it had always been his plan to teach at a 'full course in law in the University' by saying,

If you mean by the phrase 'full course in law in the university' the development of a full Faculty of Law here, I must say candidly that I think, first, that it will never come except through a liaison with Osgoode Hall (I am convinced that that solution is in the minds of the Board) and secondly, I think that that eventuality is as far off, if not farther off than ever. Osgoode is now developing full-time Professors on a larger scale, and I hear that one or two are about to be added whom they have trained.[31]

What Kennedy had in mind for his school is clear: he was interested in undergraduate and graduate programs in law modelled after those at Oxford and Dublin. Kennedy published extensive descriptions of his program, once in 1932 in the English *Journal of the Society of Public Teachers of Law*,[32] and again in 1934 and 1937 in the *Scots Law Times*.[33] In each of these pieces Kennedy candidly acknowledged that his school and the few other, far less developed, university undergraduate law programs in Canada were not designed as competitors to the law societies' professional schools: 'We do not believe that it is the function of a university law school to prepare students for practise.' Kennedy's program was not expressly intended for those who wished to practise law, although a great many did go on to do so; he wished to treat law as a university discipline, not as a professional calling. Laskin's memories of the early years of the school were consistent with this:

Kennedy had a good deal of imagination. He realized, as all of us realized who were in the law course, the deficiencies of the professional programme at Osgoode Hall Law School, and because it was so narrow, narrow even when you consider it as a professional programme; for example, there was no jurisprudence taught at Osgoode Hall Law School ... so that the very narrow professionalism of Osgoode Hall Law School left a very, very large gap which the Department of Law tried to fill. There was some duplication in subjects. For example, we had a course in the History of English Law which Clyde Auld gave. When I went to Osgoode as a student there was also a course in the History of English Law. There was some duplication – property law – but at Toronto it was taught in those days more from an historical perspective and not so much geared to the professional aspects of the ... subject.[34]

Kennedy's school had a wide selection of courses in its four-year program, courses taught by the four staff members as well as by members of the political science, philosophy, history, and economics departments. As Laskin noted, there were obvious gaps in the Osgoode Hall curriculum that Kennedy thought his school could fill. He could with truth claim that his was the most complete university law school in the country, and he was clear about his model: 'Here again we have deliberately worked out our own scheme, which is along English and European lines and not along American.'[35]

Kennedy's school was one of the few in Canada that offered master's and doctoral degrees in law (Laskin himself received a master's degree at Toronto while he was attending lectures at Osgoode Hall and articling). Students from Kennedy's school did well at Osgoode Hall. Between 1930 and 1943 169 of the 213 graduates of the University of Toronto honours law course went on to Osgoode Hall; these students constituted about 12 per cent of Osgoode Hall population in those years. Of the Osgoode Hall students who failed during this period, only a little over

1 per cent were Kennedy's graduates; of those who graduated with honours, one-third were from Kennedy's school.

There had always been a degree of formal co-operation between Kennedy's school and Osgoode Hall, and Kennedy and Falconbridge were on relatively good terms; none the less, there was tension. In his 1932 article on legal education in Canada, Falconbridge admitted to his English audience that 'cultural courses' such as jurisprudence, Roman law, and comparative law did not find a place in the crowded curriculum at Osgoode Hall. They were taught at the University of Toronto, but 'personally I am somewhat doubtful whether an arts course in which legal subjects predominate is as good a preparation for the professional study of the law as a course in English, history, languages and what not.'[37] Falconbridge did not outline the actual purpose of Kennedy's program, leaving it to Kennedy himself to describe, in another issue of the same journal, the rationale of his school:

The Honour School of Law in the University of Toronto was deliberately created with certain definite ideas behind it, to which Lord Haldane lent his constructive skill in the actual drafting of the courses. First of all, it is a University course ... Secondly, its *raison d'être* is the study of law as a social science, a process of social engineering, in which the knowledge of practical work ... is deepened by an educational purpose, by an inquiry into the social worth of legal doctrines, and, above all, by the critical attempt to find out if law in its various aspects is in reality serving the ends of society.[38]

In other words, Kennedy was trying to create a law school that took Pound's views – the views to which Wright was firmly committed – seriously. Falconbridge and Wright were highly sceptical of the possibility of satisfying this aim within a program that was not designed to prepare students for the actual practice of the law. They were right to be sceptical: Kennedy's school was a hybrid, an idiosyncratic attempt to do several things at once, a kind of idealized Harvard program fit into an Oxonian mould. Kennedy's students were younger and less mature than the average Osgoode Hall student, and the program's success probably was due to the high calibre of the teaching staff.

Yet Wright's objections to Kennedy's school went some distance beyond the fact that the school was a variant of what Wright himself sought. Wright did not think highly of some members of the school, and an incident in 1933 reinforced his negative view. Wright discovered that Jacob Finkelman was using a mimeographed casebook on contracts, bearing Finkelman's name, that contained material taken without acknowledgment from Wright's casebook. At Wright's insistence, Falconbridge sent a strongly worded letter of protest to Finkelman in April 1933, with copies to M.H. Ludwig and Kennedy. The next day, Kennedy wrote to Falconbridge, 'Your letter ... has caused me extreme personal regret,' and sent Finkelman to see Wright and resolve the dispute. Wright continued to fume about the matter to his closest friends, although he did not make his feelings known publicly.

That summer, another incident brought to the surface Wright's animosity towards Kennedy himself. Wright expressed his anger in a long and vituperative reply to a letter from Smith at Dalhousie. In the past year Kennedy had stepped up his activities to establish the credibility of his program. To gain recognition from English scholars, he had publicized his school in several English newspapers. He had also tried to persuade the law society's legal education committee to send Osgoode Hall students to his program to take specific courses for credit at Osgoode Hall. Kennedy began to increase the substantive law courses he offered, a move that gave the appearance, despite his expressed disclaimers, that he was hoping to provide a professional legal education. Smith's letter and Wright's response were provoked by Kennedy's attempt to circumvent a law society ruling that required graduates of English universities with English legal qualifications to take the full three-year program at Osgoode Hall in order to qualify to practise in Ontario. Kennedy apparently had written to Dean Smith at Dalhousie to see if it was possible for Kennedy's graduates to enter the second year of studies there. If Kennedy could get recognition in England for his program, then he could promise his students admission to the bar – via Nova Scotia – after only six years instead of seven.

Larry MacKenzie had written to Smith in early June on behalf of G. Gordon Bradshaw, a recent graduate of Kennedy's school, asking Smith if Bradshaw could enter second year at Dalhousie. Smith politely wrote back that 'the Pole Star of your BA course is different from that of our LL B course.'[39] Smith then wrote to Wright about the affair, saying that MacKenzie 'sent along a screed written by W.P.M. [Kennedy] for the Journal of the Public Teachers of Law on the law course in the University of Toronto, founded, framed and sponsored by Lord Haldane himself, etc. etc.' As for the Bradshaw case, Smith reported, 'I was annoyed ... with the very suggestion.'

Wright replied in July, 'I can plainly see that the wheels which I have long been waiting to see put in motion have at last started. I think the whole thing is quite plain, but it is the damnably underhand methods adopted that gets my goat.' One of those methods was to use MacKenzie as an intermediary with Smith, which Wright saw as Kennedy's attempt at 'trying a double game ... picking on him as a friend of yours as well as a graduate of Dalhousie [he] has insisted on him working the combine with Dalhousie to swat us in the eye.' Wright went on:

[Kennedy] has for some time past, been blowing off steam about his working arrangements with Oxford and Cambridge. As a matter of fact, he is, and has been, shooting all his best men to England for their law. The idea, of course, is the glorification of K. and K.'s 'Honour Department of Law' ... I have no doubt these men do well: not because of K. or his satellites, but simply because they are good men ... At any rate, K's scheme is to establish this English connection and then, as I see, use the Ontario ultra-enthusiasm for all things English for the acceptance of his own school.

Wright was probably correct about Kennedy's machinations, but one wonders why Wright was so hard on him; after all, Kennedy was merely attempting to secure in Ontario a genuinely academic law program, something to which Wright was so committed. But Wright was utterly unsympathetic to Kennedy's plan. At one point he told Smith, 'As a matter of fact, it has always been my contention, and I have tried to get the Dean here to take some action on it, that K's course should not even entitle a man seeking entrance here to admittance as a graduate student.' Coming from Wright this is indeed a harsh assessment, and a wholly unwarranted one. Although Kennedy's program may not have counted as a substitute for professional legal education, it offered an effective introduction to important areas of legal scholarship. In a calmer vein, Wright argued that it would be far preferable for a potential law student to spend his undergraduate career reading something other than law: 'It is self evident to me, that law can no more be a foundation for law, than one building can serve as a foundation for another ... To take a High School student and begin to teach him subtantive law seems to me to be absolutely contrary to everything that has been gained in the last few years.'

Wright, as a teacher of law, found it frustrating to face students from Kennedy's program who claimed to know contract law when their exposure to it, at least at the level taught in a professional law school, was less than adequate. The University of Toronto student, Wright commented, is 'exactly what you might expect from such a catapulting of immature minds into law. They come down here with a few half-baked principles which, for example in Contracts, they have memorized from Anson.' They were difficult to teach, Wright wrote, because of their attitude of self-satisfaction, which prevented them from appreciating that 'what they have taken, for example in Contracts, in about 20 lectures, I should worry them with for 90.'

Some fuller explanation is necessary for Wright's hostility towards Kennedy, and the reason for Wright's castigation of Kennedy and his school is not difficult to find. In his letter to Smith, Wright addressed his underlying complaint against Kennedy:

I feel quite sure that it will not be long before K. obtains his Law School. The Dean does not, or says he does not believe it. K. is a clever man. Tilley [William Norman Tilley, treasurer of the Law Society], who is dead against raising standards might very well be induced to fall for this 'bastard' system of shortening the so-called law course. I think you know my own personal views regarding University Law Schools. I am quite convinced a University is the proper place. I am equally sure that its place should be *after* and not concurrent with an Arts course. What I do fear, is that we may be shoved into the same position as England if K. gets his way. I think that is bad, because our conditions here are so different. After all, the largest part of our law school work consists in doing what the English barrister does for some years as a junior in chambers. We have not got that. To take the weak English system without it, seems to me even a further retrogression than we have as yet had.

Clearly, Wright saw in Kennedy not only a dangerous competitor who might establish the kind of university law school Wright wanted in Ontario, but the proponent of a false path that might do considerable damage. Despite his remarks in 'An Extra-Legal Approach to Law' suggesting that law was a social science that should be taught as a university discipline, Wright was firmly committed to a profesional law school geared to producing practising lawyers. The two views were not incompatible, of course, and Wright always upheld the example of Harvard as the most desirable type of university law program. But Wright rejected out of hand the idea that Kennedy's school could meet the standards of a professional law school created in the Harvard image. The controversy would continue for years. Ironically, it was one of the few issues on which the senior benchers and Wright were in agreement.

In the fall of 1932 Wright wrote to Felix Frankfurter asking if he would be willing to visit Toronto. Frankfurter detected in the letter 'an undercurrent of pessimism about our profession – I mean the lawteaching profession ... I think I know a little something about the special difficulties that are encountered in Canada, but study the early history of American Legal Education – even the recent days of Langdell, Thayer and Ames, and take heart. If right standards are ever to prevail, we must be ready to invest something of our own lives in their realization.' Wright was willing to make that investment, but it is unlikely that in 1932 he appreciated how long the struggle to achieve 'right standards' would last.

In 1933 the first skirmish in the inevitable struggle between Wright and the Law Society of Upper Canada began in earnest. The legal education committee's decision to lower the law school entrance requirements led to various forms of protest. One of the first responses came from students. As the 1932–3 school year began, M.H. Ludwig requested student opinion on the change in admission standards. The Legal and Literary Society appointed a committee to consider the matter. It soon responded with a memorandum[40] indicating that, as far as the students were concerned, the requirement of completion of two years of university should have been retained, if not increased to a mandatory BA. The students reminded the benchers that the entrance standards in Ontario were the lowest in Canada, and were lower than those in England and the United States. Their report indicated that 89 per cent of the students then enrolled at Osgoode Hall were university graduates; among the new entrants, the percentage had fallen to 49 per cent. 'Such a policy can result only in the gradual conversion of a learned profession into one filled with men of very limited education.' The report was signed by Donald D. Carrick, a first-year student.

Donald Carrick was born in Port Arthur, Ontario in 1906. He received an honours BA in English and history from the University of Toronto in 1927. Carrick was four times intercollegiate heavyweight boxing champion, and represented Canada in the 1928 Olympics. At Harvard Law School he obtained an LL B degree in 1931. Carrick wanted to practise law in Ontario, and he was amazed to discover that Osgoode Hall gave him no credit for his Harvard degree. He was forced to enter the law school in 1931 as a first-year student. Needless to say, he was no ordinary student. Although we have no record of any direct association between Wright and Carrick, the events of the next two years made it clear that Carrick's protests must have been actively supported by Wright. Carrick's own situation represented the absurd extreme of the law society's attitudes towards legal education, and Carrick, whose athletic and academic background made him what would now be called a 'media star,' used that absurdity against the benchers.

Carrick first came to the attention of the benchers, the profession, and the public at large when he wrote an article for *Obiter Dicta*, the student magazine, on 26 January 1933. The article, 'Wasting Three Years at Osgoode,' contained some of the most powerful criticisms of the school that had ever been made in public. Carrick directly assaulted those in the profession who, 'like those who substitute a Latin maxim when they cannot think of an adequate reason … dub as "theoretical" what is learned in law school, and worship at the shrine of the practical.' The profession ought to be a learned one, and 'lawyers ought not to be in law for the sole purpose of making as much money as possible.' None the less, the law society '[insisted] on keeping Osgoode Hall a trade school where we memorize a lot of rules of thumb to throw out on examination papers … if we were given the opportunity to study law in a liberal way instead of scurrying to an office at eleven o'clock and trying to concentrate for a couple of hours in the evening after a weary day of writ-serving, some conception would soon be gained of the nobleness of our calling.' The focus on practical experience in law offices, Carrick wrote, was grossly misdirected; not only did the student turn into a 'glorified office boy,' he was lucky to earn five dollars a week for his efforts. After three years of this, the student was as helpless at handling the affairs of a client as when he began. 'The theory on which the present system is conducted,' Carrick concluded, 'is that by keeping a man at the office long enough to prevent him learning anything at the law school, and by keeping him at the law school long enough to prevent him from learning anything at the office, you turn out a duly qualified practitioner.' One can imagine the annoyance Carrick's article must have caused the benchers and the pleasure it must have given Wright, who probably would have liked to fire many of the same broadsides. A number of Carrick's views of work at law offices were shared by his student colleagues, many of whom would have agreed 'that the motives of those who support the present system are not altogether philanthropic.' The situation had become so serious in Toronto that some students (perhaps as many as 16 per cent)[41] did not bother working in offices at all, and tried instead to find gainful employment to finance their education. The law society apparently turned a blind eye to this and other infractions of the Solicitors Act, which required office attendance attested to by affidavit. The situation could be remedied, Carrick argued, only by abandoning the concurrent scheme and initating office training at the end of three years of uninterrupted law school attendance. This and other changes were required, but there was 'little use in making an appeal to the legal profession because it has seen fit to adopt a reactionary policy in regard to the law school ... In the future, when we are the powers that be, we may have the opportunity of making the changes advocated a reality.'

The *Mail and Empire* carried the headline 'Osgoode Hall School Methods Assailed by Donald Carrick,'[42] and reported that the *Obiter Dicta* article was a 'bombshell' that 'promptly resulted in a sell-out [of that issue of the magazine].' The law society's treasurer, Norman Tilley, its secretary, Holford Ardagh, and Dean Falconbridge were reached by the newspaper, but each refused comment. The next day, M.H. Ludwig was quoted by the newspaper in an article headlined 'Agrees with Carrick on Standards Issue.'[43] Ludwig chaired the legal education committee, and typically voted with the majority on all of its decisions, but he was generally sympathetic to Carrick's views, and had gone on record at the 1931 CBA meeting as being in favour of the consecutive scheme of legal education whereby one year of articling followed three years of law school.[44]

Ludwig was reported as 'expressing regret' that Carrick had written his article without discussing his opinions with members of the legal education committee, and extended a 'special invitation for Mr. Carrick to drop into his office and have a talk.' Ludwig agreed that admission standards ought not to have been lowered, but defended the change on the ground that one less year of university education would not seriously affect a student's literary knowledge, and in any event standards should not be so high as to prohibit the entrance of 'poor boys.' Mr Carrick, Ludwig remarked, 'perhaps knows very little of the difficulties many young men had to overcome to enter a learned profession.' Ludwig also took exception to Carrick's charge that the number of disbarments and defalcations among lawyers was on the increase. Ludwig assured the reporter that each student was required to provide two detailed character references from competent persons, and that these references were carefully scrutinized. He denied that the legal education committee hampered in any way the dean and his lecturers in the choice of subjects taught or the kind and number of lectures given – which was true enough at the time, although the committee was soon to change its mind on the matter. Ludwig ended the interview by saying that he was 'much more familiar with the workings of our school than Mr. Carrick and I have no hesitation in saying that many of his complaints are not well founded. In the eyes of some people, everything is wrong but such people are rarely able to suggest remedies.'

Ludwig and other prominent benchers were greatly embarrassed by the episode and hoped that the matter would be dropped; but this was not to be, for members of the profession soon entered the fray. Once again, the county and local bar associations were the most vocal. The day after Carrick published his condemnation of the law society, G.A. Urquhart,[45] representing the York County Bar Association, sent a memorandum to Convocation protesting the lowering of admission standards. It was the association's feeling that 'our standards of education should be as high as [those] in the first-rate law schools in the United States.'[46] Lawyers from other parts of Ontario soon became aware of the row in Toronto. W.S. Middlebro' of Owen Sound wrote to Ardagh in February asking for the statistics on the proportion of entering students who were university graduates (in that year, 54 per cent): 'You will notice there is some agitation among the students and profession against what is called the lowering of the standards for entrance to the law society.'

Soon there was a flood of protests. The York County Bar Association, traditionally active in opposing the benchers, sent a circular to other county associations asking for reactions to the legal education committee's decision. In March 1933 the bar associations of the counties of Brant, Norfolk, Welland, Waterloo, Kent, and Oxford sent strong protests to Ardagh. Most associations deplored the legal education committee's move and demanded that the entrance requirement be increased to the completion of a BA degree. Charles W. Sims, the secretary of the Welland Law Association (who had been the only member of the legal education committee to vote against the proposal to lower admissions standards), wrote on 7 March 1933 that his association was of the opinion 'that the whole system of educational structure in the Law School, including the election of benchers, requires to be thoroughly reviewed.' A beleaguered Ardagh sent a letter to E.B. Titus, secretary of the York County Bar Association, asking for the reasons for the protest. Titus answered that it was demeaning for the legal profession to lower its standards when other professions were raising theirs, and that lower standards could only have the effect of increasing enrolments, which would produce more lawyers who could not be absorbed into the profession.

The prospect of an overcrowded profession was frequently used as an argument against the law society's policies, but few association members felt strongly enough about the issue to pursue it very far. The county bar associations were always on the alert for reasons to object to the way the law society ran the profession. The associations, which were almost exclusively made up of young lawyers (a great proportion of whom were Wright's students), tended to reflect current u.s. attitudes on legal education. Overcrowding was merely one of several problems cited as reasons for changing educational policy.

It was clear now, if it had not been before, that the controversy created by the legal education committee's decision had to be dealt with. On 15 June 1933 Convocation created 'the Special Committee of the Legal Education Committee' to 'investigate the subject of Legal Education in all its aspects and report their conclusions and recommendations.' The special committee was composed of Ludwig, Norman Tilley, J. Shirley Denison, W.S. Middlebro', W.F. Nickle, R.S. Robertson, H.J. Sims, G.L. Smith, and McGregor Young. The special committee, which met four times and heard dozens of submissions, issued a report that was adopted by a general meeting of Convocation on 21 February 1935. The recommendations of the report were to bring to an end, and to a considerable extent undo, a decade of Falconbridge's reforms.

The first meeting of the special committee was scheduled for 1 December 1933. A full agenda was tabled, including the issue of admission standards, the need for practical training, methods of teaching, curriculum, and examinations, as well as more mundane matters such as the accommodation of staff and students and the state of the Phillips-Stewart Library. The entire staff of the law school was in attendance at that initial meeting. Dean Falconbridge, MacRae, and Wright all presented submissions that consisted primarily of summaries of the courses they taught and the teaching methods they used. Falconbridge made extensive recommendations to the special committee. He urged that the admission standard be raised to the BA level, that the number of lectures at the school and the number of full-time lecturers be increased, that the examinations be toughened, and that the practice of allowing students to write an unlimited number of supplemental examinations be stopped. This last matter was of serious concern to the staff. Over the last few years Falconbridge had repeatedly come before the legal education committee to object to rule 116, which allowed a student who had failed his first-year courses to petition Convocation for a supplemental examination. Supplementals were routinely allowed, much to the teaching staff's displeasure, who saw the practice as yet another example of their lack of control over educational matters.

At the second meeting, held the following week, the part-time instructors presented reports, which were in the main descriptions of what they taught and their methods. Lecturer Kenneth Morden ventured the opinion that obtaining a university degree would make a law student more mature and more capable of independent thinking. He supported a suggestion that the student might do office work during the summer, thereby freeing the school year for full-time legal instruction. G.A. Urquhart presented the submission of the County of York Law Association, which emphasized the cultural advantages of obtaining a university degree.

Ludwig had earlier asked county law associations and the Osgoode Hall Legal and Literary Society to prepare submissions in time for the third meeting, to be held in February. Many of the associations reiterated the matters raised in their earlier letter of protest. L.Z. McPherson of the Osgoode chapter of the legal fraternity Phi Delta Phi submitted a brief to Ludwig in early February calling for the attainment of a BA as an entrance requirement. At the third meeting, held on 27 February, the Brant County Law Association presented a long submission arguing that the law school affiliate with the University of Toronto so that law students could be exposed to courses in jurisprudence, Roman law and the history of law. The most extensive brief came from the students. Signed by Donald Carrick and six others, it was entitled 'Report of the Special Committee of Students of Osgoode Hall' and was later published in the *Canadian Bar Review*.[47] We do not know to what extent the report represented the views of the majority of the students at the law school, although at various points votes were taken on certain issues. The report is interesting as a glimpse into the operation of the law school from the perspective of at least some of the students.

The report dealt with three issues: law school admission requirements, concurrent law school and office work, and courses and hours of lectures. It acknowledged that the purpose of a legal education was to prepare students for the practice of law, and the importance of practical training in a law office was not questioned. The report insisted, however, that legal education must also prepare the student to live up to his obligation to his community, and this preparation entailed a liberal education that would instil ideals and inspire the student to place his legal talents at the service of the community. Given this purpose of a legal education, the report concluded, the requirement for admission to law school should be at least two years at a university. The report argued both that the profession was overcrowded, and that because there was some evidence that professional misconduct was higher among those lacking university training, the law society should not contribute to making the path to the profession easier.

The report was unrelenting in its criticism of concurrent classroom and office work. The law student faced the prospect either of articling in a poor law office, in which case little practical knowledge was acquired, or, if he was lucky, of finding a good office and working for no pay owing to the competition among students for good jobs.[48] The number of available offices in Toronto, where the student was forced to look for articling jobs, was too small for the market. The articled student would in any case not be given much responsibility, since part of his day had to be spent at the law school. A law firm would rather hire a young lawyer: 'Young barristers are a drug on the legal market and their services can be procured at a very small wage.' In addition, the concurrent scheme had effectively destroyed the potential value of the education available at the law school. The student did not have enough time to devote to his studies, and the available courses did not provide him with the liberal background necessary to a proper professional education. The consecutive approach would make it possible for the student both to learn the law and to understand the necessary economic and social conditions responsible for the creation of rules of law. It would also solve the problem of obtaining adequate practical experience. The student would be able to serve in legal offices in all parts of Ontario, and his day would not be divided between law office and law school.

The students' report carefully surveyed the range of reforms that the Canadian Bar Association and legal academics had been recommending for years. Shrewdly, it drew on M.H. Ludwig and Shirley Denison's own published remarks supporting the consecutive scheme and more academically oriented law school courses. It ended with a series of complaints that probably reflected the views of more mature students, such as Carrick, who resented the law society's attitude towards students: 'The lectures are conducted, generally speaking, in a very elementary manner, and students are not trained to think for themselves.' The students tended to do little preparation for class, and class time was taken up with questions that would never have been asked if the students had taken the time to read the materials. In addition, 'there is a rumour current in the law school that the lecturers must cram sufficient knowledge into the heads of the students to enable them to pass the examination, because the lecturers will not be permitted to fail the students.' Another complaint was that lectures were compulsory. This paternalism was insulting, and served to undermine the whole endeavour of preparing students for the profession: 'Probably the most serious objection to conditions in the law school is the complete failure of the governing body to require the students to think and act like men ... It is, indeed, performing a cruel service to students to delude their minds and inculcate habits of mental dependence.' Behind these and many of the other criticisms found in the report was a more basic premise, never expressly stated but clearly implied: the law society should not be allowed to control legal education in Ontario.

After the third meeting of the special committee, Ludwig apparently planned to spend the next two or three months preparing a preliminary report for discussion so that the committee's business would be over by autumn. In a letter to Ludwig dated 18 June 1934, H.J. Sims of Kitchener insisted that the matter not go to Convocation at that time. Sims, it appears, was the only member of the special committee who supported the idea of a university law school, a view that may have flowed from his general dislike of the law society controlled by Toronto-based practitioners. Shirley Denison also asked W.S. Montgomery, long a follower of the legal education debate,[49] if he would write to representatives of other provincial bars for their views. Ludwig apparently was convinced by Sims that it would be more appropriate to defer writing the preliminary report until this material was available, and tentatively scheduled the next and last meeting of the special committee for early 1935.

Montgomery's requests bore immediate fruit, and he was able to send Denison a package of letters during the summer of 1934. The representatives of the various provincial law societies were nearly unanimous in their support for the completion of at least two years of university as an admission requirement, and several wrote to say that moves (so far unsuccessful) had been made to increase the requirement to the completion of a BA degree. These letters illustrate the lively interest of other law societies in the Ontario controversy. There is some suggestion that if Osgoode Hall decided to stand by its decision to lower the admission the standard, other provinces might have to follow suit. A.E. Bence of the Law Society of Saskatchewan wrote that he was 'shocked' by the decision of the Law Society of Upper Canada to lower the law school admission requirement, but added that before too long his own law society probably would follow Ontario's lead.

In the ensuing year, the law school's business was carried on as usual. In his dean's report of 20 September 1934, Falconbridge restated some of the recommendations he had made to the special committee months before and expressed again the staff's increasing frustration with 'the unlimited liberty allowed to the students of presenting themselves at the supplemental examination and of repeating their years, and by the privilege given to them of continuing their course notwithstanding their failure in two subjects at the supplemental examinations.' The dean also reported that, as part of the ongoing exchange lecture program, Caesar Wright would give another series of lectures at McGill on the subject of contract and quasi-contract in common and civil law, and G.H. Crouse of Dalhousie would give a lecture at Osgoode Hall on criminal law.

Reaction to the matters being considered by the special committee was mixed. The Canadian Bar Association expressed support for the Osgoode Hall students, and in September 1934 the committee of the junior bar presented a report containing a resolution 'that the Junior Bar Section of the Association regards with apprehension the tendency in some provinces to lower the standards of entrance to the legal profession, and recommends that a university degree in Arts, Science, or the equivalent thereof, be adopted as a preliminary condition to admission to the Bar.'[50]

At the other end of the spectrum, A.G. Burbidge of Toronto published a piece in the *Fortnightly Law Journal* attacking the Osgoode Hall students' report.[51] Burbidge ridiculed the idea that a university education was in any way necessary to practise law; it was merely a waste of good years that could be spent building up a practice: 'In order that a man may attain the position, in society, that his profession commands, with as little delay as possible, all but the most essential academic studies should be eliminated.' The suggestion that a university education built character was 'based upon idealism of the most ultramundane nature.' Putting university courses into the law student's education would be like a mechanic putting faulty parts in a machine to perfect it. The students had argued that the legal profession should follow the example of medicine and dentistry, both of which had increased their preliminary requirements; but did the medical profession 'insist upon four years at carpentry for prospective doctors?' Burbidge concluded huffily that the high school graduate was better equipped than the university graduate to enter law school: he still had some common sense.

While the education debate smouldered, Caesar Wright was gaining recognition on another front. In 1935, Sidney Smith, who had been appointed president of the University of Manitoba,[52] resigned as assistant editor of the *Canadian Bar Review*. A replacement was found in Caesar Wright. Wright, who now had several publications to his credit, took on the job of filling the pages of the review's 'Case and Comment' section. For the next eleven years, ten as editor of the review, Wright wrote hundreds of case comments and book reviews, signing his initials to them at first, but later writing anonymously. Arthur Goodhart, in a letter to Wright in 1938, said of the case comments, 'I consider them the best and most original work now being done in any legal periodical.'

It appears that Wright's appointment as assistant editor and later as editor was in part the work of Smith. In a letter to Smith in 1937, Wright remarked that Smith was 'the moving party in obtaining the editorship of THE CANADIAN BAR REVIEW for me,' and disclosed what may have motivated him to accept the job: 'I know that you will recall the queries at the time I was appointed as to whether I would endeavour to make THE CANADIAN BAR REVIEW into a Harvard Law Review.' Wright indeed did all he could during his years as editor to bring American writers and legal innovations to the attention of the Canadian profession. The editorship also provided Wright with a forum for his campaign to reform legal education.[53] It is ironic that the first volume of the *Review* that Wright helped to edit contained the report of the special committee, which was to turn back the clock on legal education in the province.

That report was adopted by Convocation on 21 February 1935, a week after the special committee's last meeting. Despite the submissions made to the special committee, which generally advocated higher admission standards, more lectures, more academically originated course work, and the abandonment of the concurrent scheme, the report recommended moves in precisely the opposite direction. The report was met with dismay by the teaching staff and many members of the profession when it was published, first in pamphlet form and then in the *Canadian Bar Review*.[54]

The report opened by arguing that the members of the special committee aligned themselves with the English tradition: 'Ontario lawyers will naturally incline towards English opinion and practice which we believe we are well advised to follow in principle as far as different conditions warrant.' The report then noted that in 1934 the Right Honourable Lord Atkin had presided over a committee on legal education established by the English Law Society. Lord Atkin's report affirmed all that the traditionalists on the special committee believed, especially the principle 'that it is for the professional bodies alone to decide what degree of professional knowledge shall qualify for admission to the profession.'[55] The special committee, bolstered in its own beliefs by the precedent of the Atkin report, then made its recommendations.

Admission requirements. The special committee declined to raise the admission requirements beyond the middle school examination with additional subjects of the upper school examination – that is, senior matriculation (equivalent to grade 13). This had been the recommendation of the Atkin report, a fact that 'fortified' the opinion of the special committee. The special committee also made it known that not only could it not recommend the two-year university standard, it wished to go on record as casting a degree of doubt on the value of a university education: 'The emphasis laid upon the importance of a university degree has to some extent obscured the advantages which students may and ought to derive from five years' experience in actual practice in an office.'

Matriculants. The special committee responded in part to Falconbridge's complaint that first-year failures (who were almost always matriculants rather than university graduates) were allowed to continue. The special committee recommended that the present passing grade of 50 per cent should be raised to 60 per cent. The special committee also recommended that matriculants be required to pursue a course of preliminary study and satisfy prescribed tests prior to the first year at the law school.

Training in offices. The most unexpected of the special committee's recommendations dealt with practical training. Everyone expected the special committee to reaffirm the importance of training in offices, but few anticipated the actual recommendations, which were prefaced with the remark, 'The Law School work is undoubtedly of great importance and value but your Committee is of opinion that the tendency has been to emphasize unduly the academic training at the expense of efficient office training.' The special committee accordingly recommended (1) that lectures be split into two sessions, one at 9 AM and the other at 4:40 PM, so that students would be available for office work during office hours; (2) that the curriculum at the law school be reduced by cutting the number of lecture hours in several courses; and (3) that the provisions of the Solicitors Act requiring students under articles to be 'actually employed in the proper practice of a solicitor' be strictly adhered to.

Methods of study. The special committee felt that the casebook method of instruction was acceptable, although 'the great favour with which the case method of teaching law has been regarded is somewhat on the wane,' and noted that 'the advantage of a study of authoritative text books and the orderly arrangement of general principles of law should not be unduly minimized.' Underscoring its preference for the English approach to legal education, the special committee recommended both that a specific course on English common law be added to the curriculum and that greater stress be laid upon 'the reading and study of standard elementary works on various branches of the law which have been written for purposes of study, some of which are also of high literary merit.'

So that there would be no mistake, the special committee's report ended by stating that 'the responsibility resting on the benchers with regard to Legal Education cannot be discharged properly without the exercise of a real control over the work of the Law School and if this report is adopted its recommendations can only be carried out ... by a continuance of full and hearty co-operation between the Legal Education Committee and the faculty.' The Old Guard had spoken.

The June issue of the *Canadian Bar Review*, the last edited by Charles Morse, reprinted the report and followed it with nine responses. Also included was a resolution of the Osgoode Hall Legal and Literary Society, supported by 96 per cent of the students, objecting to the reinstatement of the late afternoon lectures. From the students' perspective this was by far the most objectionable of the special committee's recommendations. It would destroy the effectiveness of the lectures at the law school, and would impose substantial logistic and practical problems.

The responses to the special committee's report came from various sources: there were articles by F.A. Brewin and R.F. Wilson of Toronto, Alfred Z. Reed of the Carnegie Foundation, Dean F.C. Cronkite of the University of Saskatchewan, Walter S. Johnson of Quebec, R.A. Ritchie of Nova Scotia, Lindley Crease of British Columbia, C.R. Smith of the University of Manitoba Law School, and an extract from a circular letter from the dean of law at the University of Minnesota to the law alumni. For the most part the responses from the other provinces merely described the programs in effect there, providing a basis for a comparison to the Ontario system. All of the contributors agreed that the special committee's recommendations were unfortunate and retrograde. Reed reminded the profession that whatever could be said of the recommendations, they were 'a logical outgrowth of convictions which have been implanted and nurtured for many years in Ontario soil.'[56] This was true enough: the Ontario profession had always been strongly influenced by the English profession. The fight against the benchers was all the more difficult because of the entrenched tradition out of which the established views arose.

The most eloquent reply came from Cronkite, long an active supporter of educational reform in the CBA. He was optimistic despite his realization that the report expressed the underlying attitude of the legal profession of Ontario to the lawyer as 'merely an office craftsman.' Cronkite pointed to the changing roles of the lawyer in Canadian society and the greater educational requirements that such roles demanded. He insisted that the demands to be made on the legal profession in the future would require it to become a scholarly, learned profession:

The question will be asked, can the ideal of a scholarly profession in the best sense, a scholarly profession giving service to society, be realized? The answer is that it can and will be realized. It will be realized when the law schools and professional societies take stock of the situation with a determined desire to put the legal profession at the top as a group of cultured gentlemen qualified to give the service that the modern world requires. If the other trend be followed one might make the prediction that thirty or forty years from now the lawyer will be regarded merely as an odd survival, the priest of a discarded religion.

In Cronkite's words, 'The fight is on and indications are not lacking that a group of determined individuals will carry it through.' That turned out to be true, but only after nearly a decade of frustration had passed.

5

The Decade of Frustration:
1935–1944

The 1935 report of the special committee on legal education of the Law Society of Upper Canada marked the end of many of Dean Falconbridge's reforms at Osgoode Hall Law School. Although Falconbridge was to continue as dean for another thirteen years, he never regained the ground he lost in 1935. Indeed, on a number of occasions he had to plead with the benchers for many of the same concessions granted him when he began his tenure as dean in 1923. The recommendations of the special committee reflected the views of the very conservative, old-school practitioner – men like M.H. Ludwig, Shirley Denison, and W.N. Tilley. These were the leaders of their profession, men who held firmly to the view that the true lawyer was an experienced and successful practitioner.

Had the war not intervened, it is likely that the battle between the university-minded legal academics and the benchers would have flared up in short order. But the depression, pre-war uncertainties, and the war itself made legal education issues seem unimportant. Even the legal education committee of the Canadian Bar Association, apparently stunned by the 1935 episode, was unable to rekindle its earlier enthusiasm for reform. In its 1935 report the CBA committee voiced a weak protest against the concurrent school-and-work scheme, but concluded that 'local conditions may nevertheless make such a practice desirable.'[1] The war caused the bar association to cancel many of its midwinter and annual meetings, and the topic of legal education was not explicitly discussed for several years. For the reformers, the years from 1935 to 1945 were a decade of frustration.

Few felt this frustration more acutely than Caesar Wright. His first seven years as an instructor at Osgoode Hall Law School began at the height of Falconbridge's successful reforms and continued through a period of what appeared to be a gradual progression towards the eventual triumph of the reformers. Falconbridge took the 1935 defeat quietly; he carried a heavy teaching load, fulfilled his administrative duties, and maintained a prodigious scholarly output. Wright, however, was a fighter who was happiest when battling giants. In 1935 it appeared that the giants had won, and when, in the next few years, it seemed that events would forestall the next battle, his patience was strained. As he carried on his fight in correspondence, at CBA meetings, in the press, and in the pages of the *Canadian Bar Review*, Wright began to wonder whether he ought to leave a hopeless situation and find other employment.

Despite his growing frustration, or possibly because of it, Wright was at his most active academically in these years. Between 1935 and 1945 he edited the *Canadian Bar Review*. Primarily in his capacity as editor of the *Review*, he wrote nearly 90 per cent of what he was to publish in his life: more than a thousand pages of his articles, case comments, book reviews, and editorials filled the eleven volumes of the *Review* edited by him. From 1942 on he edited both the *Dominion Law Reports* and *Canadian Criminal Cases*. He wrote frequently to friends, to those who admired him, and to those whom he admired in half a dozen countries. In addition, he was consulted by practising lawyers for advice on cases,[2] and in the mid-1940s he served as a labour arbitrator. All of these activities were ancillary to his teaching responsibilities, which included 130 to 190 hours of lectures each year.

Although in these years Wright produced numerous articles and comments on tort law, most of what he wrote, from case comment and book review to full-length article, dealt in one way or another with legal education. On occasion he would publicly criticize Osgoode Hall Law School and be chastised for doing so. It is possible to discern in Wright's editorials and writings from these years a growing impatience with the Canadian legal profession; he pleaded repeatedly for the adoption of American views on legal education and legal reform, only to have his pleas ignored. Many like-thinking scholars from around the world wrote to encourage him, but by the early 1940s Wright's frustrations began to emerge clearly in his writings. By the end of this period, in late 1944 and early 1945, he would come to perceive the possibility of a decisive battle that would settle the issue of legal education as he thought it should be settled once and for all, and would begin to fight with a new vigour. In 1935, however, Wright's attention was fully occupied by his writing and teaching responsibilities.

The benchers' policies as expressed in the 1935 report were immediately put into effect. At the law society's annual meeting in September, Dean Falconbridge announced that in accordance with the benchers' desires lectures would again be held at 9 AM and 4:40 PM, and the total number of lecture hours would be reduced from 1,014 to 900. To acquire the practical experience demanded by the benchers, matriculants would attend the law school in their first year, after which they would article for two uninterrupted years before returning to complete their remaining two years of school. Practice lectures were extended, and academic courses were cut back or combined. The only change in the teaching staff was the replacement of a part-time instructor, James C. McRuer, who had decided to return to practice, with James Weir McFadden, the Crown attorney for York County. No new courses were added, and Falconbridge did not even bring up the possibility of increasing to four the number of full-time instructors.[3]

The students at the law school continued their protest against the reinstatement of the late afternoon lectures, the change that most directly impinged on their lives. The Legal and Literary Society resolved in April 1936 to petition for the abolition of the afternoon lectures. Soon thereafter, G.G. Bradshaw, on behalf of the student society, informed the outgoing treasurer of the law society, Newton Wesley Rowell, that 'the Executive desires me to point out that the main conclusion in [the Legal and Literary Society's report] is that the concurrent system of school and office work, at present in use in the province, is an unhappy failure, resulting mainly in a supply of office-boys for solicitors in Toronto.'[4] These protests were referred to Shirley Denison, the chairman of the legal education committee, for study.

Wright's response to the situation was to throw himself into his job as editor of the *Canadian Bar Review*, a post the benchers were pleased to have him accept. Wright had clear plans for the *Review*. He wanted to use it as a vehicle for the introduction in Canada of American ideas on law and legal education. He published an article in the first issue of the *University of Toronto Law Journal* on the American Law Institute's Restatements on the law of contracts and agency.'[5] In the article he

compared the u.s. and English approaches to legal education, legal scholarship, and reform, and strongly urged that Canadians would do well
to look to the United States for a satisfactory model of the legal academic.
'The function of the law teacher and writer is to show the way,' Wright
argued, and that is precisely what had been accomplished in the United
States; the *Restatements* were a clear example of what legal scholars could
accomplish in law reform. American legal academics, 'by [their] teaching
and writings, have served to assist courts in ascertaining proper principles, and to carry on a type of law reform which the bar is either too
busy or has too little interest to perform.' The same could happen in
Canada, he wrote, but only when legal education was considered as
involving something more than the teaching of a trade.

Wright clearly hoped that under his editorship the *Canadian Bar Review*
would show by argument and example that there was much of value in
academic work. In October 1935, Wright began to write to legal academics throughout the world in an effort to bring the *Review* to the attention
of the international legal academic community. Wright wanted it to be
known that he was eager to publish examples of 'scientific' scholarship
in the law. In his letters he also campaigned for reform in legal education;
he hoped to keep the small but important community of scholars aware
of the situation in Ontario, and to solicit its support in the inevitable
confrontation with the law society.

In a letter to his mentor, Francis Bohlen, Wright admitted that the
Review 'of late years seems to have sagged considerably.'[6] He was referring
to the editorship of Charles Morse. Morse had continued a tradition
established in the days of the journal's predecessors, the *Canada Law
Journal* and the *Canadian Law Times*, when the principal function of a
professional journal was to report on social and professional activities,
new books, current judicial decisions, and, in general, the lawyer's view
of contemporary events. Morse's column, 'Topics of the Month' (later
called 'Marginal Notes') – a chatty review of current events written in
a nineteenth-century style complete with excerpts from poetry and literature – continued to appear (as the prerogative of the editor emeritus)
throughout Wright's tenure as editor. Wright, however, wanted the
Review to be an academic journal, not a mere digest of English law. He
wrote to Bohlen, 'The only way that I can see of making the REVIEW of
some value to the profession and the law teachers, is by an attempt to
bring home to their consciousness the fact that all the Common Law is
not to be found in the decisions of the House of Lords and that the
teaching of law, to use your own expression, is more than a mere "exegesis

on sacred texts culled from judicial opinions." ' For Wright, the Canadian lawyer's dependence on English law was symptomatic of the general weakness of Canadian legal scholarship. He felt it was his job, as he remarked in a letter to Karl Llewellyn of Columbia University, to enlist the support of all who could do something 'to jar the complacency with which, I am afraid, the legal profession regards the English law.'[7]

Wright told Roscoe Pound that he recalled Pound's 1927 comment that the *Review* was 'badly in need of reorganization and intellectual uplift.' He hoped that as editor he 'might perhaps be able to do something towards improving the condition of affairs which has existed in this country for so long.'[8] Wright asked the distinguished American to try to find the time to write an article for the *Review*, perhaps on the topic of legal education: 'The whole subject of legal education in Canada is a most distressing one and conditions at the present time are most chaotic.' The law societies held 'peculiar conceptions' as to the nature of the law. 'Certain retrogressive steps which have been taken in Ontario recently [have succeeded] in transforming Law Schools into little more than technical training schools.' Regrettably, Pound never obliged Wright with an article.

To Warren Seavey of Harvard, who had been the principal editor of the *Restatement of Contract*, Wright mentioned that he hoped to 'do something to buck up that periodical [the *Canadian Bar Review*] and to stimulate a little interest in legal scholarship in this country.'[9] Some months later, he was more explicit: 'I am most anxious to make an attempt at acquainting the Canadian profession with things American,'[10] including Seavey's own contributions. In another effort to find American allies, he assured Samuel Williston of Harvard that *Williston on Contracts* had become much better known in Canada because of Wright's efforts.[11]

Wright understood that his attempts to bring American law to the attention of the Canadian profession would not be easily accomplished. He admitted to the Australian scholar, Julius Stone, then at Harvard, 'I am afraid there is a tendency in this country to belittle any work that is being done in the United States regarding law.'[12] Seavey, in his reply to Wright's request for an article for the *Review*, seemed to agree: 'I am afraid your barristers will look with suspicion upon ideas emanating from the United States and perhaps you will be more effective than I as a reformer.'[13] Wright did not confine his correspondence to American scholars; he wrote also to A.D. McNair of Cambridge[14] and to the Australian scholars Alexander C. McLean of Victoria and G.W. Paton of Melbourne,[15] asking whether they could find time to contribute articles.

In October and November 1935 Wright informed his Canadian colleagues that the *Review*, under his editorship, would take a distinctly academic turn, one that would show the value of American ideas.[16] Wright hoped that members of the Canadian legal community, academics and practitioners alike, would supply him with high-quality, publishable material. Many academics responded to his request, but far too often he was forced to reprint articles from American and English publications.

On occasion, Wright's efforts to attract scholarly writers to the *Review* met with criticism. In one instance, G.W. Paton of the University of Melbourne wrote a short piece for Wright on the tort doctrine of *res ipsa loquitur* in which he expressed doubts about the value of the notion, citing leading Australian cases as examples.[17] In the same issue, Wright used Paton's analysis to criticize a recent Ontario Court of Appeal decision.[18] A few months later, R.M.W. Chitty, who emerged as the foremost spokesman of the 'practical' lawyer and who was to be one of Wright's strongest opponents on matters of legal education for the next two decades, wrote on the topic in his own *Fortnightly Law Journal*.[19] Chitty's article illustrates the kind of criticism Wright faced even on purely legal questions. He scolded Wright for his 'vulgar parlance,' adding that 'a critical article such as the one under review should not be so full of misprints and clerical errors.' Settling down to a discussion of the criticism of the Court of Appeal decision, Chitty dismissed Wright's contention that there was a distinction to be drawn between negligence and strict liability: 'It may be that academically tort may be broken down into theoretically separate branches of law. But the practical lawyer ... cannot find any real line of division between for instance negligence and nuisance.' As for Paton's and Wright's worries about the application of the rule of *res ipsa loquitur*, Chitty wrote, 'The professors have taken the various cases and analyzed the Judge's language in each case to a point of hair splitting. Very few Judges are so meticulously accurate that the language of each of their sentences can be analyzed to its elements.' There might be a theoretical distinction involved in the application of *res ipsa loquitur* of the sort drawn out by 'the professors,' but 'the practical lawyer will, we think, find the distinction, a distinction without a difference.'

Although this particular editorial seemed petty and vituperative, Robert Michael Willes Chitty was in many respects a worthy opponent of Caesar Wright. Chitty was born in England on 13 October 1883, the son of Sir Thomas Willes Chitty, KC, the editor of the first edition of *Halsbury's*

Laws of England. He was educated at private schools and at Marlborough College in England. He came to Canada in 1912 and studied at Osgoode Hall. After he was called to the bar in 1920, he combined an active practice with a tremendous amount of writing and editing. From 1923 to 1929 he edited the *Dominion Law Reports*, and in 1931 he started his *Fortnightly Law Journal*. In addition, he compiled numerous practitioners' guides and handbooks, such as *Chitty's Abridgment of Criminal Cases* and the *Ontario Annual Practice*.

A few days after Chitty's article appeared, Dean Vincent MacDonald of Dalhousie wrote to Wright, 'I shall cease to have any use for you whatever if you allow Chitty to get away with what he said about yourself and other law professors at page 88 of the current Fortnightly Law Journal.'[20] Wright responded: 'I had already seen the remarks of the very learned editor of the Fortnightly Law Journal, and was debating whether he rated a reply or not ... His article was so exceedingly stupid, however, that I must admit my first reaction – after I had cooled down a few degrees – was to leave it alone. I may be able to control my language sufficiently to write a reply for November.'[21] That reply was never written.

There were many who supported Wright's attempt to change the focus and upgrade the standards of the *Review*; but he was forced to do battle with the spectre of the 'practical' lawyer over the value of a professional class of legal academics and the importance of university-level legal education. Ironically, Wright himself was as 'practical' a lawyer as Chitty. To Wright, for whom the law was both a craft and a scholarly endeavour, the practically minded lawyer was one who was mindful of the rationale behind the legal rules and of the full range of interests those rules were meant to serve. Wright objected to the benchers' view of law school as trade school, because being a lawyer required far more than a knowledge of practice; it required an understanding of the social purposes of the law. In his teaching, Wright was hard on students who lacked the ability or desire to see the law in all its dimensions. When he discerned talent in a student, as he did with such bright lights as Moffatt Hancock and Bora Laskin, he was supportive, and often tried to push the student down the educational path he himself had travelled.

As the editor of the official organ of the Canadian Bar Association, Wright was obliged to attend the midwinter and annual meetings of the association so as to be able to report the events. The meetings gave Wright an opportunity to meet his fellow academics, although he was frustrated by the bar association's ever-weakening position on legal education. Wright wrote to F.C. Cronkite, the chairman of the association's legal education committee, who had not attended the 1936 annual meeting in Halifax: 'I am sure you would have enjoyed the Legal Education Committee and John Read's attempts to avoid the Ontario shoals.'[22] That year the committee passed five resolutions that were ranked in order of importance. The first was that 'legal education should primarily be designed to train students for the practice of law; the last was that 'some attention should be given to the social implications of law.'[23] No thought was given to the possibility of challenging the fundamental structure of legal education.

The 1936–7 academic year was uneventful. Wright concentrated on his duties as editor of the *Canadian Bar Review*. After completing his first year in that position, Wright prepared a report for the Canadian Bar Association that was harshly critical of the profession. In it he strongly hinted that the *Review* was in danger of being eclipsed by the *University of Toronto Law Journal*, which W.P.M. Kennedy had single-handedly established in 1935, and which was already gaining a substantial reputation as a scholarly journal devoid of gossip columns, editorials, and current events. Wright insisted that the *Review* must not degenerate 'into a chronicle of personal events occurring throughout Canada, which can be done by other commercial projects,' nor should it 'consist of a series of pseudophilosophical articles dealing remotely with law, but chiefly concerned with the aggrandisement of the writer's own ego.' He argued that Canada, with its two legal systems, was an ideal environment for comparative legal scholarship, and regretted that no one appeared to be interested in writing such material.

Soon after the beginning of the school year, in response to complaints from students and practising lawyers, the law society's legal education committee, under the chairmanship of Shirley Denison, struck a subcommittee, also headed by Denison, to consider the question of concurrent articling and law school training. In March 1937 the subcommittee strongly reaffirmed the importance of office training. Indeed, it considered that practical training was of such central importance that an additional year should be added to the overall program. Matriculants should receive three years' training at a lawyer's office, and university graduates one year, prior to enrolment in law school. In the first two years of law school, the student would attend classes part-time while continuing his office training. Attendance at law school in the third and final year would be full-time. These recommendations answered at least one perennial complaint: because part of the articling requirement would take place prior to law school, students would not be required to find positions in

Toronto, but could stay in their own communities. The suggestion that articling should take place after law school was rejected by the subcommittee on the grounds that the student would then be ready to compete with the very solicitor who was training him, and that competition might reduce the solicitor's clientele.[24]

In 1937, a short piece by Wright entitled 'Legal Reform and the Profession' was published in the *Canadian Bar Review*.[25] In a letter to Kennedy, Wright light-heartedly described its genesis: 'Feeling energetic over the week-end, I wrote an article on Legal Reform and the Profession, in which I make some very uncomplimentary remarks about the attitude of the profession in establishing proper law faculties, etc.'[26] It is unlikely that the piece was thrown together as casually as this remark suggests. It was carefully crafted to be at once an argument for the importance of developing a class of persons qualified to engage in legal reform, and a series of frontal attacks on many of the cherished beliefs in the virtues of the 'practical lawyer' espoused by Wright's opponents. In some ways it was a belated reply to Chitty's lambasting of Wright's and Paton's views on torts more than a year before.

Wright began by referring to the report of the English Law Revision Committee (published in the same issue of the *Review*), which recommended changes in the law of contracts. When, Wright asked, would Canada engage in much-needed reforms of private law instead of merely waiting until England had reformed its law and then adopting the reform in Canada? The answer was that no such reforms would occur until there were people who had been trained to think about reform and who had the time to do so. Those very people bore the brunt of the 'practical' lawyer's attack: 'To many lawyers our "theoretical law schools" and our "academic teachers" are viewed as things which certainly do little good and possibly do a lot of harm. What we want, some say, is a sound "practical" training, little realizing that by such a demand they may in reality, though quite unconsciously, be exposing themselves to the jibe of Disraeli that "the practical man is the man who practises the errors of his ancestors." ' Law reform could not be expected from legislatures, since much that was in need of reform was devoid of interest to the electorate: 'The man in the street cannot be induced to cheer a pungent sally at the doctrine of *Tweddle* v. *Atkinson* and an election slogan based on the Statute of Frauds, 1667, could not be counted on to win many votes.' Reform could come only from within the profession, through the efforts of reform-minded lawyers. But legal education was not designed to produce such individuals; rather, it was designed to produce the lawyer who knew 'how to do things' the way they had been done in the past. Canada would catch up with the rest of the world only if it had people trained to study the law scientifically. But in Canada academics were called 'theoretical,' and 'the word "theoretical" is deemed sufficient to condemn them.'

'Legal Reform and the Profession' showed Wright at his polemical best. The article was one of the few pieces in which he expressed political views. Partly as an example, and partly to convince his readers that the professional attitudes he was arguing against in the context of legal reform were politically ultraconservative, Wright discussed the debate over President Franklin Delano Roosevelt's New Deal 'experimentation' in government. He pointed out that, as a class, lawyers had been the first to express alarm at the growing bureaucracy that had resulted from New Deal social measures. Yet few lawyers were able to provide hard evidence of the evil to which their 'oracular pronouncements' pointed. If the transfer of power from courts to administrative tribunals was a growing phenomenon, could lawyers tell us whether this was a good or a bad thing? The question had to be addressed in law schools, but 'do we want the students to be told without investigation that the "new despotism" must be stamped out, because the law books have said it was a bad thing?'

Within a few weeks of the appearance of Wright's article, the Toronto *Star* ran a column headed 'A Toronto Barrister Speaks Out.'[27] The paper quoted Wright, and concluded that lawyers as a class were apathetic about law reform, ultraconservative, and not particularly interested in social change. As always, once reports of dissent in the ranks reached the newspapers, the benchers were forced to act. Wright was ready for a fight. Indeed, in a letter to Sidney Smith, he seemed eager for one:

I have reason to believe the shot went home and I am looking forward with some pleasure to being on the carpet as having uttered 'disloyal' comments concerning my employers ... I do hope that I am not disappointed in my expectations, but in view of the fact that the Dean has already been questioned by the Chairman of the Legal Education Committee, I think it will all depend on whether the latter can rally enough support to attempt anything. Frankly, I should welcome a showdown, as I think it must come sooner or later and at the moment I am not particularly concerned with the outcome one way or another.[28]

Smith quickly replied from Manitoba: 'Your article was great. I would like to have the time to try my hand at the same topic – there are some things in my soul that I would like to get off my chest ... about [the] Law Society of Upper Canada.'[29] A few other sympathetic letters reached Wright. He reiterated that although he was 'in danger of encountering some official opposition,'[30] he was ready for the battle. But either that opposition never materialized, or its manifestation was so uneventful that it was never mentioned again, in private correspondence or in public. Perhaps the benchers, realizing that any overreaction on their part would only play into Wright's hands, decided not to pursue the matter. No doubt he was disappointed that his provocative act had failed to provoke.

As the 1937–8 school year progressed, Wright worked on an address to be presented at the August meeting of the Canadian Bar Association in Vancouver.[31] He decided to write directly to Shirley Denison to express his views. He sent along a recent report by the Harvard faculty committee on curriculum,[32] which proposed a series of substantial changes to Harvard's curriculum and the reasons for them. In a cordial reply, Denison explained the rationale for his and the benchers' views on legal education.[33] Denison was not unaware of the problems with Osgoode Hall Law School. He himself had taught there, and in 1922 he had severely criticized the school for its inadequate facilities, its low morale, and the superficial level of training it provided.[34] But Denison was still of the view that the Harvard model was inappropriate for Ontario, and his reasons seemed compelling:

Ours is a small school poorly endowed, serving a sparsely settled and scattered area, and all candidates for the bar must attend it. Most of our students, when they graduate, must fill quite humble positions during much or all of their lives, either in a rather obscure practice in Toronto or our larger cities or in smaller places. Of course we are most interested in our few brilliant men, but we owe as much to all the others. We can not choose men like Harvard and fit them to be leaders of their various bars in their several states. We must train all that come to us to be decent, efficient and careful practitioners in their various niches in the community. We can do that by knowing them, thinking of their future needs, seeking to inspire them with some interest and enthusiasm for a pride in their profession, and we have two great advantages (1) that they have a chance to get actual office experience, a thing which we have almost entirely neglected in our teaching, and (2) it is a small school and we have a chance of knowing and making friends with our students, and I feel sure that one can do far more with the average student by knowing him and impressing the personality of the teacher upon him than we can by studying the methods of Harvard or Oxford or other great schools.

These sentiments were difficult to challenge. The attitude displayed, for example, by Chitty – that the practical lawyer knew best and did not need the assistance of the woolly minded theoretician who had no idea what took place in the day-to-day life of the law – Wright could refute with ease, as he often did. But Denison's careful and realistic assessment of the role of Osgoode Hall Law School was a different matter. Wright could not deny that Osgoode Hall, as the only law school in the province, had to teach those whose lifetime experience with the law probably would involve nothing more exotic than drafting the occasional will and conveying real estate. Wright's law was law in the broad sense, law as a social instrument. He maintained his opposition to the benchers' conception of legal education because there was indeed a need for advanced legal thinking in Canada, yet he could not easily counter Denison's argument. In the next round of his battle with the law society, he attempted to accommodate his 'higher vision' to the realities of legal education in the province by arguing, in effect, that every lawyer required a more rigorous legal training because every legal activity had direct social importance.

In July and August 1938 the Wrights took one of their infrequent long vacations. They travelled to the west coast, where the annual CBA meetings were being held. On 17 August Wright read a paper entitled 'Law and the Law Schools,'[35] which was to become one of his more influential discussions of the subject. The paper was more temperate than his previous polemical pieces, although it expressed many of the same complaints about the law society. To Wright's amazement, Mike Chitty was so taken with it that he applauded it in an editorial and extracted and published portions in the *Fortnightly Law Journal*.[36]

In his paper Wright did not underestimate the value of the practical training that the average solicitor required to perform his duties. None the less, his message was that law at every level concerns the administration of justice, and in its broadest sense 'the administration of justice is merely the solution of social problems.' To master the technical and practical aspects of the law, the lawyer must be aware of the conflicting interests at stake. The lawyer must be practical; he must know and appreciate the relevant facts of the case at bar, but this required going beyond the narrow technicalities of the law. To know the law meant more than 'finding' it in ironclad rules and principles inherited from the past. It was foolhardy to present a static picture of the law without providing a means by which the student could come to terms with changes in social realities and political structures. The student-at-law, in short, must be trained as a professional and equipped with a sense of public responsibility. The concurrent school-and-office scheme in operation in Ontario failed to provide either adequate practical training or an academic education. The future of legal education lay in what might appear to be opposite directions: 'in improving the technical branch of our training by some method of supervised and rounded practical work, and with that a teaching of every course with some view of the social purpose that law serves, how it might be improved, how it ought to function.'

At the CBA meeting in Vancouver, Wright learned that the University of British Columbia was contemplating opening a law school in the near future, perhaps as early as 1939. Delighted by the pleasant environment of British Columbia, and gratified by the warm reception he received, Wright left for home reluctantly. Once again he began to think that the time had come to give up on Ontario and look for employment elsewhere. There were two possibilities: he might teach at the new University of British Columbia law school, or he might follow up on his acquaintance with Arthur T. Vanderbilt, a past president of the American Bar Association and a professor at New York University Law School, who had been a guest speaker at the CBA meeting.[37]

In September 1938 Wright pursued both these avenues. He wrote to Senator J.W. deB. Farris, then president of the CBA: 'I am exceedingly interested in the contemplated school, and after having been to Vancouver my interest is perhaps much more personal. I was very much taken with the thought that your new contemplated school presented an opportunity for work on legal education untrammeled as we are here by the dead hand of Ontario tradition.'[38] Wright then made a direct overture: 'if I were to remain in academic work in this country I might be personally interested in the possibility of new fields of endeavour outside Ontario.'

Writing to Mr Justice H.H. Davis of the Supreme Court of Canada, a previous president of the bar association, Wright used similar language: 'In view of the extremely unpleasant attitude of some of the benchers here, it has occurred to me that if I am to remain in the teaching game the situation in Ontario is conducive neither to decent work nor to a settled state of mind which is necessary for that work.'[39] Wright asked Davis to advise him in confidence on whether he should manifest an interest in 'the new venture' to the authorities in British Columbia. Davis promptly replied, saying that he would be inclined to speak to Senator Farris about the matter; however, he offered Wright a warning: 'I do not think you can afford to make a direct contact yourself and it would be unwise for you to allow the impression to go out that you are in any way dissatisfied and are seeking some new field.'[40] Although Wright had already done what Davis was now telling him not to, he did not pursue the matter with Senator Farris. In fact, the school at the University of British Columbia did not become a reality until 1945, when the return of war veterans made the need for a law school in British Columbia apparent to all.

On the other front, Wright told Vanderbilt that the state of affairs in Ontario was 'most disheartening to one who has invested some dozen years in an effort to put legal education in swaddling clothes at least,'[41] and he would appreciate advice about the possibility of his moving to a school in the United States. Vanderbilt responded with encouraging news: 'I certainly do think that you would have a real opportunity in law teaching here. Indeed, I know of one possibility already.'[42] For some reason Wright's answer to Vanderbilt, written nearly a month later, was less enthusiastic, saying that he could not, 'at the present time, state definitely, one way or another, whether [he] should take advantage of the opportunity if it ever presented itself.'[43]

Like the Bohlen job offer of a decade earlier, Wright's first major attempt to leave Ontario came to nothing. The flurry of activity was probably only a manifestation of the frustration he experienced daily at Osgoode Hall. There was, of course, much to keep Wright in Ontario. Despite all the problems connected with teaching at the law school and trying to make the *Canadian Bar Review* into a scholarly journal, he was still an active and respected lawyer in Toronto. Soon after this episode, he was named king's counsel at the age of thirty-five. His altered status and heightened respectability helped make him feel more comfortable at Osgoode Hall, especially since he shared the honour with his former lecturers and close friends, Henry Borden and John Tory.

Wright's spirits were also lifted by remarks made about him by two men he respected. Early in November Wright had sent James J. Landis, the dean of Harvard Law School, a copy of 'Law and the Law Schools.' 'I rather harbour the belief,' he told Landis, 'that persons who heard it here believe more firmly than ever that I have been contaminated by insidious American influence.'[44] Landis replied, 'It is ... important that someone like yourself should be the mouthpiece of the effort to make the study of the law a scholarly matter.'[45] A few days earlier, Arthur Goodhart of Oxford had congratulated Wright on his case comments in the *Canadian Bar Review*: 'I consider them the best and most original work now being done in any legal periodical. They are worth more – and are certainly more interesting – than most of the lengthy articles in the American periodicals.'[46]

In 1939, despite the progression of events that was leading towards the Second World War, Osgoode Hall Law School was still active, and the question of practical training was on the minds of the benchers. In January they once again decided to try to strengthen the practical side of legal training, this time by initiating a system of oral examinations on 'practical' matters for students in the first and third years of their articling terms.[47] The oral exams were conducted by three practitioners. The exams achieved little: most of the students barely passed, and those who failed had to go through the process again.

In 1938 the Osgoode Hall building underwent structural changes, the first major improvements to be made in a hundred years. The Great Library was expanded, and faculty offices and an assembly hall were added. The changes were made necessary in part by the large number of students enrolled in the 1939–40 school year – 325 in all three years. As the war gathered momentum, student enrolment dropped rapidly to a low point of 109 in 1943–4. The possibility of radical changes to the curriculum, or any other aspects of the school, diminished accordingly. Wright appears to have resigned himself to waiting out the war. Life at Osgoode Hall was proceeding as usual, he told Sidney Smith, with the benchers pressing for a more 'practical' law school; although they were still annoyed by his articles and speeches, he said, 'they saw fit to reward me by a considerable advance in salary.'[48]

In contrast, the early war years saw a burst of activity at the law department of the University of Toronto. Since Osgoode Hall Law School, to all outward appearances, was not about to change its stand on legal education, W.P.M. Kennedy thought the time was right to persuade would-be law students to come to his school. In the *University Bulletin* for 1938–9, Kennedy described his honours course in law in attractive terms:

The course is ... specially designed not merely for those who propose to practice law – and for them it is of first class importance – but also for those who might look forward to public administration, to the Dominion and Provincial Services, and to commercial life. It forms the finest training for a student whether he looks forward to practicing law or to these other activities. There are scholarships, prizes and medals offered throughout the course, and within its short life two of the graduates have gained Rhodes Scholarships at Oxford.

Kennedy held out the prospect of studying the law as a social science in a first-rate university, and also promised a relatively speedy route to two degrees and qualification for the bar: 'Students who graduate in the Honour Course in Law are admitted to the fourth year of the Bachelor of Laws Course, which they can complete in two further years instead of the usual five. Thus, a student can obtain his Honour BA in Law, his LL B and his call to the Bar in seven years.' Kennedy boasted of 'an intimate relationship between staff and students,' the extensive use of the case method of instruction, and the absence of formal examinations, as well as moot courts, a good law library, and the Law Club. Kennedy's salesmanship was successful, and a steady stream of students came to the University of Toronto before going on to Osgoode Hall.

The honours course in law had been devised by Kennedy in consultation with other members of the Department of Political Economy in 1928. Kennedy, who previously had been an instructor in history at the university, was a prolific writer. He turned to law after the publication of his books, *The Law and Custom of Reservation: 1549–1661* and *Elizabethan Interpretations*, in the early 1920s. He taught constitutional law and medieval economics in the Department of Political Economy, and in 1924 he persuaded the university to allow him to head a subdepartment in law. When the new subdepartment was established, Kennedy taught constitutional history, John Davidson taught Roman law and jurisprudence, and part-time Osgoode Hall lecturers A.R. Clute, J.F. Harold, and H.W.A. Foster offered classes on various topics.

By 1930 Kennedy had added F.C. Auld, Jacob Finkelman, and N.A.M. MacKenzie to his staff, and a general reorganization of the political science and economics departments took place. Kennedy formed his own Department of Law, and offered both a four-year honours BA in law and a three-year LL B degree. In 1934 the programs were combined for a five-year joint LL B–honours BA in arts and law. A master's program was initiated, and in time the Department of Law underwent two symbolically important name changes – first to the School of Law in 1941 and then to the Faculty of Law in 1944. During the war, the English Council on Legal Education designated the University of Toronto School of Law as an examination centre for admission in absentia of West Indian students to the inns of court. By 1942, the school was offering an SJD degree; F. Eugene LaBrie and Morris Schumiacher were the first recipients. Kennedy was officially named dean of the Faculty in 1944.

The success of the school was regarded with dismay and some disdain by those at Osgoode Hall Law School. 'Kennedy's school' was one of the few things on which Wright and the benchers were in full agreement. In response to an inquiry for information about the University of Toronto School of Law, Wright had once said, 'There is no such thing as the University of Toronto Law School. What poses under that name is in reality nothing more nor less than a department of the Faculty of Arts.'[49] In 1941 Arthur Vanderbilt asked Wright what Kennedy had meant when, in response to a questionnaire on legal education prepared by Vanderbilt, Kennedy had said, 'I worked this course out many years ago with Haldane, and it has been publicly referred to by Wright and MacMillan.' Wright replied, 'I refrain from making any comments, although I can assure you that at the drop of a hat I am capable of several which are not particularly complimentary.'[50]

Kennedy's salesmanship extended to many fronts; not only did he promote his school in correspondence and articles, he used the University of Toronto Law Club to bring in illustrious legal scholars to enhance his school's prestige. In 1942 Kennedy invited Mike Chitty as guest of honour for the twelfth annual University of Toronto School of Law dinner. Chitty went away impressed by the spirit of the school, and became, if not an advocate of Kennedy's school, a reluctant defender of it.[51] Apparently, Kennedy also decided to use the legal education committee of the CBA to gain recognition. Wright described the scene at the 1941 committee meeting in a letter to Vincent MacDonald: 'At this meeting about the only members who attended were the entire staff of the University of Toronto and as I told you some time ago they have been milling about, raising cain generally, with a view to promoting something more active, as they put it, than has been done before. I was very much afraid if they were left on the loose they would ultimately lever W.P.M. in the driver's seat and for many reasons I did not think this was a good thing.'[52]

Wright was particularly sensitive to Kennedy's adventures since, as editor of the *Canadian Bar Review*, he was fully aware of the prestige that the *University of Toronto Law Journal* was developing. The *Journal* was in many respects serving the scholarly purposes that Wright had hoped the *Review* would fulfil, and with considerably more success. Wright did all in his power to persuade scholars to write for the *Review* instead of the *Journal*. To G.F. Curtis of Dalhousie, Wright wrote, 'I am amazed that you are writing for Kennedy rather than for The Canadian Bar Review.'[53] He told J.A. Corry, who had submitted an article for 'W.P.M. Kennedy's new venture,' that he had 'fond expectations that you are not going to desert the pages of The Canadian Bar Review,'[54] adding some months later, 'It seems rather a pity that there should be any competition in Canada for articles ... and I am quite free to admit that The Canadian Bar Review committee is not a little perturbed at the eruption of the new Toronto journal into the legal review field in Canada.'[55]

Throughout the late 1930s and early 1940s there was an ongoing controversy about whether graduates from Kennedy's school did better or worse at Osgoode Hall than those who came from other backgrounds. This dispute put Wright in an ambivalent position. Although he was unwilling to accept Kennedy's success in teaching law as a social science, he did not want to be seen to be agreeing with the benchers, who typically criticized Kennedy's school by saying that the performance of its graduates showed conclusively how futile it was to believe that university training made one a better lawyer. Wright hardly wished to subscribe to that view; equally, he could not to bring himself to praise Kennedy's efforts.

By 1943, the student enrolment at Osgoode Hall had declined by nearly 60 percent from what it had been in 1938. Many of the complaints the students had raised against the law society's articling requirements no longer applied; now there were more positions than students to fill them. Objections to the benchers' conception of legal education continued to be raised, however, and the benchers continued to defend themselves against their critics.

The pettiness of much of the dispute was illustrated again in 1942, when a memorandum of the legal education committee of the Law Society of Alberta was published as an appendix that year to the report of the CBA legal education committee. The Alberta committee described the law program at the University of Alberta, and concluded that 'the opinion of the Benchers of the Law Society of Alberta is that the system of Legal Education followed in this Province is superior to that followed in Osgoode Hall or in similar schools in Canada where legal education is carried on by means of lectures morning and evening with service under articles in an office in the interval.'[56]

The Ontario benchers, and Shirley Denison in particular, felt that this slight had to be answered. In late March 1943, Denison responded. In a memo to the law society's legal education committee, Denison dismissed the claim that Osgoode Hall Law School would benefit from an alliance with a university by claiming that no university in Ontario had ever proposed such an alliance; 'the fact that no such proposal has come from any University is sufficient evidence that such an idea does not exist in academic circles, otherwise it would be made known through the usual official channels to the Treasurer and the Chairman of the Legal Education Committee.'[57] This was, of course, a complete fabrication: the University had made a variety of proposals to the benchers with respect to taking on the burden of legal education, and had on each occasion been rebuffed.

Denison went on to argue that under the Solicitors Act the law society had no power to delegate its legal education duties to any other organization, adding that in any case it would not be a good idea to do so. He insisted that Osgoode Hall Law School taught about as many students as all the other provinces (except Quebec) combined, and was the largest law school in the country. During its fifty years of existence the school had gained valuable experience in dealing with problems affecting the education of students. Denison concluded that what might be possible and successful in Alberta would not work in Ontario.

Finally, without mentioning the University of Toronto School of Law by name, he stated that 'it would never do for universities to describe a law course as a course in arts and thus lessen the wholesome practice of taking an arts course in the true sense before studying law.' Denison then remarked that although the law society was in favour of potential law students taking a university degree before beginning their studies at Osgoode Hall, statistics indicated that as many graduates as matriculants failed their Easter exams. This fact, he insisted, undercut the argument that a pre-legal university education would be a significant improvement on the law society's existing program.

The dispute over the performance of university graduates at Osgoode Hall, and in particular the performance of the University of Toronto School of Law graduate, was to continue. It was marked by an amazing lack of agreement over the actual statistics. Wright rarely participated in this argument, since in his heart he tended to agree with the benchers about the low quality of Kennedy's program. In 1943, much of his attention was directed toward the fate of the *Canadian Bar Review*. He had edited eight volumes of the *Review*, and virtually all of his efforts to persuade practitioners to contribute articles had failed. His frustration with the profession's lack of response turned to anger when, during the Calgary Bar Association meetings in April 1943 (attended by several officers of the Canadian Bar Association), two speakers criticized the *Review* for failing to be as helpful to the profession as it might be, and for being 'rather too academic.'[58]

Wright immediately issued an editorial in response. He was clearly furious: 'We are delighted to hear criticism,' he began, 'since it indicates that the BAR REVIEW is at least looked at in Canada by some persons, a matter on which from time to time we have entertained doubts.' Wright acknowledged that he had been unhappy with some of the pieces he had published, but remarked that 'we may be forgiven ... for suggesting that the most constructive type of criticism would lie in manuscripts received for publication rather than in speeches. We ourselves have pleaded for contributions for the REVIEW at every Council Meeting of the Association we have attended since taking over the editorship of the REVIEW. Such pleas, to date, have produced no results.'[59]

Characteristically, Wright saved the full force of his wrath for a personal letter. Before he published his editorial, he wrote to Mr Justice C. Campbell McLaurin of the trial division of the Supreme Court of Alberta, who was vice-president for Alberta of the Canadian Bar Association and who had been at the Calgary meeting. Wright bluntly told McLaurin that he did not know what his critics at the meeting were talking about, and doubted that they did either. He then suggested that the criticism of the *Review* was representative of the general attitude of the Canadian profession:

First and foremost it seems to me indicative of the fact that we are content in this country to accept the law as handed down for us in England; to think about it as little as possible and certainly not to concern ourselves with anything that may cause trouble in developing that law. That is why, I believe, that to date Canada has contributed practically nothing to the advancement of common law doctrine in any way commensurate with her general position in the world ... It is another reason why meetings of the Canadian Bar Association have been, from a constructive standpoint or from the standpoint of anything along lines of legal development in a large measure, complete flops.[60]

Wright speculated that members of the association were becoming interested in the *Review* because it now contained articles by academics from fields other than law. The association, Wright thought, was troubled by the fact that 'other agencies are beginning to interfere with what many lawyers feel is their God given monopoly!!' The contributors who had written the kind of articles that had been criticized as 'too academic' or not useful to the profession were 'doing much more for the improvement of the ultimate ordering of society by law than the number of persons who are chiefly interested in telling each other and the public that they, because of some nonsense about Magna Carta, are being overlooked in the adjustment of present and future problems.'

Within a year Wright announced his intention to resign as editor of the *Canadian Bar Review*. The *Review* had not become the learned journal he had hoped it might be: 'At the moment I take a very dim view of the future of the *Review* and I feel that I have had it long enough and that the editorship should circulate.'[61] In the end, he reluctantly agreed to stay on for another year, and formally submitted his resignation in December 1945.[62]

By 1944 the decade of frustration had reached its nadir. The benchers had restated their support for the concurrent scheme of legal education and their belief that practical training played an essential role in the process. There was little likelihood that Osgoode Hall Law School would be able to expand its curriculum to add more 'academic' subjects, and there was no chance that the preliminary education requirements for entrance into the law school would be raised. John Falconbridge, now in his seventies, had been unable to bring the legal education committee around to his views. Caesar Wright, who had spent the greatest part of the decade in a fruitless effort to turn the *Canadian Bar Review* into a respectable scholarly journal, admitted defeat and lost interest in the project. Wright's attempts to find employment elsewhere had not worked out to his satisfaction, and he faced the prospect of completing his teaching career in an environment, and constrained by an attitude, that he violently opposed. The expansion of the University of Toronto School of Law was no cause for optimism: he saw 'Kennedy's school' as intellectually ill-conceived and Kennedy as an interfering rival.

At this point, however, the great events of the outside world began to intrude into the benchers' narrow universe. By late 1943 it was clear that some provision had to be made for the re-establishment of soldiers returning from the war. In November of that year the benchers established a special committee to study the problem, and Falconbridge asked Wright to take charge of designing a series of 'refresher courses' for veterans who had had to interrupt their legal education. Wright told Falconbridge that in his view the refresher courses should be wholly practical; he doubted whether he could be of much assistance in the actual teaching of these courses, but agreed to gather information about what the Americans were doing to solve the problem of returning soldiers.

Many benchers realized that providing extra courses, and even sum-mer courses (as Denison had recommended earlier), would not solve the problems posed by a rush of new students. The number of new admissions would soar (total attendance at Osgoode Hall went from 109 in 1943–4 to 445 in 1945–6), but all of the newcomers would have to find articling positions, and the Toronto bar could generate only a limited number of jobs. There was also the obvious problem of where to put all the new students. It was easy to see that the pressure from students and the profession that the law society had managed to avoid during the war would soon recur.

At what point did Wright realize that the end of the war would see the whole question of the proper approach to legal education raised anew? The concerns of the war would no longer pre-empt the issues troubling the legal academics, and public discussion of the proper role of the legal profession in reconstructing the country could open the door to a reconsideration of the law society's grip on legal education. In an address delivered at the Canadian Bar Association's summer meeting, Vincent MacDonald issued a call for law societies to 'emancipate their students and the law schools from the thralldom of purely vocational education.'[63]

Wright must have felt that the post-war years would mark the begin-ning of a renewed battle. In February 1944 John Willis, the acting dean of Dalhousie Law School, wrote to him inquiring about the prospects of a lectureship at Osgoode Hall. The two men had met at Canadian Bar Association meetings, and Willis was one of a handful of Canadian academics on whom Wright could count to help fill the pages of the *Canadian Bar Review*. Wright wrote back, saying: 'Regarding working at Osgoode Hall, much could be said on both its pleasant and disagreeable sides. I think the greatest change you might notice would be the com-parative lack of freedom from control to which one is accustomed in a university and the lack of school spirit due to the office work and the general tendency in the profession and the benchers to belittle the work of their own school ... This, of course, can be, and I hope will be changed.'[64] Within two weeks of writing this letter Wright was once again battling the law society.

The midwinter meeting of the Ontario section of the Canadian Bar Association, held in mid-February 1944, was well attended, and pro-vided Wright with an audience for the reopening of the battle between the legal academics and the Law Society of Upper Canda. D'Alton Lally McCarthy, the treasurer of the law society, had prepared an address on legal education to be presented to the meeting. The address was intended to air the benchers' views on preliminary educational requirements for admission to law school. McCarthy used the occasion to defend the benchers' perception of legal education and to express their disdain for the University of Toronto School of Law. One of his themes was that if the reason behind the school's growth was to prepare for taking over the task of legal education, the university should reconsider its plans forthwith. McCarthy tried to impress upon his listeners the seriousness with which the benchers viewed the question of the 'suitability' of a would-be law student. The present admission system, which required two character references, was designed to keep a tight control on the calibre of entering students. (McCarthy did acknowledge that he was unaware of any case in which an application for admission had been refused.)

McCarthy then moved to the crux of his address, the encroachment of the University of Toronto School of Law:

In the graduate class the men come to us from the Universities, more particularly Toronto University, who have now established an honour law course, in which they deal with almost the identical subjects that we do in our Law School. They have their case books, they have identical text books, and year by year they appear to be encroaching upon the rights and undertakings of the Law Society. This may have been done deliberately with the hope possibly that some day the lawyer will get his degree in law at a university and then have to pass the Council in the same manner as is prescribed for the medical profession, and get his practical training later on.

The university graduate came to Osgoode Hall Law School thinking he had learned it all before, and that law school was a waste of time. The results of the examinations belied this, however: 'I have seen many of the papers of fourth year honour graduates of Toronto University and I was not impressed, in fact I was surprised at what little grasp some of them have of the very plain and simple questions submitted to them.' What was needed was reciprocity between the university and Osgoode Hall, whereby the university would teach preliminary subjects and Osgoode Hall would provide practical training. University graduation was no guarantee that a student would turn out to be a good lawyer: 'It is a remarkable fact that the head man in the last three years at Osgoode Hall was a matriculant.' That did not mean that a university graduate would be a failure, 'but when I look at the early days in my practice, I can count at least ten leaders of the Bar who were not graduates.' The law society was obliged to train everyone whom it admitted, the brilliant and the mediocre alike; to accomplish that end successfully, the training had to be practical.

There was nothing new in McCarthy's address; the old arguments were refurbished for the occasion. But this time they met with a hostile response. When the meeting was thrown open to the audience, discussion turned at once to McCarthy's address. The first speaker was Gilbert D. Kennedy, W.P.M. Kennedy's son, who questioned the accuracy of the figures given for the performance of the University of Toronto School of Law graduates on the Christmas examinations.[65] Kennedy's question caught McCarthy by surprise. As Chitty reported in *The Fortnightly Law Journal* a few weeks later, 'Mr. McCarthy tried to find the Legal Education Committee report from which these figures had been given to him but was unable to do so. It was then that the doubt arose as to whether he meant that the majority of graduates had failed or that the majority of those failures were graduates.' Kennedy pressed on, claiming that eight of the first ten in the examination results were School of Law graduates. As the *Journal* put it, 'the meeting had the distinct impression that the figures given to Mr. McCarthy for his report were incorrect.'[66]

The next person to object to McCarthy's address was a familiar figure. As Chitty reported the event:

The hour was then growing late and the meeting had considerably dwindled in numbers – in fact there were only a hardy handful left – when C.A. Wright, K.C., speaking as he said as a member of the profession and not as a member of the Law School staff, made a virulent attack upon the Law School as at present constituted. The gist of his remarks was that it was no damned good. It has lost any *esprit de corps*. The students used to crowd his room from the close of the morning lecture until lunch time and into the afternoon, but now he never saw them between the morning and afternoon lectures. You could not teach law to students that were only at the school during the two daily lecture periods.

McCarthy rose to defend the school, but it was so late that the meeting soon broke up. Chitty noted that Wright's remarks led one to conclude that there was 'something rotten in the State of Denmark and the meetings of the Legal Education Committee and Convocation will be full of interest.' They were indeed; Wright was once again in the news, and the benchers began to debate the best means of defusing another of the crises that Wright had precipitated.

Surprisingly, the first person to come to Wright's defence was Chitty.

Chitty's own sentiments about legal education were well known, but he was also quick to rise on behalf of the underdog determined to fight the system. In his editorial in the *The Fortnightly Law Journal* Chitty harshly criticized McCarthy for not verifying his facts (although he said that the blame probably should be assigned to McCarthy's advisers). What was needed was co-operation between the university and Osgoode Hall Law School, but 'compromise does not result from actions that can only give rise to antagonism.'[67] As for Wright, Chitty took pains to dissociate himself from the view that some benchers must have expressed – that Wright was acting disloyally by criticizing Osgoode Hall: 'No one can doubt for a moment the sincerity of purpose that prompted the attack. No one can doubt the risks that reprisal for the attack might engender. No one can suggest any person better qualified to criticize than a man who has had first hand experience of the working of legal education at the Law School over so long a period.' Accusations of disloyalty would not dissipate the force of Wright's criticism, Chitty insisted. There was something wrong with Osgoode Hall Law School, and 'it seems to us that Dr. Wright has brought the whole house of cards tumbling about our ears.'

Kennedy, who had not been at the midwinter meeting, was soon brought into the controversy. He wrote to Harold Fox, KC, one of his part-time instructors, to say that McCarthy's statements were quite incorrect: 'As a matter of fact, at the Christmas examinations our students did brilliantly. Only one failed and she was a failure here.'[68] Kennedy cited his own statistics: since 1930 the University of Toronto School of Law had sent 169 students to Osgoode Hall, about 11.5 per cent of the total number of students enrolled there. Out of a total of 254 failures, School of Law graduates accounted for 3, or less than 2 per cent. On the other hand, of the total of 182 degrees awarded, School of Law graduates accounted for 61, or more than one-third.

As for McCarthy's claim that he had tried to enlist the co-operation of the University of Toronto School of Law, that was 'completely and finally incorrect ... He has never made the slightest attempt to do so. Indeed, two attempts were made in the history of this University to co-operate with Osgoode many years ago and on both occasions, the University was severely rebuffed.' Kennedy then informed Fox that his policy of co-operation with Osgoode Hall was governed by two conditions: first, that the university should be able to teach any law subject it wished; and second, that it would not co-operate to the point of jeopardizing the integrity of the School of Law: 'It is the distinct policy of the University that we are not going on our hands and knees to ask Osgoode to recognize our degrees or credits.' Further, 'Dr. Wright's statements fully bear out the situation downtown.' As Kennedy was writing this, the benchers had agreed that the situation was important enough to investigate.[69] W. Earl Smith, the secretary of the law society, asked Falconbridge if he 'would be good enough to arrange with Dr. Wright to be available when and if the Committee wishes him to attend.' Wright was on the carpet once again.

The legal education committee of the Law Society of Upper Canada met four times in March and April 1944. During that period John Willis was hired as a lecturer at Osgoode Hall Law School, and on 5 April Wright wrote to him with news of events. Wright's letter is very different in tone from his earlier letter to Willis; indeed, his obvious enthusiasm and optimism strongly suggest that he was thoroughly geared up for a renewed battle with the law society. In his letter, Wright described the committee meetings: 'I was on the carpet and prosecuted by one of the benchers, who was appointed to act in that capacity, and the suggestion was made that I should apologize to the benchers. Naturally, I refused. There has been a good proportion of the old guard amongst the benchers who were out for blood and still are out for blood with a view to firing me forthwith, one of the leaders, of course, being our friend the chairman [Shirley Denison].' The ploy failed miserably. The benchers had gotten themselves into a bad mess, Wright wrote; yet he expected that 'considerable good will come out of this, because there is now a general movement to investigate and reorganize the whole law school. I have hopes that this will result in cutting out the afternoon lectures and generally obtaining more control over academic matters for the faculty than has been customary.' Eventually, McCarthy called Wright into his office for a chat. The discussion was affable enough; in Wright's words, McCarthy had been delegated to ask Wright 'how the whole thing could be white-washed without the benchers losing face.' Wright suggested that the best way to proceed would be to have him 'politely spanked, but without any apology from me whatever.' Wright was willing to put up with the 'spanking' as long as he gained his point and some blueprint was laid down for the future.

Wright told Willis that prior to his appointment some of the benchers had wanted to ask Willis about his views on legal education. To the law society's credit, that plan and all it implied were quickly rejected. But what should Willis expect in the future? Wright's mood remained upbeat: 'All in all, you are stepping into a situation which has infinite possibilities now, which I do not think it had a month ago. There has been much talk in other circles of university co-operation and I have had several conversations with persons interested from that end. As this is a delicate subject, I refrain from going into it further with you, but no doubt when I see you we can discuss these and many other extremely important matters which have to be solved and I believe and hope will be solved in the not too distant future.'

As the 1944–5 academic year began, Wright approached his many duties with renewed vigour. In November he turned down an invitation from Paul Sayre to contribute an essay to a volume of essays on legal philosophy in honour of Roscoe Pound: 'Under existing circumstances the prospect of writing on legal philosophy, or even the prospect of thinking about it, is so far beyond the state of turmoil in which I am living that I am afraid I shall have to refuse your more than kind invitation. One of these days I would like to find some of that "academic quiet" which law professors are supposed to enjoy.'[70]

Of the many things occupying Wright's mind, one of the most important was the question of legal education. Now that he could realistically expect the debate to begin again, he spent some time clarifying his thoughts on the subject. He was engaged in preparing a report for the law society's legal education committee; George H. Steer, an Edmonton lawyer who was chairman of the CBA legal education committee, wrote to Wright in October asking to see the report. Wright refused his request, but agreed to give Steer some idea of what it would contain.

The greatest need in Canada, Wright said, was for 'at least one really excellent school with a faculty of at least nine to ten full time professors, each of whom should be an outstanding authority in his field and in which school law should be taught in the only satisfactory way of teaching any subject, as considerably in advance of law as it is currently practised.'[71] Wright was clearly thinking of a Harvard of Canada, a national school that would be a centre for legal research and writing, and also a training school for lawyers. In the United States it had been decided that law schools would concentrate on academic, university-style legal education, and leave the student to acquire his practical training on the job. Wright was realistic enough to know that the complete abandonment of practical training would never be acceptable to the Canadian law societies. Moreover, he was strongly of the opinion that legal education could not ignore practice completely. Ironically, despite the prevailing belief among the benchers that Wright was wholly academically minded, he was not a true academic in the sense of being a detached theoretician. He was not a deep, abstract thinker, but rather a pragmatic, practice-oriented teacher fully convinced of the necessity of practical training. His primary goal was to expose students to rigorous and socially relevant legal training uninterrupted by their law-office apprenticeship. Although he acknowledged the value of practical training, Wright thought that the apprenticeship scheme was a failure. In addition, he was greatly concerned that Canada was not producing legal writing of any sustaining value, and believed that only legal academics, devoting their full time to teaching and research, could fill that glaring need.

Wright refused Steer's request that he present a paper at the CBA meetings in the summer of 1945. If changes were to be made, Wright said, it would be better not to have his plans aired in public prematurely: 'To stir matters up and then have them fall flat does not seem to me to be in the interests of the plan on which I think you and I are pretty well agreed.'[72] As the summer of 1945 approached, he was looking towards ultimate success; 'because of that ... I am inclined to make haste slowly, although it is my own personal conviction that the time has now arrived for really going after this matter.'

The prospects did look exciting. Wright now had the promise of a measure of co-operation from Kennedy and the University of Toronto; the benchers had failed in their attempt to bully him into apologizing; and even Chitty was sympathetic to his views. The scene was almost set for the revolution. All that remained was the appearance in Toronto of the one person who, in a position of power, could unite Wright's public presence and political savvy with his own innate capacity for compromise and organization. That person was Sidney E. Smith.

6

The Summer of 1945

The summer of 1945 represented a turning-point in Wright's campaign for a professional university law school and the academic freedom that such a school would entail. Words were no longer his only weapons. For eighteen years he had developed his program for reform, preached his concept of law and legal education, and nurtured his many friendships. By the summer of 1945 he was certain that it was time for action. He was ready to challenge the benchers.

Sidney Smith's appointment as president of the University of Toronto was an important factor in convincing Wright that now was the time to act. Over a year before, when Wright had heard that Smith would assume the presidency of the university, he had been overjoyed. His telegram to Smith was an emotional outpouring:

Allah be praised. Lassie come home. Never happier in my life. Love to Harriet.
Caesar[1]

To Wright, Smith's coming meant that he would be reunited with an old and dear friend, the man to whom he was closest. Smith, a large, boisterous, fun-loving man, got along extremely well with Wright, who, although he may have looked like a bookworm, could be quite outgoing with people he respected. Wright and Smith could once again share their ideas and enjoy each other's company. Soon the Smith and Wright families were spending so much time together that Smith became 'Uncle

Sid' to Wright's three children.[2] Smith's appointment also meant that Wright would have an ally in a crucially important position. If his plans for a professional university law school were to succeed, he would need the support of the large and prestigious University of Toronto.[3] Smith could provide that support. Moreover, Smith was an avenue to political power. He was a highly regarded member of the Conservative party, which had come to power in Ontario in 1943 under the leadership of George Drew.[4] If, as Wright was inclined to believe, the benchers would not voluntarily accept his reform proposals, Smith's political connections might prove valuable in forcing them to do so.

Smith came to Toronto in the summer of 1944 for a one-year stint as principal of University College, one of the university's constituent colleges, on the understanding that he would succeed the Reverend H.J. Cody as president on 1 July 1945.[5] The year at University College was intended to give Smith a chance to familiarize himself with the university personnel and administrative structure before he assumed the presidency. The year also enabled him to refresh his memory about the problems of Ontario legal education. He met frequently with Wright, and found Wright's paper on the future of legal education 'thought provoking.'[6] He also taught property law part-time at 'Kennedy's law school.'[7]

Wright was somewhat disappointed in Smith's attitudes in that first year. Smith, for example, told Wright that he supported the concept of a national law school, but that he would not openly lend his support to the effort to turn Osgoode Hall into such a school. Smith was concerned about how such support from him would be seen by the law schools at Dalhousie and the University of Manitoba, with which he had previously been associated. Smith also seemed unwilling at this stage to join Wright in an outright assault on the benchers. As Wright put it, Smith was reluctant 'to put his foot into troubled waters.'[8] This attitude is hardly surprising. Smith was well aware of the long history of the University of Toronto's unsuccessful attempts to establish a university law school. He was also aware that the benchers regarded the university with some suspicion. Earlier in 1944, the news had leaked out that President Cody had offered Wright a position on the faculty of the university.[9] The benchers, conscious of Wright's views on the need for a university law school and of the university's past efforts at establishing such a school, reacted angrily. Kennedy described the incident to Smith: 'The Benchers were very mad at us trying to "force their hand," as one of them said, adding "it won't help you a bit if he does go to you." '[10] Although

Kennedy was in favour of Cody's offer and thought that he and Wright were allies facing a common foe, Wright continued to resist close association with Kennedy or his school. It was Wright's understanding, moreover, that Cody had Wright in mind as a replacement for Kennedy, who was talking of retirement.

Smith wanted to get settled and become more familiar with the university environment before taking any steps that might have serious repercussions. The law society had been resisting all initiatives by Ontario's universities for the reform of legal education for almost a century. Smith undoubtedly wanted to be firmly in the saddle before leading his university in another assault on the benchers' citadel of 'non-cooperation.'[11]

The events of July 1945 gave Wright the chance he needed to win Smith over. On the first day of the month, Smith learned from Kennedy that Moffat Hancock, a brilliant and popular member of the university's law faculty, had been lured to Dalhousie Law School by an offer of more money. Word then reached Smith from Jacob Finkelman that Bora Laskin,[12] another of the law faculty's bright young members, had received a job offer from the benchers of Osgoode Hall who were looking for someone to take over the full-time teaching post of the retired Dr MacRae. Smith was concerned; the loss of Laskin and Hancock meant that the university's full-time law staff would be severely depleted. There would remain only Kennedy, who was soon to retire, Clyde Auld, who was past his prime, and Jacob Finkelman, who was thinking of leaving to join the Ontario Labour Relations Board.

Smith moved swiftly to address his own school's problems. He told Wright that he thought it was in the best interests of 'the cause' for Laskin to stay at the University of Toronto and explained that he would talk to Laskin and urge him to stay. He also had a proposal for Wright: would he come to the University of Toronto to replace Kennedy as dean in 1946? This offer, he explained, was based on the 'grim' situation at Osgoode Hall and was made because Dean Falconbridge, despite his advanced age, had decided to stay on as Osgoode's dean for another two or three years, thus depriving Wright of the deanship which both Smith and Wright thought he deserved. Smith stated that he was 'prepared to try the direct approach to the Benchers' by offering to join forces with them under a reasonable scheme of co-operation to rationalize legal education in the province.[13]

Wright had different ideas about what was best for 'the cause,' however, and he had a proposal of his own. To understand why Smith eventually agreed to adopt Wright's ideas, it is necessary to look in some detail at the hectic days of early July 1945. On Friday and Saturday 6 and 7 July, Laskin discussed his Osgoode Hall job offer with Jacob Finkelman. Finkelman had been teaching law at the University of Toronto since his graduation from Osgoode Hall in 1930, and had known Laskin as both a student and a colleague. They shared a strong interest in labour law. Finkelman was somewhat distressed by Laskin's receptiveness to the Osgoode offer. He did not want to lose his young colleague, nor did he want to see Dean Kennedy hurt. Kennedy, Finkelman knew, loved Laskin like a son. After his talk with Laskin, Finkelman immediately wrote to Sidney Smith to inform him of Laskin's desire to accept the Osgoode Hall offer and to suggest to Smith that it might be wise to prepare Kennedy for the shock of losing Laskin.[14]

Laskin did not want to act before discussing his decision with both Wright and Kennedy. He was concerned about how his move would affect the 'balance' between Osgoode Hall and the university and how it would change his personal relationship with Kennedy. Laskin had studied under both Kennedy and Wright and was deeply indebted to both men. Wright and Kennedy had helped to get Laskin admitted to Harvard and to secure a scholarship,[15] and Wright had published some of Laskin's early work in the *Canadian Bar Review*.[16] After Laskin graduated from Harvard, Kennedy and other members of the University of Toronto helped him find part-time work,[17] while Wright made it possible for him to pick up extra money by writing for the *Review*.[18] It was Kennedy, though, who contributed most to Laskin's development in these early years of his career. In 1940, when Norman ('Larry') MacKenzie had left the University of Toronto to become president of the University of New Brunswick, Kennedy had offered Laskin MacKenzie's teaching position. The job was an important step in Laskin's career, for it helped him overcome the barrier his Judaism represented to his advancement in law.[19] Thus, it was not surprising that Laskin should have sought to discuss his proposed move to Osgoode Hall with the two men who had been so helpful to him in the past. Nor was it surprising that Laskin was reluctant to take any step that might hurt Kennedy. On Monday, 9 July Laskin travelled north from Toronto to visit Wright at his rented cottage on Lake Ahmic near Magnetawan where Wright and his family rented a cottage each summer. On Monday evening and Tuesday they discussed the job offer and its implications.[20]

Wright did his best to persuade Laskin to accept the position, and offered to go with him to see Kennedy. Laskin, somewhat apprehensive of meeting with Kennedy alone, was glad of Wright's company.[21] On

Wednesday, 11 July Laskin and Wright set out to get Kennedy's blessing. They had to travel thirty-odd miles from Wright's cottage to Beaver Lake, near Kearney, where Kennedy had a summer cottage. When they arrived, they walked with Kennedy along a winding path through the woods along the lakeshore. As the three of them walked along single file, with Kennedy leading the way with his walking-stick, Wright and Laskin began to explain why they thought Kennedy should approve Laskin's acceptance of the Osgoode Hall job.[22]

At first, Kennedy was quite disturbed. A few weeks earlier when he had heard rumours that Laskin might receive offers from other schools, he had written to Sidney Smith suggesting strongly that Laskin be promoted to associate professor and given an eight-hundred-dollar raise to entice him to stay at the University of Toronto. Smith, who thought that he could still do something to keep Laskin, had not prepared Kennedy for the shock of losing his brilliant young colleague. In Wright's words, Kennedy 'raved about.'[23] A few weeks before, Kennedy had to face the loss of Moffatt Hancock to Dalhousie.[24] Laskin knew nothing of this, and Kennedy did not want to tell him. Although Hancock, who would later become a leading conflicts scholar, was already recognized as a brilliant academic and a teacher much loved by his students,[25] his methods were too 'democratic' for Kennedy's taste. While Hancock's departure was of some concern to Kennedy – he was, in Kennedy's words, 'a good and stimulating teacher'[26] – Laskin's leaving was a much greater blow. To Kennedy, Hancock was not 'in the same class in value to us as Finkelman and Laskin.' Now Kennedy had to face the fact that Laskin wanted to leave to join the staff at Osgoode Hall.[27]

Although Wright and Laskin had a difficult time with Kennedy at first, they did their best to convince him that Laskin's move to Osgoode Hall had the potential of furthering both Laskin's career and the cause of legal education in Ontario,[28] both of which were important to Kennedy. Osgoode Hall offered Laskin the opportunity to teach more mature students and to work closely with three of the most eminent legal scholars in Canada – Falconbridge, Wright, and John Willis.[29] The addition of Laskin to the staff would mean that for the first time the teaching staff at Osgoode Hall would be university-oriented: Willis, Laskin, and Wright had all studied at Harvard and were familiar with the advantages of a professional university law school. Laskin would also be the first University of Toronto professor to be accepted by the benchers to teach at their law school.[30] Wright and Laskin suggested to Kennedy that by joining the staff at Osgoode Hall, Laskin could work from the inside with Wright and Willis to persuade the benchers to establish closer ties with the university and perhaps even to co-operate in the establishment of a professional university law school. Laskin could act as a bridge to bring the two schools together, a goal that Wright and Kennedy now shared.

Reluctantly, Kennedy agreed that there might be something in what Wright and Laskin were saying. He made Laskin agree to drop in to see Sidney Smith at his Rossclair cottage on his way back to Toronto, and he gave Laskin a note for Smith. In the note Kennedy recommended to Smith that Laskin be informed about Hancock's resignation and that 'the very highest offer possible be made to Laskin to retain him.'[31] He went on to say, 'Wright and [Laskin] both think that the offer is of some significance and may do much to help to bring Osgoode and U of T together. From my point of view, my chief aim has been and will always be to improve and benefit legal education and scholarship and I feel that if Laskin's going would help that purpose, I shall be satisfied indeed. It may be that the time has come if he goes, for you to take such action as may bring matters to the point of discussion with the benchers.' He added that in his opinion Smith might well find that the benchers would delay any action on a proposal such as the one Wright had in mind and would postpone 'the hoped for event ... *sine die.*' In this he would prove to be correct.

Wright, perhaps fearful that Kennedy's note, whatever it might contain, would encourage Smith to try to change Laskin's mind, cabled his old friend to explain that he was of the view that Laskin should accept Osgoode's offer both for Laskin's own advancement and because of the broader implications for legal education. The next day Wright sat down and composed a lengthy letter to Smith to explain his views more fully. After briefly outlining what had taken place at Kennedy's cottage, Wright explained why he favoured Laskin's acceptance of the job offer.[32]

My own feeling about the Laskin thing is that for the first time now with him and Willis the faculty at Osgoode is preponderantly university-minded and is in a position to execute concrete action if the opportunity arises. Further, the taking of a Toronto man at Osgoode is a tremendous advance for Osgoode – it recognizes more than anything else could do the fact that U of T faculty can be 'trusted' by the profession and in the event that either with or without legislative action an honest to God law school can be established in Toronto. How can the Benchers object to a staff which they themselves have approved?

Wright and Smith had been discussing the need for a university law school in Ontario for years, and Wright had made his views about the limitations of Kennedy's undergraduate school quite clear. What he wanted was 'an honest to God law school.' Wright, of course, was convinced that a professional law school affiliated with an institution like the University of Toronto was the only real solution to the problems of legal education in Ontario.[33] He also knew that this solution, which he had frequently proposed to the law society without effect, might have to be forced on the benchers by legislative action.

In his letter of 12 July Wright made his views clear to Smith: 'You ask me re taking over Kennedy's place in '46. I think you know my views on that. Like many other things it is *yes, provided* we can go places. I have put up with a lot from some of the Benchers because I really believe that eventually we could do a job. I still believe it. It will, of course, need (1) money, (2) support of the profession, (3) support of the Gov't & (4) support of the Governors [of the University of Toronto].'[34] Wright's reference to the 'support of the profession' shows that that he was looking beyond the benchers for support; the benchers had acted as a roadblock to his reforms for so long that he no longer expected to win them over.

Wright told Smith that he was confident about gaining the support of the government and the university board of governors. Although he expected opinion in the profession to be divided, he believed that enough supporters could be found:

On that score I think that if Robertson cj comes up to the Lake here this Summer [Chief Justice R.S. Robertson of the Ontario Court of Appeal, like Wright, had a cottage on Lake Ahmic] I will invite him over and put the thing to him squarely. I have a 'hunch' he may be for it – if so we gain immeasurably. If not, we know, at least, where we stand. In any event we get the benefit of his views which are bound on such a matter to carry much weight with your own Board.

... I have given it the best thought I can – I don't know whether you will agree. In any event, I feel more than ever that you and I must have a good 'gass' about it all – preferably sitting in the sun. Too bad we can't have Henry Borden with us – I think he and several others known to you will be of tremendous help not only as Benchers, but with the A.G. and others ...

... wpm, I am convinced, will go if I indicate that I will come up. I am not interested in the present setup. I am interested in a good professional school. I *will go* – provided there is hope – and enough money to live on – and I am sure I can take Laskin and Willis – both of whom should be there.

On this basis, my suggestion would be to attempt to obtain a temporary senior man for this year at Toronto ... As I see it, however, the University has all the talking points on merit – with Laskin at Osgoode ready to move with Willis and myself we strengthen rather than weaken the bargaining position. When I talked to Cody a year ago I would have had to go alone – and would have. Are we not better with three?

Ironically, Smith was forced to make up his mind on Laskin's departure without the benefit of Kennedy's note or Wright's telegram and letter. While Kennedy, Wright, and Laskin were debating the wisdom of Laskin's acceptance of the job offer, Smith was hurrying back to Toronto from his cottage to inspect his house, which had been broken into. When Laskin stopped at Rossclair, Smith was not there. Not knowing whether he would be able to see Smith in Toronto, Laskin left Kennedy's note and Wright's telegram at the cottage with Mrs Smith.

On Friday Laskin visited Smith in his Simcoe Hall office, and the two had a 'frank discussion' about Laskin's plans and the law school.[35] Laskin outlined what had transpired at Kennedy's cottage and how his going would help 'the cause.' Smith did his best to persuade Laskin to stay. He offered him more money, only to be told that it was not a matter of money; Laskin wanted 'to cut his teeth on a new job.' Smith, who was no stranger to such feelings, was understanding. Although he found it difficult to do, he accepted Laskin's resignation and offered him good wishes for his future. He expressed the hope that Laskin would 'play a part in a finer and better and bigger scheme for legal education in Ontario' and said that he would be 'prepared to open up the legal education tangle, first, through the Board of Governors and then by approaching the Benchers.'

Smith returned to Rossclair later on Friday, and finally read the messages from Kennedy and Wright. He was upset by the losses he had suffered in the Toronto burglary, and very concerned about the future of his law school. The weekend did little to relieve the terrible tension he felt, and it was a tired and discouraged Sidney Smith who wrote to Wright on Sunday night.[36] Smith said that after Laskin had told him about the meeting with Kennedy and had listed the advantages of his leaving, Smith 'was *about* convinced that his going might – would – help the cause.' He added, 'I hope so.' He was not optimistic that a replacement would be found for Laskin: 'Where can we get a man even for a year?' He was also concerned about Finkelman ('I fear now that Finkelman will go into practice when he learns of Bora's leaving'). Without Hancock, Laskin, and Finkelman, the university had 'not many cards or any cards of worth *in praesenti*.' The university's only 'talking points' with the benchers would be 'in futuro.' That was not a position Smith liked to be in when he approached the benchers. He encouraged Wright to approach Chief Justice Robertson, but again he saw little reason for optimism: 'I have a hunch that the cj will be Osgoode-minded!'

As Smith suggested to Wright, Jacob Finkelman was concerned about his future at the university. He had been moving more and more into the field of labour relations, and during the academic year 1943–4 he had taken a year's leave of absence from the school to act as secretary to the short-lived Ontario Labour Relations Court. He had returned to teaching because he thought it important that future lawyers have some training in labour law. No labour law course was offered at Osgoode Hall, and if students were to receive such training it had to come from the University of Toronto's law program. Laskin's presence at Osgoode would change all of that, and Finkelman did not 'relish the prospect of continuing teaching law at the University when the students would get an adequate course at Osgoode.'[37] The news of Wright's plans for an amalgamation of the University of Toronto School of Law and Osgoode Hall captured Finkelman's interest; that would be something worth staying around for. He wrote to Wright on Monday, 16 July and asked to see him on Friday or Saturday. He explained that he needed Wright's advice on his future: 'Unless there is a definite move for an amalgamation within the next year with considerable hope of success, there is no use in my staying on at the University.'

Wright, Smith, and Finkelman got together and reached a 'bargain.'[38] It was decided that Wright would test the waters by discussing the planned amalgamation with Chief Justice Robertson; Smith would seek the support of the university's board of governors; and Finkelman would agree to stay on and help Kennedy with the administration of the law school.

When informed of all this, Kennedy took a selfless stance, leaving Smith totally free to do whatever he thought was in the best interests of legal education: 'I trust that Cecil and [Laskin] are right and the *consolidated* and *firm* action by the three may do much. I sincerely trust so; and I want you at once to know that, if it is wise, if changes *come*, I am willing indeed to do only my teaching and writing and serve under anyone else as Dean. I am alone interested in the School of Law and the administration is freely and gladly in your hands. I am not worrying.'[39]

The man Wright was to talk to, Robert Spelman Robertson, was then seventy-five years old, and had been chief justice of Ontario since 20 December 1938. Prior to being appointed chief justice, he had been a senior partner in the Toronto law firm of Fasken, Robertson, Aitchison, Pickup and Calvin. Although he had received little formal education, he had developed a reputation as one of Canada's leading counsel in constitutional matters. It was Robertson who had argued in support of the Bennett reform legislation of 1935 before the Privy Council in London. His views on legal education were of special interest, because he had been a bencher of the Law Society of Upper Canada and its treasurer in 1937 and 1938. He had also been a member of the law society's special legal education committee, which produced the 1935 report; moreover, he had been appointed to the Board of Governors of the University of Toronto in December 1942, and had received an honorary doctor of laws degree from the university in September 1943. His brother, John Charles Robertson, was a professor emeritus of Greek at the university. Because Chief Justice Robertson was a highly respected member of the legal community and was able to view legal education from both the perspective of the benchers and that of the board of governors, his opinions would carry great weight with both the benchers and the university.

Wright fulfilled his part of the bargain with Smith and Finkelman in August. He had been unable to see Chief Justice Robertson in the Lake Ahmic area, and he wrote to Robertson to ask that they 'have a chat' about legal education.[40] The chief justice responded quickly, suggesting that he visit Wright's cottage on Wednesday, 1 August. In his letter Robertson stated, 'There is no simple solution [to the problems of legal education] short of scrapping what we have and starting all over.'[41]

The chief justice kept his appointment, and, in Wright's words, they 'gassed from about 3–5:30.'[42] After the meeting Wright summarized Robertson's position for Smith: '(1) he thinks and says legal education in Ontario is lousy; (2) something must be done; (3) I *believe* he is with us. *This threw me*. He has apparently been moving to the idea that the best thing to do is give a lawyer "a good education" and he will know how to go about this practical work. At one stage he even indicated that practical work was unimportant, I, of course, took the contrary view. (4) I have a feeling he likes me!!!'

Wright saw the meeting as a 'softening up.' In his discussion with Robertson he emphasized the present problems of the legal education system and his hopes for a national law school with a top-notch faculty. He explained his concerns about the policy of admitting high school graduates with no university training to Osgoode Hall. He briefly remarked on the university's potential role in remedying the ills of the existing scheme. When he did ask the chief justice how he would react to the university's establishing a professional law school, Robertson ducked the question. Nevertheless, Wright was of the view that Robertson would go along if a plan was worked out.

Smith was greatly encouraged by Wright's summary of the Robertson meeting. His enthusiasm for legal education reform was revived, and he told Wright that he really felt 'ready for a fight with the Benchers.'[43] He said that he had sent Wright's description of the meeting with Robertson to Henry Borden, the vice-chairman of the board of governors. He gave Wright the good news that Eric Phillips, the chairman of the board, had been talking about the proposal to members of the bar and was now ready to back Smith and Wright. Phillips, like Smith, favoured a direct approach to the benchers.

At his meeting with Chief Justice Robertson Wright had agreed to send the chief justice a copy of the recommendations on the future of legal education that he had prepared for Lally McCarthy in April 1944. Wright thought it politic to 'leave him for a few weeks' before sending the material to Robertson.[44] About 10 August, however, before Wright sent the recommendations, he received a letter from Robertson. The chief justice had been mulling over Wright's ideas and wanted Wright to know how he thought the benchers would respond to them.[45] He explained that while he personally saw the merit of a national law school, the benchers would be slow in accepting any such scheme for Ontario. His letter is an excellent summary of the attitudes of the benchers:

I do not see how it can be expected that, before such a school of law is established and has given assurance practically that it is of the character and accomplishes the kind of results that prove its superiority over what we have had, such a body as the Benchers of the Law Society at Toronto will commit themselves to any definite course of action in regard to it. They would require to have something more than mere hopes and promises of something much superior to what they already have before taking action. That in brief makes my first point which is that it seems to me that whatever the University of Toronto initiates along this line will largely if not wholly require to be undertaken on its own responsibility and independently of any supporting provinces ...

Assuming that the university has established such a school of law as is contemplated or is under discussion then what might it be expected reasonably that the Law Society would do in the matter. First of all I think the Benchers would wisely think twice before abandoning control of legal education. The university might do very well for a turn and later might not do so well. That sort of thing does happen. The results of the university's course in law might also in experience be proven to produce only an inferior type of lawyer of the practical type or it might be found impossible to coordinate the academic teaching of law with the necessary training in practice. These are such obvious difficulties that the Benchers would need to safeguard their position in case of any such result. That would seem to involve some limitation upon any undertaking or bargain into which they might enter and to preclude their entire abandonment of the right to have their own school of law when they want it.

The case of the matriculant is another problem ... as a matter of principle it was always strictly maintained by many that as trustees for the public of the right of admission to the practice of the law Benchers should always keep the door open to the student of limited means to enter without having first obtained a university degree. While there may be a few students affected, the principle is one that cannot be pushed aside lightly. It maintenance is some guarantee that the lawyers are not using for their own advantage the privilege of determining who may practise law as I think the medical profession are endeavouring to do in the practice of medicine.

The important question of training in the practice of law I could say much about. That problem is not being solved under the present system and I have no solution to suggest as to it in case a change were made in the law school. It is a most important matter. Law is a business as well as a profession. Lawyers have to deal with and to advise businessmen – and they cannot do it unless they know in a practical way something about business. They may learn more or less in actual practice but usually at their client's expense. I am convinced that the lack of skill in the business-like transaction of affairs does more than actual dishonesty to impair the good reputation of the profession. A solution of this problem is I think just as important and just as pressing as an improvement in the teaching of law. I greatly doubt whether the use of demonstrators in a university course will meet the need. It would be too much like teaching medicine with dummies instead of with patients in a hospital. The contact with the actual conduct of real affairs is what is needed and it is what law students today do not get very much of.

We do not know how Wright responded to this letter, except that he sent the chief justice his 1944 paper.[46] It is unlikely that Wright found anything startling in Robertson's analysis. He knew the attitude of the leading benchers well, having tried for years to convince them they were wrong. He must have found the letter somewhat discouraging, however. Although Robertson implied that he agreed with Wright's aims, he did not say that he would offer any assistance in trying to persuade the benchers to assist the university in establishing a professional school.

Robertson was of the view that the benchers would not commit themselves to a definite course of action and that the university would have
to go it alone for a long enough period to convince the benchers that
its way was better. This, of course, is what eventually happened. At
this point, however, Wright was still hoping that some sort of agreement
could be worked out, although he recognized that it might prove necessary to appeal beyond the benchers to the profession and the Ontario
government to achieve such an agreement.

While Wright was 'testing the waters' with Chief Justice Robertson,
Smith, Finkelman, and Kennedy were busy finding part-time lecturers
to take Laskin's classes for the fall term. Eugene LaBrie had already been
hired on a full-time basis to fill Hancock's position, but until it was
known what would come of the initiative to establish a professional law
school within the university, Smith did not want to hire any more full-
time faculty, nor did he want any changes in curriculum.[47] For the next
four years the university's law faculty was in a virtual state of suspended
animation, awaiting the outcome of the Smith–Wright initiative.

Smith was also busy pondering how best to present Wright's ideas to
the board of governors and the benchers. Some of his jottings and notes
reveal what was running through his mind.[48] The existing system, with
both an undergraduate and a 'graduate' law school, was expensive and
made little sense. There was unnecessary duplication: many students
took similar courses at both the university and Osgoode Hall on their
way to the bar. The granting of degrees was also a problem. The university gave an honours BA and an LL B, but its students received no
credit from the law society and could not practise without graduating
from Osgoode Hall; Osgoode Hall qualified students to practise, but
could not give a degree. By combining the two schools into a professional
university school much could be gained: one could reduce expenses,
eliminate duplication, and grant a professional LL B degree. Such a system would also permit the university to offer pre-law students a better
general arts degree, since the specialized law courses could be left to
the law school and the student would be free to take the broader and
more traditional liberal arts courses. There remained two serious problems, however: the need to combine the teaching of practical and theoretical laws and the fact that the benchers were the only ones who
could license an individual to practise. The first problem, as Wright had
suggested in 1944, could be dealt with through the establishment of
clinics in the law school; practitioners could instruct and supervise students in such matters a real estate closings and will drafting. The licen-

sing power of the bencher under the existing scheme was the more pressing concern. At times, Wright seemed to think that the only road to reform was legislative – a government-imposed revamping of legal education. Smith thought that a direct approach to the benchers would be better. In his words, they had nothing to lose. If the benchers rejected the proposal, it would still be possible to appeal to the Ontario government. Smith seems to have been less inclined than Wright to attempt any solution that bypassed the benchers. Smith, of course, had not been directly involved in Wright's past attempts at reform, and was less cynical. Moreover, as a politically active person he realized how explosive such a challenge could be, and how difficult it would be to obtain suitable legislation in the face of bencher opposition.

But if the benchers were to be approached, what should be suggested to them? Smith pondered the possibility of establishing a partnership between the law society and the University of Toronto modelled along the lines of the University of Manitoba Law School; he was intimately familiar with that situation, having been president of the University of Manitoba before coming to Toronto. A second alternative would involve a division of teaching responsibilities, with the university teaching theory and Osgoode Hall teaching theory and procedure. As we shall see, he would later present both of these proposals to the law society for discussion.

When the summer of 1945 ended, Wright was in a position he had never known before. His dream of a professional university law school serving all of Canada had never been nearer to realization. He stood at the head of a movement for reform that included as active participants the president of one of Canada's leading universities, members of the university's board of governors, and teachers at Osgoode Hall and the university. Surely he must have thought that it was only a matter of time before his long-sought goal would be reached.

7

Negotiations and Manoeuvres

During the fall of 1945 Sidney Smith began to put the grand plan into action. On 2 October he told W.P.M. Kennedy that he intended to raise the matter of legal education at the next meeting of the University of Toronto board of governors, and asked Kennedy to supply him with 'ammunition.'[1] What he sought was detailed information about the University of Toronto Faculty of Law. Within two weeks Kennedy responded with a lengthy memo outlining such things as the history of the teaching of law at the university, the degrees offered, and the makeup of the teaching staff. Kennedy explained that the English Council of Legal Education had excused University of Toronto law graduates from all English bar exams except the final one – a dispensation usually given only to graduates of selected law schools in England and granted to no other non-English school. Kennedy also noted that the University of Toronto was the only centre for graduate work in law in Canada.[2] This information was exactly what Smith wanted, and it permitted him to go to the board of governors well armed.

The members of the Board of Governors of the University of Toronto were political appointees.[3] Under the University of Toronto Act, the twenty-two man board was appointed by the Ontario cabinet. The president of the university was an ex officio member, but he did not preside over meetings. That task fell to the chairman of the board, another political appointee. The board, which consisted primarily of prominent businessmen and lawyers, was charged with the appointment of the

president and the administration of the finances, property, and buildings
of the university. Responsibility for academic affairs rested with the
president and the university Senate.[4]

Smith had to persuade the board of governors to take action regarding
legal education. He had already recruited the support of the newly
appointed chairman, Colonel W. Eric Phillips, who was a close associate
and supporter of Premier George Drew.[5] Phillips held an undergraduate
degree from the University of Toronto, and had a reputation as a shrewd
and tough-minded businessman. As one Toronto lawyer put it, 'If you
cut Eric up into little pieces, you'd have a thousand razor blades.'[6] In
the 1920s and 30s Phillips had run Duplate Canada Ltd, an Oshawa
glass factory; during the war he had been one of C.D. Howe's dollar-a-
year men, heading a Crown corporation, Research Enterprises Limited.[7]
After the war, his friendship with E.P. Taylor led to his appointment
as a senior partner in Taylor's newly created Argus Corporation.[8]

During the fall of 1945 Smith and Phillips, both recent appointees,
were learning about each other. They were soon to develop an excellent
working relationship, and together would reorganize the university's
administration.[9] The law school question became one of their first major
tasks. They went to the board in the late fall of 1945 and presented the
following proposal: Phillips would appoint members of the board to a
committee, which would then consult with Premier Drew and his attorney-general and ask them to suggest to the benchers of the law society
that they designate representatives to confer with the university's committee.[10] This plan had two advantages: it would apprise the government
of the proposed changes in legal education, and would solicit its aid in
promoting discussions with the law society. The benchers might shun
an overture from the university, but not one from the government. By
13 December Smith had persuaded the board to pass the necessary
resolution.[11]

Just two days after the resolution was passed, Smith wrote to Phillips
recommending that the committee consist of himself, Phillips, Chief
Justice R.S. Robertson, Mr Justice John Andrew Hope, Henry Borden,
KC, and Arthur Kelly, KC. Smith explained that since Robertson and
Hope might be reluctant to chair the committee, he would accept that
position.[12] On 24 January 1946 the board accepted these recommendations.[13] So far, things were going according to plan.

With the exception of Phillips, all of the members of the university
committee were either lawyers or judges. All except Chief Justice Robertson had been appointed to the board of governors in 1945. Mr Justice

Hope was a recent appointee to the Ontario Court of Appeal, having been a Supreme Court trial judge for twelve years. Hope, aged sixty-five, chaired the Royal Commission on Education in Ontario.[14] Arthur Kelly, forty-five, who had served with Hope on the royal commission, was affiliated with Osgoode Hall Law School, and supervised the conduct of oral examinations.[15] He held a BA from St Michael's College at the University of Toronto and was a partner in the law firm of Day, Ferguson, Wilson and Kelly. Henry Borden was a close friend of both Sidney Smith and Caesar Wright and the son-in-law of Dr D.A. MacRae.[16] He was a senior partner in Borden and Elliot, a firm he had helped found in 1936. Like Eric Phillips, he had been one of C.D. Howe's dollar-a-year men during the war,[17] serving for the last three years of the war as chairman of the Wartime Industries Control Board. In 1946 Borden became president of Brazilian Traction, Light and Power Company, a post he would hold for seventeen years. He was forty-four years old.

Shortly after the appointments were made, Chief Justice Robertson asked to be relieved of his place on the committee because of his heavy workload. Beverly Matthews, KC was chosen to replace him. Like the rest of the committee, Matthews was a recent appointee to the board of governors. He held a BA from the University of Toronto, and had studied under Wright at Osgoode Hall, where he had been the gold medallist in 1930. During the Second World War his heroism had earned him the OBE and CBE, as well as the rank of brigadier. At forty he was the youngest member of the committee.

The committee seems to have been inactive until June. Perhaps Smith, who was to be its motivating force, found that the job of administering the university, which had begun to receive the flood of returned veterans, was enough to keep him busy during the academic year.[18] In June, however, the committee met and began to discuss the draft of a letter to be sent by Premier Drew to the law society. Smith did the bulk of the work; he prepared the draft letter, copies of which were sent to Borden, Kelly, and Matthews for comments.[19]

The care with which the committee approached its task is evidenced by a comment made by Arthur Kelly. He objected to the wording of the last sentence of the second paragraph, which read, 'I am convinced that there is an opportunity to develop in this province the outstanding law school in Canada and one of the leading law schools in North America.' Kelly wrote to Smith, 'I am afraid that the Benchers might read from this sentence an intention that the Law School at Osgoode Hall should be absorbed as the indication is that there should be one Law School in

Toronto. I agree entirely that this is the result to be desired but question the wisdom of so stating at the present stage.'[20] Smith revised his draft accordingly.

The draft was presented to Premier Drew by Phillips. Phillips was the obvious choice, since he and Drew were friends and had been working closely on fund-raising activities.[21] On 8 October 1946 Drew sent letters to Phillips and J. Shirley Denison, the treasurer of the law society. The text was similar to Smith's draft.

The position of the University of Toronto in relation to legal education was brought to my mind when I noticed that the operating costs of the School of Law are estimated as $31,433.00 for the year 1946–47.

I am aware that the University of Toronto has been directly interested in the field of legal education since the Honourable W.H. Blake was appointed Professor of Law in 1843. So far as legal education is concerned, however, the profession and the public generally are more inclined to think of Osgoode Hall.

In my official capacity and also as a member of the Bar, it occurs to me that if there is to be a School of Law at the University of Toronto it should perhaps assume a more important role than it has occupied in the past. It seems possible that there is a duplication or perhaps lack of co-ordination between the two courses.

I understand that the Benchers of the Law Society have a Legal Education Committee and that there is a similar committee of the Board of Governors of the University. May I suggest the advisability of a joint committee being set up with say five representatives from each of these committees under an independent chairman, whom they would appoint, and that the joint committee consider the possibility of improving legal education under some plan of effective co-operation between the Law Society of Upper Canada and the University of Toronto.

I would be pleased to know if this suggestion commends itself to you and if so whether the Law Society would agree to take such joint action.

But something went wrong. By late October Smith had still not received a reply from the law society. He was becoming impatient. He wrote to Kennedy asking him to update his memo on the University of Toronto School of Law so that it would be current should it be needed.[22] He also wrote to Henry Borden explaining that although there was 'some ferment' in the ranks of the benchers, which indicated that they had received the premier's letter, there had been no official response.[23] This lack of response worried Smith. He did not want the matter to 'go by default' and he asked Borden to advise him on what the university's next step should be. It is not known what, if anything, Borden recommended.

While waiting for the benchers to respond, Wright and Smith, together with their wives, went on a short trip to New York City.[24] It was meant as a holiday, but Wright used one afternoon to talk shop and renew his friendship with Arthur T. Vanderbilt, the dean of the law school at New York University.[25] For almost a decade the two men had been sharing their thoughts and hopes for law reform and changes in legal education.[26] Vanderbilt was one of a number of American academics to whom Wright frequently turned for advice, support, and encouragement. Wright wanted to share with him the 'exciting plans' that he and Smith had made. Vanderbilt, pleased and supportive, promised to treat the discussion 'very confidentially.'

On their return from New York, Smith and Wright learned that the law society had established a special committee to study Osgoode Hall Law School and legal education in general. This was not the liaison committee they had encouraged Premier Drew to suggest. The new committee's mandate was to investigate the physical condition of the law school, additional facilities for students, pre-legal education, service under articles, and legal education in general. The special committee initially consisted of the treasurer of the law society, Shirley Denison (in an ex officio capacity), Percy D. Wilson, KC, C.W. Reid Bowlby, KC, Cyril F.H. Carson, KC, and John Cartwright, KC. Over the course of its deliberations the committee was expanded to eight with the addition of Gershom Mason, the new treasurer of the law society, who replaced Shirley Denison, Hamilton Cassels, the chairman of the legal education committee, H.J. McLaughlin, and Park Jamieson; Percy Wilson, the official guardian for Ontario and a man known for his diligence, integrity, and objectivity, was appointed chairman. The committee, in attempting to fulfil its broad mandate, was to receive oral and written submissions from the teaching staff at Osgoode Hall, as well as from members of the Ontario bar. It was also proposed that members of the committee visit other law schools in Canada and the United States.[27]

Wright, weary of law society special committees, saw the creation of this committee as another manoeuvre to defeat his plans.[28] Although that may have been true in part, there were reasons for appointing the committee that had nothing to do with impeding Wright's plans. Osgoode Hall was overcrowded with the influx of war veterans, and short-term measures had to be taken to accommodate the large number of students.

Moreover, in the preceding year Dean Falconbridge had convinced the legal education committee that curriculum changes were needed. Courses in tax, administrative law, and labour law had been added. The afternoon lectures had been rescheduled in the morning.[29] These temporary measures did not fully meet the concerns of Dean Falconbridge or those expressed by Wright in his 1944 submission to Lally McCarthy. In their decision to appoint another special committee, the benchers may have hoped to obtain long-term solutions to these problems.

On 2 December Wright and Smith received another indication that their plans were not welcomed by the benchers. Mike Chitty, the editor of the *Fortnightly Law Journal* and a bencher, wrote a lengthy editorial calling for continued control of legal education by lawyers. It was one more salvo in what was a long-running battle of words between Chitty and Wright.

The trend of the present type of course at the school is headed in the wrong direction. New subjects are constantly being added in the endeavour as we have said to accomplish the impossible task of teaching the student all the law. If that were the object of so-called legal education the job would be much better left to the universities where cloistered minds might live in the fond delusion that they not only could but in fact would achieve the impossible. The reason that the lawyer must retain control of the training of students for the practice of law is because the lawyer alone knows how a student must be trained to enable him to be qualified to serve the public in the practice of the law. It must be realized that the law schools have not time to educate the student. The student must come to the school with all the education he hopes to get from a school. The law schools can only give him a modicum of vocational training sufficient to enable him to go out and serve the public in the practice of the law ... [30]

Chitty made it clear that he did not want to see control of the law school in the hands of academics like Wright.

The academic school has for too long had its way because as the schools grew in size and importance it became more and more necessary to resort to full time staffs who for the most part had no practical experience. We have no quarrel with these men whose natural aim was to try and turn out students who were academic world beaters. Their reputation hinges on the reputation of the school they serve and the more individual academically-learned students they can turn out the greater their kudos among the other academicians. But that is not the concern of the governing body of the profession responsible for the school. The

Benchers' interest and responsibility is to turn out as many students as they reasonably can who are qualified to serve the public in the practice of the law and the emphasis must be on that word practice.

The timing and the nature of these remarks, and especially the references to the 'cloistered minds' of the university and the need for legal education to be controlled by the profession, must have made Smith and Wright suspect that a concerted effort was being planned to ensure that their own scheme to create a university law school did not succeed.

In early December, shortly after Chitty's editorial appeared, Smith began to think that either the benchers had not received their copy of Premier Drew's letter or that they had decided not to act on it, not realizing that the university had also received a copy. To force an official response, he decided that another copy of the letter should be sent to the benchers. Smith drafted a covering letter for Phillips to send to the law society which explained that Phillips had received the attached letter from the premier in October, but had been tardy in sending it along to the law society because he had been in England and on the continent in October and November. On 11 December Smith sent the draft to Borden, who passed it along to Phillips for his signature.[31] By 16 December the letter was sent, and it had the desired effect.[32] In late December, Shirley Denison wrote to Phillips explaining that he would bring the matter up with the law society's legal education committee in early January. On 14 January 1947 Premier Drew's letter was discussed by the committee, which recommended to Convocation that the premier's suggestion be followed. Two days later, Convocation appointed a liaison delegation consisting of Cyril Carson, John Cartwright, Shirley Denison, Gershom Mason, and Percy Wilson, all of whom were among the more powerful members of the Law Society.

It is not surprising that John Shirley Denison, the seventy-six-year-old treasurer of the law society, was chosen chairman. He had been a bencher for over fifteen years and had practised law for fifty-five years.[33] He was a quiet, soft-spoken man who was noted for his kindness to and concern for students and young lawyers. Like most of his colleagues on the committee, he had never attended university, having gone directly to Osgoode Hall from Upper Canada College. He and his colleagues on the committee were of the old school – they had graduated from Osgoode before Wright had begun to teach there. Denison considered himself knowledgeable about legal education at Osgoode Hall, since he had lectured there part-time between 1910 and 1925, but his views on legal education had been formulated at a time when the teaching of black-letter law was the norm. Although he had written two articles in the early 1920s criticizing the school's poor facilities,[34] he was not an ally of Wright's. He was firmly convinced that 'good office training is the best experience the student can have.'[35] When, in 1938, Denison had expressed his views on Osgoode Hall to Wright, he contended that what was being done at Harvard Law School had 'very little relation to our own Law School problems.'[36] Unlike Harvard, which could choose bright young men and 'fit them to be leaders of their various bars in their several states,' Osgoode Hall must 'train all that come to us to be decent, efficient and useful practitioners in their various niches in the community.'

By 1947 Ontario and Osgoode Hall had changed, but Denison's opinions had not. He was still of the view that '90% of teaching is the impact of personality upon personality: methods don't matter.' He was critical of Wright's pride and his advocacy of American teaching methods; he considered that what was required for successful teaching was 'some humility and a sense of humour: I think sometimes that humility and humour have fled from our halls of learning, as "pedagogy" as a science has made its fatal approach.'[37] As Denison was later to admit to Percy Wilson, he saw himself as having 'a conservative mind' at a time when the world was 'crazy for change.' These were the attitudes of the man who led the law society's delegation – attitudes that no argument from Wright or Smith would change.

Gershom W. Mason, the chairman of the legal education committee, was a powerful figure among the benchers. At sixty-nine, he was the senior partner in the firm of Mason, Foulds, Davidson and Gale. In the spring of 1947, when Denison's term as treasurer of the law society ended, Mason was elected to succeed him. After his graduation from high school, Mason had taught elementary school and taken courses at Queen's University by correspondence. Eventually, he attended Queen's University full-time and received his BA. He was a member of the Queen's board of trustees, and had received an honorary LL D from the university. A man of deep religious conviction, he did not drink, smoke, swear, or engage in small talk, and he prided himself on being a man of integrity and honour. Despite his university training, Mason too was of the old school and shared Denison's view of the proper nature and function of the law school.

Cyril F.H. Carson, forty-six, was significantly younger than Denison and Mason. He was no less powerful a figure, however, and he shared their attitudes towards legal education. Bora Laskin once described him as a man who took 'the old fashioned approach ... that the only way to become a good lawyer was ... to go through a law office.'[38] This was, of course, the route Carson himself had taken. Like Denison, he had gone to Osgoode Hall straight from high school. He had excelled in his legal studies, and had won the gold medal for his year. In 1921 he was called to the bar, and went into practice with the firm of Tilley, Johnston, Thomson and Parmenter. The senior partner in the firm, Norman Tilley, perhaps the most outstanding lawyer in Ontario, had been one of the principal authors of the special committee report of 1935. It seems likely that Tilley's conservative views of legal education influenced Carson. Tilley has been described as a 'very hard fisted character in court and out.'[44] Like his senior, Carson was a man of strong views. He was a large, ponderous man who took himself seriously and prided himself on his methodical thoroughness. When he came to a conclusion it was extremely difficult for anyone to change his mind. In argument he pounded his points home one by one. Despite his relative youth, he had been a bencher for eleven years and was considered one of the dominant figures in the law society. In 1950, he would follow in the footsteps of Denison and Mason and become treasurer of the law society. Significantly, the three most conservative members of this delegation would hold the law society's highest office for the next eleven years.

The other two members of the delegation, John Robert Cartwright and Percy Dixon Wilson, were to prove more sympathetic and less intractable in their dealings with the university. But they lacked the power and influence of Denison, Mason, and Carson. Cartwright, who later became chief justice of Canada, was fifty-one and had only recently been elected a bencher. He had never attended university, but went directly from Upper Canada College to Osgoode Hall, from which he graduated in 1920 as the silver medallist. Cartwright was quiet, courteous, and extremely talented. He was in practice with the firm of Smith, Rae, Greer and Cartwright, and made frequent use of Caesar Wright as a consultant.[39] He and Wright were friends and members of the same fraternity. Although Cartwright was highly regarded as a legal practitioner, he had never played a major role in Convocation.[40]

Percy Wilson, who had held the post of official guardian of Ontario since 1937, had first been elected a bencher in 1941. He had been called to the bar in 1913 and had been named king's counsel in 1934. Wilson was a slow-speaking, sensible, down-to-earth person, and was highly respected throughout the profession. He was not as powerful as either

Mason or Carson, but he exerted a moderating influence. Of the benchers' delegation, he would prove to be the most willing to compromise.

In a letter of 20 January W. Earl Smith, the secretary of the law society, informed Phillips of the establishment and composition of the liaison delegation.[41] Phillips was pleased to hear the news. He told Earl Smith that the University of Toronto board of governors had also appointed a delegation, and he proposed that the two groups meet on 4 February at Simcoe Hall, the administrative building of the university. (He was quick to add that his committee 'would be glad to meet in any place which is more convenient for your committee.')

The first meeting of the joint committee of benchers and university governors achieved little, other than to acquaint the members with each other and to give each side some indication of the other's concerns.[42] To facilitate more substantive discussions in the future, each side undertook to provide details of their law school's operation.

Sidney Smith was determined to make the negotiations of the joint committee a success. Before the first meeting he had met with the university delegation to plan strategy.[43] The day after the meeting, Smith asked Kennedy to supply him with copies of the 1947–8 law school calendar, a revised memo on the workings of the law school, registration figures, and other relevant materials.[44] By 19 February every member of the joint committee had copies of these documents.[45] Shortly after the materials were distributed, Shirley Denison sent committee members the Osgoode Hall student handbook for 1946–7, along with a memorandum on legal education. The memorandum was less a description than a historical justification of the existing scheme of education at Osgoode Hall.[46] It left little doubt that the benchers still placed great importance on the retention of concurrent office training.

While the sincerity of the benchers' beliefs cannot be doubted, there was also a strategic importance to their support of such training. Denison wrote to Cyril Carson, 'If concurrent office training were divorced from Law School work, it might be quite a strong argument that the University could handle as well, or better, the academic portion of a lawyers training.'[47] Although the benchers, at the suggestion of Premier Drew, had agreed to negotiate, they believed that any problems that existed in the legal education system were merely temporary, a result of the influx of war veterans. Tinkering might be in order, but major reform was not. Above all, the law society did not intend to give up its control over legal education.

While Sidney Smith was handling negotiations with the law society, Wright and the other full-time teachers at Osgoode Hall were busy giving evidence before the special legal education committee. In January 1947 the teaching staff received a list of the matters to be considered by the special committee.[48] These included such topics as whether the school should be part-time or full-time, the structure of the curriculum, the hours of lectures, entrance requirements, the use of oral examinations, and, perhaps most important, who should control the school. Full-time members of the teaching staff were asked to appear and present their views. Dean Falconbridge, the first member of the Osgoode Hall staff to do so,[49] advocated a full-time three-year program followed by a year of office training. He told the committee that he would be seventy-two in June of that year, and while he expected to teach for a few more years and to continue as dean, he could no longer carry the burden of the administration of the school. He made it clear that Caesar Wright was his logical successor and the best man available for the deanship. He also stated that if Wright was not chosen as his successor, the full-time staff were likely to resign. He suggested that Wright be made vice-dean immediately and dean in September 1948. He also suggested that Wright be permitted to attend meetings of the special legal education committee.

During the week of 3 February Wright appeared twice before the special committee to present his ideas on legal education.[50] He reported that he had been made even more aware of the need for change during the latter part of January. He had corresponded with Professor T.R. Powell, the chairman of the graduate studies committee of Harvard Law School, in an effort to convince Harvard to accept an Osgoode Hall student for graduate work.[51] The student was refused admission. Wright was dismayed that his alma mater would not accept his students. Powell explained to Wright that Harvard did not think that Osgoode Hall met the standards of the Association of American Law Schools. Harvard was willing to admit Osgoode graduates who had attended the University of Toronto's undergraduate law program. Knowing Wright's feelings about Kennedy's school, it is not surprising that he was 'amazed at this attitude' on Harvard's part. He informed Powell: 'The effect of your ruling would be to bar the great majority of law graduates in Ontario since by far the larger proportion of such graduates take, and in my opinion wisely, courses in their Arts work of a wider range than is possible in the University of Toronto's present law course, which is based to a large extent on the English system.'

In a letter of 27 January, Wright asked and was given Powell's permission to show their correspondence to the special committee. He held the correspondence in reserve until March,[52] however, preferring to make other, more basic points at his early meetings with the committee.[53] He recognized that facilitating graduate study was not a principal concern of the benchers; his immediate goal was to establish 'a full-time school with proper faculty control and responsibility.' If he was to achieve this, he would have to make the members of the committee aware of the broader benefits of such a school. That such a school would make graduate study at Harvard easier would not impress the 'hard-boiled practitioners' on the special committee. In those early meetings, Wright re-emphasized the main points of his 1944 memo, revised copies of which were presented to committee members. He explained why it was necessary to give students a better academic grounding in law in order to prepare them to serve a rapidly changing society. He also explained that lawyers had to be educated to think about the law so that they would not be confounded when the legal rules they had been taught were changed, as they surely would be in the future. He appealed to the benchers' role as trustees of the society's interest in legal education (a responsibility the benchers were fond of stressing). Wright concentrated all his efforts on achieving a full-time school and faculty responsibility, and decided, 'for purely political reasons,'[54] to leave the issue of affiliation with the University of Toronto to Smith and his committee.[55]

Much to Wright's surprise, during his second appearance before the special committee, he was asked to prepare 'facts and figures as to costs, size of faculty, building equipment, classrooms, etc. on [his] proposed scheme.' He was unprepared for such a request, and, having little experience in such things, he turned to his American confidants, Dean Pound of Harvard and Dean Vanderbilt of New York University, for assistance.[56]

The possibility of a full-time school was in itself, Wright explained to Vanderbilt, 'such a complete change in the Ontario picture' as to be 'revolutionary.' Aware of the attitude of such powerful benchers as Denison and Mason towards a full-time school, Wright told Vanderbilt: 'We will need all the help we can get.' Benchers such as Mike Chitty were ardently opposed to Wright's and Smith's proposals. Chitty had been busy in those first few weeks of 1947. In the 17 January issue of *The Fortnightly Law Journal* he again wrote a lengthy editorial on legal education.[57] He praised a scheme of 'vocational training' for lawyers, and implicitly criticized Wright's suggestions that more emphasis be placed on academic training. 'The real question,' he stated, 'is how to turn out the largest number of properly qualified practitioners or perhaps even only to see that no unqualified practitioners are turned out as being qualified.' He added that all modern legal education 'is so-called because it is not education at all but simply vocational training.'

Wright undoubtedly found Chitty's statement that legal education was 'not education at all' ludicrous. Nevertheless, Chitty's views could not be lightly dismissed. They were the views of a respected member of the bar, an intelligent, thinking person who himself took an 'academic' approach to law, as evidenced by his many publications. Moreover, many other benchers shared his views, powerful men such as Denison, Mason, Carson, and Hamilton Cassels. These men took their responsibility to society seriously. They wished to ensure that those called to the bar were capable of practising law, that they could draft pleadings, convey property, and draw up wills. These were things that one learned by doing, as they themselves had learned to do them. They approached with caution any proposal that would put less emphasis on the practical aspects of training for legal practice. They were of the view expressed by Chitty, in another editorial, 'that the lawyer with only academic training is not qualified to practise, whereas the lawyer with only a practical training is of some service to the public.'[58] Wright later summarized the situation: the leadership of the law society was 'unduly conservative' and representative of the thought of an earlier era.[59]

In early March 1947, Chief Justice Robertson again appeared on the scene. Out of a sense of duty, he agreed to act as chairman of the joint committee.[60] Smith was delighted; he still regarded Robertson as a potential ally. Robertson, however, was not to prove as supportive as Smith and Wright expected him to be.

On 26 March the joint committee held its third meeting in the boardroom of Simcoe Hall.[61] Like the two previous meetings, this one did not achieve anything substantive. Discussion continued to be general, with the law society members emphasizing the importance of service under articles and the value to students of the concurrent system. Denison was disturbed by the meeting. He later wrote, 'If I can properly appreciate the tenor of the suggestions coming from the University side, some quite drastic changes ... are in the minds of some members of this joint committee.'[62] Smith too was becoming increasingly impatient, and was concerned about the committee's lack of progress. He told the university delegates that 'we must soon get down to the consideration of concrete proposals ... the time for vague and general discussion is past.'[63] To further the discussion of concrete proposals, Smith prepared a memo, which he appended to his letter. The memo set out the choices available to the joint committee. First, the law society could abolish Osgoode Hall Law School and leave legal education to the university, as had been done at Dalhousie Law School and at the universities of Saskatchewan, Alberta, and British Columbia.[64] For historical reasons, and because of the law society's responsibility and experience, he knew this proposal would not be acceptable to the benchers. Second, the university could abolish its school of law and leave legal education entirely to Osgoode Hall. Third, the university and the law society could establish an autonomous institution governed by a board of trustees, as had been done in Manitoba. The board would consist of representatives from the university and the law society, and would have an independent chairman. The university would grant a bachelor of laws degree, and the law society would admit the graduates to practice. Instruction in academic subjects could be given on the university campus, and Osgoode Hall would be used for clinical instruction. The fourth possibility, a variation of the third, had originally been suggested at the last meeting of the joint committee by Arthur Kelly. Osgoode Hall Law School could become affiliated with the university, just as certain hospitals were affiliated with the Faculty of Medicine.[65] Under the terms of an agreement with the university, Osgoode Hall would offer instruction in clinical subjects, such as criminal and civil procedure, evidence, and real estate. The university would teach academic subjects, such as torts, contracts, and philosophy of law. The university professors and the Osgoode Hall teaching staff would be cross-appointed and would report to the same dean. It was clear that Smith saw only the third and fourth choices as viable. He, like Wright, was certain that the university had much to contribute to legal education.

In his memo Smith included the two points on which Wright had lobbied the special committee: under any proposal the teaching staff must have greater responsibility than was then the case at Osgoode Hall, and the students must be required to devote their full time to their legal studies. On these two issues Smith and Wright presented a common front.

The joint committee decided in April that Smith and Percy Wilson would work together to prepare a plan for discussion.[66] The first meaningful discussion between Smith and a bencher would finally take place. On the evening of 6 May, Wilson met with Smith and discussed Smith's proposals.[67] Wilson seemed to favour an unwieldy scheme that incorporated aspects of Smith's third and fourth alternatives without adopting either of them in its entirety. Wilson seemed to want the two schools to continue as at least semi-autonomous institutions, each under its respective governing body. The teaching staff at Osgoode Hall and the law professors at the University of Toronto would constitute a single faculty council under a single dean. The council would be responsible for academic affairs; its decisions and recommendations, however, would have to be sent to a joint committee on academic policy composed of representatives of the university Senate and the law society. This body would in turn make recommendations to the Senate and the law society. Non-academic matters would be dealt with by a joint administrative committee consisting of representatives from the law society and the university's board of governors. This committee, like its academic counterpart, would be empowered only to make recommendations to the law society and the university administration. It was unclear what would happen if only one body approved a joint committee recommendation; presumably, unanimity would be required for any recommendation to be implemented.

Under this compromise scheme, students would attend school full time, but would have to travel back and forth between the University of Toronto and Osgoode Hall for their 'academic' and 'clinical' classes. Office work would be undertaken during summer vacations and in a twelve-month articling period after graduation. The university would pay a part of the dean's $10,000-per-year salary and the salaries of eight of the ten full-time faculty members. It would also provide teaching facilities for its own courses, a law library, and necessary office and secretarial services.

Smith drafted a memo setting out the compromise proposal. Wilson wanted it made clear that the existing admission requirements for Osgoode Hall would apply to the two schools: high school matriculants were to be accepted as candidates for the bachelor of laws degree.[68] Smith, somewhat surprisingly, stated that he had not contemplated changing the existing admission qualifications.[69] Wright, of course, felt that law students needed a good liberal arts background, but he regarded admission standards as a secondary issue.

At a lunch in July, Smith and Wright agreed to hold onto the memo they were jointly preparing until the next meeting in the fall, at which time Wilson would present the compromise proposal orally.[70]

On 7 October 1947 Wilson and Smith presented their proposal to the joint committee.[71] It was decided, however, that the best course would be to mimeograph the memo outlining the proposal and distribute it, on a confidential basis, to members of the joint committee who could then study it and prepare comments. Giving the committee members time to think about the proposal and its rationale would make a quick rejection less likely. Smith later explained to Phillips, who had been unable to attend the meeting, that there seemed to be some limited support for the proposal: 'I have reason to believe that John Cartwright and Wilson are favourably disposed to the general ideas embodied in the memorandum while, on the other hand, the Chairman of the Joint Committee, the Chief Justice, and perhaps the Treasurer of the Law Society, Mr. Mason, have obvious doubts with respect to any co-operation between the Law Society and the University. Mr. Denison, I understand, is fundamentally opposed to any liaison. No one seems to know how Cyril Carson, the other member of the Law Society panel, will react.'[72] Smith told Phillips that his plan was to have Chief Justice Robertson call a meeting to deal specifically with his memorandum. It would then be obvious whether 'the representatives of the Law Society are adamant in their refusal to discuss the exploration of avenues towards co-operation.' If they were, it would be useless to waste any more time 'talking around the subject,' and Premier Drew could be so informed. When Arthur Kelly learned of Smith's views, he told him, 'I feel that the attitude of the Benchers is to evade a decision and that our best policy is to force them to take a position.'[73]

Smith got his meeting on 4 December,[74] but it did not prove to be as decisive as he had hoped. The Wilson proposal was discussed, but the law society representatives again refused to take a firm stand. They said that they had not yet been able to discuss the memorandum, a reminder that the benchers, as senior practitioners, had much more on their minds than the reform of legal education. Carson and Cartwright had been away (Carson because he was appearing before the Supreme Court of Canada, and Cartwright because he was prosecuting the Gouzenko-related spy trials). In addition, the law society's special committee on education had not yet reported, an omission that handicapped the discussions.[75] There now seemed little reason for Smith to be hopeful.

Wright too was becoming discouraged. In November, he told Horace Read, who was then teaching at Minnesota, that 'nothing had been achieved,' and, as for the results, 'your guess is as good as mine.'[76] Wright had other reasons to be unhappy. With Osgoode Hall flooded with veterans, his workload was immense. He was teaching six days a week, and had no time for outside legal activities. Because of his crowded schedule, he had had to resign from the Uniform Law Commission.

Moreover, the work was taking its toll on his health. Twice in that 'rather hectic fall' he was away from school for extended periods because of illness.[77]

In mid-December Wright got some good news: Percy Wilson and Hamilton Cassels of the law society's special committee had visited Columbia and New York University law schools in New York as he had suggested. When Wright had heard in late November that such a trip was imminent, he had written to Vanderbilt, who stressed the need for clinical work in law schools and who had some admiration for Osgoode Hall's method, and who, Wright feared, might inadvertently encourage the benchers to stress practical work at the expense of the academic. Wright's lengthy letter to Vanderbilt provides a glimpse of his thinking in late 1947. In Ontario, he said, legal education was in the hands of members of the practising bar who had never attended or even seen a 'proper law school.' The result of such control was a loss of academic freedom for Ontario law teachers. Wright acknowledged Vanderbilt's belief in the desirability of clinical work at law schools, and stated that he too saw the value of such work; but the benchers' lack of awareness of the u.s. experience with full-time academic law schools would cause them to misinterpret Vanderbilt's position. He did not want the benchers seeing Vanderbilt's call for more clinical work as some sort of justification of the existing Ontario scheme of legal education. Echoing the remarks of Felix Frankfurter more than a decade before, Wright pointed out to Vanderbilt that the benchers were in about the same position with regard to legal education as the American bar had been at the time of Langdell's appointment to Harvard.[78] Vanderbilt assured Wright that his 'instructions' would be carried out on how to handle the benchers 'sympathetically and implicitly.'[79]

Wilson and Cassels were treated courteously during their brief visit to the two New York law schools, and they were afforded the opportunity to see the American university law school system in operation. They do not seem to have been impressed. When the committee's final report appeared in January 1949, there was little mentioned of the American visit. Some of the benchers, at least, were convinced that Ontario required a unique solution to its problems of legal education and could not profitably adopt a scheme from another jurisdiction.

January 1948 brought a sudden development: John Falconbridge, pleading old age and the heavy workload of the deanship of Osgoode Hall, expressed an 'urgent desire to be relieved of the office and duties of Dean forthwith.'[80] One has to wonder about the timing of this resignation, coming as it did when Smith and Wright had virtually abandoned hope for a negotiated settlement between the university and the benchers. Although Falconbridge had earlier discussed his retirement with the benchers' special committee, his resignation came unexpectedly in mid-term, when the special committee was still studying the problems of the law school. Wright had long thought that he himself should be dean of Osgoode Hall. Was Falconbridge in failing health, or was he acting at Wright's suggestion in an attempt to put pressure on the benchers to either accept Wright's proposals or declare their opposition openly? There is no doubt that Falconbridge had long been sympathetic to Wright's ideas. Perhaps he had finally been convinced that with the younger, more dynamic Wright in the deanship, the benchers would have to reach some accommodation with him.

Falconbridge's resignation put the benchers who favoured a more practical law school in a difficult position.[81] Wright was the only serious candidate for the job who was on the full-time staff at Osgoode Hall. He had been teaching there for twenty years, and had a world-wide reputation as a legal scholar. Besides Falconbridge and Wright, the only other full-time teachers at Osgoode were Bora Laskin and Stanley Edwards – John Willis had left Osgoode in the spring of 1947 to join the International Monetary Fund in New York. Laskin, although bright and capable, had been teaching for only seven years. Moreover, he was very close to Wright and it is unlikely that he would have accepted the deanship had it been offered him. Edwards, a twenty-six-year-old Albertan, had just come to Osgoode Hall after obtaining his LL M at Harvard.

In February Wright met with Percy Wilson, the chairman of the special committee, Gershom Mason, the treasurer of the law society, and Hamilton Cassels, the chairman of the legal education committee.[82] He was asked whether, as dean, he would co-operate with the benchers. Wright described his response in this way: 'I knew, of course, that some Benchers were opposed to a full-time school, but had no means of knowing what the attitude of Convocation was, nor could I have known since the Special Committee was considering the matter and presumably the issue had not been settled. I indicated that it was unsatisfactory to appoint a Dean unless policies had been clearly settled, but I did say that I would co-operate with the Benchers until such time as their actions became completely incompatible and inconsistent with my views, at which time I would resign.'[83]

Wright later said that, in response to his doubts about the advisability of appointing a dean before a clear policy regarding legal education had been established, he was given assurances that he would be able to sit in on the sessions of the special committee or participate in some way in the work of that committee. It was on this understanding, Wright said, that he accepted the offer of the deanship.

He assumed the post at the beginning of March. If he and Falconbridge had hoped to force the benchers to accept his proposals as part of filling the vacancy, they were disappointed. Nevertheless, Wright, whose strong views on legal education were well known, had become dean, and Osgoode Hall might now finally become a full-time school. Already first year was full-time, with first-year 'practice groups' having replaced the requirement of office work.[84] Moreover, the special committee had asked Wright the year before for spending estimates for a full-time school.[85] These were encouraging signs.

If Wright had reason to be optimistic about achieving his immediate goal of a full-time law school, such was not the case with the longer-range goal of a professional university school. It seemed highly unlikely in early March that any negotiated settlement would be reached between the benchers and the university. This proved to be the case when the meeting held on 18 March again failed to produce any agreement and the joint committee was abandoned.[86]

Dean Wright was asked by the law society's special committee on legal education to submit a summary of his views on curriculum, staff, and other academic matters. Wright called a meeting of the teaching staff, both full-time and part-time, on 12 March. They gathered in the faculty library and discussed each of their courses and possible curricular changes.[87] This was the first of the monthly faculty meetings Wright called as dean.[88] By 7 April Wright had produced an eighteen-page memorandum reiterating his views on legal education and discussing how they could be put into practice.[89] Again he explained that he wanted a full-time school with a full-time teaching staff that had responsibility for academic matters. Office training was to be replaced by clinical instruction at the law school and a one-year articling period after law school. Wright's proposed curriculum will sound familiar to modern law students. He wanted the first-year practice groups moved to second and third years, and the first year dedicated exclusively to academic study. During first year, the student was to take 'certain basic concept courses' that would introduce him to large bodies of law and show him that 'all legal questions are problem questions, that there are no "right" answers, and that his proper function is to analyze, diagnose and seek solutions within the frame of an existing technique.' There would be year-long courses in contracts, torts, property, and remedies, and half-year courses in criminal law and agency. Legal writing skills would be taught in small groups. Second-year students would take year-long courses in constitutional law, corporate law (which was then being taught in a 'sketchy 36 hour course ... given by a part-time lecturer'), commercial law, and, perhaps, security transactions (in which Wright included both mortgages and forms of personal property security). Wills and trusts might be moved from third year to second year, and a half-year course in family law would be offered. Wright was willing to permit students to choose from a group of optional courses in third year. Some subjects, such as administrative law and conflicts, would be required. Optional courses might include tax, labour, corporate finance, competition law, industrial property, consumer relations, 'and eventually Jurisprudence, Comparative Law and Public International Law.'

Wright noted that he wished immediately to obtain permission to increase the hours of instruction and to hire two or three more full-time lecturers. Ultimately, he wanted eight to ten full-time teachers. The money for these teachers and the other changes would come from the annual profit the law society realized on its legal education activities – estimated by Wright to be $200,000. If this amount proved insufficient, then either student tuition fees or law society membership fees would have to be increased.

Wright stated that, ideally, a university degree should be required to gain admittance. In this way, 'we could avoid the wastage and the large percentage of failures which we have in the first year.' For the time being, however, he was 'satisfied to insist on the maintenance of a rigorous standard within the school.'

Although Wright made his views known to the benchers, he did not believe that he could persuade them to adopt his proposals. On 20 April he wrote to Horace Read, who had declined an offer to join the faculty at Osgoode Hall[90] unless arrangements could be made with the University of Toronto to make it a university law school, saying,

It was good of you to write me as you did and you may be sure that I fully appreciate your reasons for the line which you took. In fact, if it is any comfort to you, I think there seems very little hope of any effective co-operation with the University and within the last couple of days my expectations of establishing a full-time school have received a severe jolt from the governing body who seem disinclined to depart from the practices of their primordial ancestors. I am not completely despondent, however, and it may be that things will be worse before they get better. It is with that in mind that I am particularly grateful to have your letter, and I know that both Sidney Smith and myself would be very happy to see the culmination of the plans which you indicate are of interest to you. Whether those plans will be reached peacefully or as the result of bloody revolution is another question which time alone can solve. I will keep you advised or perhaps I should say you will be notified whether I return bearing my shield or on it.

The battle that Wright contemplated did not come immediately. Indeed, the benchers made some important concessions voluntarily. In June, Wright was given permission to hire two new lecturers, to extend the school term from ten to fifteen weeks, and to add a third hour of lectures per day.[91] Mike Chitty later wrote that the benchers 'unwisely' made those concessions, because, 'having appointed him as Dean ... they felt themselves forced to bow to his demands.'[92] If such was the case, it was an attitude that was not to last long. Significantly, the benchers did not ask Wright to sit in on the special committee's sessions, or take any further part in their deliberations. The special committee's decision would be made without any further direct input from him.

Wright was resolved, however, to have at least an indirect impact on that decision. He soon began to take whatever steps he could as dean to put his ideas into practice. Walter Williston, his first staff appointment, was a young practitioner who with Arthur Kelly had organized and supervised the practice-group program at Osgoode Hall.[93] Wright also managed to rehire John Willis. Furthermore, he implemented his policy of maintaining 'a rigorous standard within the school.' As if to prove his point that the present admission standards resulted in 'wastage' and a 'large percentage of failures,' he and his staff failed 104 out of the 323 first-year students, and 90 of the remaining 219 had to write supplementary exams.[94] This 'purge' of the first-year class and his other actions as dean had the effect of bringing the problems of legal education to the attention of the public. Wright certainly succeeded in attracting publicity. In July the Toronto papers were full of stories about the exam results. Wright was on holiday at his cottage and was unavailable for comment. Some of the benchers saw Wright's moves as a way of pressuring them into accepting his proposals, and said as much to the newspapers. An unnamed member of the legal education committee was quoted as saying in one newspaper story, 'There is no doubt the present Dean is out to make a full-time school of Osgoode Hall. That has never been my viewpoint or that of many Benchers.' The same bencher was also reported as saying that the examination results were a reflection of the 'academic and theoretical outlook of the present faculty.' He added, '[The law society's job] 'is not to teach anyone anything. Our job is to qualify them to practise law.' For the first time, the benchers were making public their fundamental disagreement with Wright – and their determination not to be bullied by him.[95]

The examination results led the legal education committee of the law society to call a special meeting to investigate the failures, but little came of it. The students demanded the Ontario government set up a royal commission and talked of launching a Supreme Court action against the law society. This too proved fruitless. Veterans appealed to the Department of Veteran Affairs, but with no success.

Wright was not without his supporters. The *Financial Post*, in an editorial of 24 July 1948, stated that the number of failures was 'a normal-to-low per cent flunking in any self-respecting institution dedicated to "higher learning." ' In response to the benchers' complaints, the editorial asked rhetorically:

Do they want a lower reputation for Osgoode Hall as a 'seat of learning'? Do they want to let youths without the 'stuff' or without the willingness to apply themselves continue in the delusion that the law is for them?

The public has in its own interest taken over the education of its doctors, engineers and most professional men. In Ontario, the training of lawyers has so far been left in the hands of the legal 'trade union.'

Complaints that Osgoode Hall standards aren't low enough justifies the public wondering how well the responsibility of training our lawyers and judges is being carried out.

While the controversy was raging around him, Wright was ill with gall-bladder problems. He spent much of August in hospital, and in September he underwent surgery.[96] He had been home only a short while when his incision became infected and he was forced to return to hospital. He did not begin work until 25 October. Nevertheless, he continued to direct the implementation of his new policies from his sick-bed.

The law students who were sympathetic to Wright's ideas found themselves in a difficult position. In second and third year they were expected to spend most of their day at a law office; Wright's new curriculum, however, required them to spend more and more time preparing for classes. In their words, they were 'caught between the upper and nether millstones.' The following editorial appeared in *Obiter Dicta* in mid-October:

The new Osgoode Hall, with its Harvard Law School complex, is regarded almost with scorn by many practising lawyers. In turn the burden of work prescribed by an increasingly heavy syllabus certainly disregards the time which must be devoted to practical training! Our Law School is becoming the classic illustration of new wine in a very old bottle. We have talented instructors lecturing on an inadequate time schedule to overly large groups of students who have not prepared their work. We have hard-working principals demanding an equal standard of industry in their offices, and howls of protest go up when time off is asked to study for examinations. 'When I was at Osgoode I didn't need four weeks to pass exams.' But Osgoode is not a legal kindergarten. Today, if a student is adequately prepared, it indicates either exceptional ability or, more probably, time spent in school work at the expense of office work. Real education requires more than uncritically attended lectures; it requires study and thought on the part of the student. Honest study and thought are deliberate processes which demand leisure time and a fresh mind. Under the present circumstances a student who has leisure time or a fresh mind is either failing his duty to his principal or is blessed with the endurance of a dray horse. It is just conceivable that two schools of thought, one determined to foster legal education in its broadest sense, and the other clinging to an incompatible system, have both had their way without the necessary corollary of giving ground on one side or the other. Whatever the case may be the result is painfully illogical.

The editorial concluded, 'If something isn't done soon, there should not be undue dismay if the plea for help makes itself heard beyond the walls of the mill.'

The Toronto *Globe and Mail* picked up the story in its issue of 20 October. The newest member of the teaching staff, Walter Williston, was quoted as saying, 'Students can't possibly do justice to their studies or their office work under the present setup.' He added that if articling followed law school, students could be dispersed across the province. As it was, they had to be crowded into Toronto offices.' Kennedy, whose planned retirement in the summer of 1949 had already been announced, was quoted as saying that the law school should be part of the university. Arthur Kelly was quoted as being in favour of a full-time school. He cited the practical considerations of a practising lawyer: 'I would rather have one student full-time than three students part-time. He is more valuable to the lawyer, and his work is not broken up by dashing off to lectures.' Not surprisingly, Gershom Mason, the treasurer of the law society, disagreed; the same newspaper report quoted him as saying that the students were exaggerating the amount of work required of them and that 'office practice and school work should be simultaneous.'

When Wright returned to work after his illness, he was weak and hardly in condition to fight with the law society. Nevertheless, he began to speak publicly in favour of the long-awaited reform of legal education. At the midwinter meeting of the Canadian Bar Association, he sharply attacked the existing educational system.

In December, Gershom Mason met with Wright in an effort to get him to stop his public criticisms. The reform of legal education was still being studied, and many benchers considered Wright's public attacks disloyal and improper. Nevertheless, on 14 January Wright delivered a blistering denunciation of Ontario legal education to the York County Bar Association. He began that speech with a biblical quotation: 'And he will be a wild man: his hand will be against every man's hand against him: and he will dwell in the presence of his brethren.'[97] By this time, Wright was frustrated and upset; the special committee had been study-ing the matter for two years. He was certain that the only solution to the problems legal education was facing was to adopt his scheme, and he was tired of trying unsuccessfully to convince the benchers of that fact. He had decided to take his case to the public.

In the speech Wright was at his provocative, polemical best. He stated that Ontario's 'law schools have never been given the opportunity of doing a decent job.' The legal education scheme was not working, but he 'refuse[d] to be charged and found lacking for inability to work a system which we have never been permitted to operate.' He contended that the law schools were 'infested by narrow professionalism.' One heard 'much of the teaching of the existing rules of law,' he said, and 'if this be the memorization of text-book rules they could be learned by a parrot and persons advocating this [approach] have not yet wished to admit parrots as such.' He explained that if all that was desired was to teach law students 'where to find or manipulate rules,' then he would be advocating a cookbook approach: 'It is not yours to reason why – you follow the instructions.' Reflecting on his own legal training and the lack of a centre for legal research in Canada, Wright asked, 'Must we in Canada send men to foreign countries to consider ... questions [of legal reform] and have them return to butt their heads into a stone wall of professional indifference?'

This was Wright's last speech as dean of Osgoode Hall Law School. Within the week, he resigned. At last, Caesar Wright was going to get the public debate he had long been trying to provoke.

8

Confrontation

The benchers' special committee on legal education met on 30 December 1948 to decide what recommendations should be made to the January Convocation.[1] The key issue was whether to adopt Wright's proposal of a full-time school or to retain the existing scheme of a part-time school and concurrent office training. The special committee had been collecting information and opinions for over two years; they had met with all of the full-time teachers as well as two student representatives (R.W. Macaulay and W.L.N. Somerville), three practitioners (John Arnup, Walter Williston, and Cecil Robinson), and three professors (Horace Read, Moffatt Hancock, and J.A. Corry). They had read written submissions from Mike Chitty, Arthur Kelly (on the oral examinations), Caesar Wright, Osgoode Hall students, and several angry practitioners; they had received questionnaire replies from seven provincial law societies; and several committee members had visited u.s. law schools.[2] Now, a number of things seemed clear: Ontario was virtually alone in requiring concurrent articling and law school attendance; the concurrent system was not functioning well; and full-time law teachers, whether on staff at Osgoode Hall or elsewhere, favoured a full-time academic program, as did the students at Osgoode Hall. The committee had also learned that at least some practitioners were adamantly opposed to more academic study at the expense of practical training. It was now time for the eight members of the committee to decide what should be done.

When it came time to vote on the issue, the committee split into three groups. Gershom Mason, Cyril Carson, Hamilton Cassels, and H.J. McLaughlin strongly favoured the existing concurrent system. Percy Wilson and John Cartwright were equally convinced that the time had come for a full-time school. The other two members of the committee, Park Jamieson and Reid Bowlby, both of whom were known as sensible, conciliatory individuals, suggested that it might be best to give a full-time school a try, but they both had some serious reservations.

After discussion and further meetings, it was decided that a separate report representing each of the three divergent views would be presented to Convocation on 20 January.[3] The 'majority' report was prepared by Hamilton Cassels, the chairman of the legal education committee. Cassels, known from his university football days as 'Laddie,' was a conservative bencher of the old school, and was unshakeable once he had made up his mind. 'Minority' reports were prepared by Percy Wilson and Park Jamieson.[4]

The 'majority' report was, in a polite fashion, highly critical of Wright and his supporters. It was more a profession of faith in the existing system than an objective appraisal of the facts gathered by the committee. The report rested on two basic propositions. First, 'there was no fundamental difference in the situation since the report of a special committee was adopted by Convocation on February 21, 1935.' The belief, expressed in 1935, that legal education had become too theoretical and needed a greater emphasis on practical training to create a balanced system of instruction was reiterated. Second, 'the situation in Ontario differed from that in any other jurisdiction in Canada and the United States.' Therefore, it was irrelevant that Ontario was largely alone in North America in requiring the concurrent system. No evidence was given to support either of these two propositions.

While the 'majority' conceded that Ontario had some large centres that permitted a degree of legal specialization, they believed that 'the vast majority of the profession ... entered into general practice.' The main task of the law society was 'to provide a good general training in Law and Practice.' They acknowledged that there were defects in the functioning of the concurrent system, but attributed these 'to the extraordinary condition resulting from the war,' and stated that they would 'largely disappear when the situation became more normal.' They criticized the teaching staff for requiring 'a degree of research and study beyond the capabilities of the average student,' and suggested that the disagreement between the teaching staff and the benchers over the desirability of a full-time school was detrimental to the students. The teachers should not 'have given public expression to their opinions'; the benchers 'must be able to count on the loyal co-operation of the staff.' In a scarcely veiled threat, they recommended that 'steps ... be taken immediately to remedy this situation.' What they had in mind is unclear. Part of the problem, they believed, was that the teaching staff wished to follow an American rather than an English model. This they attributed to the teachers' American training. They recommended the hiring of 'a lecturer who is a member of the English bar.' The majority report concluded with a nine-point program:

1 That a system of concurrent law school and practical training be continued and that no change be made in the present entrance requirements or the length of service under articles prescribed for graduate or matriculation students.
2 That the present curriculum of the law school be reviewed by the legal education committee in collaboration with the dean and that such modifications and changes be made therein as may be deemed necessary to provide a better balanced course of training as between the academic and practical branches of the course.
3 That the course of the law school be limited to 10 50-minute lectures a week, of which two will be held each day from Monday to Friday inclusive at 9 A.M. and 4:10 P.M.
4 That the practice group system be continued for first-year students.
5 That steps be taken as expeditiously as possible, having regard to the problems of war veterans, to enforce the rule under which students are required to work in legal offices during the Christmas and long vacations except for reasonable holidays.
6 That the practice of holding the Christmas examinations prior to the Christmas holidays be restored.
7 That oral examinations be held in all three years. In the first year these could take the form of tests as now presented to ensure that the students are working satisfactorily under the practice group system. We recommend that in the second year oral examinations of at least 15 minutes duration be held and in the third year such examinations be of not less than 30 minutes' duration.
8 That a member of the profession be appointed as a salaried official of the society on a full-time basis to superintend the system of service under articles to keep in touch with the offices in which students are working, to interview principals and students when necessary and generally to ensure that students are receiving the requisite practical training.

9 That consideration be given the establishment of a post-graduate course in law.

Clearly, the four benchers who signed the majority report were convinced that few lawyers in active practice desired a full-time law school or believed that such a school would develop better lawyers.[5] The opinions these benchers valued were those of fellow practitioners. The people who were pushing for the full-time school were law teachers who, in a sense, had a vested interest in increased academic instruction, and law students, who, as Hamilton Cassels said, were 'notoriously prone to attack the existing order of things.'[6] The four benchers who constituted the 'majority' were certain that no one knew better how to educate an aspiring lawyer than a practising lawyer.

The 'majority' seems to have had a fundamental distrust of law teachers who had little or no practical experience. The noted English jurist A.V. Dicey wrote in 1883 that many English lawyers were convinced that 'English law must be learned and cannot be taught and ... the only places where it can be learned are the law courts and chambers.'[7] The 'majority' firmly believed this. They recognized that there was a place for academic instruction, but they regarded office training as the crucial element in legal education. They perceived American legal education, as seen at Harvard and other university schools, as fundamentally in error, and they drew great comfort from the critical comments of such Americans as Jerome Frank, practitioners who apparently saw the fundamental flaws of the U.S. academic legal education.[8] To the 'majority,' England was the proper model for Ontario.

These benchers were aware, of course, of the numerous differences between English legal education and what they required of Ontario law students. They realized that England had a divided profession, with separate systems of legal education for barristers and solicitors. Nevertheless, both of those systems emphasized practical instruction. Students intending to be barristers were required to eat a specified number of meals at the inns of court, where they came into contact with practitioners. Then, after having passed an entrance examination, they spent a year in pupillage with an established barrister. Those students who wished to be solicitors had to spend three years under articles as apprentices to practising solicitors. In each case, practical training was an essential feature of legal education.

Although Wright had stressed to the committee that he did not want to turn Osgoode Hall into Harvard Law School and that he regarded

Harvard as lacking in the teaching of practical skills,[9] the 'majority' seem to have thought that he and his teaching colleagues had been too much influenced by the American system. Langdell's belief that law was a science that could be learned from books was unacceptable. The 'majority' did not intend to let Wright succeed in introducing such a belief into their law school at the expense of the longstanding English emphasis on practical training.

The recommendation that a post-graduate school be established also, in a sense, reflected English attitudes; namely, the English separation between academic and practical training. In England the universities taught academic law courses outside the mainstream of legal education; the profession governed the training of the practitioner. The 'majority' seem to have thought that if Wright and his colleagues wanted to teach academic law they should be permitted to do so, but such instruction should not form part of the standard education for lawyers. Just as law students in England could study academic law at the university, but were not required to do so to practise, in Ontario those who wished to undertake academic study would be permitted to do so if they wished.

Although the 'majority' were convinced that concurrent training was essential to legal education, they realized that if steps were not taken to improve the training students were getting in the law offices, the system would have to be abandoned. Hamilton Cassels, in a report to Convocation in September 1948, had warned of the threat 'of those who seek to change the existing order of things and to establish a full-time school.'[10] Cassels had studied Wright's articles on legal education, and recognized that 'there was no use shutting one's eyes to the fact that he had put forward a strong argument for a full-time school.' He noted that 'the strongest count in Wright's indictment of the current office and law-school system' was that students were not getting 'an adequate practical training in offices.' Wright's criticisms of office training had been confirmed, Cassels pointed out, by the annual reports of those conducting the oral examination of law students. These exams, which were meant to assess what the students had learned in their law offices, revealed that many students were not being equipped with even the minimum knowledge necessary to practise.[11] In Cassels's words, 'drastic action' was 'imperative.' The Law Society of Upper Canada was 'one of the very few ... on this continent which had retained the system of concurrent office and law school training.' To Cassels, this was not 'a valid argument for a full-time school.' In his view, 'the main reason other societies had departed from the current system' was 'that the

Profession had fallen down in the fulfillment of its fundamental part in the system.' Ontario was 'dangerously close' to doing the same thing. He issued a call to the profession to live up to their obligation to make office training effective. To go along with those who wanted a full-time school would be the easy but irresponsible way out.

Percy Wilson, the chairman of the special committee, presented a 'minority' report that was a startling contrast to the 'majority' position. Wilson sought a system that would deal with a changing legal and social environment: 'I favour a full time law school, or as close to such a system as financial and other conditions of the Law Society of Upper Canada will permit. I believe that the part-time system cannot in practice be worked to the best interests of the student-at-law.' Wilson was convinced that the 'break-down of the concurrent system' was not a result of temporary post-war conditions; rather, the system failed because of the pressures of practising law in a more complex society. Apprenticeship worked best when the numbers in the profession were small and students could be personally supervised by their principals. The increased demands on a lawyer's time and the larger number of students now meant that such personal supervision was seldom possible. It was not that lawyers were lazy or irresponsible, but that their practice left no time for them to give proper attention to the needs of students.

This failure of the apprenticeship system, Wilson believed, was aggravated by the increased intellectual demands placed upon the lawyer in the urbanized and industrialized world. As the economic system grew more complex, negligence law, taxation, labour law, constitutional law, and international law became more important. The study of these and other subjects required 'at least three years [of] full time lectures.' But even Wilson did not want to abandon office training completely. Students could work in law offices during summer vacations, and they should be required to work with a practitioner for one year after law school. Teachers would also benefit from office training. Wilson counselled all law teachers to develop practical as well as academic experience. This could be accomplished by allowing lecturers leaves of absence to work in law offices.

Unlike Hamilton Cassels, Wilson felt that 'too much administrative work' was undertaken by the legal education committee. The committee's chief duty was 'to define policy'; everyday administration should be left to the dean and his staff. Wilson ended his report by agreeing with the 'majority' that a graduate program should be established; he went further, however, and suggested that it be a 'joint undertaking by the University of Toronto and the Law Society.'

The report prepared by Park Jamieson completed the trilogy of recommendations of the special committee, and eventually proved to be the most influential of the three. He agreed in part with each of the other reports, but seemed to suggest yet another compromise. Like the 'majority,' he felt that 'the ideal set-up for the Osgoode Hall Law School was a "part-time" school with lectures and service under articles in offices taking place concurrently and with a majority of the faculty being composed of members of the profession in active practice or who have had considerable previous experience in active practice.' In his opinion, 'in essence, Osgoode Hall Law School is a vocational or trade school.' He doubted, however, whether it was possible or desirable to maintain the concurrent system in the circumstances. A part-time school could not function with a faculty 'whose sympathy with, and desire for a "full-time" law school is well known.' Moreover, as Cassels had pointed out, the members of the profession had 'not co-operated and carried out their part in making the "part-time" school the success it could and should be.'

Jamieson recommended that the dean and faculty be given an opportunity to try out their ideas and to show what results could be achieved. He suggested that Osgoode Hall be made a full-time school for a five-year trial period. His idea of 'full-time,' however, differed from Wilson's or Wright's. He envisioned a four-year program, of which only the first two years would consist of full-time study. The third year was to be devoted to full-time office training, and the fourth year to concurrent articling and law school attendance. Although he stopped short of seconding Wilson's proposals for a true full-time school, he agreed that the Legal Education Committee should be restricted to establishing policy; that the teaching staff should be given periodic leaves to obtain practical experience; and that a graduate program should be established in conjunction with University of Toronto.

These then were the three proposals put before Convocation on 20 January 1949. Twenty-six benchers were in attendance, including all of the members of the special committee, with the exception of Cyril Carson. After the reports had been presented, Hamilton Cassels, seconded by a bencher who had not sat on the committee, moved that the 'majority' report be adopted in principle. Percy Wilson, seconded by Park Jamieson, moved an amendment that the system of education set out in the two 'minority' reports be adopted in principle. The debate on the three reports was lengthy. In the end, Wilson's amendment was lost and Cassels's motion carried; the benchers rejected Wright's proposed full-time school in an attempt to preserve the concurrent system.[12] Convocation then considered the nine points proposed by the 'majority.' After some discussion and minor amendments to three points, they were adopted. The nine-point program was then referred to the legal education committee 'for such further consideration as may be required.'

Incredibly, Wright was not informed of the contents or even the existence of the reports submitted by the special committee, nor was he told of Convocation's adoption of the nine-point program. He first learned of the decision in a report that appeared in the *Globe and Mail* the next morning.[13] How surprised and shocked was Wright by what he read? There is some evidence that he expected the January Convocation to receive the special committee report; he had said as much to Larry MacKenzie in December.[14] Judging from his correspondence and his speech of 14 January, he also seems to have expected that the committee would not recommend the establishment of a full-time school. Evidently he was expecting things to get worse before they got better. Nevertheless, he probably was both surprised and upset at the extent of the backsliding in the nine-point program, at the absence of any notice to him (he was, after all, the dean of Osgoode Hall), and by the quick acceptance of the report by Convocation. There can be no doubt that, surprised or not, he was adamantly opposed to the proposals, and that he intended to escalate his public assault on the benchers' concurrent system. Wright, who revelled in combat, must have been pleased that the battle was about to begin in earnest.

The benchers' decision to issue a news release before informing Wright, who would have to co-operate in the implementation of the proposed changes, illustrates the extent to which he had alienated the governing body of his profession. In a sense, he was a victim of his own rhetoric; in his efforts to convince the benchers that his was the best way to educate law students, he had ridiculed and emphasized the faults of the existing system. But the benchers were products of that system, and had demonstrated in their own careers that it could produce competent legal practitioners. Proud and sincere men, they resented Wright's public attacks. Many saw his criticisms as acts of disloyalty and his legal education policies as pressure tactics intended to force the adoption of American ideas. They refused to bow to that pressure: since Wright had treated them with disdain, they believed they owed him no courtesies. They found, however, that Wright was not reluctant to exploit their treatment of him in order to win sympathy for his own position.

When he arrived at Osgoode Hall the next day, Wright acted quickly. By 9:30 A.M. he had dictated a memorandum to W. Earl Smith.[15] In it he stated:

I have read in this morning's newspaper a report concerning certain action taken by Convocation with regard to an alleged report by the Special Committee on Legal Education.

Will you please confirm immediately whether

(a) a report has been presented to convocation;

(b) whether the recommendations as printed in this morning's newspaper are accurate and;

(c) when I may expect to see a copy of the report.

In view of my position as the person in charge of administration of the School, I must request immediate action on the above matters for my information.

Smith's response was equally prompt and equally brusque:

I acknowledge receipt of your memorandum of this date. With reference to your enquiries

(a) a report has been presented to Convocation;

(b) the recommendations as printed in this morning's paper are substantially correct;

(c) I have instructions that no copies of the Report are to be given out by my office.

I enclose a copy of the recommendations of the Special Committee as adopted by Convocation. I understand that a copy of this was handed by the Treasurer to the press.

Why did the law society refuse to release the special committee's report? Wright told Dean C.S. LeMesurier of McGill University that the benchers' decision was a 'policy of silence in an attempt to create an appearance of unanimity which is far from the truth.'[16] It seems likely that he was correct. When the minutes of Convocation were published, mention of the 'minority' reports and the Wilson–Jamieson motion was omitted.

The law society's policy of silence was yet another error in judgment. It did not prevent Wright from learning that only four of the eight committee members had signed the report, and it gave the law society's actions an aura of conspiracy and intrigue. The policy also made life difficult for Percy Wilson. Because he had served as chairman of the special committee, his name was associated with recommendations with which he strongly disagreed. Despite the uneasiness he and the other dissenters must have felt in the face of public criticism of the 'majority' recommendations, they never issued a public statement of their views. Convocation then, as today, followed the cabinet model. Only the final decision was made public; it was thought inappropriate to reveal the nature of the debate, or even the possibility of dissent. Consequently, the dissenters suffered whatever discomfort they felt in silence.

Meanwhile, Wright was not alone in hurrying to the law school after reading his morning newspaper. Bora Laskin recalled that all of the full-time teachers rushed to work that morning as if shot out of a cannon.[17] Twenty minutes after the newspaper story had been confirmed, they decided that they should resign en masse. An exception was made for Falconbridge, who would soon retire; little would be gained by putting him through such a trying experience at his age.

Wright drafted a lengthy letter of resignation that outlined his views, shared by his colleagues, of what the law society's decision to adopt the report meant. The letter was then sent to the treasurer, Gershom Mason. The next step was crucial. A press conference was held in the early afternoon to release Wright's letter of resignation and to announce that Professors Willis, Laskin, and Edwards were joining Wright in resigning in protest over the decision taken by Convocation. Walter Williston did not add his name to the list, since it was already known that he planned to return to practice at the end of the school year. He was later quoted in the *Toronto Telegram* as saying that it would have been 'overdramatic' for him to have resigned a position he did not hold. Nevertheless, he made it clear in the *Telegram* interview that he agreed with Wright and the others. When the *Toronto Star* and the *Telegram* hit the streets that afternoon, the report of the faculty resignations appeared alongside that of Convocation's decision.

The law society may have thrown down the gauntlet, but it was Wright who chose the weapons and the field of battle; he had decided that the struggle over the direction of legal education should be fought on the pages of Ontario's newspapers. It was a battle that the law society, with its policy of secrecy, would have difficulty winning. Wright's strategy was effective: as the *Financial Post* pointed out, 'the society (which hates publicity) found itself in the newspapers in big bold type.'

Wright's first salvo was the release of his carefully worded letter of resignation. Although the letter was addressed to Gershom Mason, Wright was writing for the benefit of the members of the Ontario bar and the general public, and he deployed all of his extensive skill in advocacy to win the support of both those constituencies. The tone of the letter was polite but firm. It was the statement of a dedicated man who had only the public good in mind, and who, after being mistreated and misunderstood, had been forced into taking this regrettable step. Wright stressed that he had never been advised of the activities of the special committee, and knew nothing other than what he had read that morning in the *Globe and Mail*. He had not been permitted to read the report or even afforded the 'common courtesy' of being informed 'of such a startling departure from all [his] recommendations to the Benchers before publishing them in the press.' Since his appointment in 1927, he had 'constantly striven to maintain and to provide for the Ontario profession and the Ontario public a law school of which both ... could be proud.' The recommendation of the special committee 'set back legal education in this province at least 25 years.' The benchers had left him no alternative but to resign; he had done so because he had 'an abiding faith' that the principles he advocated were 'in the public interests as well as the interests of the profession.'

After reviewing the shortcomings of the concurrent system of legal education, Wright closed with two final criticisms: first, the law society had a monopoly on legal education; second, students were a source of revenue for the law society and of 'cheap labour' for the profession. Wright implied that the benchers were motivated at least in part by self-interest in maintaining the existing system – a motivation that stood in sharp contrast to his own desire for a more democratic system that would better serve both society and the legal profession.

In the struggle for public opinion, the *Globe and Mail* proved to be Wright's staunchest ally. On the morning after the faculty resignations were submitted to the law society, the *Globe* published a front-page story, accompanied with a bold-face headline: 'Hall Pushed Back 25 Years, Osgoode Dean Says, Quits.' There were large pictures of Wright, Willis, Laskin, and Edwards and a lengthy account of Wright's motives, drawn primarily from his letter of resignation. To the extracts from the letter were added choice phrases taken from Wright's remarks at the press conference: 'If medical education was controlled by the medical profession as law is by the legal profession, we would be back in the days of leeches ... it's an awful strain on loyalty in maintaining this standard of mediocrity.'

As dean of the law school and spokesman for the other three who resigned, Wright was the centre of attention. But the decision to follow Wright in leaving Osgoode Hall must have been a difficult one for Willis, Laskin, and Edwards. Willis was a recognized scholar, but Laskin and Edwards were young and only beginning their careers. None of them had expected that their resignations would be accepted. John Willis later recalled, 'What we hoped and expected (but we turned out to be wrong) was that the resignations of all the full-time teachers (except Falconbridge, who was going to stay and ... Walter Williston ... who was going into practice) would force the Benchers to reverse their decree and we should stay at Osgoode. How could they run the School, said we, without teachers?'[18] Wright began to receive job offers the day after he resigned,[19] but the other three men were faced, at least temporarily, with the unappealing prospect of unemployment.

The resignations rocked the Ontario legal community, and public opinion seemed to favour Wright's position. Letters and telegrams of support began to pour into his office, and newspaper stories and editorials criticized the benchers' stand and especially their policy of secrecy.[20] But not everyone supported Wright. The *Telegram* reported on 22 January that lawyers were divided on the issue; some criticized and others defended Wright's stand. One veteran bencher was quoted as 'asserting that the resignation was the "best thing that could have happened." '

Nevertheless, the publicity soon convinced the benchers that their refusal to release the special committee report and to answer the questions of the press was working to Wright's advantage. His views were being widely circulated, and people believed that the law society was hiding something. A meeting of the legal education committee was called for the afternoon of 24 January to determine how best to deal with the situation. On the morning of the same day, Wright addressed the student body of Osgoode Hall. His brief remarks set out what was to be his theme throughout the next several months: 'The action of the Benchers was taken in the utmost good faith in the interest of the students and the profession ... the resulting action of myself and other lecturers ... was also taken because of our honest belief that under the proposed system our efforts in your behalf would be futile and of little value. In other words, this is not a dispute over personalities.'[21] Although Wright was undoubtedly aware that his personality *was* an issue for at least some of the benchers, he knew that fundamentally the disagreement was over how best to train lawyers. He did not want the public to be sidetracked by other issues, nor did he want to resort to the discourteous tactics some of the benchers were using. Although his feelings were running high, he held himself in check. For Wright, who could throw verbal punches with the best and who often became extremely upset by what he regarded as personal affronts or just plain wrong-headedness, this was no easy task. Over and over during the next few months he would try to ensure that the debate focused on the issues and did not degenerate into personal vituperation.

After Wright finished his speech, the students gave him an ovation. Afterwards, William Somerville, the president of the Legal and Literary Society, announced that an emergency meeting of students would be held on Wednesday, 26 January, to decide whether a formal statement of their views would be issued. The *Globe* commented that 'the Dean's reception had left little doubt as to what those views would be.' (On the evening of 26 January a meeting of about 300 students at Osgoode Hall debated the controversy for two hours, and then voted 3 to 1 in favour of a resolution disapproving of the benchers' policy.)[22]

When the legal education committee met later in the day on 24 January, it was obvious that some explanation of the law society's position would have to be given to the press. Five of the eight members of the special committee – Hamilton Cassels, Percy Wilson, John Cartwright, C.W.R. Bowlby, and H.J. McLaughlin – were among the ten people at the meeting. Mike Chitty, who had served on the special committee for a brief time, was also present. The meeting lasted two hours and resulted in two recommendations. First, the resignations of Wright and the other lecturers should be accepted (the resignations of Willis, Laskin, and Edwards were to take effect at the end of the school year; Wright's resignation was effective immediately, but his offer to continue to teach for the rest of the term should be accepted). Second, an official statement from the legal education committee should be released to the press and copies sent to all members of the law society. That statement, which was released on 25 January, essentially reproduced the 'majority' report, with two notable additions. First, a paragraph was added: 'The system of concurrent training has been of immense value to students from outside of Toronto. Many of them have been enabled to become lawyers because of it. Care should be taken that concentration of the work of students at Toronto does not cut off access to the profession of students from distant parts of the Province who have ambition but little money.'[23] The other addition was aimed directly at Wright:

It is not the intention of the Legal Education Committee to enter into any personal controversy with Dr. Wright but the following must be said:

1 No assurance was given to him that he was to participate in the work of the special committee.
2 He was in fact invited to appear and did appear on two occasions before that committee and was given a full opportunity to present his views.
3 He, immediately prior to his appointment as Dean, knowing that Convocation was not in favour of a full-time law school, promised to co-operate with the Benchers.[24]

Wright received a copy of the statement on the same day it was released. He was struck by the remark made in the statement that Osgoode Hall's academic standards were considerably higher than those at comparable institutions and were actually on a post-graduate level, an assertion used by the benchers to buttress their contention that academic work had been overemphasized and that legal education was 'out of balance.' Wright was eager to demonstrate that Osgoode Hall required no more academic work than other Canadian law schools. He sent telegrams to the deans of Canada's other law schools quoting the benchers' claim and hoping for their ardent disagreement.

The response of Dean LeMesurier of McGill University was especially heartening to Wright: 'I cannot believe that a student attending two lectures a day and spending the rest of his time in an office can possibly acquire the same mastery of the field as one who is giving his whole time to study ... It seems ... quite ridiculous to suggest that students, many of whom are not even university graduates, attending lectures a couple of hours a day are doing work of "post-graduate" quality.'[25]

LeMesurier did not stop there. In a letter to Gershom Mason, he explained that his son Ross was attending Osgoode Hall, and thus LeMesurier had both a personal and professional interest in the legal education controversy. When his son had decided to attend Osgoode, he wrote, he had been concerned because of its 'reputation as a school emphasizing technical training with too little opportunity for a liberal education in law. However, when it seemed settled 'that Dr. Wright was taking over as Dean and that John Willis was returning,' LeMesurier had assumed that the law society 'had accepted the whole philosophy of education for which they stood.' He thought it unfortunate that such was not the case, and he warned Mason that 'this difference between the Benchers and Dr. Wright and his staff may have very serious consequence for the future of legal education across Canada.' Although most of the other provinces had some form of university law school, Ontario, as the largest and wealthiest province was looked to for leadership. What happened there could, and often did, have an impact beyond the province's own boundaries.

Meanwhile, the battle continued to rage in the Toronto press. Frank Molinaro, a practitioner who had studied under Wright, wrote a letter to the *Globe* deploring 'the absolute monopolistic domination which the oligarchy of thirty tyrants exercises over legal education and the legal profession in the Province of Ontario.' He called for the establishment of a royal commission to enquire into the existing system, which compelled [students] to accept whatever the principal chose to give them, often nothing at all, for the somewhat dubious privilege of being glorified office boys and legmen.' J.F.C. Whalley, KC had a different view. In a letter to the Toronto *Telegram* he asserted that the University of Toronto was behind the controversy; the university had 'long had a hankering for the Law School.' If it succeeded in its scheme, 'all the other universities would set up similar departments and in what possible way could a university add anything to the training of lawyers?'

Whalley's letter was the first public indication of what a number of members of the legal profession were coming to believe: Sidney Smith, acting on behalf of the University of Toronto, and Casesar Wright had precipitated the crisis so as to force the benchers to move the law school to the university. There was an element of truth in this: certainly, Smith and Wright had been trying to respond to the complaints of the academics since at least the summer of 1945, and there can be little doubt that Wright, consciously or unconsciously, had provoked the old-school benchers into taking a hard-line position. There is no clear evidence, however, that Smith and Wright actually conspired in the way Whalley and others suggested.

It was clear that the time for discussion had passed. Neither side seriously considered trying to work out their differences. The leaders of both factions were firmly committed to their positions and had no intention of compromising. The Osgoode students encouraged Wright to negotiate with the benchers, but he continued to focus his attention on influencing the legal community at large and the general public. In an address to the Toronto Lawyers' Club,[26] he made his first public comments on the benchers' official statement. He advised his audience that if they were expecting a 'pyrotechnic display' they should go home. The issue was too serious to leave room for charges and countercharges. If the benchers' proposals were implemented, 'dictated lectures descriptive of past and present experience [would] be given, written in note books and regurgitated word for word on examination books.' A good law school would not settle for so restricted a role: 'law and lawyers do not sell information. Law and lawyers deal with facts.' The school should emphasize the acquisition of skills of analysis and problem-solving. They should develop in their students a consciousness of the importance of facts, a sense of relevance, an ability to see all sides of a problem and to anticipate future developments, a mastery of language, a capacity to look beyond verbal solutions that merely conceal problems, and a 'self discipline in habits of thoroughness.' He emphasized that he had no wish to ignore totally the development of practical skills. His aim was not to establish a Harvard at Osgoode Hall; he wanted to do even better.

In the last half of his speech Wright focused his attack on two of the benchers' assertions: first, that the breakdown of the concurrent system was due to post-war conditions and, second, that he had known of Convocation's opinion when he accepted the deanship. In refuting the first statement, he noted that what was happening in Ontario was not new; similar disputes over office training had taken place in the United States in the nineteenth century, and indeed in Ontario itself. He listed the disputes that had taken place in the 1920s and 1930s: the 1923 recommendations of the Toronto Lawyers' Club – the very body he was addressing – Shirley Denison's criticisms of the law school in the 1924 *Canadian Bar Review*, R.W. Lee's report to the Canadian Bar Association, and M.H. Ludwig's remarks to the same association in 1931. He then turned to the second statement. How, he asked, could he have known of Convocation's views prior to his appointment? He was not told, nor could he have been told, 'since the Special Committee was considering the matter and presumably the issue had not been settled.' He concluded his speech with a challenge: 'Each member of the profession must face the individual responsibility of either advancing or retarding the growth of legal education.' He and his colleagues would advance, not retreat. He hoped that all members of the profession would advance together.

By now, Wright was the darling of the press: he was, in the words of the *Telegram*, 'pestered for statements and opinions.' The day following his speech to the Toronto Lawyers' Club, he gave his second press conference. He reiterated a number of the points he had made in his speech, commented on the benchers' official statement, and sought to correct certain false impressions given by that statement. While the *Globe*, the *Star*, and the *Telegram* reported Wright's press conference (under headlines reading 'Full-Time Hall Not New,' 'Law Society Decision Reverses Osgoode History,' and 'Full Academic Training Urged in 1923'), the *Financial Post* gave him the most extensive coverage. In bold-face type, on its front page, it asked, 'Which Makes the Best Lawyer: Scholar or Apprentice?' The reader did not have to finish the lengthy article to know that the *Financial Post* thought that Wright knew the right answer to that question. In an editorial in the same issue, the benchers were said to be seeking to impose a 'lower standards' policy. This should be of concern to the entire Canadian public, since lawyers held many important positions in society. The paper also published a long letter from Donald Carrick, who years before had led his own fight with the law society. Carrick had not changed his views: he stated that the weaknesses of the concurrent system and the strengths of a full-time school had been 'obvious for 25 years.'[27] The benchers' hope that less academic instruction would cure the ills of the apprenticeship system was 'a decision of despair.' If the legal community did not act to correct the situation, he warned, 'the time may come when the public will step in and demand that the Government' do so.

On 30 January Carrick debated the issue with Mike Chitty on a local radio station.[28] Carrick pointed out that graduates of Osgoode Hall could not gain entry to Harvard Law School because of Osgoode Hall's low standards. This prompted the moderator to ask Chitty what the standing nationally and internationally of Osgoode Hall was. Chitty replied, 'That is no concern whatever of the Benchers. They simply have the responsibility put upon them to certify that every graduate from the School is competent to practise law. Osgoode Hall is, therefore, not an educational institution but a vocational school for lawyers. Its comparative standing is quite irrelevant provided it turns out competent lawyers.' The *Globe* jumped on this comment in an editorial,[29] as did Wright in a statement he prepared for distribution to members of the legal profession.[30] Was it indeed the position of the benchers, he asked, that Osgoode Hall was not an educational institution? If so, the law society should so inform the public. By the end of January Wright had rallied a great deal of support against the benchers,[31] and newspapers throughout Ontario had come out in support of at least a reconsideration of the province's legal education system.

Inevitably, the dispute continued at the February meeting of the Ontario branch of the Canadian Bar Association. Wright was glad to have another public forum for his views. Recognizing the significance that the support of such a gathering would have for his cause, he encouraged his supporters to make their opinions known. The membership in the law society and the bar association overlapped, and the benchers would ignore a CBA resolution at their peril.

Again, Donald Carrick led Wright's supporters at the meeting. At the Friday evening session Gershom Mason presented a brief review of the activities of the benchers over the past year. Then Carrick, seconded by Arthur Kelly, moved a resolution to the effect that the benchers' resolutions of 20 January were 'inadequate to meet the problems of legal education in Ontario and that they should be reconsidered by the Benchers.' In introducing his resolution, Carrick referred to the law society's action as 'folly,' and renewed his warning that if something was not done to correct the situation the profession might be deprived of its control over legal education. In effect, he was calling for a demonstration of non-confidence in the benchers. Mason and Hamilton Cassels spoke in defence of the law society, but were unable to sway majority opinion. Although Donald Guthrie of Toronto and Mike Chitty also defended the benchers, the eminent Joseph Sedgwick, himself a bencher, concluded that it was obvious that the meeting could not accept the law society's position on legal education as it stood.

As the debate raged on for three hours, Wright, Willis, Laskin, and Edwards sat in silence. They knew that their position would be accurately presented by others, mostly younger members of the bar. When a vote finally came, Carrick's resolution was carried by an estimated ratio of twenty to one. A motion declaring that no censure was implied was defeated. Caesar Wright and his colleagues had demonstrated that the benchers were isolated from their constituents.

Now it was important to keep up the pressure. Again, the Toronto newspapers proved to be Wright's allies. The day following the CBA debate, the papers gave prominent coverage to the Carrick resolution.[32] These stories were followed by editorials. The *Globe* declared the question of legal education 'wide open for discussion' after the bar association's 'vote of censure and non-confidence.' Ignoring the minority position, the *Globe* termed the 'non-confidence' vote 'unanimous' and stated that 'the Benchers could not possibly ignore it.' The newspaper called for a revival of the law society–University of Toronto liaison committee, or, alternatively, for a royal commission of inquiry, and warned the benchers that their proposed course of study must be revised or their monopoly would be ended forthwith. The *Star* too called for the question to be reconsidered in the light of the 'overwhelming expression of opinion by the Ontario section of the Canadian Bar Association.'

Meanwhile, Wright was busy dispatching letters explaining his stand. To Harry Hazell, a Hamilton solicitor who had been quoted in the newspapers as saying Wright had 'done the worst possible thing in the circumstances,' Wright wrote that he had tried negotiation and conciliation for twenty-two years before placing this matter 'of public concern before the real parties interested.'[33] To Dean A.T. Vanderbilt and other legal academics, Wright sent a package of materials that included an eight-page summary of the controversy.[34] He also replied to the hundreds of letters of support he had received. He repeated over and over that the controversy was not to be regarded as a personality clash and that he was not against practical training.

One of Wright's letters is of special interest. On 14 February he wrote to Alex Corry of Queen's University with a prediction: 'My guess would be that the Benchers might strive for some compromise arrangement, having got rid of the troublesome spirit which hovers over them in me, but I feel that the compromise would be extremely difficult for any academic man to accept here. In light of that fact, it may be that if a liberal education in law is to continue in Ontario some other institution or institutions will have to accept the challenge and it is not entirely impossible that this may come about.'

Wright was encouraged by a letter from his old friend John Tory, who had been recently appointed a governor of the University of Toronto. Tory pledged his 'continued support till the battle is won and beyond,' and promised that he would be in it to the end, 'come hell or high water.'[35] If Wright was to succeed in establishing his professional university law school, he would need many more supporters like Tory.

On 17 February the benchers assembled in Convocation to receive the report of the legal education committee. It soon became obvious that the CBA resolution and the press coverage had had an effect. J.W. Pickup moved the following resolution:

1 That a special meeting of Convocation be called to be held at the call of the Treasurer, when Convocation in Committee of the whole will review the decision of January Convocation and consider the representations received or to be received on the subject of Legal Education in Ontario.

2 That all County and District Law Associations in Ontario be requested to submit their views on the questions in controversy so that they may be fully considered by Convocation at such Special Meeting.

3 That the resignation of Dean Wright be accepted as tendered and that Convocation concur in the recommendation of the Standing Committee on Legal

Education that Dr. Wright be requested to continue his lectures to the end of the present term as suggested by him.

4 That action on the resignation of Messrs. Willis, Laskin and Edwards be deferred until after review of the whole situation by the Special Meeting of Convocation.[36]

J.J. Robinette objected to the way in which the motion singled out Wright for special adverse treatment, and he successfully moved an amendment: 'That action on the resignations of Dean Wright and Messrs. Willis, Laskin and Edwards be deferred in view of this decision to review the whole situation by the Special Meeting of Convocation.' After the amended motion was passed, the treasurer was authorized to appoint a special committee to obtain the views of the county and district law associations. Gershom Mason appointed Pickup chairman and William Beaton, Mike Chitty, Gordon Shaver, and A.R. Willmott members. Convocation also resolved to give Wright an opportunity 'to make such statement as he may wish' at its next meeting.

None of this meant that Wright's struggle was over. On the evening of Convocation's sitting Wright made another public address, this time to the Women's Law Association.[37] He said nothing new; he repeated that he was not against practical training, but thought that it should come after law school, and he listed again his complaints about the nature of the office work required of students.

On 21 February Wright wrote to Earl Smith for clarification of his status. The resolutions of 17 February had left everything up in the air, and he had not been asked to withdraw his resignation. He asked permission to read the minutes of Convocation of 20 January and 17 February. Finally, he asked whether his 'conduct, qualifications or suitability as Dean were put in issue before Convocation.' A week later, when no response or acknowledgment was forthcoming, he wrote to Gershom Mason: 'Up to the present time, I have refused to consider or deal with any offer concerning my future because of a very sincere hope that my long association with Osgoode Hall might continue under new policies to which I could give my full support and cooperation. I feel, however, that as matters stand at the present time there is no assurance that this will be possible ... After March 1st, I consider myself free to make whatever arrangements for the future may appear to be in my own interests.'[38]

If Wright hoped this deadline would push the law society to clarify its position, he was disappointed. On 1 March Mason sent Wright a copy of the resolution granting him the right to address Convocation:

If you desire to be heard at that meeting I suggest, personally and without instructions from Convocation to so suggest, that you are likely to be asked about statements made in your recent addresses to various organizations of lawyers, your conversation with a committee of three of the Benchers immediately prior to your appointment as Dean, and any conversations with the Chairman of the Legal Education Committee or the Treasurer touching upon your giving addresses on subjects which were under consideration by the Special Committee on Legal Education and by Convocation.

Mason was unwilling to overlook what he regarded as Wright's disloyalty in the past. The letter confirmed Wright's suspicions that 'allegations, accusations, charges or other matters personal' to him had been made before Convocation. He told Mason that his views were well known and repeating them before Convocation, especially in answer to unknown charges, would be pointless.[39] For Wright, there was 'nothing further that could usefully be said.'

On 10 March 1949 the University of Toronto announced that Wright, Laskin, and Willis were joining the law faculty. The break with Osgoode Hall and the benchers was now complete. Wright's feelings are expressed in a letter he wrote to Roscoe Pound. In 1948, Pound, quoting Isaiah 28:16, had reminded Wright that 'he that believeth shall not make haste,' and had advised him: 'In such a task as yours well planned attrition is often a better policy than immediate, direct, heavy attack.'[40] Now, Wright reassured Pound that he had not ignored that advice:

I can only hope that when you read this you will not think that I completely disregarded the admonition in Isaiah ... I think that my record of twenty-two years of what you called well planned continuous attrition should be some indication that our action was neither hasty nor dictated by a desire to make radical changes overnight ... I am hoping to establish a full-time professional law school ... I am hoping that eventually in the not too distant future the University and the Law Society will be able to work out some mutually satisfactory arrangement whereby the Law Society still retains control over discipline and admission to practice and the University provides the academic training in a full-time law school.[41]

Wright could not know that it would take eight more years to reach a 'mutually satisfactory arrangement' with the law society.

9

'An Honest to God Law School'

In 1945, when Sidney Smith suggested that Caesar Wright replace W.P.M. Kennedy as dean of the University of Toronto School of Law, Wright replied that he would accept the post only if the school could be converted into an 'honest to God law school.' In March 1949 Wright finally did accept the university's offer on the understanding that he would undertake that conversion.

A revealing glimpse of the changes Wright planned to make is found in a letter to the university superintendent's office explaining what he wanted done in the 'Law Building'.[1] Kennedy had been first and foremost a legal scholar, and his large office on the second floor of the building reflected this. There were six bookcases on the north wall, four more along the south wall, and another in an alcove. In all other respects the office was Spartan. In Wright's opinion, the furnishings were 'antiquated': there were plain dark green blinds on the windows, army folding chairs, and a 'noisy typewriter.' It seemed that efficient administration had not been one of Kennedy's priorities: his secretary was on the third floor, with her one lonely filing cabinet; she and the dean shared the only telephone line in the school.

Wright too was a scholar, but he also had a business-like manner and was a practising lawyer. He found the conditions in which Kennedy had functioned unsatisfactory. He wanted to split the dean's office in two to create a secretary's office and a reception room. He ordered the removal of all of Kennedy's bookcases and the installation of a carpet, a large desk and chair, two armchairs, a chesterfield ('preferably leather'), drapes, and a valance box over the front window. There were to be at least two telephone lines for the school, and one was to be reserved for Wright's exclusive use. His secretary would have three filing cabinets, and there would be several 'occasional chairs: for visitors.' He also asked that a working library room be established for the law faculty and the lighting improved.

The letter to the superintendent, which was written within twenty-four hours of Wright's visit to the law building at 45 St George Street, demonstrates that he was a man who knew what he wanted, and what he wanted was a business-like approach to the running of a law faculty. Wright was not interested in a scholarly retreat; he wanted a professional school, an institution narrowly focused on the education of students for the practice of law. He hoped to bring the faculty into the mainstream of the professional legal community, and he recognized the importance of organization and efficiency in bringing that hope to fruition.

Wright's most significant initiatives were undertaken in the Faculty of Law's degree programs. At the time of his appointment the principal degree program was the four-year honours law course taught in the Faculty of Arts.[2] This course was taken by those intending to enter the legal profession. It had provided an introduction to legal studies for Bora Laskin, William Howland, G.A. Martin, and Edwin Goodman. None the less, Wright found it unsatisfactory. The honours program was also part of a five-year combined course leading to an LL B degree; graduates of the four-year course were admitted to a one-year LL B program for a fee of one dollar. The departmental regulations required students to write examinations in five subjects. In practice, students who graduated with a BA in law wrote the exams over a number of years, often while attending Osgoode Hall. In addition to these programs, there was a three-year graduate course leading to a bachelor of laws degree. It was open to university arts graduates, but very few students enrolled in the course since it did not qualify them to practise law in Ontario; moreover, the courses offered were virtually identical to those given in the popular undergraduate program.

The University of Toronto Board of Governors accepted all of Wright's proposed changes. First, the existing LL B program was discontinued, although those students who had already entered the program were permitted to complete their courses of study and receive their degrees. Second, the four-year honours law course was discontinued. Finally, a new three-year LL B course began in the 1949–50 academic year. In Wright's words, this course was 'designed to furnish an adequate liberal and professional education for persons contemplating the practice of law or dealing in public or private affairs where a sound knowledge of law and legal method is indispensable.'³ To gain admission to the new LL B course, candidates were required to submit proof of completion of at least two years of university study after grade 13 graduation. Students who were enrolled in the four-year honours law course and who had successfully completed their second year were permitted, at their option, to elect to transfer to the second year of the new LL B program.

The *Law School Calendar* set out the courses that were to be offered:

FIRST YEAR

1 *Contracts* – Offer and acceptance; consideration; Statute of Frauds; contracts under seal; capacity of parties; performance of contract including conditions, breach, frustration; illegality. 3 hours per week.
2 *Torts* – Intentional interference with the person, land, and chattels; privileges; negligent interference with the person and property; liability of occupiers of land; strict liability; nuisance; defamation. 3 hours per week.
3 *Property* – Personal and real property; possession and ownership; gifts; bailments; liens; pledges; scheme of estates; common-law future interests; Statute of Limitations; Statute of Uses; rights in land; landlord and tenant. 3 hours per week.
4 *Judicial Remedies* – The historical development of the courts, judicial procedure, legal and equitable remedies. 2 hours per week.
5 *Criminal Law and Procedure* – General principles of criminal responsibility; elements of particular crimes; exemptions from criminal responsibility; procedure relating to the arrest and trial of accused persons, including procedure on appeal. 2 hours per week.
6 *Agency* – Agent's authority or power to bind principal by contract; vicarious liability for torts; ratification; rights and duties between principal, agent and third parties; undisclosed principal; delegation. $1^1/_2$ hours per week.

SECOND YEAR

1 *Constitutional Law* – The Crown in the Canadian federation; distribution of legislative power between Dominion and Provinces. 2 hours per week.
2 *Real Estate Transactions* – Problems arising from the relation of vendor and purchaser and equitable and legal remedies therefor; mortgages; the Registry Act and related problems. 2 hours per week.
3 *Commercial Law* – Problems relating to sales and the financing of sales of

goods; negotiable instruments; banking; conditional sales; chattel mortgages; bills of lading and other documents of title. 3 hours per week.

4 *Administrative Law* – Interpretation of statutes; legal liability of public authorities including the Crown; judicial control of the legislative, judicial and quasi-judicial discretions of public authorities; judicial and extra-judicial review of administrative action. 2 hours per week.

5 *Civil Procedure* – The institution of actions; the function of drafting of pleadings and preparation for trial. This course will consist partly of lectures and partly of actual practice court work. 2 hours per week.

6 *Family Law* – Marriage; divorce; annulment; separations; married women, infants and lunatics; deserted wives and children. 1$^1/_2$ hours per week.

7 *Company Law* – Partnerships and syndicates; incorporation, operation and winding up of limited liability company; capital stock; directors, shareholders and bondholders. 2 hours per week.

8 *The Law of Industrial Property* – Patents, copyrights, trade marks; industrial designs. $^1/_2$ hour per week.

THIRD YEAR
(Not given in the year 1949–50)

1 *Taxation* – Ontario and Dominion Succession Duties; Dominion Income Tax; persons taxable; income; deductions; selected corporate problems; selected problems of accounting. 2 hours per week.

2 *Conflict of Laws* – Jurisdiction of courts; characterization of question, and selection and application of proper law; marriage, annulment and divorce; wills, administration and succession; contracts; torts. 2 hours per week.

3 *Wills and Trusts* – The distribution of accumulated wealth by trust and will; problems pertaining to life insurance and succession duties; inter vivos gifts with testamentary operation; intestacy and the testamentary power; establishing a valid will; mistake; drafting problems in wills; problems of administration; lapse; future interest and vesting problems; class gifts; perpetuities. 3 hours per week.

4 *Labour Law* – History of trade-union legislation; status of trade unions; trade action; strikes, boycotts, lockouts, picketing; the labour injunction; conciliation and arbitration; collective bargaining. 2 hours per week.

5 *Evidence and Trial Procedure* – Judicial admissions; judicial notice; affidavits; burden of proof; presumptions; degree of proof; admissibility; relevancy and circumstantial evidence; exclusionary rules including hearsay rule; competency, compellability and privileges of witnesses; privileged communications; corroboration. Combined with the lecture course students will be compelled

to participate in groups involving the actual preparation of cases for trial. 2 hours per week.

6 *Jurisprudence* – Theories of law and legislation; law reform and problems of comparative law; legal principles considered in the light of analysis, history, philosophy and the social ends to be served. 2 hours per week.

7 *Public International Law* – Nature, sources and functions; jurisdiction of states; recognition and succession; treaties; pacific settlement of international disputes; war; neutrality. 2 hours per week.

8 *Comparative Common and Civil Law* – Development of legal institutions in Quebec; a study of selected titles from the Quebec Civil Code; appropriate comparisons with the common law. A comparative study of the principles underlying the judicial administration of justice in civil and common-law jurisdictions. 2 hours per week.

The curriculum was not particularly imaginative or radical; it drew much from both the Osgoode Hall and the 'Kennedy school' curricula. Wright was never to prove innovative in making curriculum changes; he was no revolutionary in either the theory or the practice of legal education. Even in 1949, his attitudes still reflected the thinking of the Harvard professors of the late 1920s.

As Wright had frequently told the benchers, he was not unmindful of the need to teach the practical aspects of the law. In addition to taking the academic courses listed above, first-year students participated in the preparation and arguing of moot court cases. Students in second and third years were required to participate in 'group work conducted by members of the practising bar concerned with problems of practice and pleading in the courts, conveyancing, incorporation of companies, etc.' Similar 'practice' courses continue to be offered today.

Wright and Smith recognized that the new degree program would not qualify students to practise law. The university, therefore, issued the following caveat, which reflected the hope that the Faculty of Law would become a national law school: 'The degree of LL B does not in itself admit to practice and students registering for this course should communicate with the Secretary of the Law Society in any given province as to the requirements for admission to practice in that province.'

Although Wright was eager to dismantle the 'Kennedy school' and turn it into an 'honest to God law school,' Kennedy seems to have been happy that Wright was chosen to succeed him as dean. On 29 May he wrote:

My dear Caesar:

Just a line now that my work is done to give you a very warm and sincere welcome to a faculty which has been my life's work. I can think of no one whom I could desire more to be my successor and to play out my hand. If ever you want me you have only to ask me, in of course an entirely personal way between you and me. At any rate, I know you will never sell down the river to the 'barbarians' the heritage and goals of a real university legal education and that you will not allow any 'official' committees of an 'inter' nature [to] destroy these purposes. You carry with you every unqualified atom of my sincerest good will; I can say no more than that had the selection been mine, I should have unequivocally asked you to be my successor. It is not often in life that one can hand over one's job as I now do to one in whom lies one's fullest confidence and admiration.[4]

Kennedy was either unaware of or unconcerned by Wright's less than charitable assessment of his 'life's work.'

Shortly after he accepted the deanship, Wright told Arthur Goodhart that he had done so 'with the ultimate aim of expanding it into a first class professional school with the hope, and it is only a hope at the moment, of receiving recognition from the Law Society for its LL B degree.'[5] Wright knew that if he was to win recognition from the law society, he would have to convert some of his old opponents. On the same day that he wrote to Goodhart, he told G.V.V. Nicholls, the editor of the *Canadian Bar Review*, that he did not want to write an article on the Faculty of Law for the *Review* just yet:

Under the circumstances, I do not think it would be particularly wise if I printed a statement at this time. It is true that we have gone to the University but more than ever, I think we need the eventual cooperation of the profession and I would not like to do anything which might in the slightest lead to any misunderstanding on the part of the Benchers. The situation is still ticklish and while I can understand your point of view as to the general Canadian public, at the moment I am more concerned with the immediate Ontario situation and I think you will probably agree with me if you can submerge your editorial ardour.[6]

Wright also wrote to G.W. Mason, the treasurer of the law society:

I know that the last two months have been distressing to you – they certainly have been to me. By this note I merely wanted you to know that nothing in the

recent controversy has in any way altered or changed my sincere admiration –
and, I hope friendship – for you personally.

I can assure you that after coming daily to Osgoode Hall, as student and
lecturer, for a continuous period of over 25 years, I feel that there is a large part
of me in the very fabric of the building itself. Under these circumstances I would
ask you to believe me when I say that I have never sought to destroy that to
which both you and I have given so much.

If there have been misunderstandings on your part or mine, I can only hope
that, as in the past, we can together dispel them. Meanwhile, I did want you
to know that, unpleasant and trying as the winter has been, nothing has changed
my personal regard for you, or my admiration for the long tradition of Osgoode
Hall in which I have been privileged to share.

This note does not require an answer. It is simply from me to you.[7]

Wright saw the future of his new law school as 'problematical.' As he
explained to A.L. Goodhart, 'It may be that we will need enabling legislation to permit Toronto graduates to be called to the Bar after some
period of apprenticeship to a practicing solicitor, or it may be that eventually the Law Society and the school of law may be able, as I would
hope, to work out some mutually satisfactory arrangement.' Wright
made a similar remark in a letter to Edwin Patterson of Columbia University: 'The Benchers have been forced to reconsider their decision but
what the outcome will be, I do not know ... the difficulty is that our
graduates may not even be accepted into Ontario practice and unless
this is done, the fight will still continue. In the end, enabling legislation
may be necessary but the political situation here is so obscure that this
may be difficult for a few years.'[8]

Wright may have been determined to mend fences, but he was soon
reminded of the vehemence of his opponents. In a letter to *The Solicitor*,
an English publication, Mike Chitty bitterly attacked the 'academicians.'[9]
He began with a brief history of 'legal education – so-called.' The emphasis
on academic instruction, he said, had begun with Falconbridge's appointment as dean of Osgoode Hall Law School. He could not deny that
Falconbridge had actually practised law, so Chitty alleged that he 'had
only carried on a consultation practice and had had little or no active
office practice.' Similarly, Falconbridge's two assistants were 'men of no
practical experience.' Chitty claimed that pressure to make Osgoode Hall
more academic had been brought to bear upon the benchers in the 1930s,
but that pressure was resisted, as evidenced in the benchers' 1935 report.
He added, 'Despite that report the full-time staff of the school persisted

in their efforts to stress the academic side and introduced many of the methods of teaching in vogue in the law schools of the United States.' Full-time lecturers 'over-persuaded the Benchers to allow the students to take two lectures in the morning, with the immediate result that the students arrived at the office too late to take part in the day's work and much of the benefit of office training was in consequence lost.' The establishment of the special committee to study legal education in the 1940s was as the result of the 'great influx of students coming from the armed forces and ... the feeling of unrest consequent on the over-taxing of the facilities of the school and the unrelenting pressure of the academicians.' Dean Falconbridge had tendered his resignation before the committee reported, and in the circumstances 'the Benchers' hands were practically forced into appointing the next man in line in the faculty – as they had begun to call themselves – and he was the outstanding proponent of the academicians and had freely expressed himself on many occasions as dissatisfied with the part-time school.' Chitty added that the benchers 'unwisely felt themselves forced to bow to [Wright's] demands' and had increased the length of the school term and the number of lectures, 'thus completing the disruption of any possibility of the students obtaining any benefit from office training.' This overburdening planted the 'seeds of discontent' among the students. 'It was into this atmosphere ... of discontent on all sides, that the Committee of the Benchers injected their report on the 20th of January.' The result was that 'the fat was ... immediately in the fire. The Dean resigned in a huff, and with him three of the full-time staff.' Chitty was confident 'that the Benchers' views [would] in the long run prevail,' and though it would be an arduous task to repair 'the sabotage of the academicians and correct the insidious propaganda that they had spread,' it must be done, 'because throughout Canada and the United States no one has yet found the solution for bridging the gap between academic legal education and practical legal training. Universities and academics can teach law but their graduates are not competent to practise law. *Experientia docet.'*

Wright was incensed by the letter. Despite his resolve not to do anything that might be misunderstood by the benchers, he could not let Chitty's remarks go unanswered. In a letter to G.J. Keeton, the editor of *The Solicitor*, he expressed his surprise that such a publication 'would print an article of the kind in question without checking on the accuracy of the facts and in particular publish statements which ... come under the head of actionable libel.'[10] The least *The Solicitor* could do was to publish a short response by him; he enclosed a ten-page typewritten article entitled 'The Legal Education Controversy in Ontario.' The first five pages of the article carefully set out the history of legal education in Ontario, pointing out the places where Chitty had erred. Wright stressed that the changes that had been made to the Osgoode Hall curriculum were in keeping with developments in other Canadian law schools. He also said that even practising lawyers had criticized the concurrent system, and cited the 1923 recommendations of the Toronto Lawyers' Club. The last five pages of the article set out Wright's views of the controversy. He described the problem as follows:

[It] is not one of 'academic' as against 'practical,' nor is it a matter of the internal management of a corporation. The question is essentially one whether a sound and liberal professional education in law is to be a possibility in Ontario. No one questions the right of the Law Society to admit anyone it chooses to practice, but to insist that the only method of obtaining a legal education in Ontario is to compel students to serve as glorified office boys in Toronto offices seems to us definitely wrong. Our graduates are not, because of our concurrent system of office work, accepted as of right in the better American law schools such as Harvard. This is unfortunate since there is little doubt that the Faculty of Osgoode Hall is, always excluding myself, of the highest calibre to be found in the Dominion. The unfortunate feature is that their efforts have been largely frustrated by the confining atmosphere in which they have been forced to work. If these difficulties are to be increased by reverting to the outmoded system of what is in reality a poor quality night school run during two hours of the day, it seems obvious that legal education in Ontario is in serious plight.

Keeton apologized to Wright for the publication of the Chitty letter, and expressed his regret 'that our intervention can only have complicated your own position.'[11] He readily agreed to publish Wright's response.

Sidney Smith was busy trying to placate the benchers. On 10 March, when the university announced the appointment of Wright and his colleagues, he had written to Gershom Mason informing him of his intention to recommend to the university board of governors that Wright be named dean of the Faculty of Law and Willis and Laskin hired as professors. During the period of turmoil immediately following Wright's resignation from Osgoode Hall, Smith had assured Mason on several occasions that the university had had no part in the actions of Wright and the others and that it did not wish to assume control of legal education in Ontario. In his letter of 10 March, Smith reiterated that his proposal to recommend the hiring of Wright, Willis, and Laskin had been decided upon after those three men had declared themselves free agents.

On 17 March, the day on which a large farewell dinner was held for Dean Kennedy, the benchers gathered in Convocation. They faced the formidable task of trying to salvage their own law school after the severe blow dealt it by the resignations of Wright, Willis, Laskin, Edwards, and Williston. Only the aging Falconbridge remained on the full-time staff. On the recommendation of the legal education committee, the benchers appointed two new committees. The first, consisting of the chairmen and vice-chairmen of the standing committees – Hamilton Cassels, W.J. Beaton, Peter White, H.J. McLaughlin, J.W. Pickup, Gordon Shaver. G.T. Walsh, and J.R. Marshall – together with Percy Wilson, was to 'consider the field with reference to the appointment of a Head of the Law School and staff.'[12] It was told to report to the special convocation on legal education to be held on 20 April. Not surprisingly, the second committee's task was to manage public relations. The law society had suffered badly as the result of Wright's well-orchestrated and highly public campaign; the society seems to have decided that it was time to make a public defence of its position. The treasurer appointed W.J. Beaton as chairman of public relations committee and Hamilton Cassels, Mike Chitty, Park Jamieson, and George Walsh as members.

J.W. Pickup then reported to Convocation on the actions taken by his special committee. He informed them that a circular had been sent to all county and district law associations and other legal associations in Ontario asking them for opinions on the concurrent scheme of school-and-office training, what might replace it, and how practical training might best be provided. Pickup reported that fifteen briefs had been received containing a wide range of opinions. These briefs would be 'perused and collated' by his committee and presented to the special convocation on 20 April.

The benchers now faced a new challenge – how to deal with the newly invigorated law school at the University of Toronto. Sidney Smith had suggested in his letter of 10 March that he and university representatives meet with representatives of the benchers to discuss ways in which the two bodies might co-operate. Park Jamieson, seconded by Mike Chitty, moved that the treasurer be requested to inform Smith that when Convocation reached a decision as to the 'changes,' if any, to be made in Osgoode Hall, a committee of benchers would meet with representatives of the university. Smith quickly followed up on this offer. At a board of governors meeting on 14 April he proposed that a new special committee be appointed to confer with the law society.[13] The board approved this recommendation, and two weeks later W. Eric Phillips, the chairman of the board, appointed Smith, Wright, Henry Borden, Arthur Kelly, and Mr Justice Hope to the committee.[14] When Kelly declined the nomination because of other commitments, Beverley Matthews was appointed in his place.

The benchers' special Convocation on 20 April was well attended.[15] J.W. Pickup reported that 35 of the 42 county and district law associations had filed briefs; the membership of these associations represented 2,620 of the 3,120 practising lawyers in the province. The briefs were said to contain 'very divergent views.' Cyril Carson reported on the efforts made to find a new dean for Osgoode Hall in Canada and England. His committee recommended that two benchers be sent immediately to England 'to survey the field there.' The recommendation was accepted, and a discussion of legal education policy began.

After lengthy debate, Convocation adopted what was in essence Park Jamieson's compromise position of three months earlier. The resolution called for a five-point program. First, the period of training was to be four years in the case of university graduates, with an additional period of from one to two years' preliminary service under articles in the case of students admitted after high school. Second, the instruction in the law school was to proceed on a system of teaching that gave emphasis to principles of law illustrated by reference to leading cases, somewhat on the pattern of a well-written textbook rather than the case system, which put emphasis on the extraction of principles from a close analysis of numerous cases. Third, during their first two years students were to attend law school full time. The curriculum for those two years was to consist of an introduction to law and principles of law, using practice groups and other methods of instruction in practice. Fourth, during their third year students-at-law would be required to work full time in a law office in Ontario under articles to gain practical experience. Fifth, during their fourth year students would be required to attend lectures while concurrently serving under articles in a law office in Toronto. The curriculum in the fourth year was to consist of special lectures on specialized subjects.

Had Convocation adopted Jamieson's position in January, the crisis precipitated by Wright's resignation probably would have been avoided. Certainly Wright would have had difficulty attacking the resolution, although he would have objected to parts of it. But Wright's unyielding opposition to the status quo had led the benchers to reject any idea of compromise, and by offering him less they put him in a position to win more. The result was that the benchers found themselves appointing still another liaison committee to confer with the University of Toronto on matters of legal education, and authorizing a special committee on staffing to hire 'such full-time and part-time lecturers as may be required' for a one-year period. Wright, who realized that the benchers would need to hire law teachers, and knowing the benchers' preference for things English, had anticipated as early as mid-March that they were likely to seek the services of English professors. In a letter to A.L. Goodhart he had suggested that English law professors not accept any offers from the law society.[16]

Despite Wright's letters, Beaton and Chitty, with the assistance of Frank Gahan and Sir Norman Birkett, managed to find someone who seemed admirably suited to the deanship of Osgoode Hall. Charles Ernest Smalley-Baker, a Canadian, was born near Saint John, New Brunswick in 1891.[17] He received a BA from Acadia University in 1912 and an LL B from Harvard in 1915. After his call to the New Brunswick bar, he enlisted in the Nova Scotia Highlanders. In 1917, while serving in France, he was wounded and discharged as medically unfit. He moved to England, and, using his legal training did a considerable amount of court-martial work and was soon appointed dean of the law department of the Canadian Army Educational Scheme in London. In 1918 he received a Rhodes Scholarship to Oxford. He attended St John's College and eventually graduated with honours in jurisprudence. He was called to the English bar in the Inner Temple, and won the Yarborough Anderson Scholarship. For four years he practised law in London. In 1924 he became the first professor of law of the University of Birmingham; he developed the law faculty at that university, and later was appointed dean.

When Smalley-Baker accepted the deanship of Osgoode Hall he was fifty-eight, and his best years were behind him. He had never achieved much repute as a scholar. When Wright was informed of his appointment, he had to write to his friends in England asking for information about this unknown Canadian.[18] Nevertheless, Smalley-Baker was an important find for the benchers. He had impressive credentials and gave Osgoode Hall some much-needed academic credibility. Moreover, he was familiar with the English system so much loved by the benchers and was a Canadian by birth. He also had experience in law school administration and in building a faculty. The benchers were proud of the 'splendid work done by Mr. Beaton and Mr. Chitty in obtaining a Dean of such remarkable distinction.'[19] To resurrect the school, Smalley-Baker needed to hire a staff to teach the 700 or so students. He brought with him David L. Smout from Birmingham, who was appointed a full-time lecturer. Smout was highly thought of and credited with the survival of the school in the difficult years after the resignations.[20] The rest of the teaching staff was made up of part-time lecturers, from establishment figures such as Mike Chitty and H.W.A. Foster to young barristers with solid academic backgrounds such as W.Z. Estey and S.L. Robins. In 1950 the full-time staff was increased with the appointment of H. Allan Leal and Donald B. Spence.

On 3 May 1949, while the benchers were engaged in the search for a new dean, the University of Toronto officially informed the law society of the establishment of its own professional law school, and requested that its LL B graduates be given at least two years' credit under the society's new 'four-year plan.' This proposal was adopted by the benchers at a special Convocation on 29 June.[21] The benchers stipulated that in order to be eligible for the two-year credit, University of Toronto graduates had to hold a pre-law university degree; those who graduated from the law school after completing only two years of university would not be eligible for the credit.

It seems likely that the university's proposal was meant as a compromise that the benchers could readily accept. University of Toronto graduates would have to complete one full year of articles and one year of combined articles and training at Osgoode Hall, and the benchers would not be able to say that they were not receiving practical as well as theoretical training. But it soon became clear that the university had given up too much. While Osgoode Hall graduates would be called to the bar four years after entering law school, University of Toronto graduates would have to wait an additional year. Wright and his colleagues soon learned that only a handful of students were willing to invest an extra year of their life to acquire the legal education that the University of Toronto offered, and the one-year 'penalty' at times seemed to threaten the very existence of the law school.

By the summer of 1949 Wright could feel some satisfaction at what he had accomplished at the University of Toronto and indirectly at Osgoode Hall, but he was soon reminded that open defiance of the law society carried a price tag. In August he attended the CBA annual meeting in Banff, Alberta, accompanied by his seventeen-year-old son John.[22] He later recalled the 'most unpleasant experience' that occurred during his trip: 'From the time I boarded the train until the time I returned, I was literally forced from car to car by certain members of the Association who seemed to treat me as some kind of moral leper and who were fairly vocal about it in my presence and in the presence of my son.'

Wright would remember the treatment he received from the members of the association, and that he was 'hastily dropped' from the CBA committees on which he had been serving prior to his resignation from Osgoode Hall. He never again attended a CBA annual meeting.

In September, representatives of the University of Toronto met with Gershom Mason to reopen the issue of recognition of its LL B graduates.[23] It was agreed that the matter would be referred to the joint committee. Notwithstanding this mandate, the joint committee does not seem to have met during the academic year 1949–50. It seems likely that Sidney Smith and Caesar Wright were simply too busy with the running of their new law school to worry about committee meetings. The benchers, of course, were happy to let matters remain as they were.

Wright did find time in October to attend a symposium on legal education at the University of British Columbia. The paper that he presented there, which dealt with the need for university law schools, was not of the same quality as his earlier lectures. For Wright, the most important event of the symposium was his introduction to Dean Erwin Griswold of Harvard University. Over the next few years Wright was to use Griswold as a sounding-board for his ideas, much as he had done with Arthur Vanderbilt. Griswold was born in East Cleveland, Ohio, in 1904.[24] After obtaining his AB and AM degrees at Oberlin College, he enrolled in Harvard Law School. He was there when Wright was, but the two men seem not to have met. Griswold received his LL B from Harvard in 1928 and his SJD in 1929. From 1935 to 1946 he was a professor of law at Harvard, and from 1946 to 1967 he served as dean.

Wright sent Griswold a package of reports and clippings dealing with the Ontario legal education problem. Griswold's reply buoyed Wright's confidence and enthusiasm:

I want to tell you that I greatly admire your courage in this matter, the ability with which you stated the problem, your skill in handling it, and the forebearance and restraint with which you state your position. I put the papers down with the feeling that they disclosed a really important episode in the history of legal education, and that you have been a great protagonist for the right view. I wish your problem and what you have done about it might be much more widely known in this country.

You deserve a hearty thanks and [the] appreciation of all of us who are engaged in legal education.[25]

When Wright and Griswold met again in December 1949 at the Chicago meeting of the American Law Teachers Association, Griswold repeated that Wright's struggles were part of an important chapter in the history of legal education.[26] Griswold believed that American law teachers could profit from the story of Wright's dealings with the law society, and he suggested that Wright prepare an article for the *American Journal of Legal Education*. Griswold knew that Robert Kramer, the editor of the journal, was at the conference; one morning he and Wright 'went on a prowl' for Kramer. They were unable to find him, but the idea of an article was not dropped.[27] On 4 January, after Wright's return to Toronto, Wright wrote to Kramer, telling him the story of his meeting with Griswold and Griswold's suggestion that he write an article. Was Kramer of the opinion that there would be an American audience for such a story? Kramer said that he would be happy to have a paper from Wright on the subject.[28]

Wright's article was entitled 'Should the Profession Control Legal Education?'[29] In a letter to Mr Justice Ivan Rand of the Supreme Court of Canada, who was writing an article of his own on legal education, Wright said, 'I have tried to make the article as objective as possible and it is slanted to the American problem of an integrated bar but I have no doubt that I may not have entirely succeeded. I am confident, however, that all facts mentioned are capable of proof.'[30]

An important development of the academic year 1949–50 was the recruitment by the University of Toronto of Wolfgang Friedmann and James B. Milner. Friedmann was recognized as a leading scholar in the field of jurisprudence. He was born in Berlin in 1907, and practised in Germany from 1924 to 1933.[31] In 1933 he left Germany to live in London. From 1938 to 1947 he lectured in law at the University of London, but had enough spare time to act as a senior executive in the political intelligence department of the British Foreign Service and, after the war, in the allied military government of Germany. He then moved to Australia, and lectured at the University of Melbourne. Friedmann undertook a lecture tour of Canadian and American universities during the academic year 1949–50.[32] One stop on his tour was the new law school at the University of Toronto. Wright had known Friedmann for a number of years and had published several of his articles in the *Canadian Bar Review*. In a letter to Sidney Smith recommending that Friedmann be hired, Wright pointed out that Canadian law schools had 'devoted themselves almost exclusively to the technical minutiae of positive law ... [and] left a gaping void in the development of juristic and jurisprudential thought.'[33] The statement was one that could reasonably have been applied to Wright's own legal scholarship.

While Friedmann's appointment brought the University of Toronto a distinguished international scholar, the acquisition of Jim Milner was, in the long run, an even more important gain.[34] Friedmann's writings had gained him international recognition (and eventually a position on the staff at Columbia University), Milner was a law teacher par excellence, and 'an internationally recognized authority on town planning law.'[35] Milner was born in 1918 in Amherst, Nova Scotia. In 1939, after obtaining an LL B from Dalhousie University, he worked with the Foreign Exchange Control Board in Ottawa. In 1945 he joined the faculty at Dalhousie Law School, where he taught until 1949. Milner then attended graduate school at Harvard.

Friedmann and Milner brought the number of full-time teaching staff at the Faculty of Law to eight; seventeen practitioners taught or helped with clinical work on a part-time basis. The law school now had a staff 'second to none' in Canada.

In June 1950 the university reopened the issue of recognition by the law society, and pushed for the first time for 'full recognition' of its three-year LL B program. On 9 June Henry Borden, on behalf of a university committee, wrote to Cyril Carson, the new treasurer of the law society.[36] After briefly reviewing the developments at the law school and the school's program of 'theoretical' and 'clinical' instruction, Borden stated, 'the University feels that its programme of instruction and teaching staff are such that three years' full time attendance at the University school should be considered as at least equal to three years' attendance at Osgoode Hall Law School, one year of which is part-time only.' The University of Toronto asked the law society

(a) to require no further law school work by students who enter the University school of law as graduates of a recognized university in an approved course and who graduate from the university with the degree of Bachelor of Laws and,

(b) to admit such students to the practice of law in Ontario after they have spent one year under articles of apprenticeship with a solicitor at any place in Ontario.

Carson's response was abrupt: the matter of recognition had already been 'settled and approved,' although the benchers would give the matter full consideration.[37] Borden replied on 23 June that the University of Toronto Faculty of Law was intended to be a 'national' school. Students from across Canada were enrolling, and the 'course was designed to provide a well rounded, three year professional course in law which would be sufficient for admission to practice after an appropriate period under articles.'[38]

No meetings between the university and the law society were held until October. At that time, it was decided that informal meetings between Henry Borden and Beverley Matthews, representing the university, and Cyril Carson and Gershom Mason, representing the law society, would be more appropriate than calling a formal joint committee meeting.[39] On 13 October Borden, Matthews, Carson, and Mason discussed legal education in general, not the specific issue of law society recognition of the University of Toronto LL B program. Over the next six months three more informal sessions were held. Like the first meeting, they dealt with the broader issue of the future of legal education in Ontario. At the April 1951 meeting it was generally agreed that further meetings would not be fruitful unless the suggestions that had been made in the informal sessions were committed to writing. Henry Borden offered to prepare such a document. On 29 August he sent a draft to Cyril Carson, but added that in his view it did not approach the matter in the way the four participants in the informal sessions had intended. Nevertheless, Borden asked that the document be considered. Although no copy of the draft seems to have survived, its substance is discussed in a letter from Cyril Carson to Henry Borden, in which Carson states that he gave the letter careful consideration and sent a copy to Gershom Mason.[40] Both Carson and Mason shared Borden's view that the document did not serve the intended purpose. Although Carson's letter says that Borden had promised to try to have a new document prepared along the lines of what had originally been contemplated, no such document seems to have been prepared. Borden told Carson, 'I do not refer at this time to the other matters mentioned in your letter because, as you indicate, our discussions were informal and carried on between individuals without reference to our respective committees and because I feel that no useful purpose would be served by doing so at this time as you and I are both going to be away for several weeks.'[41]

This incident suggests that there may have been some differences of opinion among the members of the university committee. It seems likely that Borden did not prepare the 29 August document after all. Carson pointed out in his letter to Borden of 4 February that it was Borden and Matthews who steered the informal discussions away from consideration of the university's request for full recognition and towards 'much broader questions relating to the future of legal education in Ontario.' Could it be that Wright and Smith were unhappy with the direction that the informal discussions had taken? If so, it would explain why Borden emphasized in his letter of 7 February that the discussions were informal and carried on 'between individuals without reference to our respective committees.'

Be that as it may, there is no question that the informal discussions did not achieve the result hoped for by the university. On 31 January 1952 Borden, as chairman of the university committee, asked that the request made almost two years before be dealt with by the law society so that 'these matters should be cleared up as soon as possible in order that the uncertainty of plans for the future of legal education in Ontario should be clarified for the University, the Law Society and prospective students at law.' In contrast to his statement in the letter of 7 February, Borden was careful to point out that the university's legal education committee had reviewed the whole question of recognition and had instructed him to write this letter. He took care to set out the position of the university and to avoid any references to his own opinion.

Following the 17 April Convocation, the law society special committee met to deal with the two University of Toronto requests. The special committee, which consisted of Cyril Carson, Gershom Mason, Park Jamieson, W.J. Beaton, J.W. Pickup, and J.J. Robinette, decided to reject the university's requests. Cyril Carson drafted a report, which, after review, was presented and adopted by Convocation on 14 May 1952.[42] The report unanimously recommended that Convocation not grant the university's request. The report reiterated the benchers' long-standing position that a student was not properly qualified to practise until he had received adequate practical training and experience. It noted that in the four-year Osgoode Hall course begun in 1949, students served the last two years under articles of apprenticeship. The first of those years was served in a law office. During the second year, the student was in 'full-time service of a law office in Toronto except for two lectures of fifty minutes each during five days of the week.' If the university's request was granted, graduates of the University of Toronto law school would serve a period of office apprenticeship approximately one-half as long as that served by Osgoode Hall students. The four-year Osgoode Hall course had several advantages. During his third year the student could serve his apprenticeship at a law office at any place in Ontario. In his fourth year he had to article in Toronto, but this was advantageous since various administrative offices, such as the offices of the Supreme Court of Ontario, the public trustee's office, bankruptcy court, and the master's chambers, were located in the city. All law students would have the opportunity to become acquainted with practice in these various offices. The committee was also of the view that the fourth year at Osgoode Hall had another advantage of 'very great importance to the prospective lawyer.' Law was a profession 'deeply rooted in time-honoured traditions and inspired by the spirit and brotherhood of the law.' In Ontario, those traditions and that spirit were upheld and fostered in students by the law society and by Osgoode Hall itself, 'the home of the profession in Ontario.' To grant the university's request would be to deprive University of Toronto students of the advantage 'of their first direct association with the home of the profession and the seat of the administration of justice for the province of Ontario.' What real benefit, if any, direct association created was unclear; such arguments, however, revealed the romanticized view many benchers had of Osgoode Hall as Ontario's inn of court.

Carson's draft included one paragraph that did not make its way into the final version of the report.[43] Paragraph 19 stated that the committee was prepared to recommend that some concession be made to the university in addition to that granted in June 1949 – namely, that University of Toronto graduates be required to take only those courses offered in the fourth year of the Osgoode Hall program that were not covered at the University of Toronto. These included bankruptcy, bookkeeping and accounting, and administration of estates. University of Toronto graduates would be required to write all fourth-year exams, however. W. Earl Smith wrote to Park Jamieson on 22 April asking if paragraph 19 was what the committee had decided upon. In passing, he noted that J.W. Pickup had suggested that university graduates take their fourth year as an articling year, not necessarily in Toronto, and then write the bar exams. Park Jamieson responded that he did not believe that paragraph 19 set out accurately what the committee had decided; the committee did not want University of Toronto graduates to skip lectures in the fourth year because they would miss the advantages of being in attendance at Osgoode Hall. He cited the treasurer's analogy to the advantages of attendance at the inns of court.

Carson's and Pickup's suggested compromises never made their way into the final report. Instead, the report supported the status quo and offered the university nothing it did not already have.

10

The Road to Compromise

The 1952 special committee report destroyed any hope that the Law Society of Upper Canada would voluntarily grant the University of Toronto full recognition for its three-year legal program. Sidney Smith and Caesar Wright resolved to use different tactics. They considered at least two approaches: public pressure, which had worked effectively in 1949 to force change upon the benchers, and legislative action.

Wright had mentioned the possibility of a political solution as early as the summer of 1945. He and Smith had discussed in March 1949 the necessity of seeking legislative intervention, and there is some evidence that in March 1950 Wright was attempting to marshal the arguments in favour of a legislative solution.[1] In November 1950 he sent a copy of an article he had published in the *Journal of Legal Education* to Premier Leslie Frost of Ontario, yet another indication that he was seeking political support.[2]

Wright set out the university's reaction to the special committee report in a letter to Professor Julius Stone of Australia:

For two years we have had outstanding a request with the Law Society of Upper Canada that our students be exempt from further academic work so that we would be treated on a basis of equality with the school conducted by the Law Society itself. About three weeks ago, the Law Society got around to answering our request with a very cold 'no' which means we are again placed in a position of inequality where prospective students entering our School must contemplate five years after graduation in Arts before being admitted to practice which, as you can readily see, would mean at least eight or nine years after high school leaving.

The implications from this might be serious unless our Board of Governors at the University is prepared to fight and, in particular, attempt to obtain some kind of assistance from the Government. I feel reasonably confident that the morale of the Governors has been stiffened, if anything, by this action but I do think that this is a critical period in the struggle here.[3]

On 25 October Wright spoke on the legal education controversy to a group of lawyers in Oshawa.[4] Remington White, a Beaverton lawyer, set out the audience's reaction to Wright's remarks in a letter to Wright.[5] When he had attended Wright's lectures at law school, he said, the class had in essence been divided into those who looked forward to Wright's lectures and those who were contemptuous of them; 'at the meeting the other night, we simply saw and heard those same two divisions of thought and values more sharply emergent.' He was 'greatly concerned' when he heard a bencher publicly charge Wright with 'deliberate misrepresentation of everything stated so far.' He equated the remark to a 'stink-bomb' thrown into the audience. The audience was 'unruly and partly antagonistic,' and Wright's address was marred by 'interruption and assault.' White suggested that in similar situations the chairman of the meeting ought publicly to name each heckler, 'his status as a bencher or otherwise and his home town, for the enlightenment and appraisal of the audience.' In this way people would be able to put the remarks of the heckler into perspective, and meetings might be made more orderly and constructive.

The reception Wright received at the Oshawa meeting underlined the strong negative reaction he elicited from certain members of the legal community. For many, feelings of personal animosity towards Wright prevented them from objectively assessing the merits of his case. Wright was abrasive and domineering in public, and this demeanour made more enemies than friends. In terms of achieving a workable compromise with the law society, Wright had become a liability to the university.

The intensity of the university's publicity campaign increased in February 1953 with the publication of the president's annual report to the Ontario government. Sidney Smith delivered a scathing attack on the injustice of the law society's rejection of the university's request for recognition. By denying that request, he said, the benchers 'equated arbitrarily' three years of legal education at the University of Toronto to two years at Osgoode Hall; but 'in education, as in mathematics, three is greater than two.' Once again Smith was careful to point out that the university recognized the need for practical experience; he cited the 'clinical teaching' or 'field work' offered in such courses as trial practice, conveyancing, and company law. He then suggested that University of Toronto graduates might be required to serve a period of articles of apprenticeship equivalent to the third year of the Osgoode Hall curriculum and to the portion of the fourth year that Osgoode Hall students spent working in a law office. Such a regulation 'might be less indefensible than the present one.' Smith stressed that what was most upsetting about the existing requirements was that the University of Toronto graduates, who had an additional year of classroom instruction, were required to take further classes at Osgoode Hall in their fourth year. They were 'bracketed with Osgoode students who – it must be kept in mind – have had but two years' instruction ... This is manifestly inequitable, and gives color to the charges of monopolist control of legal education in Ontario.' He failed to mention that the university itself had originally suggested the two-year credit scheme.

Ontario's newspapers quickly picked up Smith's criticisms. The *Globe and Mail*, in an editorial of 29 January 1953 entitled 'Doctor Smith Rebukes the Benchers,' criticized the law society for its lack of recognition of the university's law program. Times had changed. In 1949, Wright's charges of monopoly and self-interest had gone largely unanswered; the benchers' hard-line position and policy of silence had given Wright a strategic advantage that he exploited fully to win public support. Now, the benchers' position was no longer difficult to defend. They had adopted some of Wright's proposals and had granted a degree of recognition to the University of Toronto Law School. Moreover, the benchers themselves, through their public relations committee, now actively defended their stance. Park Jamieson and W. Earl Smith wrote letters to the editors of all the newspapers that carried articles critical of the law society.[6] Cyril Carson prepared and distributed a press release entitled 'The Law School Controversy.'[7] Copies of an article from the *American Bar Association Journal* entitled 'Law Schools and the Layman: Is Legal Education Doing Its Job?,' which was critical of the American academic approach to legal education, were sent to all members of the law society by the public relations committee.

When Wright received his copy of the article, he told W. Earl Smith that he was pleased that the benchers were circulating articles of this nature, which drew to the attention of the profession 'the need for the improvement of legal education in this province.' He noted that the period of time that Canadian law students served under articles 'should supply the answer to many criticisms made of the American scene.' He was also happy to point out that the author of the article had stated that no existing system of law teaching could be defended on the ground that it had produced splendid lawyers in the past; he added, 'I feel sure that if we are able to approach the question of legal education in this spirit, there is every hope that future discussions will produce considerably more light and less heat.'

In his press release Cyril Carson briefly reviewed the developments to date. He characterized the university's request as a 'demand,' and stated that it was difficult to understand this demand in light of Sidney Smith's statement in his annual report for 1949–50 that he recognized that University of Toronto graduates must comply with the articling requirements applicable to all law school graduates. He noted that the benchers' view that two years of articles were necessary had been confirmed by a study of the English law society requirements. He summarized the controversy as follows:

On the one side is the opinion of the Dean of the University School of Law, apparently concurred in by the President of the University of Toronto, that one year's service under articles is sufficient. On the other side is the opinion of the Benchers of the Law Society, all practicing lawyers and the duly elected representatives of their profession, that two years' service under articles is required.

Surely the practicing lawyers of Ontario are best able to judge the period required for service under articles before Call to the Bar.

The law society sent a copy of Carson's statement to its members and to the newspapers.

The law society was well aware that Smith's report would be read by the Ontario government, and that University of Toronto law students were lobbying members of the provincial legislature to support a reform of legal education.[8] Shortly after Carson's statement appeared in the press, W. Earl Smith had a lengthy conversation on the telephone with Dana Porter, the provincial attorney general. Smith was pleased to learn that Premier Leslie Frost had 'no intention of touching this question this session' and that if anything further developed that the premier 'would see the benchers before taking any action.'[9] Smith also sent Porter clippings from newspapers that supported the law society's position.[10]

The law society had learned much from its mishandling of Wright's media campaign in 1949. Then, the newspapers had quoted Wright extensively and had inferred from the law society's silence that it had something to hide. Now, the law society effectively countered the media campaign mounted by Wright and Sidney Smith. As a result, press reaction was mixed: Wright and Smith could count on the *Globe and Mail* for unqualified support, and the benchers could rely on the *Telegram* for approval.[11]

How long would the University of Toronto Board of Governors support a full-time teaching faculty of eight for a law school in which only fifty-five students were enrolled? On 18 February Sidney Smith formally asked the law society to reconsider its position.[12] Cyril Carson responded that the benchers disagreed with Smith's suggestion that the controversy really centred on the overall number of years required before university graduates could be called to the bar. The benchers believed that the issue arose from a fundamental difference of opinion on the amount of practical training required and the time that should be spent in the milieu of Osgoode Hall. He stated that the fourth year of the Osgoode Hall program could not be considered separate and apart from the course as a whole. He then repeated the law society's least convincing argument (and its most firmly held belief) – that law students derived special benefits from direct association with Osgoode Hall, Ontario's equivalent to the English inns of court.

On 27 March Sidney Smith informed the university's board of governors that Convocation had refused to budge.[13] After a lengthy discussion the governors decided to remove Wright from their legal education committee. This was the university's first open acknowledgment that Wright had become a stumbling-block in its efforts to deal with the law society. In the university's files there is a handwritten note from Sidney Smith indicating that this was a message that Smith wanted to deliver to Wright personally. Smith recognized that his old friend who so thrived in battle would need some convincing that 'they also serve who only stand and wait.'

While the law society was dealing with Sidney Smith's request for a reconsideration of its position, the controversy between the University of Toronto and the law society finally became a subject of discussion in the legislative assembly of Ontario. The issue arose not out of any lobbying by Smith or Wright, but as a result of actions taken by the students at the University of Toronto Law School. The students, who felt discriminated against, organized a picket line outside Osgoode Hall, distributed broadsheets denouncing the discriminatory practices of the law society, and wrote editorials in student publications criticizing the benchers.[14] They may also have lobbied individual members of the provincial legislature.[15] All of this activity led Peter Manley, an opposition MPP from Stormont, to ask a question in the legislature of W.J. Dunlop, the education minister: Why were University of Toronto law graduates obliged to study one year longer than Osgoode Hall graduates before their call to the bar? Dunlop replied briefly that the Law Society Act enabled the society to set the standards for legal education in the province and that so long as the act was in force such matters would remain the benchers' responsibility. Another opposition MPP, Joseph Salsberg of St Andrew, rose to state that that was hardly a complete answer. It was within the competence of the legislature to change the statute, and 'some of the outstanding educators of this province ... are asking this Parliament to change the law, so that a graduate of the Law School of the University of Toronto will be permitted to practise the law within this province ... [When students of the University of Toronto] feel compelled to engage in demonstrations, and parade down the streets with banners, I think it is time this house sat up and took notice.'

The government's position was more clearly stated on 25 March when the Liberal leader, Farquahar Oliver, asked Attorney General Dana Porter to intervene in the controversy.[16] Porter replied that the attorney general would not intervene; the matter was for the benchers to decide. He added, 'They should be complimented for the position they have taken. This does not mean that further conversations will not take place.' He later commented that the law society had taken 'a very sensible position' and that the two years of practical experience required of law students before being called to the bar constituted a protection to the public. In an editorial on 21 March 1953, the *Globe and Mail* characterized the attorney general's remarks as 'a masterpiece of fatuity.'

Although no further discussions of legal education took place in the legislature, University of Toronto files show that a good deal was being done behind the scenes to persuade the Ontario government to take action. In 1954 Sidney Smith mentioned in a letter that 'representations [had] been made over a period of years on behalf of the University of Toronto to the Premier and the Attorney General of Ontario asking for a more equitable recognition of graduates of the University of Toronto School of Law.'[17] All of those representations were uniformly rebuffed. Among Wright's papers is draft legislation to amend the Law Society Act, the Barristers Act, and the Solicitors Act, and an explanatory memorandum setting out the proposed changes.[18] The proposed amendments were designed to interfere as little as possible with the law society's powers to make rules and regulations governing admittance to practice. Graduates of approved law schools established and maintained by a university in Ontario would take the provincial bar examinations after spending one year under articles.[19] The bar examinations would be given to all graduates who applied and the same standards of fitness and qualification would have to be met by all applicants.

By the end of March 1953 it seemed clear to the university's board of governors that it was futile to make further representations to either the law society or the Ontario government. When the newly reconstituted legal education committee met for the first time on 14 April it began to examine other approaches to the problems facing the law school.[20] One suggestion was that the university establish a six-year program that would lead to the degrees of bachelor of arts and bachelor of laws. There was also a proposal to offer a three-year program together with a con-current two-year program comparable to the two years of full-time instruction given at Osgoode Hall, and consideration was again given to the possibility of a Manitoba-type arrangement whereby the university school would amalgamate with Osgoode Hall Law School under a board of trustees composed of an equal number of representatives from the university and the law society.

Dean Wright, although not a member of the committee, attended the meeting. He reported that members of the teaching staff were of the opinion that a marked increase in first-year enrolment was expected for the academic year 1953–4. The university would be in a better bargaining position with the law society if it could increase the enrolment of students of good academic calibre in the next few years. Smith replied that recruiting activities had already been inaugurated among graduates of Ontario universities. He told the committee that the teaching staff was anxious to be assured that the board of governors would continue to support the law school, and on Thursday, 23 April, the board passed a resolution expressing appreciation for the work of the staff in reorganizing and improving the school and increasing its prestige throughout Canada and abroad. The board reaffirmed its intention to support the school and 'thus ensure the development of a centre for legal education and re-search, second to none in Canada.'[21] At the second meeting of the committee on 25 May, Sidney Smith responded to the proposals put forward earlier. For various reasons he found all of them unacceptable.[22] The committee concurred with Smith's views, but did resolve to give further consideration to the possible co-operation, co-ordination, or amalgamation of the university's law school with Osgoode Hall. Little seems to have come of the committee's deliberations, however. No revisions to the law school's curriculum and no new attempts at co-operation or amalgamation were made.

Indeed, 1954 was a year of relative calm in relations between the university and the law society. There was a minor stir in the summer when Mr Justice Ivan C. Rand of the Supreme Court of Canada published an article in the *Canadian Bar Review* that was mildly critical of the benchers' stand on legal education.[23] Perhaps the most notable event of 1954 was an attempt by Caesar Wright to prove to certain members of the Canadian legal academic community that a 'situation of strain' did not exist between the law society and the University of Toronto.[24]

Nineteen-fifty-five represented a turning-point in the university's efforts to ensure that its law school graduates received equality of treatment. What made the events of 1955 so different from those of earlier years was that the initiative for change and reform came, for the first time, from the Law Society of Upper Canada.

By 1955 the law society was faced with a serious problem. The number of students enrolled in Osgoode Hall Law School was increasing. In 1949, when the law society's special committee had recommended the preservation of the concurrent system, it had suggested that the increased enrolment at Osgoode Hall following the end of the Second World War was a temporary phenomenon and that in a few years the numbers would return to the pre-war level. In this prediction, as in so many others in the 1949 majority report, the benchers were proved wrong.[25] In the years immediately preceding the Second World War the average enrolment at Osgoode Hall had been about 325.[26] After the war, the returning soldiers contributed to a substantial increase in the student population. In 1947 there were 801 students; between 1948 and 1952 the number of students fell to 624, but by 1955 it became obvious that enrolment was again on the rise. A law school built to accommodate some 300 students would now have to serve at least twice that number.

In January 1955 Park Jamieson, vice-chairman of the law society's legal education committee, declared that some firm and decisive action must be taken to improve the teaching facilities at Osgoode Hall. Jamieson's concerns led to the creation of yet another special committee, consisting of Cyril Carson, John Arnup, William Beaton, Park Jamieson, Hugh McLaughlin, and H.C. Walker. When this group met on 16 February

1955, it considered a lengthy memorandum from the Osgoode teaching staff. The committee was soon convinced that something more than renovations was needed – additional facilities seemed to be required. It asked and received from Convocation the authority to engage architects.

At its next meeting, on 4 March 1955, the special committee learned that within ten years there would be fifteen hundred law students in Ontario, more than double the present number. In an interim report, the committee concluded that 'not only was the present law school accommodation inadequate for present needs but, because of the probability of the enrolment increasing greatly in the future, the present premises would become more and more inadequate as time passed.' It was 'imperative' that, at a minimum, two new lecture halls and 'accessory rooms for study and instruction' be built as quickly as possible.

The special committee realized that planning for the future of Osgoode Hall Law School involved a determination of the school's role in legal education in Ontario. It is important to recall that Osgoode Hall Law School was a private institution not funded by the province. For years critics of the benchers had suggested that the benchers viewed their school as a profit-making enterprise. Whatever truth there may have been in that allegation in the past, there is no doubt that by 1955 legal education had become a costly enterprise. The law society faced major capital expenditures to accommodate a mushrooming student body, and the special committee wanted to settle the important matter of whether the law society 'should continue to assume the increasingly costly bulk of responsibility for legal education.' Pushed finally by the fiscal realities of modern mass education, the benchers decided that it was time to assess the possible role of the universities in legal education in Ontario.

Acting on the recommendation of Convocation, the special committee met with representatives of Ontario's universities at Osgoode Hall on the evening of 30 April 1955.[27] Mr Justice John Arnup, one of the benchers present at that meeting, recalled that 'the atmosphere at the start was electric with tension.'[28] The heads of the other Ontario universities knew of the differences that had existed between the benchers and the University of Toronto in 1949, and of the bitter debates, some in public and some in newspaper columns, that had only made matters worse. The benchers opened the discussion by referring to the situation at Osgoode Hall and to the findings of the special committee. Cyril Carson then invited a general discussion on the topic of legal education. A number of points were raised, including the 'ideal basic law course,' entrance requirements to the law school, the possibility of a university pre-law course, and the combination of university instruction with instruction at Osgoode Hall.

It was Arnup's 'distinct impression' that W.A. Mackintosh, the principal of Queen's University and the elder statesman of the university representatives, would be their leader in any subsequent discussions and negotiations. For many years Mackintosh had made his presence felt. He wanted to ensure that any political solution between the law society and the University of Toronto addressed the interests of Ontario's other universities. It was his particular desire that the door be left open for the establishment of law programs at universities other than the University of Toronto, and that the law society not grant the university any privileges that were unavailable to the other schools. He often pointed out that historically the teaching of law in Ontario had not been limited to the University of Toronto: Queen's had taught law even before the law society had established its own school.

Arnup recalled that the presence of Mackintosh encouraged him, because Mackintosh and Cyril Carson respected and trusted each other. The history of problems between Sidney Smith and the benchers meant that it would have been unwise for Smith to have taken the leadership role. According to Arnup, Queen's University was seriously interested in starting a law school of its own, provided that it would not be subject to the same limitations as those imposed on the University of Toronto. McMaster University was planning to establish a medical school, and did not intend to set up any other professional school; however, it was interested in offering a pre-law program in the Faculty of Arts. The University of Western Ontario had not seriously considered starting a law school, but it too was 'decidedly interested' in a pre-law course. The University of Ottawa, which already had a civil law faculty whose graduates practised in Quebec, was interested in the Ontario developments, but was not well versed in the mechanics of Ontario's legal education scheme.

John Arnup sat across from Sidney Smith at the meeting. It was obvious to him that Smith initially thought that the meeting was a waste of time: 'He doodled on a pad, and said very little until the conversation swung around to the possibility of university law schools.' Yet the meeting ended encouragingly, when Cyril Carson suggested that the university representatives might wish to discuss among themselves the issues raised at the meeting. Carson even called upon them to formulate a proposal for consideration at a future meeting with his committee.

It was 10 June before Sidney Smith and Caesar Wright were able to discuss 'the Benchers' overtures' with W.A. Mackintosh and Alex Corry, the vice-principal of Queen's University.[29] Wright and Smith found that their views and those of Mackintosh and Corry 'were nigh identical.' Corry, not surprisingly, believed that a three-year full-time law school was necessary for proper preparation for the bar. A lawyer by training, Corry had attended the University of Saskatchewan Law School, where he had studied under J.T. Hébert, the author of the 1921 'unsolicited report' on Canadian legal education.[30] He had then done graduate work in England and the United States, and for a time had taught law at the University of Saskatchewan.[31]

Although all four men were concerned about the length of time it took 'recruits for the Bar' to be qualified to practise, they did not want to dilute either the bachelor of arts or the LL B program. (They suspected that the University of Western Ontario might propose to the benchers that candidates be given a BA and an LL B in five years instead of the present six.) Mackintosh and Corry made it clear that Queen's University would not establish a law school unless the benchers removed the handicap under which the University of Toronto Faculty of Law then laboured. All were convinced that the benchers would have to continue to operate Osgoode Hall Law School. If, in ten years, Queen's took 150 law students, Western another 150, and Toronto 350, 850 students would still go to Osgoode Hall Law School.

The informal meeting ended with Mackintosh proposing to discuss the four academics' views with the treasurer of the law society before the beginning of the next school year. Wright said that he would attempt to explain the needs of legal education to President George Edward Hall of Western. All four thought it a good idea to call a meeting of the heads of the universities to be addressed by Mr Justice Rand, who had recently written on the needs of legal education, and by Caesar Wright and Alex Corry.

On 15 September Mackintosh told Carson that the universities were keenly interested in the issue of legal education, and that he hoped to hold a meeting shortly to discuss the matter further.[32] Carson replied that he was 'greatly pleased' to hear of the universities' concern, and that he would 'indeed be interested' to hear from Mackintosh after the university representatives had met.[33] There was no indication in Carson's letter that the benchers had taken 'any irrevocable decision or prejudiced the matter for the future.'[34]

The benchers, however, were moving ahead with their plans to construct an addition to the Osgoode Hall buildings. No word had been received from the universities, and Osgoode Hall was faced with another significant increase in enrolment. The special committee recommended in October that an immediate start be made on the addition. On 21 October the *Globe and Mail* announced that the law society had decided to proceed with the construction of a new wing at Osgoode Hall at an estimated cost of $1.3 million. Sidney Smith was disturbed by the report, and his unease grew when he learned from 'an authoritative source' that Cyril Carson had told Convocation that 'from a meeting held with representatives of Ontario universities, I can state that there is no hope of help from these institutions, and that we will have to go it alone.' Smith passed this information on to Mackintosh.[35] The university presidents must meet as soon as possible; 'after negotiating with that crowd for nine years, and having been "rolled" four or five times, I am wondering if they are now trying to take us all into camp!' Mackintosh refused to jump to a negative conclusion.[36] He told Smith that he had seen the announcement. 'I was not sure whether this represented a decision to care for all comers there or whether it represented an unavoidable increase in space even if they were to look after something like the present registration.' He was willing to meet sometime after 15 November, but only if they had 'a firm knowledge of the facts.' Perhaps the way to settle the issue was to write to Carson and 'ask him a blunt question.' Smith agreed, noting that 'with your gallic touch, the pointedness of the bluntness can be dulled (How's that for a metaphor?).'[37] Carson assured Mackintosh that the actions of the benchers had been taken because of the pressures of the present enrolment at Osgoode Hall and did not preclude the universities from playing a role in legal education in the future.

The public announcement of the addition to Osgoode Hall Law School worked in favour of the universities. In November the law society sent out a notice to its membership. The estimated cost of the new buildings, together with furniture and equipment, was $1.3 million; the law society planned to sell securities worth just under $700,000 to provide financing for the project. It was estimated that after drawing on these funds and on the additional surplus that would be earned during the period of construction, the law society would have to borrow an additional $500,000. The sale of the securities would result in a loss of interest income, and in future the law society would have to look to fees to provide for all school-related disbursements. Effective immediately, solicitors' fees were increased by ten dollars. This announcement immediately stirred up an intense interest in legal education within the profession. A number of people began to think that it was time that the law society let universities play a larger role.

On 29 November Mackintosh wrote to the heads of the Ontario universities calling a meeting for 10 December.[38] Mackintosh set out the results of this gathering in a letter to Cyril Carson.[39] There was 'complete agreement ... on the interest of the universities in having some share in legal education.' The universities were of the opinion that it was not possible to combine the arts degree with the law degree: 'We could not combine effectively the broad general education which the Faculty of Arts is expected to give and concentration on the exacting professional preparation that law students should have.' A number of universities were seriously interested in establishing law schools; Mackintosh estimated that it might be possible to provide in this way, in the next couple of years, for about 700 students, distributed over the three years of the program, in addition to those who would attend Osgoode Hall. He then set out the basis upon which such schools would be established by the universities:

(a) a B.A. or equivalent degree as a minimum entrance qualification.
(b) a three-year course in law, presumably leading to an LL.B. degree, in which the minimum prescriptions for core subjects would be agreed with the Law Society but the University Senates would be left latitude to develop specialties and variations adapted to their own staffs and opportunities.
(c) such time spent by the student under articles as a law clerk, whether or not in attendance at Osgoode Hall, as the Law Society may require.
(d) such examinations for admission to the Bar as may be prescribed by the Law Society but which desirably might follow the pattern of the Royal College of Physicians and Surgeons in not duplicating university and Bar examinations.
(e) such substantial parity of treatment for all students as will make it possible for them to qualify for the Bar in the same length of time whether they have proceeded through Osgoode Hall or through a university law school.

Mackintosh and Carson agreed that representatives from the universities and the law society would discuss all these matters further.[40]

Meanwhile, Wright was encouraging local law associations to discuss the law society's expansion of Osgoode Hall. In a letter to Morris Kertzer of the Carleton Law Association, he noted that 'within the last few months the controversy has shifted from the place where the Law Society wanted it, namely, as a squabble between the University of Toronto and the Society: or perhaps, between President Smith, myself, and the Society.' He added that the real issue remained equality of treatment for Osgoode Hall and university graduates.[41]

On 17 March 1956 the law society had its second full-scale meeting with the representatives of the universities.[42] Cyril Carson opened the meeting with a review of the events that had occurred since the law society had first met with the university representatives. Carson expressed disappointment that there had not been a proposal from the universities to shorten the preparation time for the bar. He read excerpts from Dean Wright's annual report for 1954–5 calling for the establishment of a 'good tough two years in arts in preference to a normal Pass or General Arts degree as a legal prerequisite.' Carson said that the benchers would be willing to consider such a two year pre-law course. The benchers regarded two points as essential – namely, that Osgoode Hall offer a complete course in law and that graduates of any university law course spend two years after graduation under articles before their call to the bar. During the second of those two years the student should work in a law office in Toronto and attend lectures at Osgoode Hall. In other words, the benchers wanted the final two years of the four-year Osgoode Hall program preserved. As long as the universities required three years of full-time attendance in a law school, as compared with two years at Osgoode Hall, it would not be possible to have parity of treatment for all law students.

After some further discussion of ways to reduce the total number of years required before call to the bar, both Alex Corry and Sidney Smith stressed the need for three years of full-time attendance in a professional law school. Corry and Smith also remarked that the purpose of dining at the inns of court in England 'was more formal and gastronomical than educative.' This was an attempt to counter the law society's argument that Osgoode Hall, as the Ontario equivalent of the inns of court, must be attended (if not dined in) by all law students.

Mackintosh, seeing that the benchers were adamant about the retention of the last two years of the Osgoode Hall program and that several universities, at least, were equally adamant that a three-year law course was necessary, proposed a compromise. Would it be possible to have students in attendance at a university law school articled in an office in the area during their third year? Could the third year of the Osgoode Hall law course then be telescoped into the third year of the university law course?[43]

On 18 April Mackintosh told Sidney Smith that Edward Hall had thrown a monkey wrench into the discussion with his earlier suggestion of a two-year arts program followed by a two-year law program.[44] Mackintosh was of the opinion that for the time being the universities were 'stymied.' He had no doubt that what he and Smith had suggested ultimately would be carried out, but that he was inclined to wait and see whether the upcoming election of benchers produced any shift in the balance of opinion in the governing body of the profession.

Several of those running for the position of bencher were favourably disposed towards a larger role for universities in legal education. Richard A. Bell, a prominent Conservative politician from Ottawa, had long been a supporter of the University of Toronto. In February 1953 Bell had answered Cyril Carson's letter to the profession, pointing out the advantages of the university law school. At that time Wright had told Bell that his letter 'gave us all new heart here in the struggle for recognition.'[45] In January 1956 Bell had played an important part in the Carleton Law Association's passage of a resolution calling on the benchers to delay building the addition to Osgoode Hall, and to explore the possibility of decentralizing legal education through the establishment of additional university law schools.[46]

D.A. Keith of Toronto was another candidate who supported the idea of university law schools. In March 1956 he circulated a letter to members of the legal profession pointing out that the 'vital problem of legal education' would be 'the most important matter of policy to engage the attention of the Law Society in the next few years.'[47] In his opinion, university faculties of law should be established at the earliest possible time in co-operation with the law society. In this way the cost of legal education could be borne by the public through grants from government revenue to the universities and from student fees, and would not be a charge on the practising lawyers of the province.

Wright and his colleagues also found some support from yet another candidate, Gordon W. Ford of Toronto. On 28 March he gave Wright a copy of a letter he had sent to Lewis Duncan, a prominent Toronto lawyer and municipal politician.[48] Ford said that 'the entire question of legal education in Ontario requires immediate and dispassionate reappraisal.' The academic portion of legal education should be handled by duly accredited university law schools, and the role of Osgoode Hall should be to provide a post-graduate period of essentially practical training combined with a period of service under articles.

When the election results were tallied at the end of April, Bell, Keith, and Ford had all been elected. None the less, Wright was not particularly pleased by the results, and he did not believe that the benchers were likely to provide much support for university law schools. Most of those elected were incumbents, and the three who supported Wright represented a very small proportion of the total number of benchers. In a letter to Bell, he stated, 'We were all delighted here to think that at least we have one person who will stand up and be counted when the chips are down. I really believe that there are a number of others who would take the same view as yourself if only they had a little cement behind the knees.'[49]

During the summer and the early fall Wright carried on an educational campaign. He wrote to anyone who showed any interest in the legal education system in Ontario, pointing out the possible solutions to the impasse with the benchers. He set out his views fully in letters to Stuart Ryan of Port Hope, who was preparing a report for the Canadian Bar Association.[50] He also wrote to Gordon Ford, the newly elected bencher, citing the difficulties of dividing legal education into practical and theoretical components, as Ford suggested.[51] He wrote to Horace Read, the dean of the law school at Dalhousie University, expressing his sympathy with the problems facing Dalhousie graduates who wished to be called to the Ontario bar,[52] and to Robert Reid, the deputy secretary of the law society, stressing the need for changes in the law society's regulations regarding lawyers moving to Ontario from other jurisdictions.[53] Wright was of the opinion that the regulations, as then constituted, penalized University of Toronto Law School graduates who were called to the bar in other provinces and then sought to come to Ontario. Wright also wrote to Alex Corry in Kingston and to Wilf Gregory, a bencher from Stratford, Ontario, to suggest that equality of treatment of Osgoode Hall graduates and university law school graduates could be achieved:[54] if Osgoode Hall was to require a BA degree for entrance and the universities were to require two years of university training, both an Osgoode Hall graduate and a university law graduate would be called to the bar seven years after graduating from high school.

Wilf Gregory became the means by which Wright and Corry tested their ideas on the benchers. Corry had been in correspondence with Gregory, whom he knew through his Stratford and Liberal party connections. He explained to Wright that he had tried to make it clear to Gregory and, through him, to the benchers that the universities would not accept the proposition that two years of legal training at Osgoode Hall were as good as three years at a university. On 29 October Corry told Wright that Gregory had been discussing with the benchers the possibility that the law society drop out of legal education except to supervise the year under articles and the fourth year of combined articles and study at Osgoode Hall. Gregory got nowhere with this proposal; the benchers were determined to continue to offer a full program at Osgoode Hall. Gregory was sympathetic to the idea that equality of treatment of university graduates could be achieved through differing pre-law requirements. That proposal worried Corry: 'The chief concern that I see to it is that it would tend to let the universities become loaded up with the fellows who are in a hurry to get into the practice of law where they would dilute the more interesting and scholarly types who really want to learn all they can before taking up their profession.'

Corry's letter provided some other important information. 'In the strictest confidence' Corry told Wright that Mackintosh had received 'a curious letter' from Cyril Carson. In the letter Carson asked whether the universities were close to reaching an agreement; he wanted to know the answer before he entered into discussions with individual universities. Both Corry and Mackintosh were concerned that the law society might attempt to destroy the universities' united front and seek separate deals with each school. Mackintosh had replied to Carson by saying that the time had come for the two of them to 'sit down together without the aid of other representatives and without prejudice to see if they two can come to anything which they think might be acceptable to both constituencies.' Corry assured Wright that Mackintosh did not intend to talk to Carson until Wright and Corry had had the opportunity to discuss the whole matter. Wright replied that the whole issue was becoming 'curiouser and curiouser.'[55]

Wright spent the weekend of 12 and 13 November in Kingston conferring with Corry. He summarized the results of their 'extremely good – if somewhat strenuous – weekend': 'Provided that in the contemplated negotiations the position of three full-time years is made an essential and the question of duplication made an issue, if not for immediate settlement, then as a long term objective, I am inclined to think on balance that the parity situation we discussed, a B.A. for Osgoode, two years for university, could do no harm and might, indeed, be of material assistance in bringing in more than one university to fight the further issue that would remain concerning the duplication matter.'[56]

Shortly thereafter, Mackintosh met with Carson and John Arnup. During the meeting Mackintosh suggested that a small study group, consisting of one or two representatives from the law society and from the universities, be constituted to carry out further negotiations. The suggestion was accepted by the law society special committee, and Park

Jamieson and John Arnup were appointed as that committee's representatives. The choice of the university representatives presented a problem. Corry would obviously be one; Wright was, in one sense, the logical
second representative, but he was still persona non grata with many
benchers. Arnup later recalled that Mackintosh was reluctant to have
the discussions proceed without a representative of the University of
Toronto being present. Arnup and Park Jamieson suggested that Jim
Milner be appointed; Sidney Smith, however, replied that 'there were
others on his staff who were more intimately connected with and familiar
with the matter,' and suggested Bora Laskin. But Laskin was not
approached, probably because no one wished to offend Caesar Wright.
In the end, Alex Corry was the sole university representative.

Meanwhile, the full-time faculty of Osgoode Hall Law School prepared
a report for consideration by the law society's special legal education
committee. The report was presented in November and was signed by
vice-dean Allan Leal, who was becoming increasingly involved in the
negotiations.

In the report the staff strongly recommended that admission to the
school should follow the successful completion of two years' work at
the university level. There was also a discussion of the inequality of
office training received under articles; it was argued that practical training given at the law school might be better than the articling training
acquired by some students. Finally, the report argued that the law society
should play a dual role in the province: it should first ensure that Osgoode
Hall could furnish legal training of the kind and quality that would
qualify its graduates to practise law, and, second, if universities in the
province were to establish law schools, the law society should provide
both an accrediting procedure and a mechanism for monitoring the content of the courses offered.[57]

A month later, Vice-Dean Leal wrote to Park Jamieson and John Arnup
with some further thoughts of his own. He suggested that those who
sought legal training for business, industrial, or government careers
would be required to complete two years of university work in liberal
arts, followed by a three-year full-time course of studies in law at Osgoode
Hall law school 'or any other university law faculty.' Those who wished
to practise would, in addition, be required to spend an articling period
in an office anywhere in Ontario and then a final year (or part of a year)
doing clinical and practical work in a program at Osgoode Hall under
the general direction of the Osgoode Hall teaching staff and practitioners.

Neither the report nor the Leal letter was considered in any depth by the law society as a whole. But the members of the special committee who were actively engaged in the negotiations spent many hours discussing them in preparation for what would prove to be the decisive meetings with Alex Corry.[58]

The meetings that finally produced the definitive compromise were held in Park Jamieson's suite at the Royal York Hotel on 18 and 19 January 1957. John Arnup's summary of those discussions is an excellent one:

On Friday afternoon, January 18th, 1957 Alex Corry, Park Jamieson and myself met in Jamieson's suite at the Royal York Hotel. Dr. Corry has referred to it as 'a short meeting, without any convivial preparation.' Neither reference is quite accurate (Dr. Corry also has the date wrong, placing it in March). As I recall it, we met in the early afternoon, that first day, and I am quite sure that by five o'clock, Jamieson had produced some of his deluxe Scotch. I know that we had dinner sent up to the suite; the chef was obviously aware of the Jamieson standards of culinary excellence. We continued talking until about 10 p.m. Dr. Corry with his usual modesty has left the impression that 'all [he] did was to assent to each item of the proposal as it was put forward.' My recollection of his contribution puts it on a higher level.

It is true that Corry, who had not been at either of the two prior meetings, had not fully realized how far down the road the second of those meetings, and the November meeting with Dr. Mackintosh, had carried us towards accord in principle. Nor did he know of the Leal letter, which Jamieson and I agreed with and refined in our private discussions. While Dr. Corry writes that the only point on which we had any extended discussion was whether an applicant for admission to a law school should have a university degree or only two years' university work, and he thought two years of university preparation before a student entered on his legal studies was enough, I have already shown that on the benchers' side we had reached that position months before and the law school faculty had agreed with us. We did put before Dr. Corry all of the pros and cons on this subject that we had heard expressed over the preceding twelve months, but only for the purpose of seeing that he understood all facets of the issue, and that the universities still agreed with us.

On the following morning (Saturday) we reconvened at 9:30 a.m. Jamieson summoned up a card table, produced a foolscap pad, and sat down to write, in his flowing, legible hand, what we had agreed upon the night before. Corry and I made suggestions as to the wording. A few more refinements were added. The result was a short document, less than four foolscap pages in a rather large hand, but the words were chosen with great care. The orderly arrangement was Jamieson's; that was the way his mind worked. The program outlined bore a strong resemblance to that suggested by Allan Leal only a month before, after weeks of discussion in which R.F. Reid, the Deputy Secretary, also participated. The document was eventually reproduced verbatim in a printed version of the complete and final report of the Special Committee dated February 14, 1957, which was sent to every lawyer in Ontario, and eventually, to every university in Canada. Indeed, copies were requested by legal education specialists all over the world. Doubtless most of those copies have disappeared, and in any event, the complete agreement should again be set out. It read:

> Memorandum of discussions re Law schools and Admission to the Bar in Ontario which took place at Toronto on January 18th and 19th, 1957.
>
> Present: J.A. Corry, D.P. Jamieson and J.D. Arnup.
>
> At the opening of the discussions, Mr. Jamieson indicated that the Special Committee of the Benchers had under consideration certain changes in the Osgoode Hall Law School course involving its division into an academic course and a Bar Admission Course. The meeting considered the matters before it having regard to
>
> A Admission to a Law School Course
> B Law School Courses
> C A Bar Admission Course.

The following points were thought appropriate as a basis for further discussion by the Universities of Ontario and the Law Society.

A ADMISSION TO A LAW SCHOOL COURSE

1   The minimum requirement for admission to a law school course should be
(a) Successful completion of two years in an approved course in an approved University after senior matriculation; or
(b) Successful completion of three years in an approved course in an approved University after junior matriculation.
   Note: No opinion was reached as to whether a minimum standing in any such course should be required.
2   Of course, a degree in an approved course in an approved University would satisfy the minimum requirement.

B LAW SCHOOL COURSES

1   The length of the law school course should not be less than three years.
   Under the proposals being considered by the Special Committee of the Benchers, the present Osgoode Hall Law School course would be divided

into a full-time academic course of three years and a Bar Admission Course in which the practical training would be given. Thus the two functions which the Law Society now performs as a teaching institution for Legal Education and as part of the accrediting mechanism of the Law Society would be separated.

2 A law school course should contain certain basic subjects which would be compulsory for all students in all schools.

3 Additional subjects to complete the regular course should be at the discretion of each law school.

4 It is also recognized that some law schools may desire to specialize in particular fields.

5 Successful completion of a law school course should entitle the student to a law degree.

C BAR ADMISSION COURSES

1 Graduates from the Osgoode Hall Law School academic course or from an approved law course in an approved University in Ontario would be eligible for admission to the Law Society and entrance to the Bar Admission Course at Osgoode Hall provided they also satisfied the further requirements prescribed by the Benchers such as citizenship, good character and fitness, and payment of fees.

2 Under the proposals being considered by the Special Committee of the Benchers, the Bar Admission Course would consist of a period of service under articles of not more than 15 months (June 1st to August 31st of the succeeding year) and a further period of practical and clinical training at Osgoode Hall, supervised by members of the Law School Staff and practising members of the profession, of not more than 6 months (September 1st to February 28th).

3 Upon proof of the required service under articles and the passing of such oral and written examinations as may be prescribed, the staff of the Bar Admission Course would certify to the Benchers that the student in question had successfully completed such course.

4 Call to the Bar would then follow in the usual way, which under these proposals, would take place not later than March in each year.

We had no secretarial service and no copying machine. Dr. Corry either made his own copy in longhand or took extensive notes. Jamieson kept the original. We parted, tired but happy, in the belief that we had agreed on a formula that met the principal objectives of everyone concerned. Within a couple of hours Dr. Corry had telephoned Caesar Wright and read him the agreement. Harry Arthurs has written that 'Caesar was jubilant.' Corry telephoned me at my home; the phrase I recall with reference to Caesar's reaction is 'incredulous but ecstatic.'[59]

On Monday, 21 January, Wright told Corry that he and Sidney Smith had spent the evening of that historic Saturday 'considering [Corry's] remarkable achievements.'[60] He and Smith were 'both still somewhat dazed,' but they wanted to let Corry 'know at the earliest possible moment that they were entirely and unreservedly in favour of the proposed terms.' Wright also expressed his 'pleasure, delight and some astonishment at the excellent and constructive measure' that had come out of the two days of meetings; the events had 'done so much to re-establish [his] faith in human nature.' Wright added that on Saturday afternoon, when Corry had called with the news, he had been 'stunned.' He still found it 'a little difficult to realize that the war is over,' and he and Smith had spent considerable time trying 'to convince each other on Saturday evening that such was the case.'

For Wright, this was the culmination of decades of effort. Almost twelve years had passed since he had used the occasion of Bora Laskin's departure from the University of Toronto to recruit Smith's support for the creation of an 'honest to God' professional university law school. Those had been difficult, trying years, years of false hopes and bitter disappointments, years of seemingly interminable negotiations with the law society. As the events of 1955–7 showed, both Smith and Wright had had their faith in human nature shaken. Nevertheless, they had persevered, and had ultimately been rewarded. It could not be said that they themselves had triumphed, however; what had triumphed was a spirit of co-operation, compromise, and mutual understanding. It had taken new, more objective participants in the struggle – John Arnup, Park Jamieson, and Alex Corry – to negotiate the peace treaty. But, as Wright said, the war was over.

Wright and Smith were eager to have the proposed terms accepted in principle by both the law society and the universities. Because they wanted the law society to be 'under no illusion that there is any doubt, equivocation or reservation on anybody's part,'[61] they left it to Corry and Mackintosh to decide whether a meeting of the universities should be called. They emphasized, however, that it was far more important to obtain 'speedy acceptance' than to have any 'formalized expression of united action.' It would be 'disastrous' if the 'proposed terms got noised about' before the matter was finally settled.[62]

Corry and Mackintosh decided not to call a formal meeting of the universities. Instead, Corry got in touch with each university informally, and by 4 February he was able to report to Wright that 'all approve[d] the proposal warmly without reservations.[63] On 14 February the benchers' special committee approved the report setting out the proposed terms, and the next day it was presented to Convocation by Cyril Carson. In John Arnup's words: 'Although a handful of older benchers who had not previously had detailed exposure to what was going on obviously had some lingering misgivings, it was inconceivable that the report of a Special Committee chaired by the Treasurer himself, and which included Jamieson, Robinette, Fred Parkinson, Bill Beaton, R.F. Wilson, Wilfrid Gregory and John Arnup would be opposed. It was carried unanimously.'[64]

The *Globe and Mail*, Wright's long-standing ally, used the occasion to point to the law society's 'undue delay' and to gloat over the society's surrender of its monopoly over legal education.[65] Wright himself attempted to heal wounds by expressing his gratitude to the benchers for their actions. He congratulated Carson on the blueprint for legal education in Ontario. 'Having spent some 30 years in an endeavour – however misdirected it may at times have appeared – to advance that particular cause,' he was 'delighted' with the benchers' action. Both he and Carson 'should turn [their] backs on the past and look forward to the future in a spirit of cooperation and unity of objectives.'[66]

Epilogue

By March 1957 the terms of the compromise were settled. Alex Corry, representing the Ontario universities, and John Arnup and Park Jamieson, representing the benchers' committee, met briefly to review the final details. In his memoirs Corry wrote, 'Like someone who is offered a handsome gift with no strings attached, all I did was to assent to each item of the proposal as it was put forward.'[1] The only issue in dispute was whether the applicant for admission to a law school should have a university degree or merely two years of university work. Thinking that the gains from requiring an additional year or two did not justify putting an obstacle in the way of students of limited means, Corry suggested that only two years of university work be required. The others agreed.

Everyone involved was aware that this was the end of an era for legal education in Ontario. It was now up to the universities to respond. University administrators across the province knew that the presence of a law school on their campuses could only enhance their reputations. The more astute administrators, such as W.A. Mackintosh and Alex Corry, also realized that although there were more candidates for law school than Osgoode Hall and the University of Toronto could handle, it was also likely that there were more universities eager to open up law schools than were needed to meet the demand. 'Other things being equal,' Corry remarked, 'the early bird would have some advantages.'[2]

Given Corry's role in reaching the compromise, it was predictable that Queen's University would move quickly. Amazingly, Queen's was able to open the doors to its law school in six months. Corry, who was acting dean, was blessed with a highly supportive principal and board of trustees. By halting demolition on a house that had been bought as part of a future building site, the university provided a home for the new school. Corry thought that the law school would need only two instructors besides himself to teach the first-year courses required by the law society. To his surprise, two highly qualified people applied for the jobs: D.A. Soberman, who had been teaching at Dalhousie Law School, and H.R.S. Ryan, a Port Hope practitioner for twenty-four years who was eager to teach. Soon after the law school opened, Corry managed to persuade W.R. Lederman to assume the post of dean in time for the 1958–9 school year.

At the University of Ottawa, the new legal education regime was easily accommodated.[3] In 1953 the university had re-established its faculty of law under the chairmanship of Mr Justice Gerald Fauteux of the Supreme Court of Canada. Only courses in civil law were given. But in 1957 the university secured the permission of the law society to offer courses in common law, and the autonomous common law section enrolled nine students in its first year.

In 1959 the University of Western Ontario, which, like Queen's and Ottawa, had attempted to establish a law school in the 1880s, appointed Ivan C. Rand, who had recently retired from the Supreme Court of Canada, as dean. With the assistance of Ronald St John Macdonald of Osgoode Hall, Robert S. Mackay of the University of Toronto, and a recent graduate of Yale, Douglas M. Johnston, Dean Rand welcomed thirty-five first-year students to the law school.[4]

For Osgoode Hall Law School, the years between the 1949 crisis and the 1957 compromise had been devoted to surviving the controversy and rebuilding confidence in the school.[5] Under Dean C.E. Smalley-Baker a larger full-time faculty was slowly assembled, although the curriculum remained unchanged. During these transitional years, Osgoode Hall offered a cumbersome four-year program in which the student spent two years in academic instruction, one in articles, and one in a concurrent program of lectures and clerkship.

The beginning of the 1957–8 school year saw substantial changes in the school. The transition to the three-year LL B program was easily enough accomplished, but now Osgoode Hall was competing for students with three other law schools. The law society had earlier approved the expansion of the school's facilities, including an extension to the students' library, and construction was completed by the fall of 1957.

More important, Dean Smalley-Baker had retired, and the benchers now had an opportunity to appoint a dean who could demonstrate to the universities that Osgoode Hall was ready to move in a more academic direction. The law society found such a dean in the person of H. Allan Leal, QC, who had recently completed his LL M at Harvard.

With the benchers' blessing, Leal began to increase the full-time teaching staff and to replace part-time instructors with academically trained lawyers. Leal also abandoned the traditional 'practice courses,' in which trial and appellate practice and the practical aspects of commercial law, such as drafting contracts and letters of agreement, were taught. Those subjects would be covered in what was now called the bar admission course – that is, the period of articling that now followed the three-year academic course of studies. In an article introducing the new regime at Osgoode Hall, Leal remarked, 'The acquisition of the practical skills and techniques and the inculcation of professional responsibility is no longer the sole responsibility of the Law School.'[6] The administrative structure of the school was altered so that issues such as admission standards, library acquisitions, and curriculum changes were dealt with directly by the faculty and the dean. Leal acknowledged the legal education committee of the law society the controlling body at the school, but 'neither [was] the university faculty free from the control of its senate.'[7]

At the beginning of the 1960s, the general increase in student populations began to be felt in all of Ontario's law schools. Although the enrolment at Osgoode Hall Law School had dropped from 700 students in 1956–7 to 465 in 1960–1, each year the number of first-year students grew. The university law schools, with full co-operation from their university administrations, also expanded to accommodate new students.

Yet at the University of Toronto, Wright and his staff were not always treated generously. During the transitional years 1949–57, the law school was quite small, averaging a total of 60 to 80 students. This was understandable, since prior to the 1957 compromise a University of Toronto student was required to spend an extra year at Osgoode Hall before qualifying for the profession. By 1958, however, the school's population jumped to 153, and it steadily grew through the early 1960s until it levelled off near the 400 mark. Yet, despite this growth, the university was not quick to respond to the physical and financial needs of the school.[8]

From the beginning Wright had vigorously lobbied the university for a permanent home for the law school. In 1949 the law school had been hurriedly located in cramped quarters at 45 St George Street. A few years later, in 1952, the students were moved to Baldwin House; then, with no suitable library space available on the main campus, the faculty was moved to Glendon Hall on Bayview Avenue, seven miles from the main campus, in 1956. Although the premises were pleasant, Wright and his staff felt cut off from the university. Not until 1960 did the university reluctantly offer the law school the use of Flavelle House on Queen's Park Crescent, then occupied by the Department of History. The historic house was clearly too small by itself, and it was renovated and expanded to accommodate a maximum enrolment of 450 students.[9] The law school moved to Flavelle House in 1961, and remains there today.

By 1965 Osgoode Hall Law School faced a crisis.[10] An anticipated growth in the law school population would soon make the physical plant hopelessly unsuitable. No land in the vicinity of Osgoode Hall was available for expansion, and building a new school downtown would be prohibitively expensive. But now that the school's program and philosophy were indistinguishable from those of the university law schools, and now that the profession no longer controlled legal education, no barrier stood in the way of university affiliation. The benchers were well aware that the law society could not cope with the complexities of operating a large law school, and many realized that the administrative structure of a university could best handle the financial needs of such a school. The time had come to affiliate the law school with a university.

No one involved thought for a moment that Osgoode Hall should be moved outside of the Toronto area; York University in Downsview, a northwestern suburb of Toronto, was the only possibility. After informal talks between the law society and the university, the question of affiliation was brought to the faculty in March 1965. Some members of the faculty strongly opposed affiliation, either because they thought the profession should continue to run the school, or because of a great reluctance to leave the centre of the city. In these early discussions attempts were made to reconcile the faculty; none the less, some remained firmly opposed to the idea of affiliation. Although he agreed to represent those favouring affiliation for the purposes of negotiations, Dean Leal decided in early 1966 that he would not move to York. Alan W. Mewett was elected to succeed him as acting dean.

Before it became clear that it was in the best interests of the law school to affiliate with York University, a compromise was suggested, which was designed in part to allay the fears of those who did not wish to leave the heart of the city. It was proposed that Osgoode Hall Law School and the University of Toronto Law School amalgamate to form one large law school, which initially would be operated as an autonomous institution. The school would remain in the downtown university location and would be independent from both the law society and the university, although it was anticipated that it would eventually be affiliated with the University of Toronto. This suggestion was conveyed to Wright and his staff. At a meeting of the council of the Faculty of Law held on 19 April 1965, the proposal was unanimously rejected by Wright and the thirteen other members of faculty 'on the simple ground that the Faculty could not contemplate anything that would interfere with their existing relationship with the University of Toronto.'[11]

By December 1966 the Osgoode Hall professors had come to the realization that affiliation was inevitable, and a formal agreement with York University was signed. Now the faculty faced the enormous task of designing a university law school. Professor Albert Sacks of Harvard Law School, who had been hired as a consultant, evaluated the strengths and weaknesses of the faculty and prepared a report that dealt with nearly every aspect of the new law school, from optimum class sizes and teaching loads to the size and location of faculty offices and the seating capacity of the library. York University provided nearly six million dollars for construction,[12] and 'Osgoode Hall Law School of York University' officially came into existence on 1 July 1968.

Caesar Wright must have viewed Osgoode Hall Law School's transformation to a true university law school with a mixture of personal satisfaction and regret. He had always wanted the law school in which he had invested so much of his energy to assume a position of prominence in Canada, and he had assumed that he would be the one to bring that about. Only because of the intransigence of the benchers had he taken the drastic step of leaving his law school and starting again at the University of Toronto. But his strong opinions and his acerbic personality caused him to make enemies among the benchers, and ensured that he would not play an active role in the slow process of compromise between the law society and the universities. The development of legal education in Ontario, of which he was undoubtedly the architect[13] was now in the hands of younger people, many of whom, like himself, were Harvard-trained.

Wright's prestige as a legal scholar should have led to a judicial appointment at the end of his long teaching career.[14] On 25 September 1957, the chief justice of Ontario, the Honourable John Pickup, resigned his post for health reasons. Wright's chances of being named Pickup's successor seemed particularly good after three highly placed members of the federal Progressive Conservative party called on him. After the meeting, Bora Laskin related, Wright came into his room and said, 'I guess you will be taking over here.' Yet, possibly because Wright had been a lifelong Liberal, or possibly because of his reputation as a rabble-rousing academic, the vacancy was filled on 31 January 1958 by the Honourable Dana Porter.

A week or two before Porter's appointment was announced, Mr. Justice R.L. Kellock resigned from the Supreme Court of Canada. Again, Wright's prospects looked good. Mr Justice Rand, a long-time friend and fellow educator, and Mr Justice Cartwright had telephoned Wright to tell him that they were hoping for his appointment to the highest court in the land. Besides these two influential supporters, Wright had another important, highly placed ally – Sidney Smith, who was then secretary of state for external affairs in the Diefenbaker government. Yet once again the position was given to another man, Wilfred Judson.

According to Laskin, Wright showed no disappointment at being passed over. Instead, he continued in his job as dean and professor. During the early years of the 1960s, when he was in his late fifties, Wright's health began to deteriorate. He carried on his administrative and teaching work, but his scholarly output was minimal. He was consulted by local lawyers, and became an almost legendary figure to his staff and students. He undoubtedly took great pleasure in Bora Laskin's elevation to the Ontario Court of Appeal in 1965.

During the 1966–7 school year Wright worked on the fourth edition of his *Cases on the Law of Torts*, which he had published to great acclaim twelve years before.[15] In that same year the law society's legal education committee decided that it would at last acknowledge Wright's contribution to legal education at the spring graduation exercises of Osgoode Hall Law School. When he was informed that he would receive an honorary doctor of laws degree, Wright told Acting Dean Alan Mewett, 'I need hardly tell you that I view this honour in a very special way in light of my long association with Osgoode.' Wright was finishing the revisions to his casebook and was part way through the proofs when he died suddenly on 24 April 1967.

A few weeks later, the chairman of the law society's legal education committee read the following testimonial to Wright:

Mr. Treasurer, I have the honour to present to you the following citation:
For eighteen years Cecil Augustus Wright was the Dean of the Law School

of the University of Toronto. He began his teaching career 40 years ago as a lecturer and subsequently became Dean of the Osgoode Hall Law School. He has rightly been called the architect of legal education in Ontario. The fact that this Province enjoys a system of legal education second to none in the common law world is to a considerable extent attributable to his selfless dedication. As a teacher he had no peer and generations of law students first received from him a knowledge and understanding of law as an instrument of social justice.

Never once did he compromise his standards, nor was he dismayed if his was the only voice to criticize the inadequate or to advocate reform. He lived to witness the realization of his goals and many legal reforms stand as his monuments. For him, the finest tribute is that many who were his students and colleagues remain to pursue his ideals and practise his precepts.

In March of this year, he accepted your invitation, Mr. Treasurer, to receive the degree of Doctor of Laws, honoris causa, and it is a matter of deep regret that his death intervened. It is fitting that the name of Cecil Augustus Wright be recorded among those worthy of our highest honour.

In a resolution of the council of the Faculty of Law of the University of Toronto published in the *University of Toronto Law Journal*, a more personal note was struck:

An institution, it has been said, is but the lengthened shadow of a man. A cluster of institutions is the lengthened shadow of Cecil Augustus Wright. The whole fabric of legal education in Canada – indeed, by derivation, the revival in this country of law as a thinking man's occupation – is part of this shadow. Another such institution is the *Canadian Bar Review*. Still another, to which it is appropriate more especially to address these remarks, is the Faculty of Law of the University of Toronto – more appropriate because our most intimate association with him was there and there also he was most fervently engaged.

Placidity was not his style. Wherever he saw smugness, wherever he saw obscurantism, wherever he saw unfairness, he was ready to lead a charge against it, partly from a love of the battle itself but with a particular gusto because of his loathing of smugness, obscurantism, unfairness. He devoted his energies, first to bringing law back to life as a university discipline in Ontario, then to expanding its meagre beginnings and obtaining resources to do the quality job he envisaged for the Faculty, and all along to making both the university and the wider community realize the importance of what was at issue. Each of us cherishes his own recollections of particular incidents in these campaigns but all can bear witness to how superbly he functioned both as strategist and as field commander.

He was a lawyer. Keen to maintain the dignity of his, and our, profession, he would neither tamely let it be downgraded by others nor let it degrade itself to becoming either a mechanical trade or an arid pedantry. He insisted that it respect itself and that others respect it.

While intensely serious, he was anything but solemn. What fun it was to be with him – listening to his irreverent sallies in his office, enjoying his hospitality in Toronto or at Magnetewan – wherever he was, the air sparkled. In the legal and university circles of Canada, his enduring imprint will probably be the quality of his intellect. We, his associates, remember him for that but equally for the quality of his spirit. It is hard to believe or accept that that tremendous vital force is no longer with us. Indeed, it will never be wholly gone as long as any remain who had the stimulating privilege of working with Caesar in building the Faculty of Law.[16]

In this book we have focused on Caesar Wright's life and career in the hope that by doing so we might be able to recreate the issues and concerns that made the thirty years between 1927 and 1957 so vitally important in the history of Canadian legal education. The honorary degree granted to Wright by Osgoode Hall was an official aknowledgment of his efforts to reform legal education, and the accolades from his colleagues were a testament to the tremendous force of his personality. But it would be wrong to think of the history of legal education in Ontario as merely the story of one man's personal struggle to create a full-time professional law school. More was at stake than the transformation of Osgoode Hall Law School, and the people and forces at work went far beyond one man's contribution or personality.

As we saw, one of the most striking differences between the law society's school at the beginning of this century and today's Ontario law schools is that law is no longer taught exclusively or even primarily by practitioners or retired judges; there now exists a large body of people whose full-time occupation is the teaching of law. Caesar Wright was not the first of Canada's professional law teachers. He was, in fact, a member of the second generation. He himself was taught by John Falconbridge and Donald MacRae, who were influenced by their colleague R.W. Lee. These, in a sense, were the trailblazers. They fought the early battles for recognition and a degree of influence over the educational process. Through such organizations as the Canadian and provincial bar associations, they made their ideas known to those who controlled legal education, the self-regulating bodies of the legal profession, the law societies.

No doubt change would have come eventually without the confrontational tactics of Caesar Wright. There can be no denying that in 1935, and again in 1949, the old guard of the benchers of the law society did everything in their power to resist change. Men like Denison, Cassels, Mason, Chitty, and Carson were thoroughly convinced that the old methods had proved themselves and ought not to be tampered with. One cannot doubt their sincerity and integrity, although one can suggest that they had lost touch with recent developments, such as the increasing urbanization of Ontario and the trend towards specialization. Their views were clouded by their reverence for tradition and their romanticized perception of the English system. It was their very sincerity and integrity that led to the crisis in legal education. When Wright began to appeal to public opinion, to ridicule their ideas and invite confrontation, they reacted with personal hostility and even contempt towards Wright. These were men who prided themselves on being gentlemen – men to whom an unsullied professional reputation was very important. The thought that an employee of long standing would challenge their judgment in a public forum and would resort to what they saw as personal insults was something that they could not abide. Only when they began to realize that they had misjudged the amount of public support for Wright's ideas did they begin to relent. Their strong personal animosity towards Wright was submerged, to some extent, in the face of the apparent public support for change.

The reasons for such broad public support can only be guessed at. It is likely, however, that the return of the war veterans played a significant part; those young men had experienced the rigours of war and were unlikely to share the attitudes of the older members of the legal profession. Their numbers put a pressure on the legal education system never before experienced, and they were unsympathetic when the conservative, traditional benchers sought to solve the ensuing problems by a return to old practices. Wright, who was at his best in a battle, was able to use his extensive polemical skills to rally the younger members of the profession and the public in general to his cause.

We have emphasized the importance of Wright's first-hand experience with Harvard Law School. It is clear that at Harvard, Wright first saw the possibilities inherent in the concept of the professional law teacher. At Harvard, professional legal educators determined the curriculum and the nature of legal education. They did not need to convince a group of tradition-bound practitioners of the value of their educational methods. Moreover, they saw their influence as legal educators extending into political and social spheres, as advisers to governments and as legal reformers. At Harvard Wright absorbed a vision of the independent legal professoriate, a vision of a subprofession dedicated not only to teaching and scholarly achievement but also to social service and legal reform.

It has been strongly argued by Jerold Auerbach that the development in the United States in the 1920s and 1930s of the legal professoriate should be seen in a very different light, as a conscious attempt by a white male élite to preserve its power against dilution by 'undesirables.'[17] Auerbach has argued that establishment lawyers, fearing the effects of a profession composed of immigrants, blacks, and Jews, attempted to set up barriers to entry. The university-based legal academics led the battle to 'cleanse the bar' of undesirables by aligning themselves with the developing élite of corporate lawyers and confronting the bar at large with the argument that high standards of legal education could in part be guaranteed by ridding the country of the proprietary law schools that catered to the undesirables. Employing the forums provided by the American Bar Association and its offshoot, the American Association of Law Schools, the legal academics relied on the image of the legal academic as 'scientist' whose expertise endowed him with the right to maintain a monopoly over legal education. In Auerbach's view, the legal professoriate, conspiring with the élite of the bar, used legal education as a filtering device expressly designed to secure the exclusion from the bar of immigrants, blacks, Jews, and other 'undesirables.'

Whatever may be said of Auerbach's thesis as it pertains to the United States, the history of the development of legal education in Ontario suggests that it cannot easily be carried over to the Canadian situation. It is true that racism and xenophobia existed among members of the Ontario bar, and that those attitudes had a direct effect on the composition of the legal profession. There is little doubt that in Ontario the bar was elitist, although the exclusivity of the profession was assured more by tradition than by vigilance and conspiracy. The undisputed authority of the law society helped to create a professional status early on, and, in contrast to the situation in the United States, a stratified or differentiated bar never developed: every lawyer went through the single training regime administered by the law society.

There are good reasons for thinking that it is principally the role of the law society that produced conditions that make the Auerbach thesis inapplicable in Ontario. First of all, in Ontario and indeed throughout Canada, the proprietary law school was never a force to be reckoned with, simply because the provincial law societies, in keeping with English traditions, maintained a monopoly over legal training.[18] The statutory authority over legal education vested in the law society, as well as the interest it always took in legal education, ensured that – for better or worse – the private night school was never a viable possibility. By contrast, in the United States, although the law schools at Harvard, Columbia, and Johns Hopkins had, by virtue of their reputations, little difficulty in competing with the night schools, other university law schools were constantly threatened by the cheaper, faster, and easier legal education offered by the proprietary schools. For university legal education to survive, the threat of 'private' law schools simply had to be removed.

In addition, the law society represented and promulgated a relationship between legal academics and practitioners that reflected attitudes quite different from those that appear to have been at work in the United States. There were always occasions when complaints of an overcrowded bar were heard, and, as one might imagine, the practitioner and the legal academic tended to have different views of that issue. That dispute aside, however, two general perceptions existed throughout the early part of the century that serve to distinguish the Ontario situation from that of the United States.

First, non-Toronto lawyers tended to assume that the law society would always cater to the interests of the Toronto bar. This view was often expressed as a challenge to the law society's monopoly over legal education, and as a result, when legal academics in Ontario fought to wrench control over legal education away from the law society, they often found allies in the non-Toronto bar.

Second, practitioners, especially those sympathetic to the law society, saw preparation for admission to the bar as primarily a matter of hands-on practical experience. In the United States, the legal academics joined ranks with the practitioner to convince state legislatures of the necessity for requiring *any* form of organized preparation for the profession; in Ontario, and throughout Canada, articling was (and still is) an established and unquestioned prerequisite for admission to the bar.

Differences in attitude and tradition are often difficult to isolate and substantiate, but those differences can make a great difference in how institutions function. In Ontario, English legal traditions, upheld by the law society, clearly shaped the battle between the law society and innovators like Wright. Ironically, although Wright conceived of his task as that of bringing American ideas into the Canadian context, he may have underestimated the importance of the cultural differences between the two countries, differences which in part determined the nature of the struggle he and others waged.

The crux of the Auerbach thesis deals with the motivations of the legal academics in their crusade for higher educational standards. These academics, or the more influential of them, Auerbach argues, were guided in their crusade by a hidden agenda. Can the same be said of the struggle against the law society in Ontario?

At the outset, it must be admitted that it would be naïve to suppose that the battles that waged in Ontario from 1923, when J.D. Falconbridge was named principal of the Osgoode Hall law school, to 1949, when Caesar Wright left Osgoode Hall and set up his own 'honest to god law school' at the University of Toronto, were all motivated and energized by the simple desire to improve legal education in the province. There was this desire, undoubtedly, but there was also a clear need for legal academics to secure for themselves the elevated status the law society and its defenders were denying them.

It is important to keep in mind two groups when comparing the legal professoriate in the United States during the halcyon days of the Root committee with the contemporaneous Canadian legal educational community. Until the 1940s, the number of full-time academics in Canada was very small indeed. In the late 1920s, when Wright came on the scene, there were fewer than thirty full-time law lecturers in the country. Osgoode Hall Law School had a student population as large as the larger American schools, although it operated with only four full-time instructors when Wright was hired. The legal academic community in the United States during these early decades was gigantic by Canadian standards.

Those in Canada who conceived of themselves as law professors, rather than as practitioners taking a turn at part-time lecturing, fought for recognition as a distinct and respectable aspect of the legal profession. They were neither a politically powerful nor a publicly identifiable group. It is unlikely that they felt confident enough in their power to attempt more ambitious social aims, such as 'cleansing the bar,' even if they had been inclined to do so.

In short, it might be correct to say that, in the absence of evidence to the contrary, in the three decades during which legal education was transformed in Ontario, the Canadian legal professoriate was far too occupied with the basic need to establish itself as a respected subprofession – a source of legal reform and scholarly output – to be interested in, or to have any realistic hope of achieving, more wide-ranging social or professional ends. Moreover, the alliances formed between some members of the practising profession and the legal academics in Canada seemed always to rest on admirable goals: to improve the educational standards of the profession, to produce indigenous legal texts, and to make the profession truly learned.

But if the aims of the leaders of the legal academics in Canada were more modest, and more respectable, than those Auerbach attributes to the legal academics to the south, the extent to which even these modest aims were accomplished by the crisis of 1949 remains an open question. The revolution associated with Wright's name helped to make possible the university of law schools in Ontario, and brought an element of academic freedom and respectability to the subprofession of legal teaching. Yet, ironically, Wright himself did not move very far in realizing the potential of either the institutions or the academic freedom.

When he came to the Faculty of Law at the University of Toronto, and even after the compromise of 1957, Wright did not introduce much in the way of curriculum reform. The courses offered at the school did not differ in any significant way from those offered at Osgoode Hall before 1949, or indeed in the 1960s and early 1970s. It tended to be Osgoode Hall rather than the University of Toronto that experimented with a new curriculum. Nor did Wright do much to encourage the academic, multidisciplinary, extralegal approach to law that he had at times vigorously advocated.

In some respects Wright's own school was less academic and less innovative in its curriculum than Kennedy's school had been in the 1930s and early 1940s, because Wright was at heart a practice-oriented teacher; he was not interested in delving into the intricacies of legal philosophy or examining the social scientific approach to research in the law and legal institutions. As a teacher, he hoped to turn out well-prepared practitioners; as a scholar, he was concerned with the critical analysis of particular judicial pronouncements.

In many respects, in short, Wright created a model for the type of legal teacher and scholar that was severely criticized by the Arthurs commission in the study *Law and Learning*.[19] In its report the commission argued that although legal education in Canada aims at satisfying a variety of goals – from learning legal rules and advocacy skills to developing a humane perspective on law and an understanding of law as a social phenomenon – it lacks the structure to achieve any of them. An 'eclectic curriculum' is typically offered, but inasmuch as the law faculties conceive of themselves as especially concerned with professional preparation, scholarly or social-science-oriented courses, when offered, are not seen as being essential to the educational experience.

Canadian legal scholars tend to avoid the genuinely scholarly study of the law. The needs of the profession are catered to, while legal theory and fundamental research into the values implicit in the law or the actual operation of legal institutions are neglected. Legal academics in this country have not been trained as scholars, for the simple reason that legal training is almost wholly career-oriented; non-professional and interdisciplinary legal studies have not been encouraged. The legal academic who is interested in scholarly legal research must come to terms with the perceived primary aim of legal education – the training of lawyers. The commission concluded:

The scholarly enterprise of law can flourish neither divorced from the profession, nor in its close embrace, nor in hand-to-hand combat with it. Its best prospect for growth and development is therefore to take up a position with the law faculties as a distinct and separate endeavour, with its own goals, standards and basis of legitimacy. Only such a stance will at once stimulate energies, promote sensible interdisciplinary cooperation and provide a free and equal basis for exchange between scholars and practitioners.[20]

Doubtless Wright would have reacted with some disdain to the Arthurs commission's call for an improvement in the 'scholarly education of legal researchers' and for a clarification and legitimation of the role of the non-practising legal scholar whose concerns are fundamental, theoretical, and interdisciplinary legal scholarship. Wright strongly rejected the emphasis of the Kennedy school, whose aims were quite similar to those advocated by the Arthurs commission. Wright was practice-oriented, a man of action, not contemplation.

Yet it must be borne in mind that scholarly research is not meaningful if it is distanced from or in competition with the practice of law. The problem with current legal education, according to the Arthurs commission, is that instead of a pluralistic legal academic community we have an eclectic one, one purporting to satisfy the needs of practical training and scholarly research at the same time and in the same manner. Legal scholarship of a more fundamental sort must coexist with practical legal education, but it must also be independent of the needs of professional training.

Despite the misgivings expressed in *Law and Learning*, however, Wright and his colleagues made it possible for a fundamental legal scholarship to develop in this country. Had Wright and others not fought to move legal education to universities where professional legal educators could achieve a previously unknown level of academic freedom, the recommendations of the Arthurs commission could not be implemented at all. By taking legal education at least in part out of the hands of the practising bar, the reforms of the 1940s and 1950s helped to promote a more forward-looking, reform-minded approach to law and legal education. They were a significant step in an ongoing process. University legal educators are more likely, by virtue of their training and the environment in which they work, to be aware of broader social issues and long-term consequences than are practitioners. Wright did most to make this essential transformation of legal education possible in Ontario.

The debate about the nature of legal education continues. One still hears criticisms of the overly academic approach of the law schools, of the hours wasted on menial jobs during the articling year, and of the tedious weeks spent at the bar admission courses. One still hears prominent Toronto lawyers boast that they got to the peak of their profession by dint of practical experience and hard work, not because of anything they picked up in law school. And one still hears the fainter voice of those legal academics who insist that Canada has produced all too little of scholarly value in the law.

Wright would not have been surprised. He himself might have advocated changes to the present scheme. The compromise of 1957 was never thought to be perfect, but it did represent a system that could be accepted by people holding differing views about legal education and legal scholarship. When the system ceases to be acceptable, it will change. Those changes, however, should not decrease the significance of the story told here: the story of the development of Ontario's professional law teachers, of the 'Americanization' of legal education in Ontario, and of one committed man's struggle against the establishment to introduce reform.

Appendix

THE WRITINGS OF CECIL A. WRIGHT*

1930 'Implied Agency of the Wife for Necessaries' *Canadian Bar Review* 8 (1930) 722

1931 Review of *The Public and its Government* (Frankfurter) *Canadian Bar Review* 9 (1931) 62
Review of *The Law of Canadian Companies* (Wegenast) *Canadian Bar Review* 9 (1931) 594

---

* From 1928 to 1945 Wright also wrote some 237 case comments for the *Canadian Bar Review*, some of which were of substantial length – or at least, he signed or initialled that number. It is uncertain whether other unsigned comments should be attributed to him because Bora Laskin also wrote comments for the *Review*. As Laskin recalled in his memoir of Wright – 'Cecil A. Wright: A Personal Memoir' *University of Toronto Law Journal* 33 (1983) 148, 151 – 'Wright placed great store on the Case and Comment section of the review which he and I wrote in large measure. Some of our contributions were signed with the initials C.A.W. or B.L., but many were unsigned. One of my proudest boasts, exemplifying the influence that Wright had on me, was that there were times when we would wonder, after publication, whether it was he or I who wrote certain case comments which neither of us signed or initialled.' As editor of the *Dominion Law Reports*, Wright was quite active; he wrote editorial comments on twenty or thirty cases per volume, especially during the 1940s.

1932   'An Extra-Legal Approach to Law' *Canadian Bar Review* 10 (1932) 1

1934   Review of *Essays in Equity* (Hanbury) *Canadian Bar Review* 12 (1934) 386

1935   Review of *Legal Essays: In Tribute to Orrin Kip McMurray* (Radin and Kidd) *Canadian Bar Review* 13 (1935) 425
Review of *World Court Reports* vol. 2 (Hudson) *Canadian Bar Review* 13 (1935) 613
Review of *Law and the Lawyers* (Robinson) *Canadian Bar Review* 13 (1935) 690
Review of *Res Judicatae* (magazine of the Law Students' Society of Victoria) *Canadian Bar Review* 13 (1935) 771
'The American Law Institute's Restatement of Contracts and Agency' *University of Toronto Law Journal* 1 (1935–6) 17
Review of *A Treatise on the Law of Torts* (Harper) *University of Toronto Law Journal* 1 (1935–6) 193

1936   Review of *Modern Equity* (Hanbury) *Canadian Bar Review* 14 (1936) 85
Review of *Dominion Report Service, Canadian Bar Review* 14 (1936) 174
Review of *All-Canada Digest, Canadian Bar Review* 14 (1936) 175
Review of *All England Law Reports (Annotated), Canadian Bar Review* 14 (1936) 373
Review of *A Political and Cultural History of Modern Europe* vol. 2 (Hayes) *Canadian Bar Review* 14 (1936) 561
Review of *Index of Canadian Cases Judicially Noted (1929–1936)* (Wrinch) *Canadian Bar Review* 14 (1936) 562
Review of *Fraser on Libel and Slander* (Slade and Faulks) *Canadian Bar Review* 14 (1936) 634
Review of *The Saving of Income Tax, Surtax, and Death Duties* (More) *Canadian Bar Review* 14 (1936) 636
Review of *Annual Survey of English Law 1936, Canadian Bar Review* 14 (1936) 637
Review of *Daly's Canadian Criminal Procedure and Practice before Magistrates* (Popple) *Canadian Bar Review* 14 (1936) 717
Review of *Principles of Contract* (Pollock) *Canadian Bar Review* 14 (1936) 783
Review of *A Digest of the Law of Evidence* (Stephen) *Canadian Bar Review* 14 (1936) 788
Review of *Apportionment in Relation to Trust Accounts* (Chick) *Canadian Bar Review* 14 (1936) 789

Review of *Salmond on the Law of Torts* (Stallybrass) *Canadian Bar Review* 14 (1936) 849

1937 Review of *You May Cross-Examine* (Herman and Goldberg) *Canadian Bar Review* 15 (1937) 55
Review of *Le Droit Civil Français: Livre-Souvenir des Journées du Droit Civil Français, Canadian Bar Review* 15 (1937) 117
Review of *Roman Law and Common Law* (Buckland and McNair) *Canadian Bar Review* 15 (1937) 119
Review of *Assessment and Rating* (Manning) *Canadian Bar Review* 15 (1937) 303
Reviews of *Equity: A Course of Lectures* (Maitland); *The Forms of Action at Common Law: A Course of Lectures* (Maitland); and *Selected Essays* (Maitland) *Canadian Bar Review* 15 (1937) 386
Review of *The Law of Damages* (Gahan) *Canadian Bar Review* 15 (1937) 390
'Law Reform and the Profession' *Canadian Bar Review* 15 (1937) 633
Review of *The Modern Law Review, Canadian Bar Review* 15 (1937) 671
Review of *Modern Equity* 2d ed. (Hanbury) *Canadian Bar Review* 15 (1937) 672
Review of *The Law of Wills* (Bailey) *University of Toronto Law Journal* 2 (1937–8) 189

1938 Review of *Selected Cases on Commercial Contracts* (Caporn) *Canadian Bar Review* 16 (1938) 73
'The Abolition of Claims for Shortened Expectation of Life by a Deceased's Estate' *Canadian Bar Review* 16 (1938) 193
Review of *A Text-book of the Law of Torts* (Winfield) *Canadian Bar Review* 16 (1938) 237
Review of *In the Eyes of the Law* (Mills and Dix) *Canadian Bar Review* 16 (1938) 424
Review of *A Digest of English Civil Law* 3d ed. (Jenks et al.) *Canadian Bar Review* 16 (1938) 505
Review of *Engineering Law* (Laidlaw and Young) *Canadian Bar Review* 16 (1938) 507
'Law and the Law Schools' *Canadian Bar Review* 16 (1938) 579
Review of *Payne's Carriage of Goods by Sea* (Samuel) *Canadian Bar Review* 16 (1938) 748
Review of *The Law of Negligence* (Charlesworth) *Canadian Bar Review* 16 (1938) 752

Review of *Gatley on Libel and Slander* 3d ed. (O'Sullivan) *Canadian Bar Review* 16 (1938) 819
Review of *Hints for Young Solicitors and Articled Clerks* (Gregory and Tweedie) *Canadian Bar Review* 16 (1938) 822

1939   Review of *Essays Dedicated to Mr Justice Cardozo Canadian Bar Review* 17 (1939) 146
'Newspapers and Criminal Trials' *Canadian Bar Review* 17 (1939) 191
Review of *Cases and Other Materials on Judicial Remedies* (Scott and Simpson) *Canadian Bar Review* 17 (1939) 217
Review of *Ontario Statute Citator, 1927–37 Consolidation* (Cartwright) *Canadian Bar Review* 17 (1939) 220
Review of *Stephen's Commentaries on the Laws of England* 20th ed. *Canadian Bar Review* 17 (1939) 283
Review of *Readings in Jurisprudence* (Hall) *Canadian Bar Review* 17 (1939) 365
Review of *The Life of Mr Justice Swift* (Foy) *Canadian Bar Review* 17 (1939) 464
Review of *Readings on Personal Property* (Fryer) *Canadian Bar Review* 17 (1939) 465
Review of *Liability for Animals* (Williams) *Canadian Bar Review* 17 (1939) 613
Review of *Money in the Law* (Nussbaum) *Canadian Bar Review* 17 (1939) 689
Review of *Lawyers and the Promotion of Justice* (Brown) *Canadian Bar Review* 17 (1939) 690
Review of *The 'Unauthorized Practice of Law' Controversy* (Sanders) *University of Toronto Law Journal* 3 (1939–40) 239
Reviews of *The Spirit of the Legal Profession* (Wilkin) and *Lawyers and the Promotion of Justice* (Brown) *University of Toronto Law Journal* 3 (1939–40) 487

1940   Review of *Legal Essays and Addresses* (Lord Wright) *Canadian Bar Review* 18 (1940) 71
Review of *Cases and Materials in the Law Merchant* (Thayer) *Canadian Bar Review* 18 (1940) 74
Review of *Lawyers and Laymen in Western Canada* (Stubbs) *Canadian Bar Review* 18 (1940) 75
Review of *Limitations* (Weaver) *Canadian Bar Review* 18 (1940) 145
Review of *Contracts for the Benefit of Third Parties* (Finlay) *Canadian Bar Review* 18 (1940) 235

Review of *Broom's Legal Maxims, Canadian Bar Review* 18 (1940) 236
Review of *Criminal Appeals in America* (Orfield) *Canadian Bar Review* 18 (1940) 326
Review of *The Doctrine of Unjustified Enrichment in the Law of the Province of Quebec* (Challis) *Canadian Bar Review* 18 (1940) 509
Review of *Contemporary Juristic Theory* (Pound) *Canadian Bar Review* 18 (1940) 583
Review of *The Law of Wills* (Bailey) *Canadian Bar Review* 18 (1940) 748
Review of *Organization of Courts* (Pound) *Canadian Bar Review* 18 (1940) 816

1941 'Concerning Lawyers' *Canadian Bar Review* 19 (1941) 59
Review of *The Canadian Law List* (Cartwright) *Canadian Bar Review* 19 (1941) 71
Review of *Contempts by Publication: The Law of Trial by Newspaper* (Sullivan) *Canadian Bar Review* 19 (1941) 72
Review of *Effect of War on Contracts* (Webber) *Canadian Bar Review* 19 (1941) 224
Review of *Holmes-Pollock Letters* (Howe) *Canadian Bar Review* 19 (1941) 387
'Negligent "Acts or Omissions" ' *Canadian Bar Review* 19 (1941) 465
Review of *Handbook of the Law of Torts* (Prosser) *Canadian Bar Review* 19 (1941) 551
Reviews of *Historical Introduction to the Theory of Law* (Jones) and *Law as Logic and Experience* (Radin) *University of Toronto Law Journal* 4 (1941–2) 449

1942 Review of *Success in Court* (Wellman) *Canadian Bar Review* 20 (1942) 171
Review of *Modern Tort Problems* (Eldredge) *Canadian Bar Review* 20 (1942) 172
Review of *Ontario Annual Practice, 1942* (Chitty) *Canadian Bar Review* 20 (1942) 570
'The Law of Evidence: Present and Future' review of *The Law of Evidence* (Phipson) *Canadian Bar Review* 20 (1942) 714
Review of *Cases on Torts* (Thurston and Seavey) *Canadian Bar Review* 20 (1942) 813

1943 Review of *A Historical Introduction to English Law and Its Institutions* 2d ed. (Potter) *Canadian Bar Review* 21 (1943) 333
Review of *Handbook of the Law of Real Property* (Burby) *Canadian Bar Review* 21 (1943) 334

Review of *A Textbook of the Law of Torts* (Winfield) *Canadian Bar Review* 21 (1943)
Review of *Restatement of the Law of Property* vol. 3: *Future Interests*, *University of Toronto Law Journal* 5 (1943–4) 450

1944   Review of *The Prevention of Repeated Crimes* (Waite) *Canadian Bar Review* 22 (1944) 171
Review of *Interpretation of Documents* (Burrows) *Canadian Bar Review* 22 (1944) 477
'Introduction to the Law of Torts' *Cambridge Law Journal* 8 (1944) 238

1945   Review of *What Is the Verdict?* (Gross) *Canadian Bar Review* 23 (1945) 72
Review of *Canadian Government and Politics* (Clokie) *Canadian Bar Review* 23 (1945) 73
Review of *Legal Theory* (Friedmann) *Canadian Bar Review* 23 (1945) 267
Review of *The Canadian Law of Copyright* (Fox) *University of Toronto Law Journal* 6 (1945–6) 270

1946   Review of *Law Training in Continental Europe* (Schweinburg) *Canadian Bar Review* 24 (1946) 462
Reviews of *Studying Law* (Vanderbilt) and *Materials for Legal Method* (Dowling, Patterson, and Powell) *Canadian Bar Review* 24 (1946) 935

1947   Review of *The Province and Function of Law: Law as Logic, Justice, and Social Control* (Stone) *University of Toronto Law Journal* 7 (1947–8) 227
Reviews of *Interpretations of Modern Legal Philosophies* (Sayre); *Men of Law: From Hammurabi to Holmes* (Seagle); and *Salmond's Jurisprudence* (Williams) *University of Toronto Law Journal* 7 (1947–8) 583

1948   'The Law of Torts: 1923–1947' *Canadian Bar Review* 26 (1948) 46

1949   Review of *Men and Measures in the Law* (Vanderbilt) *University of Toronto Law Journal* 8 (1949–50) 408
'The Legal Education Controversy in Ontario' *Solicitor* 16 (1949) 105
'The University Course in Law' *University of British Columbia Legal Notes* 1 (1949) 16

1950   'The University Law Schools' *Canadian Bar Review* 28 (1950) 141; reprinted in *Journal of Legal Education* 2 (1950) 409

'Should the Profession Control Legal Education? The Law Society of Upper Canada: A Professional Monopoly' *Journal of Legal Education* 3 (1950) 1

1951 Review of *The Law of Torts: A Treatise on the Law of Civil Wrongs* (Iyer) *Canadian Bar Review* 29 (1951) 555
Review of *Current Legal Problems II. 1949 III. 1950* (Keeton and Schwartzenberger) *University of Toronto Law Journal* 9 (1951–2) 136

1954 *Cases in the Law of Torts* (Toronto: Butterworths 1954)

1955 'The English Law of Torts: A Criticism' *University of Toronto Law Journal* 11 (1955–6) 84

1956 'Report of the Committee on Legal Research – Partial Dissent of Dean C.A. Wright' *Canadian Bar Review* 34 (1954) 1056
Review of *The Rule against Perpetuities* (Morris and Leach) *Canadian Bar Review* 34 (1956) 1209

1957 'The Outlook for Ontario Legal Education' *University of Toronto Law Journal* 12 (1957) 282
'The Law of Torts' *Journal of the Society of Public Teachers of Law* 4 (n.s.) (1957–8) 27

1958 *Canadian Tort Law* 2d ed. (Toronto: Butterworths 1958)

1961 'The Adequacy of the Law of Torts' *Journal of the Society of Public Teachers of Law* 6 (n.s.) (1961) 11; reprinted in *Cambridge Law Journal* 19 (1961)
'Law as a University Discipline' *University of Toronto Law Journal* 14 (1961–2) 263
'U. of T. Law Faculty Gets New Building' *Canadian Bar Journal* 4 (1961) 68

1963 *Canadian Tort Law* 3d ed. (Toronto: Butterworths 1963)
'Legal Education: Past and Present' in *Changing Legal Objectives* edited by R. St J. Macdonald (Toronto: University of Toronto Press 1963)

1967 *Canadian Tort Law* 4th ed. (Toronto: Butterworths 1967)

1968 'Res Ipsa Loquitur' in *Studies in Canadian Tort Law* edited by Allen M. Linden (Toronto: Butterworths 1968) 41

Notes

1 Bora Laskin *The British Tradition in Canadian Law* (London: Stevens and Sons 1969) 84
2 Allen Linden *Studies in Canadian Tort Law* (Toronto: Butterworths 1968) vii. See also the posthumous citation awarded at the Osgoode Hall Law School convocation in 1967, reprinted in B. Bucknall, T. Baldwin, and J.D. Lakin 'Pedants, Practitioners, and Prophets: Legal Education at Osgoode Hall to 1957' *Osgoode Hall Law Journal* 6 (1968) 138, 221 note 27, and telegram from Dean Maxwell Cohen of McGill Law School, Wright Papers, University of Toronto Archives (hereinafter cited as WP), 25 April 1967.
3 See G. Blaine Baker 'Legal Education in Upper Canada 1785–1889: The Law Society as Educator' in *Essays in the History of Canadian Law* vol. 2, edited by D.H. Flaherty (Toronto: The Osgoode Society 1983) 49.
4 See Thayron Sandquist 'The Inns of Court' in *Dictionary of the Middle Ages* edited by Joseph R. Strayer (Toronto: Collier Macmillan 1985) 477–8.
5 Sir William Holdsworth *A History of English Law* vol. 12 (London: Methuen 1903) 78–80
6 William Blackstone *Commentaries on the Laws of England* vol. 1 (Dubin 1771) 32
7 Parliamentary Papers (UK) 1846, x, xxxiv
8 Holdsworth *History of English Law* vol. 12, 90

9 See Richard A. Cosgrove *The Rule of Law: Albert Venn Dicey, Victorian Jurist* (Chapel Hill: University of North Carolina Press 1980) 51–2.

10 A.V. Dicey 'Teaching of English Law at Harvard' *Harvard Law Journal* 13 (1900) 422

11 James Bryce, quoted in Albert Coates 'The Story of the Law School at the University of North Carolina' *North Carolina Law Review* (1968) 9–10

12 James Bradley Thayer 'The Teaching of English Law at Universities' *Harvard Law Review* 9 (1895) 169

13 Ibid. 170. The history of this early period is told in Lawrence M. Friedmann *A History of American Law* (New York: Simon and Schuster 1973) chapters 11 and 12; Albert J. Harno *Legal Education in the United States* (San Francisco: Bancroft-Whitney 1953); James Willard Hurst *The Growth of American Law: The Law Makers* (Boston: Little, Brown 1950); Robert Stevens 'Two Cheers for 1870: The American Law School' in *Law in American History* edited by Donald Fleming and Bernard Bailyn (Boston: Little, Brown 1971) 404; and Arthur E. Sutherland *The Law at Harvard* (Cambridge: Harvard University Press 1967).

14 See Hurst *The Growth of American Law* 250–5.

15 See A. Chase 'Birth of the Modern Law School' *American Journal of Legal History* 23 (1979) 329.

16 Quoted in Sutherland *The Law at Harvard* 175

17 Ibid.

18 Josef Redlich *The Common Law and the Case Method in American University Law Schools* (New York: Carnegie Foundation for the Advancement of Teaching 1914); but compare Chase 'Birth of the Modern Law School.'

19 Quoted in Sutherland *The Law at Harvard* 184

20 See Jerold S. Auerbach 'Enmity and Amity: Law Teachers and Practitioners 1900–1922' *Perspectives on American History* 5 (1971) 551, and Auerbach *Unequal Justice* (New York: Oxford University Press 1976) chapter 3.

21 Auerbach *Unequal Justice* chapter 3

22 *Report of the American Bar Association* 18 (1895) 450

23 See Preble Stolz 'Training for the Public Profession of the Law (1921): A Contemporary Review' in *New Directions in Legal Education* edited by Herbert L. Parker and Thomas Ehrlich (New York: McGraw-Hill 1972) 228–30.

24 Thereby closing six of the eight black medical schools as well as drastically reducing the number of women doctors for several decades.

25 A.Z. Reed *Training for the Public Profession of the Law* (New York: Carnegie Foundation for the Advancement of Teaching 1921); *Some Contrasts Between American and Canadian Legal Education* (New York: Carnegie Foundation for the Advancement of Teaching 1925); and *Present-Day Law Schools in the*

United States and Canada (New York: Carnegie Foundation for the Advancement of Teaching 1928)

26 Quoted in Harno *Legal Education in the United States* 107–8
27 Auerbach *Unequal Justice* 117–9
28 Until recently, much of what was known about this period was found in the writings of W.R. Riddell – *The Legal Profession in Upper Canada in Its Early Periods* (Toronto: Law Society of Upper Canada 1916); *The Bar and the Courts of the Province of Upper Canada or Ontario* (Toronto: Macmillan of Canada 1928); 'The Law Society of Upper Canada in 1822' *Ontario Historical Society: Papers and Records* 23 (1926) 450; and 'The First Law School in Canada – 1742–1758' *Bench and Bar* (1932) 12. Of assistance too is D.B. Read 'The Law School of Osgoode Hall, Toronto' *Green Bag* 3 (1891) 265. This area has now been more thoroughly treated by G. Blaine Baker in 'Legal Education in Upper Canada 1785–1889: The Law Society as Educator' in *Essays in the History of Canadian Law* vol. 2, 49.
29 Baker 'Legal Education' 61
30 Riddell *The Bar and The Courts* 47
31 William Riddell 'The Legal Profession in Ontario and the Law Society of Upper Canada' *Essays and Addresses* vol. 3 (Toronto: Law Society of Upper Canada 1915) 50. Read 'The Law School of Osgoode Hall' speaks of the original 1797 act in similar terms: 'This legislation practically placed the good name and fame of the bar, its education, and future welfare in the hands of the members of the bar themselves' (266).
32 *Upper Canada Law Journal* 5 (1859) 164
33 Read 'The Law School of Osgoode Hall' 269
34 J.C. Hamilton *Osgoode Hall: Reminiscences of the Bench and Bar* (Toronto: Carswell 1904) 12
35 *Canada Law Journal* old series 1 (1855) 163
36 *Upper Canada Law Journal* 7 (1861) 140
37 H.M. Neatby *Queen's University: To Strive, to Seek, to Find and Not to Yield*, edited by F.W. Gibson and R. Graham (Montreal: McGill-Queen's University Press 1978) 106–7, and J.A. Corry 'The Queen's University Faculty of Law' *University of Toronto Law Journal* 12 (1957–8) 290
38 *Canada Law Journal* 4 (1868) 134
39 *Canada Law Journal* 9 (1873) 134
40 *Canada Law Journal* 12 (1876) 188
41 See the suggestive remarks by one 'Vindex' in a letter in *Canada Law Journal* 16 (1878) 119–20, and Baker 'Legal Education' 103–4.
42 Baker 'Legal Education'; and see Bucknall, Baldwin, and Lakin 'Pedants, Practitioners, and Prophets' 155–7.
43 See *Canada Law Journal* 15 (1879) 325, and Baker 'Legal Education' 105–6.

44 *Canada Law Journal* 17 (1881) 480
45 John Willis *A History of Dalhousie Law School* (Toronto: University of Toronto Press 1979) 31–3
46 *Canada Law Journal* 22 (1886) 275; compare E.D. Armour's disgruntled editorial in *Canada Law Times* 7 (1887) 246.
47 James J. Talman and Ruth Davis Talman *'Western' – 1878–1953* (London: University of Western Ontario Press 1953) 40–2
48 See *Canada Law Journal* 24 (1888) 130–2.
49 Ibid. 152–3
50 Ibid. 173
51 Ibid. 394–7
52 *Proceedings of Convocation of the Law Society of Upper Canada* vol. 1 (Toronto: Law Society of Upper Canada 1885) 263–6
53 Riddell *The Legal Profession in Upper Canada* 61
54 Baker 'Legal Education' 119–23
55 *Canada Law Journal* 9 (1889) 241
56 Ibid. 246–7
57 Ibid. 247
58 Ibid. 252–3
59 Ibid. 256
60 *Canada Law Journal* 16 (1880) 161
61 *Canada Law Journal* 30 (1894) 617
62 N.W. Hoyles 'Legal Education in Canada' *Canada Law Journal* 19 (1899) 261, reprinted in *American Law School Review* 1 (1902) 6
63 See W. Stewart Wallace *A History of the University of Toronto 1827–1927* (Toronto: University of Toronto Press 1927).
64 Sess. Rep. no. 42 (1906) xxxv
65 See Bucknall, Baldwin, and Lakin 'Pedants, Practitioners, and Prophets' 182.

1 WRIGHT AS STUDENT: OSGOODE HALL 1923–1926

1 In the same edition of the *Gazette* there appears a picture of Wright's future wife, Marie Therese Laughlin, whom he married in 1930. She was a year behind Wright at Western, and her achievements in English and history rivalled those of her husband-to-be.
2 *Proceedings of Convocation* of the Law Society of Upper Canada (cited hereinafter as PC). The unpublished records of proceedings prior to 1973 are housed at Osgoode Hall and are referred to here by date.

3 *Law Society of Upper Canada Calendar* (1924) 11

4 Shirley Denison 'Legal Education in Ontario' *Canadian Bar Review* 2 (1924) 85, 86

5 PC 20 March 1924, 'Special Committee of the Legal Education Committee Report'

6 See C.A. Wright 'Should the Profession Control Legal Education? (The Law Society of Upper Canada: A Professional Monopoly)' *Journal of Legal Education* 3 (1950) 1, 15, and 'Report of the Committee on Legal Research – Partial Dissent of Dean C.A. Wright' *Canadian Bar Review* 34 (1956) 1056, 1061.

7 C.S. Kenny *Cases on Contracts* (Cambridge: Cambridge University Press 1922) v

8 John D. Falconbridge *A Selection of Cases on the Sale of Goods* (Toronto: Canada Law Book 1927). See also the review by Vincent C. MacDonald *Canadian Bar Review* 6 (1928) 173. For a further discussion of early Canadian casebooks, see below at 75–6.

9 Until his death in 1922, Armour was a prominent bencher and served for many years as chairman of the law society's legal education committee. The treatise was in continuous use at the law school from 1901 to 1929, when it was replaced by a casebook.

10 Some indication of the profession's attitude can be gleaned from the comment made by a Mr Tait during a debate of the Canadian Bar Association meeting in 1922. In response to the question whether Canadian textbooks might be preferable to the English classics he said, 'It would be entirely impossible for anyone to supersede Anson on Contracts': *Minutes of Proceedings* Canadian Bar Association (1922) 58.

11 See *Canadian Bar Review* 3 (1925) 225, and 35 (1957) 607.

12 PC 21 June 1923

13 PC 20 March 1924

14 See R. St J. Macdonald 'An Historical Introduction to the Teaching of International Law in Canada' *Canadian Yearbook of International Law* 12 (1974) 67, 93, and John Willis *A History of Dalhousie Law School* (Toronto: University of Toronto Press 1979) 70–2.

15 Quoted in Willis *A History* 70

16 A 'technical' law school, to be called the Halifax Law School, was proposed but never opened.

17 Ibid. 70–1

18 Ibid. 89–90

19 Ibid. 90

20 See B. Bucknall, T. Baldwin, and J.D. Lakin 'Pedants, Practitioners, and Prophets: Legal Education at Osgoode Hall to 1957' *Osgoode Hall Law Journal* 6 (1968) 138, 185.

21 'Report of Dean John D. Falconbridge' PC January 1927

22 See G.F. Henderson 'Review of Falconbridge *Cases on the Sale of Goods*' *Canadian Bar Review* 4 (1926) 135; compare his remarks on Sidney Smith's casebook: *Canadian Bar Review* 4 (1926) 288.

23 C.A. Wright *Cases on the Law of Torts* (Toronto: Butterworths 1954) v

24 By 1925 two more high-ranking Dalhousie graduates, Norman A.M. (Larry) MacKenzie and Horace Read, had received LL M degrees from Harvard. The story of Harvard's recognition of Dalhousie is set out in Willis *A History* 88–90. A handful of Canadians received Harvard LL BS or SJDs in those years. In Wright's year (1926) three other Canadians were pursuing the SJD degree: Harold E. Carey BA, LL B (University of Manitoba), Ives Colin Campbell BA (Dalhousie), LL B (Harvard), and Roy Douglas McNutt BA, LL B (Dalhousie).

25 See the review by Horace Read *Canadian Bar Review* 7 (1929) 143.

26 *Canadian Bar Review* 4 (1926) 296

27 Willis *A History* 84

28 Ibid. 101–2

29 *Canadian Bar Review* 4 (1926) 2

30 Ibid. 374–5

31 See G.F. Henderson 'A Problem of Legal Education' *Canadian Bar Review* 3 (1925) 371, 327.

32 *Canadian Bar Review* 4 (1926) 329

33 A.Z. Reed *Some Contrasts between American and Canadian Legal Education* (New York: Carnegie Foundation for the Advancement of Teaching 1925)

34 See E.R. Cameron 'Legal Education in Ontario' *Canadian Bar Review* 2 (1924) 503, 505.

35 O.M. Biggar 'Legal Education Again' *Canadian Bar Review* 1 (1923) 864

36 The 1925 proposal and correspondence relating to it can be found in the Law Society of Upper Canada Archives.

37 See the announcement in an editorial by Charles Morse *Canadian Bar Review* 5 (1927) 281.

38 See Macdonald 'An Historical Introduction' 104–7.

39 *Canadian Bar Review* 5 (1927) 282

2 THE BAR ASSOCIATIONS AND LEGAL EDUCATION

1 From 1921 to 1926 22 of the 38 elected benchers were from Toronto; 927 of Ontario's 2,341 lawyers practised in Toronto. See A.Z. Reed *Present-Day*

Law Schools in the United States and Canada (New York: Carnegie Foundation for the Advancement of Teaching 1928) 519. This imbalance was in evidence from the earliest days of the Ontario bar; see G. Blaine Baker 'Legal Education in Upper Canada 1785–1889' in *Essays in the History of Canadian Law* vol. 2, edited by D.H. Flaherty (Toronto: The Osgoode Society 1983) 120–2.

2 See H.A. Aylen 'County Bar Associations in Ontario' *Fortnightly Law Journal* 5 (1935) 103.

3 As it transpired, the attempt to organize the county law associations came on the heels of the first unsuccessful attempt to organize a Canadian bar association in the last years of the nineteenth century. The association was the brainchild of the Honourable J.E. Robidoux, QC, the bâtonnier-general of Quebec. The preliminary conference of the new Canadian Bar Association took place in Montreal on 15 September 1896. A Canada-wide association, Robidoux argued, 'would be of service in helping to advance the service of jurisprudence, promote the administration of justice and uniformity of legislation and uphold the honour of the profession of the law in Canada': *Report of Proceedings of the Preliminary Conference and First Meeting of the Canadian Bar Association* (1896) 3. The first meeting of the CBA was by all accounts friendly, though not particularly productive. The next meeting was held in Halifax in 1897, with Robidoux presiding. In his address Robidoux referred to the example of the American Bar Association and told his audience that the aim of 'one grand association of the members of all the bars in Canada' was to create strong bonds of warm friendship: 'Our aim, then, can be resumed in one thought, which is altogether in the interest of civil society, and of agreeable social relations': *Report of Proceedings of the Canadian Bar Association, 1897–8* 4. At this meeting a committee on legal education was created, which included Aemilius Irving, QC, of Toronto, then in his fifth year as treasurer of the law society, and Benjamin Russell, Dean Weldon's right-hand man at Dalhousie Law School. The third and last meeting of the early CBA took place in Ottawa; Irving took over as president from the ailing Robidoux. There was no report from the legal education committee, and the association itself disappeared, to be reorganized sixteen years later. In 1913 the *Canadian Law Journal* 49 (1913) noted (at 23): 'It will be remembered that a Dominion Bar Association was formed some years ago, but, owing to practical difficulties in its working, it died a natural death.' It is not unlikely that the 'practical difficulties' had to do with the fact that it was not being supported in Ontario.

4 The early history of the Ontario Bar Association is found in *Canadian Law Times* 41 (1921) 126.

5 'As large a proportion of members as the New York State Bar Association,'

acting chairman F.E. Hodgins proudly reported: *Canadian Law Times* 29 (1909) 75–6.

6 Ibid.

7 *Canadian Law Times* 32 (1912) 268

8 The *Canadian Law Times* and the *Canadian Law Journal* dutifully published all other reports and proceedings of the OBA from 1909 to 1922, but only W.C. Mikel's presidential address, which was a historical review of past OBA activities, was published in 1913; see *Canadian Law Journal* 49 (1913) 78.

9 See E.H. Coleman 'The Canadian Bar Association' *Canadian Bar Review* 26 (1948) 1.

10 *Canadian Law Journal* 51 (1915) 133, 161

11 *Canadian Law Times* 35 (1915) 72

12 *Canadian Law Journal* 54 (1918) 124, 126–8

13 Ibid. 129

14 Ibid. 125

15 See *Minutes of Proceedings of the Third Annual Meeting of the Canadian Bar Association* (cited hereinafter as *CBA Minutes*) (1918) 171.

16 *Canadian Law Times* 38 (1918) 257, and see E.K. Williams 'Legal Education in Manitoba: 1913–1950' *Canadian Bar Review* 28 (1950) 759.

17 See 'In Memoriam: Robert Warden Lee' *American Journal of Comparative Law* 7 (1958) 659.

18 See H.A. Smith 'Legal Education in Canada' *American Law School Review* 4 (1921) 739–41. Lee was one of the exponents of the teaching of Roman law in Canada. In 1923 he noted that the subject was not taught in Canada because of the general perception of legal education: 'A system of instruction which aims primarily at qualifying students to practice the profession of law in the Province to which they belong is apt to assume a purely practical complexion and to condemn as useless any branch of legal study which cannot be regarded as directly conducing to this end': 'The Place of Roman Law in Legal Education' *Canadian Bar Review* 1 (1923) 132.

19 R.W. Lee 'Legal Education, Old and New' *Canadian Law Times* 36 (1916) 24, 109, 110–12

20 R.W. Lee 'Legal Education: A Symposium' *Canadian Law Times* 39 (1919) 138

21 *Canadian Law Times* 38 (1918) 262–3

22 Ibid.

23 *Minutes of the Proceedings of the Canadian Bar Association* (1919) 150 (cited hereinafter as *CBA Minutes*)

24 G.F. Henderson 'Legal Education' *Canadian Law Times* 39 (1919) 143
25 *CBA Minutes* (1918) 10
26 See Williams 'Legal Education in Manitoba' 763–4 and E.H. Coleman 'Legal Education' *Manitoba Bar News* 5 (1933) 1.
27 For a survey on legal educational schemes in Canada, see *Canadian Law Journal* 56 (1920) 201–15.
28 Ibid. 219
29 See John Willis *A History of Dalhousie Law School* (Toronto: University of Toronto Press 1979) 78–83.
30 *CBA Minutes* (1922) 262
31 See Curtis Cole 'A Developmental Market: Growth Rates, Competition, and Professional Standards in the Ontario Legal Profession, 1881–1936' *Canada-United States Law Journal* 7 (1984) 231 for a discussion of the ongoing concern about overcrowding.
32 *CBA Minutes* (1922) 39
33 *Canadian Law Journal* 58 (1922) 154
34 Some years later Ira MacKay published his views on legal education in 'The Education of a Lawyer' *Alberta Law Quarterly* 4 (1940–2) 103.
35 Harlan F. Stone 'Some Phases of American Legal Education' *Canadian Bar Review* 1 (1923) 646
36 PC 19 January 1922
37 See *Reports of the American Bar Association* 47 (1922) and *American Law School Review* 4 (1922) 812.
38 Albert J. Harno *Legal Education in the United States* (San Francisco: Bancroft-Whitney 1953) 112
39 Jerold S. Auerbach 'Enmity and Amity: Law Teachers and Practitioners 1900–1922' *Perspectives in American History* 5 (1971) 551, and Auerbach *Unequal Justice* (New York: Oxford University Press 1976) chapter 4; see also Robert Stevens *Law School: Legal Education in America from the 1850s to the 1980s* (Chapel Hill: University of North Carolina Press 1983). Compare A.L. Gordon 'The Organization of the Canadian Bar' *Oregon Law Review* 4 (1925) 200.
40 H.W. Arthurs, in his review of Auerbach's *Unequal Justice* (*University of Toronto Law Journal* 27 [1977] 513), suggests that client domination and racial discrimination in Canada were avoided, and that 'credit must go, on the one hand, to lingering British traditions of lawyerly integrity and independence, and to relatively limited economic development, and on the other to the less conspicuous presence of ethnic communities in Toronto and Montreal as compared with, for example, Boston and New York' (514).

This may be so, but at the moment no research on this issue has been done.

41 These are A.Z. Reed's figures as given in *Present-Day Law Schools*; see also Curtis Cole 'A Developmental Market.'

42 See R.J. MacLennan 'Legal Education in Canada' *Canadian Law Times* 41 (1922) 319, 325: 'The lack of adequate personal acquaintance and influence is reflected in the character and quality of our bar. We find it in the administration of our own association. We are too busy scrambling for fees to take much interest in the general development of our profession; too frequently we get up our law by proxy; we have not been inspired to aim high enough or to leave some great work behind us; we generally decline invitations to give addresses or to read papers on branches of the law in which we have become experts; too often we have to import our principal speakers; we have few text-book writers, and some of the results are best termed pot-boilers; and speaking with all respect, the quality of our bench, as a whole, might be a little higher still, had our judges, when students, been inspired by sympathetic teachers to look forward to and to prepare for a judicial career.'

43 See Julius Goebel *A History of the School of Law Columbia University* (New York: Columbia University Press 1955) 215–18 for a biographical sketch of H.F. Stone.

44 See John Henry Schlegel 'American Legal Realism and empirical Social Science: The Singular Case of Underhill Moore' *Buffalo Law Review* 29 (1980) 195.

45 Stone 'Some Phases' 657

46 J.T. Hébert 'An Unsolicited Report on Legal Education in Canada' *Canadian Law Times* 41 (1921) 593

47 According to J.A. Corry *My Life and Work – A Happy Partnership* (Kingston: Queen's University 1981) 34.

48 Ibid. 59

49 Hébert 'An Unsolicited Report' 611

50 D.A. MacRae 'Canadian Bar Association Committee Report' *Canadian Bar Review* 1 (1928) 671

51 *CBA Minutes* (1922) 101

52 H.A. Smith 'Legal Education in Canada' *Association of American Law Schools Review* 4 (1921) 734, 735–7

53 H.A. Smith 'The Function of a Law School' *Canadian Law Times* 41 (1921) 27, 28

54 See R. St J. Macdonald 'An Historical Introduction to the Teaching of

International Law in Canada' *Canadian Yearbook of International Law* 12 (1974) 72–4.

55 For a Canadian argument in favour of the imperial school, see Mr Justice John Greenshields 'Is It Desirable to Establish in London a School of Advanced Legal Studies?' *Canadian Bar Review* 4 (1926) 639. See also H.A. Smith 'An Imperial School of Law' *Journal of the Society of Public Teachers of Law* (1927) 11, and H.C. Gutteridge 'Advanced Legal Studies' *Journal of the Society of Public Teachers of Law* (1929) 1.

56 For the letter, and an editorial comment, see *Canadian Bar Review* 4 (1926) 322, 483, 492, 577, and 599.

57 The memorandum was never published, but is included in materials of the special committee on legal education in the Law Society of Upper Canada archives. See also *Toronto Daily Star* 29 January 1929.

58 Reprinted in *Law Society Gazette* 13 (1979) 343

3 WRIGHT AT HARVARD: THE SHAPING OF A LEGAL SCHOLAR

1 *Toronto Telegram* 21 March 1927

2 Letter to Professor Thomas Reed Powell, chairman of the Graduate Studies Committee at Harvard Law School, 13 January 1947, Wright Papers (hereinafter cited as WP). In 1947 Harvard was still sceptical of the quality of Canadian graduates in general and the Osgoode Hall degree in particular, and Wright was forced once again to take up the issue in support of a recent graduate.

3 See 'Report of Dean John Falconbridge' *Proceedings of Convocation of the Law Society of Upper Canada* January 1927. In 1926 Osgoode Hall ranked twentieth among 150 North American law schools in size of student population.

4 A.Z. Reed *Training for the Public Profession of the Law* (New York: Carnegie Foundation for the Advancement of Teaching 1921) 26–8

5 'Memorandum by Cecil A. Wright Concerning Matters Discussed at the Legal Education Committee, Law Society of Upper Canada Meeting December 1, 1933' WP

6 See Arthur E. Sutherland *The Law at Harvard* (Cambridge: Harvard University Press 1967) 277.

7 See G. Edward White *The American Judicial Tradition* (New York: Oxford University Press 1976) chapter 8.

8 Sutherland *Law at Harvard* 223–4

9 Wright's notebook on Roman law, purchased at the Harvard student co-op and marked with the notation 'C.A. Wright, 68 Kirkland St., Cambridge, Mass.,' and his jurisprudence notebooks are found in WP.

10 Sutherland *Law at Harvard* 295
11 *Canadian Bar Review* 15 (1937) 119
12 See Paul Sayre *The Life of Roscoe Pound* (Ames, Iowa: Iowa University Press 1948).
13 Sutherland *Law at Harvard* 293
14 Sayre *Life of Pound* 210–13
15 Josef Redlich *The Common Law and the Case Method in American University Law Schools* (New York: Carnegie Foundation for the Advancement of Teaching 1914)
16 For critiques of Redlich's assessment of the case method of teaching, see J.H. Beale 'The Law School as Professor Redlich Sees It' *Harvard Graduates' Magazine* 23 (1915) 617, and Albert Kocourek 'The Redlich Report and the Case Method' *Illinois Law Review* 10 (1915) 321.
17 See Robert Stevens 'Two Cheers for 1870: The American Law School' in *Law in American History* edited by Donald Fleming and Bernard Bailyn (Boston: Little, Brown 1971) 445–7.
18 WP
19 Ibid. 145–6
20 See, for example, 'An Extra-Legal Approach to Law' *Canadian Bar Review* 10 (1932) 1, 'Legal Reform and the Profession' *Canadian Bar Review* 15 (1937) 633, and 'Concerning Lawyers' *Canadian Bar Review* 19 (1941) 59.
21 In the 1920s Pound 'continued to apply his ideas widely, but he ceased to pursue them more deeply': David Wigdor *Roscoe Pound: Philosopher of Law* (Westport, Ct: Greenwood Press 1974) 233.
22 For a general discussion of these years, see G. Edward White 'From Sociological Jurisprudence to Realism: Jurisprudence and Social Change in Early Twentieth-Century America' reprinted in *Patterns of American Legal Thought* edited by G. Edward White (New York: Oxford University Press, 1978). See also William Twining *Karl Llewellyn and the Realist Movement* (London: Weidenfeld and Nicolson 1973) and J. Mitchell *Jerome Frank: Jurist and Philosopher* (New York: Philosophical Library 1970). Although the birth of American realism is often said to have occurred with the publication of Karl Llewellyn's 'A Realistic Jurisprudence – The Next Step' *Columbia Law Review* 30 (1930) 431 and Jerome Frank's *Law and the Modern Mind* (New York: Brentano's 1930), the seeds of the realist position were sown in the early 1920s and were well known to Pound. See Underhill Moore 'Rational Basis of Legal Institutions' *Columbia Law Review* 23 (1923) 609, W. Haines 'General Observations on the Effects of Personal, Political, and Economic Influences in the Decisions of Judges' *Illinois Law Review*

17 (1922) 96, and Max Radin 'The Theory of Judicial Decision: Or How
Judges Think' *American Bar Association Journal* 11 (1925) 357.

23 An assessment of the realist movement and an exhaustive treatment of the
'experiments' at Yale and Columbia can be found in John Henry Schlegel
'American Legal Realism and Empirical Social Science: From the Yale
Experience' *Buffalo Law Review* 28 (1978) 459, and Schlegel 'American Legal
Realism and Empirical Social Science: The Singular Case of Underhill
Moore'

24 In a review of Jones's *Historical Introduction to the Theory of Law (University
of Toronto Law Journal* 4 [1941–2] 449, 450), Wright expressed his general
dislike for impractical abstraction when he said of Jones's book that it was
an example of jurisprudence that 'remains a moribund specimen, fit
only for dissection and classification, rather than a vital and living force
which can stimulate and command action.' Wright was equally hard
on Wesley N. Hohfeld: 'The legal geometry of the Hohfeldian system of
legal correlatives has about as much connection with law as a governing
force in society as have the dogmatic prophecies of weather conditions
in patent medicine almanacs on the changing of seasons': 'Review of
Salmond's Jurisprudence' *University of Toronto Law Journal* 7 (1947–8) 586.

25 'Do We Need a Philosophy of Law?' *Columbia Law Review* 5 (1905) 339, 344

26 'Mechanical Jurisprudence' *Columbia Law Review* 8 (1908) 605, 607–8

27 198 U.S. 45 (1905)

28 'Liberty of Contract' *Yale Law Journal* 18 (1909) 454

29 'Law in Books and Law in Action' *American Law Review* 44 (1910) 12, 35–6

30 *Harvard Law Review* 24 (1911) 591, and 25 (1912) 489

31 *Harvard Law Review* 25 (1912) 515–16. See also *Outlines of Lectures on
Jurisprudence* (New Haven: Yale University Press 1928) 16–19; 'Fifty Years
of Jurisprudence' *Harvard Law Review* 50 (1937) 557, and 51 (1938) 444,
777; *Social Control through Law* (New Haven: Yale University Press 1942);
and *Jurisprudence* vol. 1 (St Paul: West 1959) 291–4. For an example of
Pound's use of the notion of 'social engineering,' see 'The Administration
of Justice in the Modern City' *Harvard Law Review* 26 (1912–13) 302.

32 'Scope and Purpose of Sociological Jurisprudence' 515, and 'Fifty Years of
Jurisprudence.' See also Eugene U. Rostow *The Sovereign Prerogative* (New
Haven: Yale University Press 1962) 22, where Rostow characterizes the
'functional approach' as the view that the 'law is *instrumental* only, a means
to an end, and is to be appraised only in light of the end it achieves'
[emphasis in original].

33 See 'Fifty Years of Jurisprudence' and *Jurisprudence* vol. 1, 292: 'Jurisprudence is thought of as one of a group of social sciences.'

34 See *Outlines* 601–71 and 'A Theory of Social Interests' *Publications of the American Sociological Society* (1921) 15; *Introduction to the Philosophy of Law* (New Haven: Yale University Press 1922) 90–6; and 'Interests in Personality' *Harvard Law Review* 41 (1928) 343.

35 White *Patterns* 115

36 See, for example, Karl Llewellyn 'Some Realism about Realism – Responding to Dean Pound' *Harvard Law Review* 44 (1931) 1222, a response to Pound's attack in 'A Call for a Realist Jurisprudence' *Harvard Law Review* 44 (1931) 697.

37 'The Theory of Judicial Decision' *Harvard Law Review* 37 (1923) 940, 955, and see *Introduction to the Philosophy of Law* chapter 2.

38 See, for example, Jerome Frank 'What Constitutes a Good Legal Education?' *American Bar Association Journal* 19 (1933) 723; 'Why Not a Clinical Lawyer School?: *University of Pennsylvania Law Review* 81 (1933) 907; 'A Plea for Lawyer Schools' *Yale Law Journal* 56 (1947) 1303; Karl Llewellyn 'On What Is Wrong with So-Called Legal Education' *Columbia Law Review* 35 (1935) 651; and Llewellyn 'The Current Crisis in Legal Education' *Journal of Legal Education* 1 (1948) 211.

39 Erwin N. Griswold 'Intellect and Spirit' *Harvard Law Review* 81 (1967–8) 292, 295. Wigdor, in *Roscoe Pound*, argues that Pound's reluctance to put into practice the implications of his jurisprudential views for legal education is explained by his strong sense of professionalism, and in particular by his desire to retain the integrity and separation (and ironically, as a result, the insularity) of the legal profession (223–6).

40 Brief of the special committee on legal education, 1949; transcript of interview with Wright, Law Society of Upper Canada Archives.

41 'Review of *Salmond's Jurisprudence*' 583, 584

42 'Stone on Jurisprudence' *University of Toronto Law Journal* 7 (1947–8) 227, 229. Compare Zechariah Chafee's remark: '[Pound's course] entirely changed my views of law and I believe the results of it will stay with me through life': quoted in Wigdor *Roscoe Pound* 261.

43 *Minutes of the Proceedings of the Canadian Bar Association* (1922) 39

44 Letter to Professor P.H. Winfield of Cambridge, 4 April 1938 (WP)

45 For a biographical sketch of Bohlen, see W.D. Lewis 'Francis Hermann Bohlen' *University of Pennsylvania Law Review* 91 (1942–3) 377.

46 G. Edward White *Tort Law in America: An Intellectual History* (New York: Oxford University Press 1980) 78–80

47 Ibid. 87

48 F.H. Bohlen 'Old Phrases and New Facts' *University of Pennsylvania Law Review* 83 (1935) 305

49 See, for example, A. Arnold 'Leon Green – An Appreciation' *Illinois Law Review* 43 (1943) 1

50 Leon Green 'The Torts Restatement' *Illinois Law Review* 29 (1935)

51 'The American Law Institute's Restatement of Contracts and Agency' *University of Toronto Law Journal* 1 (1935–6) 17. Wright's *Cases on the Law of Torts* (1954) was the first Canadian casebook to make use of the *Restatement of Torts.*

52 [1932] AC 562. See F.H. Bohlen 'Liability of Manufacturers to Persons Other Than Their Immediate Vendees' *Law Quarterly Review* 45 (1929) 343. Wright was later to cite this influence on judicial change as an example of what legal scholarship should be geared towards. See Wright 'Restatement of Contracts and Agency' 22, n. 15.

53 F.H. Bohlen 'Review of J. Frank *Law and the Modern Mind' University of Pennsylvania Law Review* 79 (1931) 822, 825

54 *Studies in the Law of Torts* (Indianapolis: Bobbs-Merrill 1926) v

55 *Canadian Bar Review* 26 (1948) 46

56 Ibid. 94

57 Lewis 'Francis Hermann Bohlen' 381

58 L. Eldredge 'Francis Hermann Bohlen' *University of Pennsylvania Law Review* 91 (1943) 387

59 *Cases on the Law of Torts* v–vi

60 This can be seen in Wright's general discussions on English tort law: 'Negligent "Acts or Omissions" ' *Canadian Bar Review* 19 (1941) 465; 'The Law of Torts: A Criticism' *University of Toronto Law Journal* 11 (1955–6) 84; and 'The Adequacy of the Law of Torts' *Journal of the Society of Public Teachers of Law* (1961) 11.

61 'Gross Negligence' *University of Toronto Law Journal* 22 (1983) 184

62 'Introduction to the Law of Torts' *Cambridge Law Journal* 8 (1944) 238

63 *Cases on the Law of Torts* 9

64 Harvard Law School records. We wish to thank the Wright family and the officials of Harvard Law School for granting us access to Wright's student records.

65 Letter to Bora Laskin, then a student at Harvard, describing Harvard Law School, 12 March 1937 (WP)

4 WRIGHT AS TEACHER: OSGOODE HALL, 1927–1935

1 A.Z. Reed *Present-Day Law Schools in the United States and Canada* (New York: Carnegie Foundation for the Advancement of Teaching 1928)

2 *Proceedings of Convocation of the Law Society of Upper Canada* (hereinafter cited as PC) 17 January 1927
3 See PC 16 June 1927.
4 *Toronto Star* 21 June 1927.
5 Rough draft of undated letter to F.H. Bohlen (probably written between 4 September and 20 November 1928) WP. Unless otherwise noted, all references to letters from or to Wright are to be found in the Wright Papers.
6 See letter from E.R. James, 21 November 1930, and letter to H.S. Dimmit, 4 December 1940.
7 Letter of 2 May 1929
8 Letter from F.H. Bohlen 4 September 1928
9 Letter of 20 November 1928
10 Bohlen to Wright, 21 January 1929
11 Undated draft of a response to Bohlen's letter of 4 September 1928
12 PC 20 September 1928
13 *Canadian Bar Review* 7 (1929) 465
14 See Jack Batten *Robinette* (Toronto: Macmillan 1984) and John Willis *A History of Dalhousie Law School* (Toronto: University of Toronto Press 1979) 101.
15 *Proceedings of the Canadian Bar Association Meeting, 1928* (cited hereinafter as Read report).
16 Ibid. 214
17 See 'Implied Agency of the Wife for Necessaries' *Canadian Bar Review* 8 (1930) 722.
18 University of Toronto Archives (hereinafter UT Archives), letter from Davison to Kennedy, 19 February 1929
19 *Canadian Bar Review* 10 (1932) 1
20 217 NY 382 (1916)
21 See, for example Jerome Frank 'Are Judges Human?' *University of Pennsylvania Law Review* 80 (1931) 17; 'Why Not a Clinical Lawyer-School?' *University of Pennsylvania Law Review* 81 (1933) 907; 'A Plea for Lawyer-Schools' *Yale Law Journal* 56 (1947) 1303; Karl Llewellyn 'On What Is Wrong with So-Called Legal Education' *Columbia Law Review* 35 (1935) 651; and Llewellyn 'The Current Crisis in Legal Education' *Journal of Legal Education* 1 (1948) 211.
22 *Canadian Bar Review* 9 (1931) 31
23 See C.A. Wright 'The American Law Institute's Restatement of Contracts and Agency' *University of Toronto Law Journal* 1 (1935–6) 17.
24 *Dalhousie Gazette* 18 March 1931
25 What follows concerning Henry Borden is based on a personal interview with Borden on 14 September 1982.

26 *Law Society of Upper Canada Calendar* 1932–3

27 See B. Bucknall, T. Baldwin, and J.D. Lakin 'Pedants, Practitioners, and Prophets: Legal Education at Osgoode Hall to 1957' *Osgoode Hall Law Journal* 6 (1968) 138.

28 *Proceedings of the Canadian Bar Association Meeting, 1932* (cited hereinafter as *CBA Minutes*) 147–9

29 John D. Falconbridge 'Legal Education in Canada' *Journal of the Society of Public Teachers of Law* (1932) 32

30 Bora Laskin interview (Robin Harris) UT Archives 8–9

31 Kennedy to Davison 25 January 1929, UT Archives

32 'Legal Subjects in the Universities in Canada' *Journal of the Society of Public Teachers of Law* (1933) 23

33 'Law as a Social Science' *Scots Law Times* (1934) 165 and 'A Project of Legal Education' *Scots Law Times* (1937) 1, 17, 21

34 Supra note 30

35 'Legal Subjects' 27

36 From a two-page chart entitled 'Record, Graduates, Honour Law, University of Toronto, at Osgoode Hall,' Law Society of Upper Canada Archives (hereinafter cited as LSUC Archives)

37 Falconbridge 'Legal Education in Canada' 36

38 Kennedy 'Legal Subjects' 26

39 Bradshaw eventually went to Osgoode Hall. He was killed in the Second World War.

40 The memorandum was published in *Canadian Bar Review* 11 (1933) 348.

41 See 'Education for the Bar: Report of the Special Committee of Students at Osgoode Hall' *Canadian Bar Review* 12 (1934) 144, 152.

42 *Mail and Empire* 21 February 1933

43 Ibid.

44 *CBA Minutes* (1932) 214

45 Later Mr Justice Urquhart of the Ontario High Court.

46 LSUC Archives, York County Bar Association. What follows is drawn primarily from the archives.

47 Supra note 41

48 Bora Laskin, who entered Osgoode Hall Law School in 1933, read law with W.C. Davidson. Laskin later recalled, 'To say that I read law with him was really a euphemism of the worst kind. All it meant was that I was an articled student, I was paid $2 a week and I was mostly in debt to the petty cash throughout the whole three years of my service under articles. We still were ... to a degree under the English tradition which even in England, I think, is now gone, where you paid your principal for the

privilege of – what – of being educated by him in the intricacies of the law. Well, I think that I was worth a hell of a lot more than $2 a week, but perhaps I was lucky. A good many of my friends got nothing, but then of course they were articled in other law offices, maybe some more prestigious, some larger.' UT Archives, Robin Harris interview 14

49 See W.S. Montgomery 'Problems of Legal Education' *Canadian Bar Review* 12 (1934) 431, 510, 639; 13 (1935) 31.

50 *Canadian Bar Review* 12 (1934) 517

51 A.G. Burbidge 'Some Other Aspects of Legal Education' *Fortnightly Law Journal* 4 (1934) 120; and see the editorial by R.M.W. Chitty 'An Educational Controversy' *Fortnightly Law Journal* 2 (1933) 343.

52 *Canadian Bar Review* 12 (1934) 366

53 Further indication of Wright's intent can be seen in two of his personal letters. He wrote to F.H. Bohlen on 18 October 1935: 'The only way that I can see of making the *Review* of some value to the profession and the law teachers is by an attempt to bring home to their consciousness the fact that all the Common Law is not to be found in the decisions of the House of Lords and that the teaching of law, to use your own expression, is more than a mere "exegesis on sacred texts culled from judicial opinion." ' To Warren Seavey Wright confessed, 'I am most anxious to make an attempt [at] acquainting the Canadian profession with things American' (30 October 1935).

54 *Canadian Bar Review* 13 (1935) 347

55 *Report of the Legal Education Committee* July 1934 (the Atkin report) Cmnd 4663

56 *Canadian Bar Review* 13 (1935) 374

5 THE DECADE OF FRUSTRATION: 1935–1944

1 See *Proceedings of the Canadian Bar Association Meeting, 1935* 210.

2 See Bora Laskin interview (Robin Harris), University of Toronto Archives (hereinafter cited as UT Archives), where Laskin describes Wright's activities: 'I can recall very eminent practising lawyers coming around to Wright's chambers asking Wright to peruse their pleadings in a case, you see, and to offer them professional advice. And then the next day these would be the people who would be traducing Wright because he [was] impractical. Well, this was the shabbiest kind of nonsense that one could possibly hear about.' Later, Laskin adds: 'Here was the man who was being traduced ... too much of an airy liberal philosopher ... who wanted to upset applecarts all over the place, and yet when they were in trouble

with difficult problems who did they come to – Wright. It's not really
a very illustrious period in the history of the Law Society of Upper Canada'
(64).

3 *Obiter Dicta* 15 May 1936, 1
4 Letter from G.G. Bradshaw to N.W. Rowell, 11 May 1936, Law Society of
Upper Canada Archives (hereinafter cited as LSUC Archives)
5 'The American Law Institute's Restatement of Contracts and Agency'
University of Toronto Law Journal 1 (1935–6) 17
6 Wright to F.H. Bohlen, 18 October 1935, Wright Papers (hereinafter cited
as WP). Unless otherwise stated, the correspondence cited in this chapter is
found in the Wright Papers.
7 Wright to Llewellyn 11 March 1936
8 Wright to Pound 18 October 1935
9 Wright to Seavey 7 March 1935
10 Wright to Seavey 30 October 1935
11 Wright to Williston 26 October 1935
12 Wright to J. Stone 30 October 1935
13 Seavey to Wright 4 November 1935
14 Wright to McNair 22 November 1935
15 Wright to McLean 10 October 1935; Wright to Paton 27 November 1935
16 Wright to J.A. Corry 16 October 1935
17 G.W. Paton 'Res Ipsa Loquitur' *Canadian Bar Review* 14 (1936) 480
18 *Canadian Bar Review* 14 (1936) 514
19 R.M.W. Chitty 'A Practical Exposition of Res Ipsa Loquitur' *Fortnightly Law
Review* 6 (1936) 88
20 MacDonald to Wright 21 October 1936
21 Wright to MacDonald 26 October 1936
22 Wright to Cronkite 14 September 1936
23 See *Fortnightly Law Journal* 6 (1936–7) 56.
24 Report of Wright's first year as editor of the *Canadian Bar Review* (undated)
WP
25 *Canadian Bar Review* 15 (1937) 633
26 Wright to Kennedy 14 October 1937
27 *Toronto Star* 8 November 1937
28 Wright to Smith 12 November 1937
29 Smith to Wright 14 November 1937
30 Wright to Paul Martin 4 November 1937
31 Wright was also busy preparing to teach a course he had never taught
before, torts. He wrote to Francis Bohlen Wright on 11 November 1937:
'Although it was eleven years ago that I had the pleasure of working

with you at Harvard in Torts, it is only this year that I have taken over that subject here and I would like you to know that the assistance and pleasure I obtained from your work in this field is a debt which, I am afraid, I will never be able to repay.' Wright had inherited the first-year course in torts from J.J. Robinette, who had decided to leave teaching. The casebook Wright prepared for that course in torts was the first version of the casesbook that eventually was published in 1954.

32 See *Harvard Law Review* 51 (1938) 965.
33 Denison to Wright 29 January 1938
34 See S. Denison 'Legal Education in Ontario' *Canadian Law Times* 42 (1922) 236, and Denison 'Legal Education in Ontario' *Canadian Bar Review* 2 (1924) 85.
35 *Canadian Bar Review* 16 (1939) 579
36 *Fortnightly Law Journal* 8 (1938–9) 130, 134
37 Vanderbilt would later become dean of the New York University Law School and eventually chief justice of New Jersey, where he was instrumental in introducing many significant reforms in court practice. As we shall see, he and Wright became close friends.
38 Wright to Farris 15 September 1938
39 Wright to Davis 15 September 1938
40 Davis to Wright 18 September 1938
41 Wright to Vanderbilt 15 September 1938
42 Vanderbilt to Wright 19 September 1938
43 Wright to Vanderbilt 11 October 1938
44 Wright to Landis 4 November 1938
45 Landis to Wright 21 November 1938
46 Goodhart to Wright 10 November 1938
47 *Proceedings of Convocation, Law Society of Upper Canada* (hereinafter cited as PC) January 1939
48 Wright to Smith 20 May 1939
49 Wright to J. Dainow of Loyola University School of Law, New Orleans 10 December 1935
50 Wright to Vanderbilt 8 December 1941
51 See *Fortnightly Law Journal* 11 (1941–2) 242.
52 Wright to MacDonald 1 October 1941
53 Wright to Curtis 25 May 1939
54 Wright to Corry 16 October 1935
55 Wright to Corry 12 February 1936
56 Quoting J.S. Denison 'Legal Education Committee Memo' 27 March 1943, LSUC Archives

57 Ibid.
58 *Canadian Bar Review* 21 (1943) 500
59 Ibid. 501
60 Wright to McLaurin 3 June 1943
61 Wright to MacDonald 28 December 1944
62 *Canadian Bar Review* 23 (1945) 785
63 *Canadian Bar Review* 21 (1943) 781
64 Wright to Willis 21 September 1944
65 Gilbert Kennedy, himself a graduate of his father's school, had recently joined the staff as a part-time lecturer, replacing Finkelman, who had taken a leave of absence to serve as registrar of the Ontario Labour Court.
66 *Fortnightly Law Journal* 13 (1944–5) 233
67 Ibid. 242
68 Kennedy to Fox 9 March 1944, UT Archives
69 Smith wrote to Falconbridge to inform him that a meeting of the legal education committee would be held on 22 March at which a resolution adopted by Convocation would be discussed. The resolution read: "Moved, seconded, and carried, that the remarks made by Dr. C.A. Wright at the mid-winter meeting of the Ontario Section of the Canadian Bar Association, with reference to the Law School, be referred to the Legal Education Committee with the request that the Committee investigate and report to Convocation.'
70 Wright to Sayre 15 November 1944
71 Wright to G. Steer 6 November 1944
72 Wright to Steer 20 June 1945

6 THE SUMMER OF 1945

1 Wright to Smith, University of Toronto Archives (hereinafter cited as UT Archives)
2 Interview with William Wright, 18 October 1981
3 Letter from Wright to George H. Steer, 16 February 1945, Wright Papers (hereinafter cited as WP): 'In order to be effective anything of this kind should have the cooperation of the University of Toronto and in particular the new president, Sidney Smith. We have discussed the matter briefly on several occasions and I do not think that Smith is, as yet, willing to put his foot into troubled waters and in light of that I do not feel that it would be wise for me, at the present time, to undertake the paper which you have in mind.' Unless otherwise stated, the correspondence cited in this chapter is found in the Wright Papers.

4 See E.A. Corbett *Sidney Earle Smith* (Toronto: University of Toronto Press 1961) 28–31, where Smith's possible leadership of the Conservative Party in 1942 is discussed. See also Peter Stursberg *Diefenbaker Leadership Gained, 1956–62* (Buffalo: University of Toronto Press 1975), where the possibility of Smith's leadership in 1956 is discussed.

5 Corbett *Smith* 33

6 Smith to Wright 9 July 1945

7 W.P.M. Kennedy Papers, UT Archives

8 Wright to George H. Steer 26 February 1945

9 Kennedy to Smith 1 July 1945, UT Archives

10 Ibid.

11 Ibid. Kennedy spoke of the 'bonds of non-cooperation' that separated the University of Toronto and the law society.

12 Hancock and Laskin were friends and classmates in Kennedy's 'BA in Law' program and Osgoode Hall Law School. Both went on to do graduate work in law – Laskin at Harvard Law School and Hancock at the University of Michigan Law School. During the war both taught at Kennedy's school before finally parting ways in 1945. Laskin went to Osgoode Hall to teach, and Hancock went first to Dalhousie Law School, then to Michigan Law School, and finally to Stanford Law School, where he taught until the 1970s. Throughout the three years they spent at Osgoode Hall Law School, Hancock and Laskin were top students, winning honours and scholarships. Hancock usually edged Laskin out for first place.

13 Smith to Wright 9 July 1945

14 Finkelman to Smith 7 July 1945, Smith papers, UT Archives

15 Kennedy's first move on Laskin's behalf was to write to Thomas Reed Powell, who was in charge of graduate admissions. Powell was confused by Kennedy's description of Laskin's degrees: 'Unless the Dean [Roscoe Pound] is familiar with your degrees, it would be well to indicate what it means with you to graduate in the Honour Course in 1933 and to take an M.A. in law in 1935 before proceeding to an LL.B. in 1936.' Powell to Kennedy 19 January 1935 UT Archives. Kennedy replied promptly, describing the degrees and outlining Laskin's interests ('he intends to work in Administrative Law'). Kennedy to Pound 27 January 1936, UT Archives. Kennedy also wrote to Felix Frankfurter asking him to assist Laskin in obtaining a fellowship.

Wright wrote on Laskin's behalf to Warren Seavey: 'I think Laskin should do well. He is a serious minded young man and has done various bits of work around here which I think show a certain aptitude for research which I would like to see encouraged.' Wright to Seavey 12 No-

vember 1935. Sometime later Wright was asked by both Laskin and
Hancock to support their applications to Harvard. In December Wright
wrote to Pound about the 'two very capable men who are anxious to
do the post graduate work.' Wright to Pound 20 December 1936. Wright
went on to say, 'It is difficult for me to pick and choose between them, but
as will be apparent from their names, the former is a Hebrew ... From
my knowledge of the two, I would say that Mr. Hancock has a more brilliant type of mind and would probably do exceptionally well in the
teaching field, which, I believe, is his ultimate goal. Laskin also has this
goal in mind I think, but I am afraid that in the limited field in this country
there would be, unfortunately, a certain prejudice against him which he
would find it difficult to overcome.'

Pound warned Wright that there would be less money available for
fellowships and scholarships in the upcoming year, but inasmuch as 'we
have always had good luck with the men who have come to us from
Canada,' Pound suggested that he would like to do something to help:
Pound to Wright 29 January 1936. Laskin was accepted and given a modest
fellowship. Hancock was also accepted and given a fellowship, but he
decided to go to the University of Michigan (with its larger fellowship)
instead. Wright also wrote to Dean H.M. Bates praising Hancock highly:
see Wright to Bates 1 May 1936.

16 At Osgoode Hall, Laskin won the essay contest two years in a row. Both
essays were on labour law topics, and both were published by Wright
in the *Review*: 'Picketing: A Comparison of Certain Canadian and American
Doctrines' *Canadian Bar Review* 15 (1937) 10, and 'The Labour Injunction
in Canada: A Caveat' *Canadian Bar Review* 15 (1937) 270.

17 Laskin left Harvard in the summer of 1937. His father was anxious for him
to return to Fort William but, as Laskin recalled, 'I just somehow couldn't
relate Holmes, Brandeis, Cardozo and Frankfurter and maybe some of
the English scholars with practising law in Fort William, although the opportunities there were certainly very, very tempting.' Laskin interview
(Robin Harris) UT Archives. After six months of looking for work, Laskin
took a job with Burroughs Publishing Co., the publisher of the *Canadian
Abridgment*. Clyde Auld was a consultant for Burroughs, and, with Finkelman's assistance, managed to convince Burroughs to hire Laskin. See
National Archives of Canada, J. Finkelman, MG 32E27 vol. 10, 15 January
1937. Finkelman told Laskin that Auld had said that Burroughs was
'looking for another full-time man and that he has you in mind for that
position, so that in any event I think you will be taken care of for the next
year.' Laskin replied, 'I am deeply grateful to you for your unselfish

interest in me and for the marvelous results of your efforts. Professor Auld is exceedingly generous in thinking of me for the position with Burroughs; it goes without saying that I should be immensely pleased to obtain it.' The job involved writing headnotes for cases from across the country, at fifty cents each. Laskin calculated that this could enable him to make more than the $131 a month that he had been receiving at the attorney-general's office.

18 Soon after Laskin's return from Harvard, he became the unofficial (and unacknowledged) assistant editor of the *Review*. Wright asked Laskin to help him put together some case comments and to write the odd book review. Laskin accepted, and his first case comment appeared in October 1937 (*Canadian Bar Review* 15 [1937] 660). Laskin later described his work at the *Review*: 'Wright placed great store on the Case and Comment section of the Review which he and I wrote in large measure. Some of our contributions were signed with the initials C.A.W. or B.L., but many were unsigned. One of my proudest boasts, exemplifying the influence that Wright had on me, was that there were times when we would wonder, after publication, whether it was he or I who wrote certain case comments which neither of us signed or initialled.' *University of Toronto Law Journal* 35 (1982) 151.

19 The fact that the future chief justice of Canada, recently returned from Harvard Law School with a brilliant academic record, made his living writing headnotes is an indication of the difficulties Jews faced in the Depression years. Wright apparently had warned another Canadian Jewish student, Maxwell Cohen, of the problems he might face. At the time, Cohen had graduated from the University of Manitoba Law School and earned his LL M at Northwestern University, and was spending a year at Harvard Law School as a special student. Cohen wrote back: 'Bora Laskin and I discussed the problem last summer and the conclusion we came to was that there were few men around Toronto that had our training, and that while we were still very green, we might be able to do something if given the chance ... I recognize that the Jewish problem in Toronto presents a serious obstacle, but personal interviews might do a little to offset the initial disadvantage of name.' Cohen to Wright 9 December 1937.

Something of Wright's realism (and his own prejudices) is apparent in a letter he wrote to Sidney Smith a few years later when a teaching job opened up at the University of Manitoba Law School. Wright heartily recommended Laskin (who was still without a permanent job), and then added: 'Unfortunately, he is a Jew. This may be a fatal regarding his chances with you. I do not know. His race is, of course, proving a difficulty facing him in Toronto so far as obtaining a good office is concerned ... Laskin is not one of those flashy Jews, and the highest recommendation which I could give him is to say that, in the absence of any overwhelming prejudice and if I had control of a decent faculty, I would have no hesitation in placing Laskin.' Wright to Smith 20 May 1939.

20 Wright to Smith 12 July 1945, UT Archives. Wright says Laskin came 'last Thursday,' but this does not fit the dates in the correspondence.

21 Laskin interview (Robin Harris) UT Archives

22 Laskin interview (C. Ian Kyer, December 1980)

23 Wright to Smith 12 July 1945, UT Archives

24 Kennedy to Smith 1 July 1945, UT Archives

25 See John Willis *A History of Dalhousie Law School* (Toronto: University of Toronto Press 1979) 162–3.

26 Kennedy to Smith 1 July 1945, UT Archives

27 For some time Laskin had been moving away from Kennedy's conception of legal education. Laskin later recalled lunching with the instructors at Osgoode Hall and having long talks with Wright on the future of legal education during his years at Kennedy's school: Laskin interview (Robin Harris) UT Archives. Perhaps because of these and other encounters with Wright, Laskin apparently was won over to Wright's view of legal education and the role of the lawyer. Laskin was also becoming increasingly concerned about the direction in which Kennedy was taking the school. Kennedy was moving towards a professional law school, or rather a mixture of professional training and an academic, social-sciences approach. To Laskin's mind, this was unfortunate, especially since Kennedy could not expect co-operation from the law society. The law society had consistently and adamantly refused to recognize Kennedy's program as being in any manner supplementary to their own, and steadfastly refused to give credit for any of the University of Toronto courses at Osgoode Hall. There appeared to be no prospect of Kennedy actually getting a professional law school. Laskin became more and more attracted to the idea of teaching in a professional school rather than in an undergraduate program in an arts faculty.

28 Wright to Smith 12 July 1945, UT Archives

29 See Laskin interview (Robin Harris) UT Archives. Willis had joined the Osgoode Hall staff in 1944, after eleven years of Dalhousie Law School. An Englishman, he had been educated at Oxford and Harvard. He was Canada's leading authority in the relatively new field of administrative law.

30 Wright to Smith 12 July 1945, UT Archives
31 Kennedy to Smith 11 July 1945, UT Archives (Smith Papers)
32 Wright to Smith 21 July 1945, UT Archives
33 As early as 1933 Wright had written to Smith to this effect; see Wright to Smith 27 July 1933.
34 Wright to Smith 12 July 1945, UT Archives
35 Laskin to Wright 14 July 1945
36 Smith to Wright 15 July 1945
37 Finkelman to Wright 16 July 1945
38 Wright to Smith 3 August 1945, UT Archives
39 Kennedy to Smith 18 July 1945, UT Archives (Smith Papers)
40 See Wright to Smith 3 August 1945, UT Archives.
41 Robertson to Wright 30 July 1945
42 Wright to Smith 3 August 1945, UT Archives
43 Smith to Wright 8 August 1945
44 Wright to Smith 3 August 1945, UT Archives
45 Robertson to Wright 10 August 1945
46 Robertson to Wright 4 September 1945
47 Smith to Kennedy 28 July 1945, 18 December 1946, UT Archives (Smith Papers)
48 Legal education file, UT Archives (Smith Papers)

7 NEGOTIATIONS AND MANOEUVRES

1 Smith to Kennedy 2 October 1945, University of Toronto Archives (hereinafter cited as UT Archives)
2 Kennedy to Smith 16 October 1945, UT Archives
3 See Claude Bissell *Halfway Up Parnassus: A Personal Account of the University of Toronto 1932–1971* (Toronto: University of Toronto Press 1974) 29.
4 The University of Toronto Act, RSO 1937, c. 372
5 Smith to Kennedy 2 October 1945, UT Archives
6 Quoted in Peter Newman *The Canadian Establishment* rev. ed. (Toronto: McClelland & Stewart 1979) 22n
7 Bissell *Parnassus* 29; Newman *Establishment* 384
8 Newman *Establishment* 384
9 Bissell *Parnassus*; E.A. Corbett *Sidney Earle Smith* (Toronto: University of Toronto Press 1961) 44–5
10 Smith, handwritten notes, undated, UT Archives
11 'Memorandum re Committee on Legal Education Bursar's Office' 26 February 1953, UT Archives (board of governors' legal education committee

file). The text of the resolution was as follows: 'Resolved that the Chairman appoint a special committee to consider legal education; to consult thereon with the Prime Minister and the Attorney General of the Province; to invite, if it deems fit, the Benchers of the Law Society of Upper Canada to appoint representatives to confer with the Committee in relation to co-operation between the Law Society of Upper Canada and the University in the field of legal education; and to report to the Board of Governors.'

12 Smith to W.E. Phillips 15 December 1945, UT Archives

13 Legal education file, UT Archives

14 For a discussion of this royal commission, see Joseph Schull *The History of Ontario since 1867* (Toronto: McClelland and Stewart 1978) 317

15 See editorial by R.M.W. Chitty in *Fortnightly Law Journal* 16 (1946), and letter from Williston to Wright 12 April 1948, Wright Papers (hereinafter cited as WP).

16 *Canadian Who's Who 1967–9* 109–10; see also W. Clement *The Canadian Corporate Elite* (Toronto: McClelland and Stewart 1975) 222, 261

17 Newman *Establishment* 379

18 For a discussion of these burdens see Corbett *Smith* 41, 44–8.

19 Smith to Henry Borden 25 June 1946, UT Archives (Smith Papers).

20 Kelly to Smith 28 June 1946, UT Archives

21 See the correspondence between Drew and Phillips in Drew Papers, National Archives of Canada, vol. 177, file 23.

22 Smith to Kennedy 28 October 1946, UT Archives

23 Smith to Borden 30 October 1946, UT Archives

24 Wright to Senator J. Haig, a member of the Canadian delegation to the United Nations, 25 November 1946 WP

25 See the correspondence between Wright and A.T. Vanderbilt, late November 1946 WP.

26 Ibid. The two seem to have first met at the conference in Vancouver in 1938 at which Wright gave his address 'Law and the Law Schools.' (See above, 145–6.) Vanderbilt visited Osgoode Hall on 27–8 February 1941. They met again briefly in Detroit in 1942.

27 From the final report of the special committee submitted on 20 January 1949. Copies of the report, which was incorporated into the Minutes of Convocation of that date, are to be found in the Archives of the Osgoode Hall Law School Library, York University, and in the Archives of the Law Society of Upper Canada (hereinafter cited as LSUC Archives).

28 In November 1946 Wright wrote to Vanderbilt: 'On my return, I found that a committee had been established from my dear friends, the Benchers, the object of which was to investigate legal education and [they] have

gathered in subterranean channels to look for some genius who would spike any possible plans of mine regarding a Deanship in particular and a reorganization of legal education in general. Things are getting quite amusing at the moment and I merely tell you this because in the wanderings of this committee, it may be that you will be one of the persons who will be interviewed. I do not know whether this will happen, but you may be sure that if I can wangle it, I shall endeavour to see that you are.'

29 B. Bucknall, T. Baldwin, and J.D. Laskin 'Pedants, Practitioners, and Prophets: Legal Education at Osgoode Hall to 1957' *Osgoode Hall Law Journal* 6 (1968) 138, 203-4

30 *Fortnightly Law Journal* 16 (2 February 1946)

31 Smith to Borden 11 December 1946, UT Archives

32 See W. Earl Smith to W.E. Phillips 20 January 1947, UT Archives.

33 Most of the following personal comments are derived from the authors' interviews with Mr Justice Arnup on 1 April 1983 and with Brendan O'Brien and John Honsberger on 4 February 1987.

34 'Legal Education in Ontario' *Canadian Law Journal* 42 (1922) 236; 'Legal Education in Ontario' *Canadian Bar Review* 2 (1924) 85

35 *Canadian Bar Review* 2 (1924) 85, 88

36 Denison to Wright 29 January 1938 WP

37 Denison to Wilson 14 November 1947, LSUC Archives. These last remarks were clearly directed at Wright himself. Wright was not a humble man, and he was regarded by his students as humourless in the classroom. On occasion, however, he displayed his human side. Gordon Nisbet, the former city solicitor of Windsor, Ontario, recalls the crap games that took place in the Osgoode Hall common room in the early post-war years. 'The crap games kept getting bigger, and then ... people started to come in off the street who had nothing to do with Osgoode Hall; they were professional dice-rollers ... [One day] Caesar Wright came in when the game was particularly big and people were talking to the bones; everybody said, "Oh, my God, it's Professor Wright!" He said, "Get over, give me room," and got down in the circle. He had more theories on how to roll dice than he had on torts. Eventually he cleaned up about half the money that was in the room, and then left. He never apologized.'

38 Laskin interview (Robin Harris) UT Archives

39 See WP for correspondence between Cartwright and Wright.

40 As John Arnup explained, it takes some time for a bencher to get the feel of what is going on in Convocation, and Cartwright simply had not been a bencher long enough.

41 Smith to Phillips 20 January 1947, UT Archives

42 The goal of the committee was to 'attempt to define what might be the
   ideal system of legal education in Ontario and to consider how close it can
   come to suggesting the setting up of such a system, having in mind, if
   possible, the avoidance of duplication of courses at the School of Law and
   the Osgoode Hall Law School.'
43 Smith to members of the University of Toronto committee 28 January 1947,
   UT Archives
44 Smith to Kennedy 5 February 1947, UT Archives
45 Smith to members of the joint committee 19 February 1947, UT Archives
46 Denison to Smith 24 February 1947, UT Archives
47 Denison to Carson, undated, UT Archives
48 Summary of meetings of committee, LSUC Archives
49 Brief of special committee. This brief contains transcripts of the oral
   evidence given by Falconbridge, Wright, Laskin, Willis, and others: LSUC
   Archives
50 Ibid. See also Wright to Vanderbilt 10 February 1947 WP.
51 Wright to Powell 7 January 1947–29 January 1947 WP
52 Wright to R.M. Sedgewick (then at Harvard) 22 March 1947 WP
53 Wright to Vanderbilt 10 February 1947 WP
54 Wright to Roscoe Pound 11 February 1947 WP
55 Wright to Vanderbilt 10 February 1947 WP
56 As he explained to Vanderbilt: 'I think it would be very helpful if you
   could find the time to let me have your views ... as to what we might
   reasonably put forward as suggested estimates based on a normal enrolment in a school of around 450. I have indicated to the Benchers that I
   would like to keep classes to a minimum of sixty, although probably the
   best we would hope for would be two sections of seventy-five each. What
   in your opinion would this involve in the way of necessary classroom
   space and what in the way of full-time lecturers?' Vanderbilt, who had
   come to full-time law teaching after developing an extensive practice, admired the way Osgoode Hall Law School utilized members of the practising
   bar in legal education. Wright was quick to point out in his letter that
   such would continue to be the case in the future if his ideas were accepted;
   the methods of utilization, however, were to be improved. 'I envision
   the base, as demonstrators, usually sharing their practical experience with
   groups rather than attempting with indifferent success the conduct of
   academic courses. I would hazard an off-hand guess of eight full-time men
   and approximately twenty-five part-time demonstrators to be used in the
   second and third years. What these part-time members should be entitled
   to in the way of salary is a question on which I have an open mind and

on which I think you can be of great assistance to me.' Wright also asked for Vanderbilt's opinion on what would be required to establish a post-graduate program, 'an essential which has been entirely lacking up to the present.' This remark, which ignores Kennedy's post-graduate program at the University of Toronto, suggests that Wright was focusing exclusively on changing Osgoode Hall at this time.

57 *Fortnightly Law Journal* 17 (15 January 1947)

58 *Fortnightly Law Journal* 17 (1 April 1947)

59 'Should the Profession Control Legal Education?' *Journal of Legal Education* 3 (1950) 1, 19–22

60 See the letter from Robertson to Smith 13 March 1947, UT Archives, explaining the earlier argreement.

61 See W. Earl Smith to S. Smith, and minutes of second and third meetings, LSUC Archives.

62 Denison to other Law Society representatives, LSUC Archives

63 Smith to Phillips, Hope, Kelly, and Matthews 1 May 1947, UT Archives

64 See John Willis *A History of Dalhousie Law School* (Toronto: University of Toronto Press 1979); A.R. Thompson 'An Introductory Course in Law at the University of Alberta' *University of Toronto Law Journal* 13 (1959–60) 274; W.B. Farris 'The New Era' *Advocate* 4 (1946) 130; Carlyle King *The First Fifty: Teaching, Research, and Public Service at the University of Saskatchewan 1909–1959* (Toronto: McClelland and Stewart 1961) 36–8.

65 The university had such an arrangement with, for example, Toronto General Hospital; see Bissell *Parnassus.*

66 See minutes of meeting, LSUC Archives.

67 Smith to Wilson 7 May 1947, UT Archives

68 Wilson to Smith 29 May 1947, UT Archives

69 Smith to Wilson 30 May 1947, UT Archives

70 Note written by Smith 10 July 1947, attached to letter from Smith to W.E. Phillips 17 November 1947, UT Archives. While preparing the memo for Wilson, Smith had been gathering other opinions about a Manitoba-type arrangement between the University of Toronto and the law society. One person whose views he solicited was Henry Borden's father-in-law, Dr MacRae, who had taught at Dalhousie and at Osgoode Hall for many years. MacRae was of the view that the law school's administrative machinery should be kept as simple as possible. He preferred a university law school along the lines of Dalhousie's. Nevertheless, he realized that concessions might have to be made to 'history.' He knew that the law society played a dominant role in legal education in Ontario and would have to be accommodated in any new scheme. In this context, he consid-

ered a Manitoba-type school desirable. He thought it best, however, to locate such a law school on the university campus, where law students could fraternize with non-law students. He ended on an encouraging note, stating that he was also of the opinion 'that the conjunction of present circumstances would be peculiarly favourable for the arranging of these matters satisfactorily to all concerned.' Smith could only hope that he was right. See MacRae to Smith 27 May 1947, UT Archives.

71 W. Earl Smith to S. Smith 16 October 1947, UT Archives; minutes of meeting, LSUC Archives

72 Smith to Phillips 17 November 1947, UT Archives

73 Kelly to Smith 24 November 1947, UT Archives

74 Memos to Phillips, Kelly, Hope, and Matthews 27 November 1947, UT Archives; Smith stated, 'In the hope that we can make some progress in this matter or learn, on the other hand, that it is not likely that we will make any progress, I do trust that we can have a full representation from the university panel.' See minutes of meetings, LSUC Archives.

75 Minutes of meeting, LSUC Archives

76 Wright to Read November 1947 WP

77 Wright to G.V.V. Nicholls 13 November 1947 WP

78 Wright to Vanderbilt 24 November 1947 WP

79 Vanderbilt to Wright 1 December 1947 WP

80 See Bucknall et al. 'Pedants' 206.

81 Mike Chitty would later describe that position in these words: 'Dean Falconbridge tendered his resignation on account of age and the increasing burden of the School. At that time, owing to post-war conditions, it was almost out of the question to find a new Dean outside of the full time staff of the school and the Benchers' hands were practically forced into appointing the next man in line of the faculty – as they had begun to call themselves – and he was the outstanding proponent of the academicians and freely expressed himself on many occasions as dissatisfied with the part time school.' *The Solicitor* 16 (1949) 70.

82 Special committee on legal education, summary of meetings, 12 February 1948, LSUC Archives

83 Wright's letter of resignation 21 January 1949, WP

84 Bucknall et al. 'Pedants' 205

85 Wright to Roscoe Pound 11 February 1947, and A.T. Vanderbilt 10 February 1947 WP

86 See draft minutes of meeting, LSUC Archives.

87 Wright to B. Laskin 4 March 1948 WP

88 The teaching staff had begun to call themselves the 'faculty' as if they

were associated with a university. See LSUC Archives, 24 September 1946, 'Petition from the Dean and Faculty.'

89 The memorandum was considered by the special legal education committee: 15 April 1948, LSUC Archives

90 Wright to Read 14 April 1948 WP

91 See Wright's letter of resignation 21 January 1949 WP.

92 *The Solicitor* 16 (1949) 70

93 See correspondence between Wright and Williston concerning practice groups (WP).

94 *Toronto Daily Star* 16 July 1948; Bucknall et al. 'Pedants' 213

95 Another newspaper reporter said that he was told by a bencher that there was a 'tug-of-war between the faculty, headed by Dean Cecil Wright and the Benchers for control' of legal education.

96 Interview with William Wright, 18 October 1986. See also letter from Somerville to Wright 6 August 1948, letter from Wright's secretary to J.R. O'Kell 1 September 1949, and letter from Wright to centenary committee, University of Ottawa 15 September 1948 WP.

97 The text of the speech is found in WP. Much of the speech was later incorporated into Wright's article 'Should the Profession Control Legal Education' *Journal of Legal Education* 3 (1950) 1.

8 CONFRONTATION

1 See the handwritten and typed minutes of this meeting of the special committee on legal education in the Archives of the Law Society of Upper Canada (hereinafter cited as LSUC Archives).

2 See brief of meetings of special committee on legal education, LSUC Archives.

3 See memos from W.E. Smith to Hamilton Cassels (17 January 1949) and to special committee members (14 January 1949) LSUC Archives.

4 Copies of these reports are found in LSUC Archives.

5 Memo prepared by Hugh McLaughlin for presentation to other committee members, LSUC Archives

6 Report to Convocation prepared by Hamilton Cassels as chairman of the legal education committee (September 1948) LSUC Archives

7 A.B. Dicey 'Inaugural Lecture as Vinerian Professor at Oxford, 1883' quoted in W.S. Holdsworth *Some Lessons from Legal History* (London: Macmillan 1928) 170–1.

8 See Jerome Frank 'What Constitutes a Good Legal Education?' *American*

Bar Association Journal 19 (1933) 723, and 'Why Not a Clinical Lawyer School?' *University of Pennsylvania Law Review* 81 (1933) 907.

9 See Wright's oral submissions to the special committee on legal education 5 February 1947, LSUC Archives

10 Cassels report to Convocation, supra note 6

11 Arthur Kelly to Hamilton Cassels 12 May 1948, LSUC Archives

12 See minutes of Convocation 20 January 1949, copies of which are found in the Wright Papers (hereinafter cited as WP) and LSUC Archives.

13 See Wright's letter of resignation 20 January 1949 WP. Under the headline 'More Practical Training Decreed for Lawyers' the *Globe and Mail* of 21 January 1949 reported:

> More practical training in law offices for Ontario law students to balance their theoretical education at Osgoode Hall was ordered yesterday after an all-day meeting of the benchers of the Law Society of Upper Canada.
>
> The benchers endorsed a nine-point program which will bring a decided change in the present system of legal education. In announcing it, G.W. Mason, treasurer of the Law Society, denied that the move was the result of [the] 'flunking' of some 86 first-year students last spring. It was charged at the time that they had failed in questions of practical law through too much emphasis on the theoretical side of jurisprudence.
>
> Mr. Mason said a special committee had been studying the question for two years and that its report yesterday was aimed at 'a better balance between academic and practical training.'
>
> The report approved the appointment of a lawyer on a full-time basis to superintend the present system whereby law students serve in law offices under articles during their course at Osgoode Hall. Consideration should also be given the establishment of a postgraduate course in law here.
>
> The curriculum of the law school also is to be reviewed ... Under the new system, Mr. Mason explained, practical work in law offices and lectures at the law school are to be carried on concurrently.
>
> 'This is the case now to a certain extent,' Mr. Mason said. 'But it is thought desirable to make a better balance between these two branches of training.'
>
> The head of the Law Society said sufficient practical training had been difficult since the war because the law school had been much over-crowded. The number of students the school could accommodate was

limited.

'It was difficult if not impossible,' he said, 'to provide more places in law offices. This position, however, is only temporary and we expect the number of students to decrease in the next two years.'

14 Wright to MacKenzie [December 1948] WP
15 Wright noted the time of dictation on his copy of the memo.
16 Wright to LeMesurier 7 February 1949 WP
17 Bora Laskin 'Cecil A. Wright: A Personal Memoir' *University of Toronto Law Journal* 33 (1983) 148, 154
18 John Willis to authors, 17 October 1979
19 One offer came from Webber Katy, the dean of the University of Chicago Law School: see 10 February 1949 WP
20 On 26 January 1949 the *Toronto Star* ran a story headed 'Inquiry Sought as Dean, 3 Law Teachers Quit, Protest Study Change.' The story explained that John Godfrey, a Toronto lawyer and a trustee of the York County Law Association, had requested an emergency meeting of the association to discuss the decision of the Law Society 'which will make the Law Society of Upper Canada the laughing stock of the legal world.' On Monday, 24 January, Wright received a telegram from Dean S.C. LeMesurier and professors F.R. Scott and Maxwell Cohen of McGill congratulating him on his 'splendid fight for liberal and scholarly standards in legal education.' The same day the *Globe and Mail* ran a letter to the editor from Irving Himel, a lawyer of ten years' standing, calling for either a new election of benchers so that the legal community could choose the course it thought best, or a public inquiry by a 'more representative committee of distinguished educators.' The *Globe* supported Himel in its editorial entitled 'The Public and Osgoode Hall': 'Is the main object of [a lawyer's] training to enable him to earn a living in a law office? Or should he have, besides this professional equipment, the breadth of culture and the special knowledge which can make him a worthy tribune of the people?' The same day the *Globe* ran a story entitled 'Policy of Secrecy: Legal Committee Silent, Answers no Questions on Osgoode Hall Split.' It was reported that the members of the special committee 'were sitting tight ... on their policy of secrecy ... Was the report from the committee of eight a unanimous one, and if not, how was the vote split? Why was the report released if it couldn't be made public immediately, and if the report [was] in order, why then, all the secrecy?' The *Toronto Star* reported on 24 January 1949 that opposition was rising swiftly to the benchers' plan.
21 *Globe and Mail* 25 January 1949
22 The resolution read: 'We, the members of the Osgoode Hall Legal and

Literary Society, respectfully disapprove of the policy on legal education
adopted by Convocation. Since we are not in a position to endorse any
other particular policy, we earnestly request both parties to the issue meet,
discuss and reconsider their previous decisions.'

23 In his copy of the statement Wright put a large question mark beside this
paragraph. He seems to have doubted that the low salary paid articling
students did much to facilitate the students' coming to Toronto to study.
(A copy of the committee's statement can be found in WP.)

24 Points 1 and 3 elicited marginal jottings from Wright on his copy of the
statement. Point 1 was marked with a vertical line, a signal Wright used to
indicate that the paragraph was of special interest. Point 3 was set off by
large square brackets, a large portion of it was underlined, and a large
underlined question mark appeared in the margin. Wright obviously
thought it ludicrous to suggest that he had known as early as March 1948
that Convocation would not support a full-time school.

25 LeMesurier to Wright [January 1949] WP.

26 A copy of this speech can be found in WP.

27 See above at 121–4.

28 The transcript can be found in WP.

29 The *Globe and Mail* 3 February 1949 stated that the public needed 'educated
lawyers, meaning lawyers who know more than the tricks and techniques
of the trade. If Osgoode Hall does not aim at educating but only at making
its students "competent," then it is high time Ontario had a school which
does produce men learned in the law and can claim admission to the
bar for them ... Mr. Chitty's formula for legal education may turn out
practitioners with sufficient knowledge of that kind to earn a good income.
Whether it will produce learned judges, great defenders of the liberties
of the subject and statesmen-lawyers who can wisely frame new legislation
is another matter.'

30 Copies can be found in WP.

31 The Toronto Lawyers' Club sent a summary of Wright's 'brilliant defence
of his position' to their members. The club decided to appoint a committee
to investigate the situation. Allin Annis, the newly elected president of
the Ontario Country Bar Association, also publicly endorsed Wright's
position.

32 The *Globe* headline read: 'Lawyers Ask Benchers to Reconsider Decision on
Cutting Class Time.' The *Star* ran pictures of the leaders of the 'junior
members of the bar' who had 'demanded reconsideration' of the benchers'
proposal, and proclaimed: 'Law Association Votes 20–1 against Proposal
to Cut Osgoode Course.' Even the *Telegram*, which had been the least

supportive of Wright's stand, announced: 'Dean Backed by Lawyers in Breach with Benchers.'

33 Wright to Hazell 7 February 1949 WP
34 Wright to Vanderbilt 8 February 1949 WP
35 Tory to Wright 14 February 1949 WP
36 Minutes of Convocation 17 February 1949, LSUC Archives
37 See the text of this speech in WP.
38 Wright to Mason 24 February 1949 WP
39 Wright to Mason 3 March 1949 WP
40 Pound to Wright 1 May 1948 WP
41 Wright to Pound 24 March 1949 WP

9 'AN HONEST TO GOD LAW SCHOOL'

1 Wright to Major E.C. Moogk 3 June 1949, University of Toronto Archives, Sidney Smith Papers (hereinafter cited as UT Archives)
2 The following summary of the degrees offered by Kennedy's law school and Wright's comments on them is taken from a memo prepared by Wright for submission to the university administration entitled 'Proposed Changes in the Courses in the School of Law Leading to the Degree of Bachelor of Laws, and the Combined Course in the Faculty of Arts and the School of Law Leading to the degrees of B.A. in Law and of LL.B.' Wright Papers (hereinafter cited as WP).
3 'Proposed Changes' WP
4 Kennedy to Wright 29 May 1949 WP
5 Wright to Goodhart 15 March 1949 WP. The same letter was sent to D. Hughes Parry, Professor J.C. Turner, and Professor P.H. Winfield.
6 Wright to Nicholls 16 March 1949 WP
7 Wright to Mason 16 March 1949 WP
8 Wright to Patterson [1949] WP
9 *The Solicitor* 16 (1949) 70
10 Wright to Keeton 6 May 1949 WP
11 Keeton to Wright 14 May 1949 WP
12 Minutes of Convocation 17 March 1949, Law Society of Upper Canada Archives (hereinafter cited as LSUC Archives)
13 Minutes of University of Toronto Board of Governors 28 April 1949 UT Archives
14 Phillips to S. Smith 22 May 1949, UT Archives
15 See minutes of special Convocation 20 April 1949, LSUC Archives.

16 Wright to Goodhart 15 March 1949 WP: 'I think that any good academic man at the moment would be rather foolish to come to the Osgoode Hall Law School in the present state of uncertainty. Certainly no Canadian academic man of any stature is likely to enter on a field which has been so badly discredited. When the picture clears a bit, I will write you further and advise you of developments. In the meantime, if you would pass this word along I would be very grateful. I am sending the same letter as this to my friend, Professor Hughes Parry and Glanville Williams of London and Professor Winfield and Cecil Turner of Cambridge.'

17 See minutes of Convocation 19 May 1949, LSUC Archives, and the *Law Society Gazette* 7 (1973) 233.

18 Wright to A.L. Goodhart 3 June 1949, and G. Williams to Wright 5 June 1949 WP

19 Minutes of Convocation 19 May 1949, LSUC Archives. Mr Justice Horace Krever quipped that, given the loss of Wright, Laskin, and Willis and their replacement with practitioners and recent graduates in 1949, the benchers put a gun to the head of Wright and his colleagues, pulled the trigger, and blew their own brains out: First Alumni Dinner, University of Toronto Law School, 30 October 1982.

20 See B. Bucknall, T. Baldwin, and J.D. Lakin 'Pedants, Practitioners, and Prophets: Legal Education at Osgoode Hall to 1957' *Osgoode Hall Law Journal* 6 (1968) 219–23.

21 Minutes of Convocation 29 June 1949; and see correspondence between Gershom Mason and Henry Borden, LSUC Archives.

22 What follows is based on a letter from Wright to Sydney Paikin, QC, of Hamilton, 26 September 1963 WP.

23 H. Borden to C. Carson 12 June 1950, UT Archives

24 Arthur E. Sutherland *The Law at Harvard* (Cambridge: Harvard University Press 1967) 261, 288, 316, 321–2

25 Griswold to Wright 23 November 1949 WP

26 Wright to R. Kramer 4 January 1950 WP

27 Ibid.

28 Kramer to Wright 27 April 1950 WP

29 *Journal of Legal Education* 3 (1950) 1

30 Wright to Rand 28 June 1950 WP

31 *Columbia Law Review* 72 (1972) 1134–46

32 On Friedmann's tour and its motivation, see Wright to F.R. Scott 7 November 1949, and G. Williams to Wright 30 December 1949 WP.

33 Wright to S. Smith 24 April 1950, UT Archives

34 See J.E. Page and M.L. Bogart 'James B. Milner: Some Aspects of His Work, Career, and Writings in Community Planning Law' *Environments* 14 (1982) 35.
35 This wording appears on a plaque erected by the Toronto Historical Board in Milner Park, Toronto, on 9 June 1984.
36 Borden to Carson 9 June 1950, UT Archives
37 Carson to Borden 14 June 1950, UT Archives
38 This correspondence is reprinted in an appendix to *Report of the Special Committee on Legal Education of the Law Society, 1952* LSUC Archives.
39 See the discussion of these meetings in the 1952 report, Ibid.
40 Carson to Borden 4 February 1952, LSUC Archives
41 Borden to Carson 7 February 1952, LSUC Archives
42 See Carson to W.E. Smith 26 April 1952, LSUC Archives.
43 See the copy of Carson's draft and the correspondence between W. Smith and P. Jamieson in LSUC Archives.

10 THE ROAD TO COMPROMISE

1 Wright had written to Arthur C. Pulling, the Harvard Law School librarian (28 March 1950, Wright Papers, hereinafter cited as WP) to enlist his help in tracking down a quotation used in an editorial on legal education by Dr Morse in the 1934 edition of the *Canadian Bar Review*. The quote was to the effect that if the inns of court made arbitrary rules for the governance of their members, abridged the period of study, and relaxed the regulations for the exclusion of improper candidates, it would be necessary for the legislature to interpose and to establish a uniform and efficient discipline. Wright explained: 'I'm most anxious to find the statement, properly authenticated, because in our present controversy on legal education, I think you will appreciate its very direct bearing.' After much searching, Pulling found the quotation in a footnote in a biography of Lord Mansfield in *Campbell's Lives of Chief Justices*. Wright was undoubtedly disappointed to discover that it was not a dictum of Lord Mansfield himself.
2 Wright to Frost 17 November 1950 WP
3 Wright to Stone 31 May 1952 WP
4 Wright's notes for this speech can be found in WP.
5 White to Wright 29 October 1952 WP
6 See correspondence in Law Society of Upper Canada Archives (hereinafter cited as LSUC Archives).
7 Ibid., memo of 9 February 1953, a copy is also in WP.
8 Memo from W.E. Smith to C. Carson 5 February 1953, LSUC Archives

9 Smith to Carson 11 February 1953, LSUC Archives
10 W.E. Smith to Porter 15 February 1953, LSUC Archives
11 On 14 February the *Toronto Telegram* ran an article entitled 'Apprentices Need Two Years Lawyers Refute "u" Charge: Law Society Contends Knows Own Needs Best.' The article, which was based on Carson's press release, noted the criticism of university law schools made by Cantrall in the *American Bar Association Journal*. It also noted that while Osgoode Hall's attendance was increasing, the University of Toronto was experiencing declining enrolment; there were twenty-seven students in third year at the University of Toronto, but only sixteen in second year and twelve in first year.
12 University of Toronto Archives (hereinafter cited as UT Archives), Board of Governors Legal Education Committee file
13 Ibid.
14 Copies of the broadsheets and the student editorials are in LSUC Archives. See also the article by William French in the *Globe Magazine*, 23 April 1960, for a picture of the student demonstrators dressed in suits and ties marching in front of Osgoode Hall.
15 W.E. Smith to C. Carson 10 February 1953, LSUC Archives
16 See *Globe and Mail* 26 March 1953.
17 Smith to R.A.F. Montgomery 30 January 1954, UT Archives
18 The Wright Papers contain a mimeographed copy of this material, which suggests that copies were distributed. All of this material is undated but is found with copies of *Report of the Special Committee on Legal Education of the Law Society, 1952*, the 1952 University of Toronto president's report, and the 1952 Legislative Debates. In a letter to W.P. Gregory dated 22 October 1956, Wright stated that he had drawn this memorandum up 'some time ago.'
19 The explanatory note stated: 'The entire scheme is contained in the amendment of Section 41 of the Law Society Act and the proposal shortly is to place graduates of both schools on a basis of equality; to permit the Benchers of the Law Society to provide an identical examination of graduates of all law schools approved by them before admission to practice; to regulate the mode of examination to preserve such equality; to maintain the Benchers' power of control over all law schools by permitting the withdrawal of approval of any school other than their own for failure to observe standards, etc. and to provide a limited right of appeal from any decision on that question of approval by the Law Society by the Board of Judges and the Attorney-General.'
20 UT Archives, Board of Governors Legal Education Committee file

21 Ibid.

22 The first proposal was that the law school curriculum be reorganized to consist of an arts program in the first year, and two years of law courses leading to both the BA and the LL B degrees. Smith noted that the university Senate, which had to approve changes in curriculum, would not sanction such a plan. He noted that there would be problems in administering the program, since the student would spend one year in the Faculty of Arts and the other years in the School of Law. He also thought it unlikely that the law society, which had based its limited recognition of the School of Law on the ground that law students had an arts degree followed by three years of law work, would allow more credits for 'an attenuated law program.' He noted that the proposal would reduce the standards of the school and would adversely affect its standing in the United States, as well as in other parts of the Commonwealth. The second proposal called for maintenance of the present three-year program, but would have allowed prospective Ontario practitioners to enter Osgoode Hall Law School after completing two years in the university's law school. Smith stated that this seemed unworkable, since the university would virtually become a full-time, two-year law school' and the 'present integrated curriculum would be destroyed.'

23 'Legal Education in Canada' *Canadian Bar Review* 32 (1954) 387. See Rand to Wright 1 July 1954 WP. Rand told Wright, 'When I wrote the paragraphs on a national School, I had in mind one directed and inspired by you.'

24 Canada's learned societies, including the Association of Canadian Law Teachers, were holding their annual meetings in Toronto in June 1955. A member of the association's executive suggested that it might be appropriate to have the law society and the University of Toronto jointly sponsor the association's meeting. There was perceived to be a 'situation of strain' between the two institutions, and the association did not want to be seen as siding with one or the other. On 30 November 1954, Wright wrote to Cyril Carson to assure him that while differences of opinion existed between the university and the law society on some matters, he and his colleagues at the university were not conscious of any 'strain.' He also assured Carson that the university would be 'more than happy to cooperate with the Law Society in every possible way to make the meeting a success.' Carson replied, on 6 December, that those at Osgoode Hall did not have any feelings of living in a 'situation of stress.' He had asked, he said, that a copy of his letter be sent to all of the law schools who were members of the association. At the same time Carson wrote to the president of the association renewing the law society's offer to have the

association meet at Osgoode Hall, but suggesting that if the association chose to meet at the university, like the other learned societies, there was 'no possibility that such a choice will be misconstrued by us.' The meeting was eventually held at the university.

25 Ironically, just at the time that the majority of the special committee were making their conservative, backward-looking predictions, J.P. Nelligan was beginning a survey of the legal profession in Canada under the auspices of the Canadian Bar Association in co-operation with the Carnegie Corporation and the Nuffield Trust. Nelligan's survey, published in two articles in the *Canadian Bar Review*, showed not only that the special committee's predictions were wrong, but that lawyers were practising more and more in large urban communities and with an increasing degree of specialization.

26 The enrolment figures cited here are derived from the report of the special committee on legal education (14 February 1957) LSUC Archives.

27 The universities were represented by Sidney Smith of the University of Toronto, W.A. Mackintosh, the principal of Queen's, G.P. Gilmour, the president of McMaster, R.A. Allen, the vice-president and dean of graduate studies of Western, Rev. René Lavigne, the dean of the University of Ottawa, Rev. E.C. Lebel, the president of Assumption College, Rev. G.S. Cousineau, the rector of St Patrick's College, and M.M. MacOdrum, the president of Carleton College.

28 John Arnup 'The 1957 Breakthrough' *Law Society Gazette* 18 (1984) 180

29 See Smith to Beverley Matthews 17 June 1955 WP, in which Smith described his 10 June meeting with Wright, Corry, and Mackintosh.

30 See above, 75–6.

31 See J.A. Corry *My Life and Work: A Happy Partnership* (Kingston: Queen's University 1981).

32 A copy of this letter can be found in WP.

33 Carson to Mackintosh 20 September 1955 WP

34 Mackintosh to S. Smith 23 September 1955 WP

35 Smith to Mackintosh 24 October 1955 WP

36 Mackintosh to Smith 31 October 1955 WP

37 Smith to Mackintosh 2 November 1955 WP

38 Mackintosh to Ontario university presidents 29 November 1955 WP

39 Mackintosh to Carson 15 December 1955 WP. The letter was also included in the report of the special committee on legal education, 14 February 1957, LSUC Archives.

40 Carson to Mackintosh 19 December 1955 WP

41 Wright to Kertzer 17 January 1956 WP

42 See memorandum of this meeting prepared by Smith (WP). Representing the law society were Cyril Carson, John Robinette, Park Jamieson, Roly Wilson, Earl Smith, and Harold Walker. Representing the universities were Mackintosh and Corry from Queen's, Hall from Western, Lebel of Assumption College, Dean H.S. Armstrong of McMaster, President R. Normandin of the University of Ottawa, Rev. F.E. Banim of St Patrick's College, Dr J.A. Gibson of Carleton College, and Sidney Smith.

43 Sidney Smith later summarized the results of the meeting as follows: 'The conclusion of the meeting, then, can be boiled down to two points: the representatives of the universities, and in particular the University of Toronto, would study the possibility of establishing a good tough two-year course in the field of Arts; and the Special Committee of the Law Society would study Dr. Mackintosh's proposal, then another joint meeting could be held.' Smith noted that it seemed to him that Cyril Carson, John Robinette, and Harold Walker 'were very sincere in expressing their desire to resolve this question.'

44 Mackintosh to Smith 18 April 1956. There is a copy of this letter in WP.

45 Wright to Bell 23 February 1953 WP

46 Bell to Wright 12 January 1956 WP

47 There is a copy of this letter in WP.

48 There is a copy of this letter in WP.

49 Wright to Bell 25 May 1956 WP

50 Wright to Ryan 18 June 1956 WP

51 Wright to Ford 17 September 1956 WP

52 Wright to Read 17 October 1956 WP

53 Wright to Reid 27 July 1956 WP

54 Wright to Gregory 22 October 1956, and Corry 14 September 1956 WP

55 Wright to Corry 6 November 1956 WP

56 Wright to Corry 19 November 1956 WP

57 Arnup 'Breakthrough' 194

58 Ibid. 195

59 Ibid. 195–8

60 Wright to Corry 21 January 1957 WP

61 Wright to Corry 23 January 1957 WP

62 Wright to Corry 21 January 1957 WP

63 Corry to Wright 4 Feburary 1957 WP

64 Arnup 'Breakthrough' 199

65 *Globe and Mail* 15 February 1957

66 Wright to Carson 19 February 1957 WP

EPILOGUE

1 J.A. Corry *My Life and Work: A Happy Partnership* (Kingston: Queen's University 1981) 154
2 Ibid.
3 See Georges Caron 'The Faculty of Law of the University of Ottawa' *University of Toronto Law Journal* 12 (1957–8) 292.
4 See I.C. Rand 'The New Faculty of Law in the University of Western Ontario' *University of Toronto Law Journal* 4 (1961–2) 107.
5 See H.W. Arthurs 'The Affiliation of Osgoode Hall Law School with York University' *University of Toronto Law Journal* 17 (1967) 194, 195.
6 H. Allan Leal 'Osgoode Hall Law School – Today and Tomorrow' *University of Toronto Law Journal* 12 (1957) 285, 286
7 Ibid. 290
8 In his interview with Robin Harris on 2 May 1977 (University of Toronto Archives), Bora Laskin suggested that after the 1949 crisis support from the university dropped 'because a good many of the members of the Board of Governors, the lawyer members, were probably more sympathetic to the Law Society than they were to their own University Faculty.'
9 See C.A. Wright 'U. of T. Law Faculty Gets New Building' *Canadian Bar Journal* 4 (1961) 68.
10 Arthurs 'Affiliation' 197–204
11 Minutes of the meeting of the council of the Faculty of Law, 19 April 1965, University of Toronto Law School files
12 Of Osgoode Hall Law School's good fortune, Laskin noted in 1977: 'The University of Toronto ended up with the worst Law building of any Law School in Ontario. Osgoode Hall … it's rather ironic that the final act in this whole sorry business was the surrender by the Law Society of its Law School to York University and York University gets a $5^1/_2$ million dollar building. I don't begrudge it to them, but I say that in retrospect we were very very meanly dealt with, very meanly dealt with.' Interview with Robin Harris 2 May 1977
13 As he had been called by Maxwell Cohen of McGill, in a telegram Cohen sent to the University of Toronto Law School on the occasion of Wright's death (Wright Papers).
14 The following account is taken from Bora Laskin 'Cecil A. Wright: A Personal Memoir' *University of Toronto Law Journal* 33 (1983) 148, 160–1.
15 In a review of the first edition of *Cases on Tort Law*, John G. Fleming wrote: 'This volume has to be read from cover to cover in order to appreciate

the finesse and thoughtfulness which [has] gone into its execution ... If this work fails to convince teachers of the superiority of the casebook method, that cause is indeed lost, since I know of no other collection which, for its inherent excellence and ready usability in British Common law countries, holds out so much attraction.' *Sydney Law Review* 2 (1956) 212, 215–16.

16 'In Memoriam, Cecil Augustus Wright' *University of Toronto Law Journal* 17 (1967) 247

17 These claims are developed in Jerold S. Auerbach *Unequal Justice* (New York: Oxford University Press 1976); and see above at 74–5.

18 See Blaine G. Baker 'Legal Education in Upper Canada 1785–1889: The Law Society as Educator' in *Essays in the History of Canadian Law* vol. 2, edited by D.H. Flaherty (Toronto: The Osgoode Society 1983).

19 *Law and Learning: Report to the Social Sciences and Humanities Research Council of Canada by the Consultative Group on Research and Education in Law* (Ottawa: The Information Division of the Social Sciences and Humanities Research Council of Canada 1983). See also Harry Arthurs 'Paradoxes of Canadian Legal Education' *Dalhousie Law Journal* 3 (1976–7) 639.

20 Ibid. 140

Index

Aikins, Sir James 55, 62
Allen, R.A. 327 n.27
American Bar Association 18, 20–2
American Law Institute
  Restatements 92, 111, 136–7, 301
  n.51
American legal education: early
  development 13–22
American legal realism: at
  Harvard 86, 88–9, 91–2, 298 n.22,
  299 n.23; influence on Wright 95,
  110
Ames, James Barr 17
Anderson, J.T. 26
anti-semitism: in Ontario 310 n.19
apprenticeship: in England 7–8,
  10–12
Ardagh, Holford 123–4
Armour, Edward Douglas 36, 43, 72,
  291 n.9
Armstrong, H.S. 328 n.42
Arnup, John 201, 248, 249–50,
  257–62, 263, 264, 314 n.40

Arthurs, Harry 261, 276–8, 295 n.40
Ashley, W.J. 35
Association of American Law
  Schools 19, 20–2, 53
Atkin, Lord 130
Atkin Report 130–1
Auld, Clyde 115, 116, 149, 164, 309
  n.17
Austin, John 9

Banim, F.E. 328 n.12
Barlow, F.H. 56, 78
barrister/solicitor: distinction in
  Canada 23, 24
Baw, James 104
Beaton, William J. 220, 231, 233, 239,
  248, 263
Bell, Richard A. 255, 256
Bence, A.E. 128
Birkett, Sir Norman 233
Blackstone, William 8–10, 13
Blake, Edward 26, 31, 35
Blake, Samuel H. 35

Blake, William Hume 25
Bohlen, Francis: influence on
    Wright 83, 90–6, 101, 102–3, 137;
    see also tort law
Borden, Henry 112–13, 147, 172,
    177–8, 179–80, 182, 232, 237–8
Borden, Sir Robert 112
Bowlby, C.W. Reid 180, 202, 213
Bradford, Samuel Hugh 42, 43, 47,
    99–100, 103
Bradshaw, G. Gordon 118, 136
Brandeis, Louis D. 83, 109
Brebner, James 57
Brewer, David J. 19
Brewin, F.A. 132
Brown, T.D. 69
Bryce, James 12
Burbidge, A.G. 129
Burgess, I.J. 26

Cameron, E.R. 56–7
Cameron, John Hillyard 25, 27
Campbell, Alexander 26
Campbell, Ives Colin 292 n.24
Canadian Bar Association: beginnings
    62, 293 n.3; Lee reports 63–9;
    MacRae's standard curriculum
    69–71, 77; depression years 105–6;
    support for changes in legal
    education 114, 123, 129, 134,
    140–1, 155–9, 199, 217–18, 234–5;
    see also Ontario Bar Association
Canadian Bar Review 62, 77; under
    Wright's editorship 129–30, 132,
    136–9, 141, 148, 150–1, 152–4
Cardozo, Benjamin 109
Carey, Harold Eric 85, 292 n.24
Carrick, Donald 121–4, 126–7, 217–18
Carson, Cyril F.H. 180, 182, 185, 188,
    191, 202, 207, 232, 272, 326 n.24;

as old-fashioned lawyer 183–4;
    treasurer of law society 237–8,
    239–40; role in compromise 243–4,
    245, 249, 250, 251–2, 254, 257, 263,
    328 nn.42, 43
Cartwright, John Robert 42, 180, 182,
    184, 191, 202, 213, 269, 314 n.40
casebook method of legal instruction:
    u.s. origins and views on 15–17,
    84–5, 298 n.16; use in Canada 27,
    32, 43, 46, 51–3, 54, 76, 82, 101–2,
    113, 131–2, 329 n.15
Cassels, Hamilton 180, 188, 192, 193,
    202, 204, 205–6, 213, 218, 231, 272
Chitty, Robert Michael Willes 150,
    196, 210, 213, 231, 233, 272, 317
    n.81; as spokesman for practitioner
    138–40, 145, 217, 218, 228–9, 321
    n.29; criticism of Wright 142, 181–2,
    187–8; defence of Wright 157–8
Clarke, A.W. 61
Clute, Arthur Roger 42, 47, 52, 99,
    149
Cody, H.J. 163–4
Cohen, Maxwell 310 n.19, 320 n.20,
    329 n.13
Coleman, E.H. 105
'concurrent approach': see legal
    education
Connor, Skeffington 25
'consecutive approach': see legal
    education
Conservative party (Progressive
    Conservative) 163, 269, 308 n.4
Cook, Walter Wheeler 20
Corbett, P.E. 105
Corry, J. Alex 76, 151; role in
    compromise 201, 219, 251, 254,
    256–62, 264–5
Costigan, George P. 101

Council of Legal Education (England) 11, 176
Cousineau, G.S. 327 n.27
Crease, Lindley 132
Cronkite, F.C. 105, 114, 132, 133, 140–1
Crouse, G.H. 129
Curtis, G.F. 150–1

Dalhousie Law School 28, 48–50, 67–8, 81, 164, 256, 291 n.16
Davidson, John 149
Davidson, W.C. 303 n.48
Davis, H.H. 146–7
Davison, James Forrester 58, 107–8, 115
Delamere, T.D. 28
Denison, John Shirley 36, 43, 47, 125, 134, 136, 141, 151–2, 177, 189; criticism of Osgoode Hall 39–42, 125, 216; criticism of 'Harvard model' 144–5; representative of 'old guard' 182–3, 185, 188, 191, 272
Dicey, A.V. 12–13, 204
Doherty, C.J. 62
Donoghue v. Stevenson 92
Draper, W. George 26
Draper, William Henry 25
Drew, George 163, 177, 178, 179, 180, 182, 185, 191
Duncan, Lewis 255
Dunlop, W.J. 246
Dwight, Theodore 27

Edwards, Stanley 193, 210, 212, 218
Eliot, Charles W. 15, 17
English legal traditions: in Canada 5, 23–4, 203–5, 274–5
Esten, James Christie Palmer 25
Estey, Wilfred Z. 234

extralegal approach to law 87–90, 92–4, 108–10, 142–4, 145–6; see also sociological jurisprudence

Falconbridge, Sir Glenholme 45
Falconbridge, John Delatre 77, 81, 103, 107, 112, 117, 128, 134–5, 136, 228, 229, 231, 271, 275; as principal and dean 36, 42, 43, 44–7, 50–1, 53, 55–6, 58–9; lobbies for academic legal education 62–3, 79, 125, 181, 186; hires Wright 98–100; resigns deanship 192–4, 317 n.81
Falconbridge, Mary Phoebe 45
Farris, J.W. de B. 146
Fauteux, Gerald 265
Finch, G.B. 42–3
Finkelman, Jacob 149, 164–5, 169, 170–1, 174, 307 n.65, 309 n.17; hired at University of Toronto 115; irritates Wright 117–18
Flavelle, Sir Joseph 36
Fleming, John G. 329 n.15
Flexner report (U.S.) 19–20, 288 n.24
Ford, Gordon W. 255, 256
Fortescue, Sir John 7
Foster, Harold W.A. 42, 47, 99, 103, 149, 234
Fox, Harold 158
Frank, Jerome 204
Frankfurter, Felix, 83, 120–1, 192
Friedmann, Wolfgang 236–7
Frost, Leslie 241, 244

Gahan, Frank 233
Gibson, James A. 328 n.42
Gilmour, G.P. 327 n.27
Godfrey, John 320 n.20
Goodhart, Arthur L. 147, 148, 227, 228, 233, 323 n.16
Goodman, Edwin 223

Green, Leon 91–2, 109
Gregory, Wilfrid 256–7, 263
Griswold, Erwin N. 89, 235–6
Guthrie, Donald 218

Hagarty, John 25
Haldane, Viscount 62
Hall, George Edward 251, 254–5, 328 n.42
Hancock, Moffatt 140, 164, 166, 201, 308 nn.12, 15
Harcourt, Frederick Weir 45, 57
Harold, J.F. 149
Hart, Henry 102
Harvard Law School: influence on Dicey 12–13; development of casebook method 15–17; recognition of Canadian degrees 53, 81–2, 186–7, 297 n.2; as model for Canadian law schools 28, 34, 43, 63–4, 65, 76, 77–8, 120, 144–5, 183, 204–5, 226, 272–3
Hazell, Harry 219
Hébert, J.T. 75–6, 251
Henderson, G.F. 51–2, 54, 66
Himmel, Irving 320 n.20
Hodgins, F.E. 61
Hodgins, Thomas 28, 294 n.5
Hohfeld, Wesley N. 299 n.24
Holdworth, William 7, 12
Holmes, Oliver Wendell 83, 87
Honsberger, John 314 n.33
Hope, John Andrew L.C. 177–8, 232
Howland, W.G.C. 58, 223
Hoyles, Newman Wright 34, 36
Hudson, Manley Ottmer 83

Imperial School of Advanced Legal Studies (London) 78, 297 n.55
Incorporated Law Society (England) 9–10, 130

inns of court 6–7, 10–11
Irving, Sir Aemilius 61, 293 n.13

James, Eldon R. 102
Jamieson, Park 180, 202, 231, 233, 239, 240, 243, 257–8, 328 n.42; prepares report on legal education 207–8; role in compromise 259–62, 264
Johnson, Walter S. 132
Johnston, Douglas M. 265
Judson, Wilfred 269

Katy, Webber 320 n.19
Keeton, G.J. 229, 230
Keith, D.A. 255
Kellock, R.L. 269
Kelly, Arthur: role in compromise 177, 178–9, 189, 191, 196, 198–9, 201, 218, 232
Kennedy, Gilbert D. 157, 307 n.65
Kennedy, William Paul Maclure 174, 176–7, 179, 198, 222, 231; and 'Kennedy's School' 58, 107–8, 114–17, 148–51, 311 n.27; Wright's animosity towards 117–20, 150–1; and Laskin's Osgoode Hall job offer 163–70; helps Laskin 308 nn.11, 15; congratulates Wright 226–7; see also 'Kennedy's Law School'
'Kennedy's Law School' 58, 107–8, 114–20, 148–52, 158–9, 163–5, 174, 226, 276, 277, 311 n.27, 322 n.2
Kerr, W.F. 69
Kertzer, Morris 253
King's College 25, 35
Kramer, Robert 236
Krever, Horace 323 n.19

LaBrie, F. Eugene 150, 174

Lafleur, Eugene 66
Landis, James M. 84, 147–8
Langdell, Christopher Columbus 15–17
Laskin, Bora 58, 140, 193, 210, 212, 218, 221, 230, 233, 258, 262, 269, 279, 329 nn.8, 12; on 'Kennedy's School' 115, 116, 311 n.27; student years 303 n.48; employment problems 308 nn.12, 15, 309 nn.16, 17, 310 nn.18, 19; Osgoode Hall job offer 164–70; on Cyril Carson 183–4
Lavigne, René 327 n.27
Law Society of Alberta 151
Law Society of Upper Canada: creation and incorporation 23–4; 1935 report 121–33; 1946 special committee 180–201; 1949 report 202–8; resignation of Wright 208–21; rebuilding the law school 231–4; negotiations 230, 235, 237–41, 248–52, 254–5, 257–63; see also Osgoode Hall Law School
law teachers: Blackstone's view 9; professionalization in u.s. 16–17; Canadian view 58–9, 275–6; see also Unequal Justice
Lawyer's Club of Toronto 78–9
Leal, H. Allan 234, 258–9, 266, 267
Lebel, E.C. 327 n.27, 328 n.42
Lederman, William R. 265
Lee, Edward T. 21
Lee, Robert Warden 51, 64–6, 69, 77, 216, 271, 294 n.18
Lefroy, A.H.F. 36, 43
Legal and Literary Society 28, 121, 126, 132, 136, 213, 320 n.22
legal education: law school admission requirements 69–70, 113–14, 121, 123, 126, 131, 173, 180, 193, 224, 260; 'concurrent approach' 27, 49, 66, 68, 70–1, 105–6, 122–3, 126–7, 146, 185, 201, 202–3, 205–7, 216; 'consecutive approach' 57–8, 106–7, 122, 127; in England 6–13
legal scholarship 78, 109–10, 133, 137–8, 160–1, 276–8
Leith, Alexander 26
LeMesurier, C.S. 111, 209, 214, 320 n.20
Lewis, W. Draper 20
Litchfield Law School (u.s.) 13–14, 17; see also private law schools (u.s.)
Llewellyn, Karl 138
Lochner v. New York 87
Ludwig, Michael Herman 47, 57, 79, 98, 100, 113, 118, 121, 125, 128, 216, 234; on the concurrent system 70–1; views on legal education 90, 123–4, 127

Macaulay, R.W. 201
McCarthy, D'Alton Lally 35, 155–8, 159, 172, 181
MacDonald, A.L. 105
Macdonald, Ronald St John 265
MacDonald, Vincent 53, 104, 112, 140, 150, 155
McFadden, James Weir 136
McGill University 40, 51, 77–8
Mackay, Ira A. 71, 295 n.34
Mackay, Robert S. 265
Mackenzie, A. Stanley 48, 50
Mackenzie, Norman A.M. (Larry) 58, 115, 118–19, 149, 165, 208, 292 n.24
Mackintosh, W.A.: role in com-

promise 250, 251–3, 254–5, 257
259, 262, 264, 327 n.27, 328
nn. 42, 43
McLaughlin, Hugh J. 180, 202, 213,
231, 248
McLaurin, C. Campbell 153
McLean, Alexander C. 138
MacLennan, R.J. 55–6, 63, 71–2, 73,
296 n.42
MacMahon, Hugh 35
McMaster University 250
MacMurchy, Angus 66
McNair, A.D. 138
McNutt, Ray Douglas 292 n.24
MacOdrum, M.M. 327 n.27
McPherson, L.Z. 126
MacPherson v. *Buick Motors* 109
MacRae, Donald Alexander 47–8, 52,
71, 80–1, 105, 112, 125, 178, 271,
316 n.70; dean of Dalhousie 50–1;
compiles standard curriculum 66,
69–70, 77; sends Wright to Harvard
80–1, 98; retires from teaching 164
MacRae, Jean Creelman (née Borden)
113
McRuer, James Chalmers 104, 136
Manley, Peter 246
Marshall, J.R. 231
Martin, Clara Brett 33
Martin, Edward 30
Martin, G. Arthur 58, 223
Mason, Gershom W. 180, 182, 188;
opposes co-operation with Uni-
versity of Toronto 191, 193, 199;
favours concurrent system 202,
210, 211, 214, 218, 220–1, 227–8,
230, 238, 239, 272
Masten, C.A. 57
Matthews, Beverly 178, 232, 238
Mavor, James 36

Mewett, Alan W. 207, 269
Mickel, W.C. 294 n.8
Middlebro', W.S. 124, 125
Middlesex Law Association 29
Mills, David 35
Milner, James B. 236–7, 258
Molinaro, Frank 215
Montgomery, W.S. 78, 128
Moogk, E.C. 322 n.1
Moore, William Underhill 74
Morden, Kenneth Gibson 112, 126
Morse, Charles 56, 58, 111, 132, 137,
324 n.1
Moss, Charles 30, 35
Moss, Thomas 27
Munro, George 49

Nash, Albert 42
Nelligan, J.P. 327 n.25
Neville, K.P.R. 80
Nicholls, G.V.V. 227
Nickle, W.F. 125
night law schools: *see* private law
schools (u.s.)
Nisbet, Gordon 314 n.37
Normandin, R. 328 n.42
North, Roger 7
Nova Scotia Barristers' Society 49

O'Brien, Brendan 101–2, 314 n.33
O'Brien, Henry 63–4
office training: *see* practical training
Oliver, Farquahar 246
Ontario Bar Association: beginnings
61–2; interest in legal education 61,
71–2, 73–5; *see also* Canadian Bar
Association
Orde, J.F. 66
Ordinance of 1785 22–3
Ormrod Committee (England) 11–12

Osgoode, William 23
Osgoode Hall: construction of 24; 'keeping terms' 25; first compulsory lectures 25; early schools of law 25–30; improvements 148
Osgoode Hall Law School: beginnings 30–6; Wright's student years 39–59, 81–8, 297 n.3; English influence on 82; Wright's early teaching years 98–134; during Second World War 148, 151–2, 154–5; rebuilding after Wright's resignation 232–4; expansion 251–2; post-crisis years 265–6, 267–8; at York University 268
Osler, B.B. 35
Osler, Featherstone 45
overcrowding of legal profession 70, 106–7, 124–5, 126, 295 n.31

Parker, Isaac 13
Parkinson, Fred 263
Paton, G.W. 138, 139
Patrick, J.A.M. 67
Patterson, Edwin 228
Phillips, W. Eric 172, 177–8, 179, 182, 185, 191; role in compromise 232, 316 n.70
Pickup, J.W. 219, 231, 232, 239, 240, 268
Pitblado, Isaac 66
Porter, Donna 244, 246, 269
Pound, Roscoe 20, 81, 83, 92, 97, 99, 117, 138, 187, 298 n.21; influence on Wright 86–90, 108, 109, 221
Powell, Thomas Reed 186, 308 n.15
Power, James 53
practical training of lawyers: need for 30–1, 34, 66–7, 70–1, 105–7, 122–3, 126–7, 131, 173–4, 181–2, 187–8, 192, 204, 230, 239, 258, 303 n.48

private law schools (U.S.) 13–14, 17–18, 20, 73, 273–4; see also Litchfield Law School (U.S.)
Proudfoot, William 35
Provincial Articles of Peace (1782) 22
Pulling, Arthur C. 324 n.1

Quebec Act (1774) 22
Queen's University 26, 29, 250, 251, 264–5

racism in the legal profession: in U.S. 14, 21, 72, 74–5; in Canada 32, 72–3, 165, 273–4, 295 n.40, 308 n.15, 310 n.19
Rand, Harriet 113
Rand, Ivan C. 236, 248, 251, 265, 269, 326 n.23
Read, D.B. 25
Read, Horace 82, 191, 195–6, 201, 256, 292 n.24
Read, John E. 50, 103, 105, 141
Redlich, Josef 84–5
Reed, Alfred Z. 20, 56, 132
Reed reports (Carnegie Foundation for the Advancement of Teaching) 20–1, 81–2, 99
Reeve, William Albert 30–4
Reid, Robert F. 256, 260
Riddell, William R. 23, 24, 30
Ritchie, R.A. 132
Robertson, John Charles 171
Robertson, Robert Spelman 125, 168, 170–4, 177–8, 188, 191
Robidoux, J.E. 293 n.3
Robinette, John Josiah 55, 104–5, 112, 220, 239, 263, 306 n.31, 328 nn.42, 43
Robins, S.L. 234
Robinson, Cecil 201
Robinson, Christopher 42, 47

Robinson, John Beverley 24
Robson, H.A. 63, 69
Roger, Henry Wade 20
Rogers, H.M. 80
Roosevelt, Franklin Delano 142
Root, Elihu 19, 20, 72
Root Committee (U.S.) 19–20, 71–2,
   81–2
Row, Walter 22
Rowell, Newton Wesley 136
Royall, Isaac 13
Russell, Benjamin 293 n.3
Ryan, H.R. Stuart 256, 265

Sacks, Albert 268
Salsberg, Joseph 246
Sayre, Paul 160
Schumiacher, Morris 150
science, law as 9, 16, 32, 67, 137,
   205, 273
Scott, Austin Wakeman 53, 83, 111
Scott, F.R. 320 n.20
Seavey, Warren 102, 111, 138
Second World War: returning
   soldiers at Osgoode Hall 154–5,
   180–1, 191–2, 196–7, 229, 248, 272
Sedgwick, Joseph 218
Shauer, Gordon 220, 231
Sims, Charles W. 124
Sims, H.J. 125, 128
Smalley-Baker, Charles Ernest 233–4,
   265–6
Smith, C.R. 132
Smith, G.L. 125
Smith, Herbert A. 51, 77–8
Smith, Sidney Earle 50, 81, 113,
   118–19, 143–4, 148, 215, 226, 235,
   236, 307 n.69, 308 n.4, 316 n.70; at
   Osgoode Hall 53–5, 98; dean of
   Dalhousie 103–4; friendship with

Wright 103, 111–12, 162–3; presi-
   dent of University of Manitoba
   129–30; president of University of
   Toronto 161–2, 307 n.3; campaigns
   for legal education reform 162–75,
   176–82, 185–91, 230, 231, 326 n.22,
   328 nn.42, 43; role in compromise
   241, 242, 244–8, 250–5, 258–62, 269
Smith, W. Earl 185, 209–10, 220, 240,
   243, 244, 328 n.42
Smith, Young B. 102
Smout, David L. 234
Soberman, D.A. 265
sociological jurisprudence 86–9
Somerville, W.L.N. 241, 273
Spence, Donald B. 234
Spence, Wishart Flett 104
Steer, George H. 160–1, 307 n.3
Stone, Harlan J. 19, 20, 71, 73–5, 89
Stone, Julius 138, 241–2
Story, Joseph 14–15
Strong, S.H. 26, 30
Sullivan, Robert Baldwin 45
supplemental examinations: student
   resentment 125, 129, 196

Taft, William Howard 19, 72
Taylor, E.P. 177
Ten Broeck, John 23
Thayer, Ezra Ripley 84, 86
Thayer, James Bradley 13, 84, 85
Tilley, William Norman 120, 123,
   125, 134, 187
Titus, E.B. 124
tort law: Bohlen's influence on
   Wright 90–4, 305 n.31; Wright's
   'Gross Negligence' 94–6
Tory, John S.D. 99, 147, 219
Treaty of Paris (1763) 22
Trinity College 29

Tweddle v. *Alkinson* 142

Unequal Justice (Auerbach) 72–3,
    273–6
Université Laval 48–9
Université de Montréal 49
University of British Columbia 146
University of Manitoba 68, 175
University of Ottawa 29, 250, 265
University of Toronto: first law lec-
    tures 25, 35; offers to collaborate
    with Osgoode Hall 28–30, 35–6;
    pre-crisis events 56–8, 152; role in
    1949 negotiations 176–80; Wright's
    law school 221–8, 234–7; negotia-
    tions for recognition 230, 235,
    237–41, 248–52, 266–7; *see also*
    'Kennedy's Law School'
University of Toronto Law Journal 141,
    150–1
University of Western Ontario
    (Western University) 29, 38–9, 250,
    251, 265
unjust enrichment: Wright's views
    on 111–12
Upper Canada: early bar of 23–5
Urquhart, G.A. 124, 126

Vance, W.R. 20
Vanderbilt, Arthur T. 146, 147, 150,
    180, 187, 192, 219, 306 n.37, 313
    nn.26, 28, 315 n.56
Van Koughnet, Philip 25
Victoria University 29

Walker, Harold 248, 328 nn.42, 43
Walsh, George T. 231
Weekes, William 23
Weldon, Richard Chapman 28, 48,
    49–50, 293 n.3

Welland Law Association 124
Whalley, J.F.C. 215
White, John 22
White, Peter 231
White, Remington 242
Whitney, James P. 36
Wigmore, John H. 19, 20
Wilkinson, Walter Butler 23
Willis, John 50, 230, 311 n.29; hired
    at Osgoode Hall 155, 159–60, 166,
    196; resignation 210, 212, 218, 221
Williston, Samuel 19, 53, 83, 138
Williston, Walter 196, 198, 201, 210
Willmott, A.R. 220
Wilson, Percy Dixon 180, 182, 183,
    184–5, 189–91, 192, 193, 202,
    206–7, 210, 213, 231
Wilson, R.F. (Roly) 132, 263, 328
    n.42
Wilson, Woodrow 19
Wood, Thomas 8
Worrell, J.A. 29
Wright, Cecil Augustus: birth and
    early education 37–8; Osgoode Hall
    Law School and articles
    38–44, 51–9; Harvard Law School
    year 79–97, 297 n.9; influence of
    Pound 88–90, 300 n.42; influence
    of Bohlen 90–6; 'Gross Negligence'
    94–6; earns sjd 96–7; hired at
    Osgoode Hall 98–9; fiasco with
    jurisprudence 100–1; job offer
    from Bohlen 102–3; marries Marie
    Therese Laughlin 105; 'An Extra-
    Legal Approach to Law' 108–10;
    Dalhousie lecture (1931) 110–12;
    views of Kennedy and his school
    117–20, 150; editor of *Canadian
    Bar Review* 129–30, 135, 136–9, 303
    n.53; years of frustration 134–61;

'Legal Reform and the Profession'
142–4; 'Law and the Law Schools'
145–6; interest in University of
British Columbia Law School
146–8; resigns from *Canadian Bar
Review* 152–4; war years 154–61;
brings Laskin to Osgoode Hall
164–70; 1949 pre-crisis manoeuvres
180–2, 186–9, 191–200; deanship
193–205, 317 n.81; resignation
208–1, 319 n.13, 320 n.20; dean of
University of Toronto Law School
221–30, 234–7; 'The Legal Education Controversy in Canada'
229–30; lobbies for recognition
241–5, 247, 250–8; resolution
260–7, 268; judicial prospects
268–9; *Cases on the Law of Torts* 269;
death 269
Wright, John 234
Wright, Marie Therese (née
Laughlin) 105, 290 n.1
Wythe, George 13

York County Bar Association 124,
199
York University 267–8, 329 n.12
Young, McGregor 125